Adobe®

Flash CS4 Professsional

1 2 3 4 5 6 7 **on Demand**

Steve Johnson

Perspection, Inc.

 Que Publishing, 800 East 96th Street, Indianapolis, IN 46240 USA

Adobe® Flash® CS4 Professional On Demand

Library of Congress Cataloging-in-Publication Data is on file

ISBN-13: 978-0-7897-3836-3

ISBN-10: 0-7897-3836-8

Que Publishing offers excellent discounts on this book when ordered in quantity for bulk purchases or special sales.

For information, please contact: U.S. Corporate and Government Sales

1-800-382-3419 or corpsales@pearsontechgroup.com

For sales outside the U.S., please contact: International Sales

1-317-428-3341 or International@pearsontechgroup.com

Trademarks

Warning and Disclaimer

Publisher
Paul Boger

Associate Publisher
Greg Wiegand

Acquisitions Editor
Laura Norman

Managing Editor
Steve Johnson

Author
Steve Johnson

Technical Editor
Adrian Hyde

Page Layout
Beth Teyler
James Teyler

Interior Designers
Steve Johnson
Marian Hartsough

Photographs
Tracy Teyler

Indexer
Katherine Stimson

Proofreader
Adrian Hyde

Team Coordinator
Cindy Teeters

Acknowledgements

Perspection, Inc.

Adobe Flash CS4 Professional On Demand has been created by the professional trainers and writers at Perspection, Inc. to the standards you've come to expect from Que publishing. Together, we are pleased to present this training book.

Perspection, Inc. is a software training company committed to providing information and training to help people use software more effectively in order to communicate, make decisions, and solve problems. Perspection writes and produces software training books, and develops multimedia and Web-based training. Since 1991, we have written more than 80 computer books, with several bestsellers to our credit, and sold over 5 million books.

This book incorporates Perspection's training expertise to ensure that you'll receive the maximum return on your time. You'll focus on the tasks and skills that increase productivity while working at your own pace and convenience.

We invite you to visit the Perspection Web site at:

www.perspection.com

Acknowledgements

The task of creating any book requires the talents of many hard-working people pulling together to meet impossible deadlines and untold stresses. We'd like to thank the outstanding team responsible for making this book possible: the writer, Steve Johnson; the editor, Adrian Hyde; the production editors, James Teyler and Beth Teyler; proofreader, Adrian Hyde; and the indexer, Katherine Stimson.

At Que publishing, we'd like to thank Greg Wiegand and Laura Norman for the opportunity to undertake this project, Cindy Teeters for administrative support, and Sandra Schroeder for your production expertise and support.

Perspection

About The Authors

Steve Johnson has written more than 45 books on a variety of computer software, including Adobe Photoshop CS3 and CS2, Adobe Flash CS3, Dreamweaver CS3, Microsoft Office 2007 and 2003, Microsoft Windows Vista and XP, Microsoft Office 2008 for the Macintosh, and Apple Mac OS X Leopard. In 1991, after working for Apple Computer and Microsoft, Steve founded Perspection, Inc., which writes and produces software training. When he is not staying up late writing, he enjoys playing golf, gardening, and spending time with his wife, Holly, and three children, JP, Brett, and Hannah. Steve and his family live in Pleasanton, California, but can also be found visiting family all over the western United States.

We Want To Hear From You!

As the reader of this book, *you* are our most important critic and commentator. We value your opinion and want to know what we're doing right, what we could do better, what areas you'd like to see us publish in, and any other words of wisdom you're willing to pass our way.

As an associate publisher for Que, I welcome your comments. You can email or write me directly to let me know what you did or didn't like about this book—as well as what we can do to make our books better.

Please note that I cannot help you with technical problems related to the topic of this book. We do have a User Services group, however, where I will forward specific technical questions related to the book.

When you write, please be sure to include this book's title and author as well as your name, email address, and phone number. I will carefully review your comments and share them with the author and editors who worked on the book.

Email: feedback@quepublishing.com

Mail: Greg Wiegand
        Que Publishing
        800 East 96th Street
        Indianapolis, IN 46240 USA

For more information about this book or another Que title, visit our Web site at *informit.com/register*. Type the ISBN (excluding hyphens) or the title of a book in the Search field to find the page you're looking for.

Contents

4 Working with Groups, Symbols, and Instances   131

Introduction

Welcome to *Adobe Flash CS4 Professional On Demand*, a visual quick reference book that shows you how to work efficiently with Flash. This book provides complete coverage of basic to advanced Flash skills.

How This Book Works

You don't have to read this book in any particular order. We've designed the book so that you can jump in, get the information you need, and jump out. However, the book does follow a logical progression from simple tasks to more complex ones. Each task is presented on no more than two facing pages, which lets you focus on a single task without having to turn the page. To find the information that you need, just look up the task in the table of contents or index, and turn to the page listed. Read the task introduction, follow the step-by-step instructions in the left column along with screen illustrations in the right column, and you're done.

What's New

If you're searching for what's new in Flash CS4, just look for the icon: **New!**. The new icon appears in the table of contents and throughout this book so you can quickly and easily identify a new or improved feature in Flash. A complete description of each new feature appears in the New Features guide in the back of this book.

Keyboard Shortcuts

Most menu commands have a keyboard equivalent, such as Ctrl+P (Win) or ⌘+P (Mac), as a quicker alternative to using the mouse. A complete list of keyboard shortcuts is available on the Web at *www.perspection.com*.

How You'll Learn

How This Book Works

What's New

Keyboard Shortcuts

Step-by-Step Instructions

Real World Examples

Workshops

Adobe Certified Expert

Get More on the Web

Step-by-Step Instructions

This book provides concise step-by-step instructions that show you "how" to accomplish a task. Each set of instructions includes illustrations that directly correspond to the easy-to-read steps. Also included in the text are time-savers, tables, and sidebars to help you work more efficiently or to teach you more in-depth information. A "Did You Know?" provides tips and techniques to help you work smarter, while a "See Also" leads you to other parts of the book containing related information about the task.

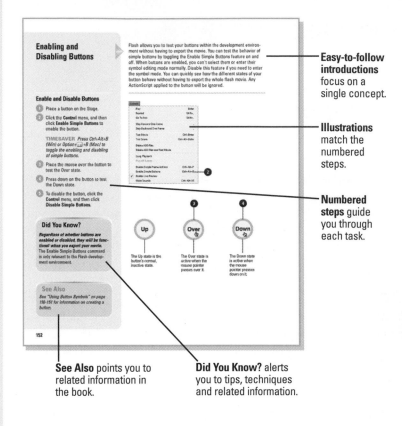

Easy-to-follow introductions focus on a single concept.

Illustrations match the numbered steps.

Numbered steps guide you through each task.

See Also points you to related information in the book.

Did You Know? alerts you to tips, techniques and related information.

Real World Examples

This book uses real world example files to give you a context in which to use the task. By using the example files, you won't waste time looking for or creating sample files. You get a start file and a result file, so you can compare your work. Not every topic needs an example file, such as changing options, so we provide a complete list of the example files used throughout the book. The example files that you need for project tasks along with a complete file list are available on the Web at *www.perspection.com*.

Real world examples help you apply what you've learned to other tasks.

Workshops

This book shows you how to put together the individual step-by-step tasks into in-depth projects with the Workshop. You start each project with a sample file, work through the steps, and then compare your results with a project results file at the end. The Workshop projects and associated files are available on the Web at *www.perspection.com.*

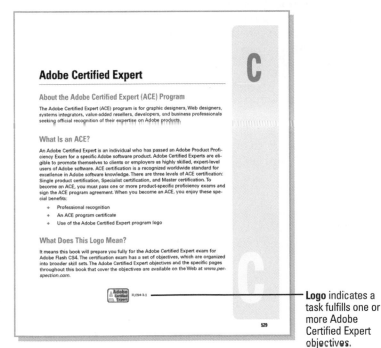

The **Workshop** walks you through in-depth projects to help you put Flash to work.

Adobe Certified Expert

This book prepares you fully for the Adobe Certified Expert (ACE) exam for Adobe Flash CS4. Each Adobe Certified Expert certification level has a set of objectives, which are organized into broader skill sets. To prepare for the certification exam, you should review and perform each task identified with a Adobe Certified Expert objective to confirm that you can meet the requirements for the exam. The Adobe Certified Expert objectives are available on the Web at *www.perspection.com.*

Logo indicates a task fulfills one or more Adobe Certified Expert objectives.

Get More on the Web

In addition to the information in this book, you can also get more information on the Web to help you get up-to-speed faster with Flash CS4. Some of the information includes:

Transition Helpers

◆ **Only New Features.** Download and print the new feature tasks as a quick and easy guide.

Productivity Tools

◆ **Keyboard Shortcuts.** Download a list of keyboard shortcuts to learn faster ways to get the job done.

More Content

◆ **Photographs.** Download photographs and other graphics to use in your Flash documents.

◆ **More Content.** Download new content developed after publication.

You can access these additional resources on the Web at *www.perspection.com.*

Keyboard Shortcuts

Adobe Flash CS4

If a command on a menu includes a keyboard reference, known as a keyboard shortcut, to the right of the command name, you can perform the action by pressing and holding the first key, and then pressing the second key to perform the command quickly. In some cases, a keyboard shortcut uses three keys. Simply press and hold the first two keys, and then press the third key. Keyboard shortcuts provide an alternative to using the mouse and make it easy to perform repetitive commands.

If you're searching for new keyboard shortcuts in Adobe Flash CS4, just look for the letter: **N**. The **N** appears in the Keyboard Shortcuts table so you can quickly and easily identify new or changed shortcuts.

Keyboard Shortcuts		
Operation/Tool	Windows	Macintosh
Add Anchor Point Tool **N**	=	=
Arrow tool (select in Toolbox)	V	V
Sub Select	A	A
Arrow tool (temporary access)	Ctrl	
Brush tool (select in Toolbox)	B	B
Constrain (ovals to circles, rectangles to squares, lines and rotation to 45-degree angles)	Shift+drag	Shift+drag
Convert corner point to curve point (Subselection tool)	Alt+drag	Option+drag
Convert Anchor Point Tool **N**	C	C
Create new corner point (Arrow tool)	Alt+drag a line	Option+drag a line
Delete Anchor Point Tool **N**	-	-
Drag a copy of selected element	Alt+drag	Option+drag
Drag a copy of selected keyframe unit in Timeline	Alt+drag	Option+drag
Dropper tool (select in Toolbox)	I	I
End open path (Pen tool)	Ctrl+click	+click

Additional content is available on the Web.

Working Together with Adobe Programs

Introduction

Adobe programs are designed to work together so you can focus on what you need to do, rather than on how to do it. In fact, the Adobe programs share tools and features for your most common tasks so you can work uninterrupted and move seamlessly from one program to another. Adobe Creative Suite is an integrated collection of programs that work together to help you create designs in print, on the Web, or on mobile devices. When you install Adobe Creative Suite or a stand-alone Adobe program, you also get additional Adobe programs—Bridge, Version Cue, Drive, ConnectNow, Device Central, and Extension Manager—to help you perform specific jobs, such as locating, downloading, and modifying images for projects, managing files and program extensions and testing files for different mobile devices.

Adobe Bridge is a program that lets you view, open, modify, and manage images located on your computer from any Adobe Creative Suite program. Adobe Bridge is literally the glue that binds Adobe Creative Suite programs together into one cohesive unit with shared tools. Bridge allows you to search, sort, filter, manage, and process image files one at a time or in batches. You can also use Bridge to do the following: create new folders; rename, move, delete and group files; edit metadata; rotate images; create web galleries and contact sheets; and run batch commands. You can also import files from your digital camera and view file information and metadata.

What You'll Do

Explore Adobe Programs

Explore Adobe Bridge

Get Started with Adobe Bridge

Get Photos from a Digital Camera

Work with Raw Images from a Digital Camera

Work with Images Using Adobe Bridge

Set Preferences in Adobe Bridge

Automate Tasks in Adobe Bridge

Share My Screen

Manage Files Using Adobe Version Cue

Work with Adobe Drive

Explore Adobe Device Central

Check Content Using Adobe Device Central

Use Adobe Extension Manager

Additional content is available on the Web.

1

Getting Started with Flash CS4

Introduction

Flash is an application for developing rich content, user interfaces, and Web applications. Adobe Flash CS4 allows designers and developers to integrate video, text, audio, and graphics into rich experiences that deliver superior results for interactive marketing and presentations, e-learning, and application user interfaces. Most major commercial Web sites have implemented Flash content because of its cross-platform consistency, rich graphics capabilities, and small file sizes. After you create and fine-tune multimedia content in Flash, you can deliver it on the Web within a browser using the Flash Player. Flash Player is a software product developed by Adobe for browsers on the Macintosh and Windows. Flash is the world's most pervasive software platform, used by over one million professionals and reaching more than 97% of Web-enabled desktops worldwide, as well as a wide range of consumer electronic devices, such as PDAs and mobile phones.

Flash operates virtually the same on both Macintosh and Windows versions, except for a few keyboard commands that have equivalent functions. You use the [Ctrl] and [Alt] keys in Windows, and the ⌘ and [Option] keys on a Macintosh computer. Also, the term *popup* on the Macintosh and *list arrow* in Windows refer to the same type of option.

What You'll Do

Prepare to Install Flash

Install and Start Flash

View the Flash Window

Create a Project Plan

Build a Flash Project

Create a New Document

Create a New Document from a Template

Open an Existing Document

Change Document Properties

Work with Document Windows

Save a Document

Save a Document in Different Formats

Get Help While You Work

Get Online Updates and Support

Finish Up

Preparing to Install Flash

System Requirements

Before you can install Flash CS4 and development content, you need to make sure your computer meets the minimum system requirements. You can create Flash content on Windows and Macintosh computers. As a Flash developer, you also need to be aware of the system requirements for viewers of your Flash movies in a browser using the Adobe Flash Player. Web users need to download and install the player in order to view and interact with Flash content. The Flash Player is free and widely distributed over the Web at *www.adobe.com*.

Some Flash CS4 features require the latest version of QuickTime or QuickTime Pro. During the installation, use the *Recommended* installation type to install the required components. You can obtain the latest version of QuickTime at *www.quicktime.com*.

For Windows Computers

You need to have a computer with the following minimum configuration:

- Intel Pentium 4, Centrino, Xeon, or Core processor or equivalent.

- 1 GB of RAM.

- 2.5 GB available disk space.

- 16-bit (thousands of colors), 1024 x 768 resolution.

- Microsoft Windows XP with Service Pack 3 or higher; Windows Vista with Service Pack 1.

- Internet or phone connection required for activation.

- QuickTime 7.x or higher; DirectX version 9.0c or higher.

For Macintosh Computers

You need to have a computer with the following minimum configuration:

- 1 GHz PowerPC G5; Intel-based Macintosh.

- 512 megabytes (MB) of RAM, 1 GB or above recommended.

- 2.5 GB available disk space.

- 16-bit (thousands of colors), 1024 x 768 resolution.

- Mac OS X 10.5.x, or later.

- Internet or phone connection required for activation.

- QuickTime 7.x or higher.

For Viewers in a Browser

Your visitors need to have a computer with the Flash Player and the following minimum configuration:

- **For Windows 98/Me.** Internet Explorer 5.5, Netscape 7.x, Mozilla 1.x, Firefox 1.x, AOL 9, or Opera 7.11.

- **For Windows 2000.** Internet Explorer 5.x, Netscape 7.x, Mozilla 1.x, Firefox 1.x, CompuServe 7, AOL 9, or Opera 7.11.

- **For Windows Vista/XP/Windows 2003 Server.** Internet Explorer 6.0, Netscape 7.x, Mozilla 1.x, CompuServe 7, Firefox 1.x, AOL 9, or Opera 7.11.

- **For Macintosh OS X 10.1.x - Mac X 10.4.x.** Safari 2.x, Internet Explorer 5.2, Netscape 7.x, Mozilla 1.x, Firefox 1.x, AOL for OS X, Opera 6, or Safari 1.x.

Installing Flash

To perform a standard application install, insert the Adobe Flash CS4 installation disc into the drive on your computer, and then follow the on-screen instructions. Because the setup process is different for Macintosh OS X and Windows platforms, general steps are provided to help you get started, and the on-screen instructions will guide you through the rest. Make sure to have your serial number handy because you'll be asked to enter it during the installation process. If you're updating from a previous version of Flash, you'll be required to verify the older version with your serial number for the previous version. The Flash installation includes all the components you need, including the Flash Player 10 (**New!**), to develop Flash content. The Flash Player is software installed on a user's computer that allows them to view published Flash movies (SWFs) in a Web page or through the player.

Install Flash CS4

1 Insert the Adobe Flash CS4 installation disc into your drive.

2 If necessary, double-click the disc icon, and then double-click the installer icon.

The installer window opens, displaying the opening screen of the Flash CS4 installer software.

3 Follow the on-screen instructions to install the product; the installer asks you to read and accept a licensing agreement, enter a serial number, indicate the language you want (**New!**), and specify where you want to store the software.

IMPORTANT *Adobe, in an attempt to thwart software piracy, now requires online or phone activation of the program. The activation occurs during the installation process, but you can postpone it for 30 days after product installation. If activation is not achieved within 30 days, Flash will cease to function. You can click the Help menu, and then click Activate to complete the process.*

Starting Flash

You can start Flash in several ways, depending on the platform you are using. When you start Flash, the computer displays a splash screen and then the Flash window. When you start a new Flash session or close all documents, a Welcome screen appears in the Document window, providing easy access links to open, open recent, create new, create from template, and tutorial actions to help you get started. You can also use the Extend link to access the Adobe Flash Exchange Web site, where you can download additional applications and information.

Start Flash in Windows

1 Click **Start** on the taskbar.

2 Point to **All Programs** (which changes to Back).

3 Point to an Adobe Collection CS4 menu, if needed.

4 Click **Adobe Flash CS4**.

5 If you're starting Flash CS4 for the first time, perform the following:

◆ Enter your serial number, and then click **OK** to continue.

◆ Click **OK** to complete the activation process.

◆ Fill in the registration form, click **Register Now**.

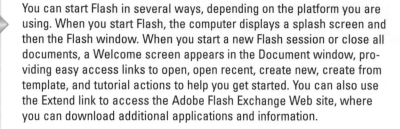

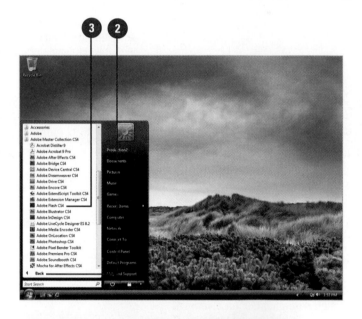

Did You Know?

You can hide the Welcome screen. On the Welcome screen, select the Don't Show Again check box.

You can set launch preferences to customize how Flash starts. Click the Flash (Mac) or Edit (Win) menu, click Preferences, click the General category, select an option from the On Launch popup, and then click OK.

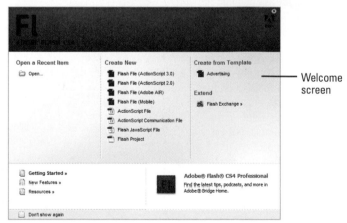

Welcome screen

Start Flash in Macintosh

1. Open the Applications folder (located on the main hard drive).

2. Double-click the Adobe Flash CS4 folder.

3. Double-click the **Adobe Flash CS4** application icon.

4. If you're starting Flash CS4 for the first time, perform the following:

   ◆ Enter your serial number, and then click **OK** to continue.

   ◆ Click **OK** to complete the activation process.

   ◆ Fill in the registration form, click **Register Now**.

Did You Know?

You can create a shortcut on the Macintosh. Drag and drop the Flash application to the bottom of the monitor screen, and then add it to the dock.

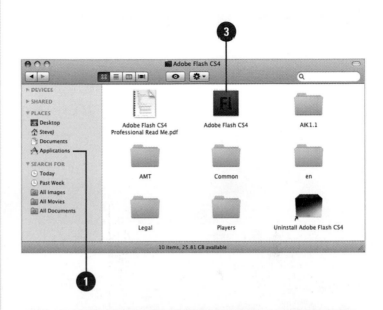

Shortcut for Adobe Flash CS4

For Your Information

Launching Flash and Opening a Document

You can also start Flash and open a Flash document at the same time. Double-click the Flash file icon in Windows Explorer or My Computer (Win) or in a Macintosh folder (Mac). You can identify a Flash document by the file icon or .fla file extension. A file extension is a three-letter suffix at the end of a filename that identifies the file type for the operating system. The Macintosh doesn't need to use file extensions, but added the feature to promote cross platform use. In the Mac Operating System (OS) 10 or later, you have the option to show or hide file extensions. When you are working on both platforms, using file extensions on the Macintosh allows Windows and Flash to recognize and open the files.

Viewing the Flash Window

Panel Windows
Gives you access to authoring tools
and attribute settings for elements.

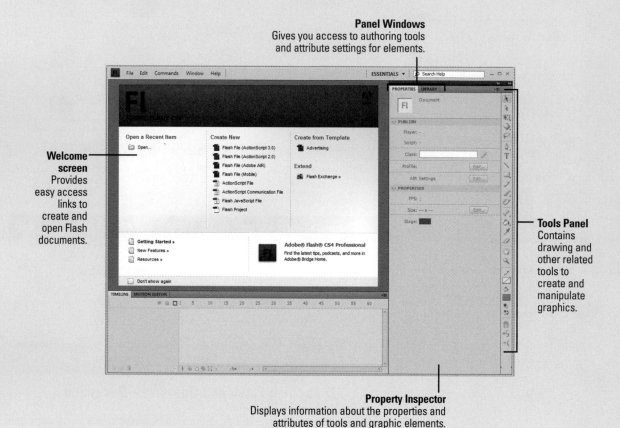

Welcome screen
Provides easy access links to create and open Flash documents.

Tools Panel
Contains drawing and other related tools to create and manipulate graphics.

Property Inspector
Displays information about the properties and
attributes of tools and graphic elements.

Document Window
Displays open Flash documents, which include an Edit bar, Timeline and Stage.

Edit Bar
Displays what editing mode you are working in and allows you to switch scenes.

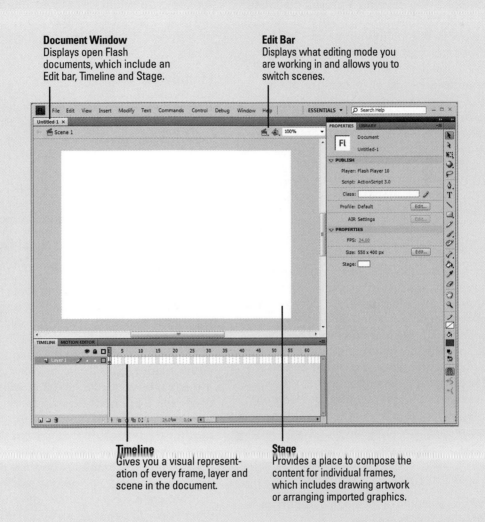

Timeline
Gives you a visual represent-ation of every frame, layer and scene in the document.

Stage
Provides a place to compose the content for individual frames, which includes drawing artwork or arranging imported graphics.

Creating a Project Plan

 FL 1.2

Before you begin to create a movie in Flash, it's important to develop a project plan first. The project plan provides a **site map** for you to follow as you build your project in Flash. Without a project plan, you'll inevitably hit road blocks, which will cause you to waste time redesigning all of or portions of the movie. Planning a movie project involves determining its purpose, identifying the audience, logically developing the content, organizing the structure of the content, developing the layout and design, and identifying the delivery computer system. With a project plan in place, you'll be ready to create a movie in Flash.

Plan a Movie

Creating a movie can take a long time; it's worth the effort to plan carefully. The tendency for most first-time Flash developers is to start creating a movie without carefully planning the project. Before you begin, you need to develop and follow a plan. Otherwise, you might end up spending a lot of time fixing or completely changing parts of the movie, which you could have avoided from the beginning. You need to figure out the goal of the project, the look and feel of your production, its length and size, how it will interact with the viewer, and how and for whom it will be distributed.

When planning a movie, it's important to accomplish the following:

Determine the purpose

Is it for training? Sales? Entertainment? Informing? The answer will determine the types of features you may want to include or exclude in the movie. If the purpose is to create a training site, you might want to include simple navigation, easy-to-use instructional material, and a help system. On the other hand, if the purpose is to create a sales promotion, you might want to include eye-catching graphics, videos, and audio to get users' attention and draw them into the presentation.

Identify the audience

How you create your movie will depend on how you classify the intended audience. If the intended audience consists of novice computer users, you will have to concentrate on making the navigational controls and layout as simple to use as possible. If the users are experienced computer users, you can include more advanced features and interactions.

Develop the content and organize the structure

The most beneficial planning tools for the multimedia developer are the script and schematic flowchart. The script tells the story of your movie production in text form. Just like in the movies, a script is used to describe each section, to list audio or video, and to provide a basis for the text that will appear onscreen. Schematic flowcharts are the best way to sketch the navigational structure of a movie and make sure that each of the sections is properly connected. After you have the script and schematic flowchart mapped out on paper, you will quickly see the correlation between what you have developed and what you will begin to set up in Flash.

Develop the layout and design of the movie

The storyboard tells the story of your movie in visual form. It helps you design the layout of each screen in your movie. The storyboard follows the script and develops visual frames of the movie's main transitional points, which help you develop the Flash media elements you will use to create your movie. A storyboard can take a long time to develop, but the media elements you assemble and create in the process will shorten the overall development time. As you develop your layout and design, be sure to keep:

- Navigation easy to understand and consistent from page to page, such as navigation bars or drop-down menus

- Text easy to read

- Sound and animation limited

- Movie file sizes as small as possible for fast downloads. Break up large files into small ones for easy management

- Color consistent and appropriate for the audience

- Content accessible to users with visual or auditory impairments

Identify the delivery computer system and browser to be used for playback

Some computers are more up-to-date than others. You need to determine the minimum computer hardware and software requirements in which your movie will be delivered. The hardware and software requirements will determine what types of media you can use and how the movie will play back.

Some hardware requirements you need to consider for the delivery computer system are (1) CPU (central processing unit), which determines the speed with which your computer can compute data; (2) RAM (system memory), which determines how fast files load and how smoothly they run; (3) Sound cards, which determine if you can use sound files; (4) Video cards, which determine the quality and speed of the graphic and video display, and (5) Monitor resolution, which determines the color display (number of available colors), size (800 x 600 is typical and 1024 x 768 is becoming the new standard, while 1440 x 900 is becoming more and more available), and overall look of your movie.

Some software requirements you need to consider are the operating system version and supported browser type and version. See "Preparing to Install Flash" on page 2 for specific details about these requirements.

Sample script

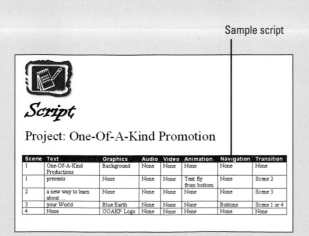

Sample flowchart

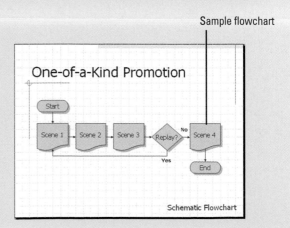

Building a Flash Project

 FL 1.2

After you develop a project plan, you can use Flash to create a movie according to the plan. Creating a movie involves six main steps: setting up movie properties, assembling media elements, positioning the media elements on the Stage and sequencing them in the Timeline, adding custom functionality and interactive elements, previewing and testing the movie, and finally publishing or exporting the movie for distribution.

Build a Movie with Flash

Before you start creating a movie using Flash based on your project plan, it's important to understand the process of developing Flash software. The basic steps for developing interactive multimedia software with Flash are listed below.

Step 1: Set up document properties

Before you start a Flash project, you need to create a new document and set up initial document properties, such as the user's viewable screen size, for how your movie looks and operates. It is important to specify document property settings that affect the entire movie at the beginning of the project, such as how colors are defined and the size and location of the Stage, so you don't have to redesign the movie later.

Step 2: Create or import media elements

Media elements include graphics, images, buttons, videos, sounds, and text. You can create new media elements in Flash or import ones that have already been developed. Flash provides several tools for creating media elements, including shape and paint tools, and text creation tools. You can also add media elements from the Library, a media storage area. Media elements are either static or dynamic. **Static** media is an element, such as text or graphics, created or imported into a movie that doesn't change unless the author makes the change and republishes the movie. **Dynamic** media is an element, such as data, MP3 sound, a JPEG image, or Flash Live Video (FLV) video, stored outside of the published movie and loaded when needed or changed by scripting, which makes updating easy, keeps file sizes down, and provides personalized information to the user.

Step 3: Position the elements on the Stage and sequence them in the Timeline

The Stage is the viewing area you use to display where media elements appear in a movie, and the Timeline is the area you use to organize what you want to occur at the time and duration you specify. You use the Stage to create the look and feel for your production; you use the Stage and Timeline together to arrange the media elements in space and time. The Stage represents the media elements' position in space (where) and the Timeline represents the media elements' position in time (when).

Step 4: Add navigational components, interactive behaviors, and motion effects

Scripting allows you to add custom functionality to your movie, such as moving objects on the Stage, formatting text, storing and managing information, performing mathematical operations, and controlling the movie in response to specific conditions and events, such as a mouse click. In Flash, scripts are written in ActionScript, a Flash-specific programming language. To help you get started scripting and save you some time, Flash comes with built-in components, and scripts called **behaviors**. **Components** are elements you can use to quickly create a user interface. For example, components can include buttons, arrows, or other navigation elements that move the viewer to different parts of a movie or to different locations on the Web. After you add a component, you can use behaviors to add functionality to the component to make it do what you want. In addition to behaviors, you can use built-in Timeline effects to add motion to elements. As you build in movie navigation and organization, it's good design to break up large projects into smaller movies, which can be quickly accessed from a main movie. This keeps Internet download times to a minimum, and it makes projects easier to update, and more manageable for a team to produce.

Step 5: Preview and test the movie

After you create your project, you use the Test

Movie command to preview and test the movie to make sure it runs the way you want it to. It's important to test the functionality of your movie early and often during the development process to catch problems while they are still minor.

Step 6: Publish the document as a movie file for use over the Internet

When the movie runs the way you want it to, you can publish your production as a Flash movie that viewers can play on a Web page, using a browser with the Flash Player. Flash publishes the movie file (.swf) and creates an HTML file with information to display the movie file. Viewers can't change the movies in the .swf format; they can only play them.

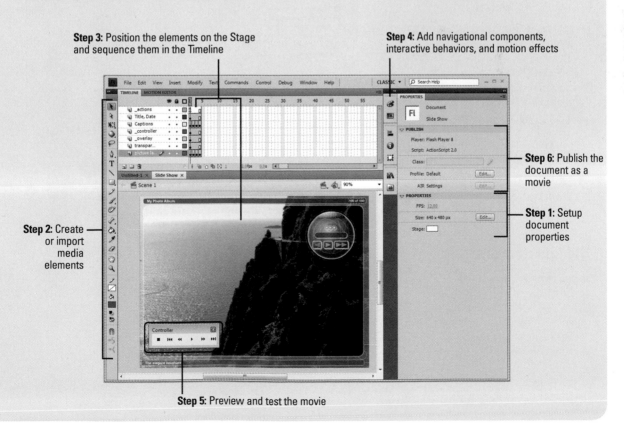

Step 3: Position the elements on the Stage and sequence them in the Timeline

Step 4: Add navigational components, interactive behaviors, and motion effects

Step 6: Publish the document as a movie

Step 1: Setup document properties

Step 2: Create or import media elements

Step 5: Preview and test the movie

Creating a New Document

A file in Flash is called a **document**. Flash documents, which have the .fla filename extension, contain all the information required to develop, design, and test interactive content. Flash documents are not the same as the movies you play with the Flash Player. Instead, you publish your Flash documents as Flash movies, which have the .swf filename extension and contain only the information needed to display the movie. When you open a new Flash document, it's blank, ready for you to create or insert text, graphics, and other media content. By default, the first Flash document is titled Untitled1. You can create new documents in several ways including using the New command on the File menu and the New Document task pane. Flash numbers new documents consecutively. You can open and work on as many new documents as you have memory (RAM) for.

Create a New Blank Document

1. Click the **File** menu, and then click **New**.

   TIMESAVER *Click Flash Document on the Welcome screen to create a new blank document.*

2. Click the **General** tab.

3. Click **Flash File (ActionScript 3.0)** or **Flash File (ActionScript 2.0)**.

   IMPORTANT *ActionScript 2.0 and ActionScript 3.0 are not compatible with each other. ActionScript 3.0 is recommended.*

   ◆ If you want to create a specific type of document, click the type you want.

4. Click **OK**.

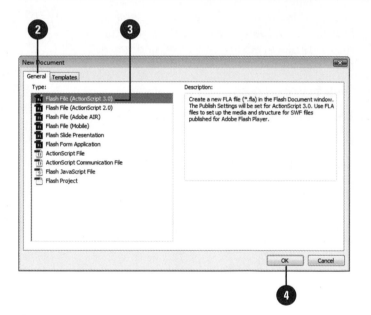

Did You Know?

You can open a new window with a copy of the current document. Create or open the Flash document you want to open in a new window, click the Window menu, and then click Duplicate Window.

Creating a New Document from a Template

Flash makes it easy to create many common documents based on a template. A **template** opens a Flash document (such as an animation or set of menus) with predefined formatting and placeholder text, graphics, and actionscripts. Flash comes with a set of templates, which includes the following categories: Advertising, BREW Handsets, Consumer Devices, Global Handsets, Japanese Handsets, Photo Slideshows, and Quiz. When you select a template category, a list of templates appears. Select a template to display a brief description. If you can't find the template you want, you can check the Adobe Flash Support Center Online Web site for more.

Create a New Document from a Template

1. Click the **File** menu, and then click **New**.

   TIMESAVER *Click a template category on the Welcome screen to open the New From Template dialog box, where you can select a template.*

2. Click the **Templates** tab.

3. Click a template category.

4. Click the template you want to use.

5. View the templates in the Preview box and read the description.

6. Click **OK**.

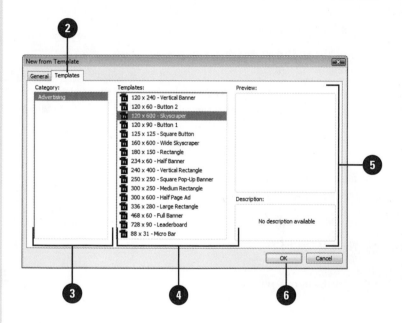

See Also

See "Saving a Document in Different Formats" on page 22 for information on saving a document as a template.

Opening an Existing Document

FL 2.5

You can open an existing document file and the Flash program at one time, or you can open the file from within Flash. In Windows Explorer (Win) or Finder (Mac), you can double-click a Flash document to open the Flash program and the document. In Flash, you can use the Open section on the Welcome screen, Open commands on the File menu, or Adobe Bridge CS4 (a stand-alone file management program that comes with Flash CS4) to open Flash documents, scripts, and movies in several formats. You can also open content from Adobe InDesign and Adobe After Effects in the XFL file format (**New!**). When you open a document, a tab appears across the top of the Document window, which you can click to display it.

Open a Flash Document

1. Click the **File** menu, and then click **Open**.

    TIMESAVER *Click Open or a recently opened Flash document name on the Welcome screen to open a document.*

2. To open a specific type of Flash file, click the **File as type** list arrow (Win), or the **File type** popup (Mac), and then select the file format you want.

3. Navigate to the drive or folder where the file is located.

4. Click the document file you want to open.

5. Click **Open**.

Did You Know?

You can view what is inside of an XFL file. (**New!**) An XFL file is essentially a ZIP package containing the XML and the assets for a FLA file. To view the actual XML and assets of the FLA file, change the .XFL file extension to .ZIP and unzip the folder.

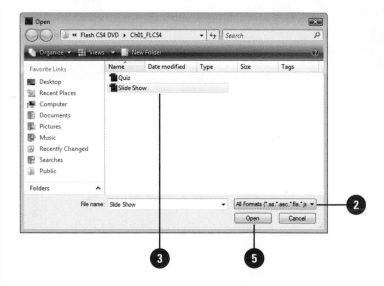

Other Dynamics

Format	Description
ActionScript (.as)	A file to store ActionScript code for a Flash document.
XFL (.xfl, .xml) (**New!**)	A packaged XML representation of a FLA file along with the assets for that file.
Communications (.asc)	A file to store ActionScript code on a computer with Flash Communication Server.
Flash Document (.fla)	A Flash document you create and save in Flash authoring environment.
JavaScript (.jsfl)	A separate file with JavaScript code to add new functionality to Flash.
Flash Movie (.swf)	A compressed movie file you publish in the Flash authoring environment.

Open a Recently Opened Document

1. Click the **File** menu, and then point to **Open Recent**.

2. Click the document you want to open.

Did You Know?

You can open a recent file quickly from the Start menu (Win). Click the Start button, point to Recent Items (Vista) or My Recent Documents (XP), and then click the file name you want to open.

Browse Documents in Adobe Bridge

1. Click the **File** menu, and then click **Browse in Bridge**.

   Adobe Bridge CS4 opens, displaying files and folder on your computer.

2. Select a workspace display to view your files the way you want.

3. Navigate to the drive or folder where the Flash file is located.

4. To open a Flash file, double-click the file icon.

5. When you're done, click the **File** menu, and then click **Return to Adobe Flash**.

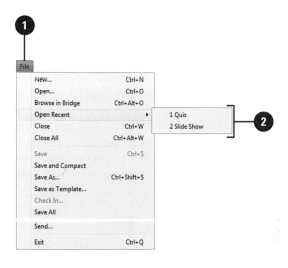

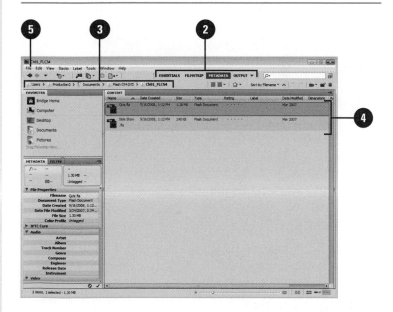

Changing Document Properties

When you create a new Flash document or open an existing one, you need to set up or change the document properties. You set document properties at the beginning of the project to make basic decisions about how your movie looks and operates. You use the Document Properties dialog box or the Property Inspector to specify document property settings that affect the entire movie, such as the background color, the size and location of the Stage, the **frame rate**—the number of frames per second in which the computer plays an animation, and the unit of measure for rulers. These settings apply only to the current document unless you set Flash defaults to apply to every document. You can use the Properties command on the Window menu to display the Property Inspector, which appears vertically (**New!**) on the screen.

View Document Properties

1. Click the **Selection** tool on the Tools panel.

2. Click the **Window** menu, and then click **Properties** to open the Property Inspector.

   TIMESAVER *Press* ⌘+F3 *(Mac) or Ctrl+F3 (Win).*

3. View the document properties at the top of the Property Inspector:

   ◆ **Stage Size.** The current size appears in the button label.

   ◆ **Background Color.** The color of the Stage background.

   ◆ **Frame Rate.** The speed at which the movie runs.

Did You Know?

You can change the background color quickly in the Property Inspector. Open the Property Inspector, click the Background color box, and then select a color from the panel.

You can change the frame rate quickly in the Property Inspector. Open the Property Inspector, and then enter the number of animation frames to be displayed every second in the Frame Rate box.

Document name

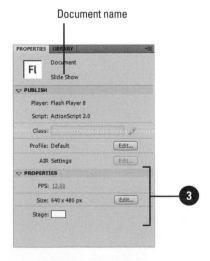

Change Document Properties

1 Create or open a document.

2 Click the **Modify** menu, and then click **Document**.

TIMESAVER *Click the Size button in the Property Inspector or double-click the frame-rate box in the Status bar on the Timeline.*

3 To set the Stage dimensions, do one of the following:

- **Specify size in pixels.** Enter values in the Width and Height boxes. The default size is 550 x 400 pixels.

- **Set size to an equal space around content.** Click Contents.

- **Set size to the maximum print area.** Click Printer.

- **Set size to default setting.** Click Default.

4 Click the **Background Color** box, and then select a color.

5 Enter a frame rate. For most computers playing from the Web, 8 fps (frames per second) to 12 fps is adequate. The default is 12 fps.

6 To specify the unit of measure for rulers, click the **Ruler Units** popup, and then select an option.

7 To set properties for all new documents, click **Make Default**.

8 Click **OK**.

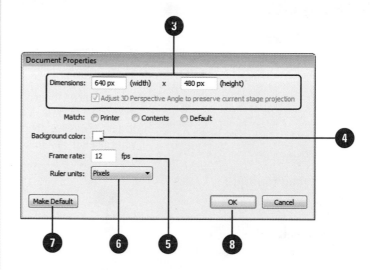

See Also

See "Displaying Rulers" on page 89 for information on using rulers.

For Your Information

Improving Searchability by Internet Search Engines

When you add a title and description to Flash document properties, you're making it easier for Internet search engines to categorize the content in your Flash movie file (.swf). The title and description boxes are metadata properties for the SWF file format. The Internet uses metadata as a standard format for gathering and transferring data. When you enter a title and description, use descriptive keywords that reflect the type of user you want to attract to your Web site.

Working with Document Windows

When you open multiple documents, you can use the Window menu or tabs at the top of the Document window to switch between them. You can click a tab name to switch and activate the document. By default, tabs are displayed in the order in which you open or create documents. When you want to move or copy information between documents, it's easier to display several Document windows on the screen at the same time and move them around (**New!**). However, you must make the window active to work in it. Each tab also includes a Close button (**New!**) to quickly close a document. If the document view is too small or large, you can change it to suite your needs.

Switch Between Multiple Documents

1. Open more than one document.

2. Click a tab name to switch to the document.

   TIMESAVER *Press Ctrl+Tab or Ctrl+Shift+Tab to cycle to the tab you want.*

   ◆ You can also click the **Window** menu, and then click a document name at the bottom of the menu.

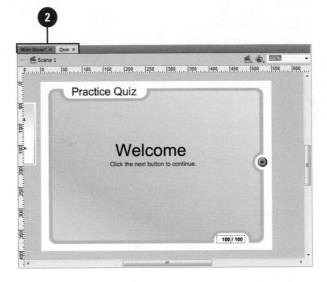

Change the Document View

1️⃣ Open more than one document.

2️⃣ Click the **View Size** list arrow in the Edit bar, and then select a view size: **Fit in Window**, **Show Frame**, **Show All**, or a percentage.

◆ You can also enter a custom percentage in the View Size box, and then press Enter (Win) or Return (Mac).

3️⃣ To display the document window in the full screen, click the **Window** menu, and then click **Hide Panels**.

◆ To show panels, click the **Window** menu, and then click **Show Panels**.

panels hidden

Move Document Windows Around

1️⃣ Open more than one document.

2️⃣ Do either of the following:

◆ **Rearrange the order of tabbed documents.** Drag a windows' tab to a new location (**New!**).

◆ **Dock or undock a document window.** Drag the window's tab out of the group or into the group (**New!**).

Undocked document window

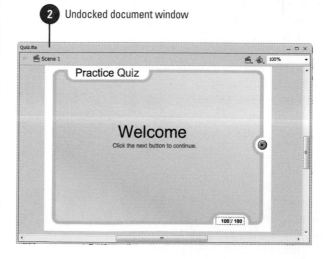

Saving a Document

When you save a Flash CS4 document within the authoring environment, the document is saved in the .fla format. If you want to display a document in the Adobe Flash Player, you need to publish or export the document in the .swf format. When you save a new document, you give it a name and specify the location in which to save the file. Name your documents clearly so you can easily locate them later. Also, creating folders and subfolders with meaningful names helps to locate files easily and saves a lot of time. When you save an existing file, the file retains its original name and folder location unless you specify a change. An unsaved Flash file displays an asterisk (*) after the name in the document name tab. To retain older versions of a document as you update it, use the Save As command and give each new version a new number with the old name, such as project1, project2 and so forth. Saving your files frequently ensures that you don't lose your work.

Save a Document

1. Click the **File** menu, and then click **Save**.

   If you are naming your document for the first time, continue. Otherwise, Flash saves the current document.

2. Type the new file name.

3. Navigate to the drive or folder location where you want to save the document.

4. Click **Save**.

5. If the file was created in Flash CS3, click **Save** or **Cancel** to convert it to Flash CS4.

Did You Know?

You can revert to the last saved version of a document. Click the File menu, and then click Revert.

You can save more than one document at a time. Click the File menu, and then click Save All.

You can save and compact an existing document to reduce the file size. Click the File menu, and then click Save And Compact.

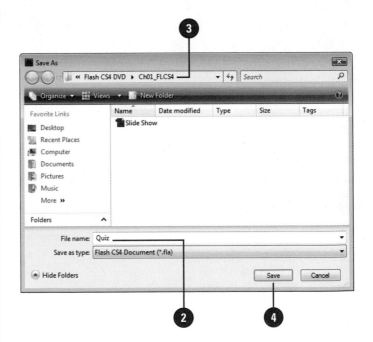

Save a Document with a Different Name or Location

1. Click the **File** menu, and then click **Save As**.

2. Type the new file name.

3. Navigate to the drive or folder location where you want to save the document.

4. Click the **New Folder** button.

5. Type the new folder name, and then press Enter (Win) or click **Create** (Mac).

6. Click **Save**.

7. If the file was created in Flash CS3, click **Save** or **Cancel** to convert it to Flash CS4.

Did You Know?

You can rename a folder in the Save As and Open dialog boxes (Win). Right-click the folder you want to rename, click Rename, type a new name, and then press Enter.

You can move or copy a file quickly in a dialog box (Win). In the Open or Save As dialog box, right-click the file you want to move or copy, click Cut or Copy, open the folder where you want to paste the file, right-click a blank area, and then click Paste.

There is a difference between Save and Save As. When you save an existing document using the Save command, Flash performs a quick save, which appends new content to the existing file. When you save a new document using the Save As command, Flash performs a complete save, which saves and compacts the content into a small file.

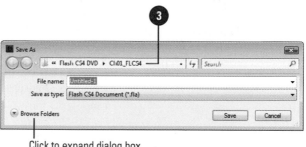

Click to expand dialog box

New folder

Saving a Document in Different Formats

A file type specifies the document format (for example, a template) as well as the program and version in which the file was created (for example, Flash CS4). You might want to change the type if you're creating a custom template or sharing files with someone who has an earlier version of Flash, such as Flash CS3. You use the Save As dialog box to change the file type for a document. The Format popup (Mac) or Save As Type list arrow (Win) displays a list of the available formats for Flash.

Save a Document in the Flash CS3 Format

1. Click the **File** menu, and then click **Save As**.

2. Click the **Format** popup (Mac) or **Save As Type** list arrow (Win), and then click **Flash CS3 Document**.

3. Type the new file name.

4. Navigate to the drive or folder location where you want to save the document.

5. Click **Save**.

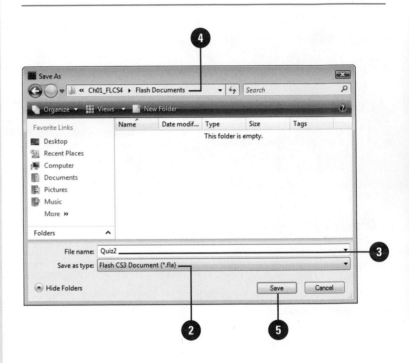

Did You Know?

You can delete a file in a dialog box (Win). In the Open or Save As dialog box, right click the file you want to delete, and then click Delete.

Save a Document as a Template

1. Click the **File** menu, and then click **Save as Template**.

2. Type a name for the new template.

3. Click the **Category** list arrow, and then click a category template.

4. Type a description for the new template.

5. Click **Save**.

6. If the file was created in Flash CS3, click **Save** or **Cancel** to convert it to Flash CS4.

See Also

See "Creating a New Document from a Template" on page 13 for information on creating a new document from a Flash template.

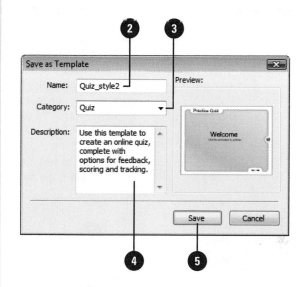

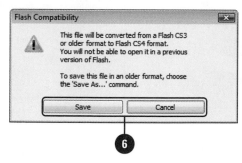

Getting Help While You Work

At some time, everyone has a question or two about the program they are using. Flash Help uses a Community Help site (**New!**) on the web at *adobe.com* (which is updated regularly) to help you find the information you need. When you start Flash Help, your browser opens, displaying a web site with Flash help categories and topics. You can search the Flash Help site by using keywords or phrases or browsing through a list of categories and topics to locate specific information. When you perform a search using keywords or phrases, a list of possible answers is shown to you from adobe.com, with the most likely answer to your question at the top of the list. Along with help text, some help topics include links to text and video tutorials. In addition, comments and ratings from users are available to help guide you to an answer.

Get Help Information

1. Click the **Help** menu, and then click **Flash Help**.

   TIMESAVER *Press F1.*

   Your browser opens, displaying Flash Help from the web. An Internet connected is required.

2. Click **Using Flash** to get help information for Flash. If you want help with ActionScript, click the appropriate link.

3. Click Help categories (plus sign icons) until you display the topic you want.

4. Click the topic you want.

5. Read the topic, and if necessary, click any hyperlinks to get information on related topics or definitions.

6. When you're done, close your browser.

Did You Know?

You can move backward and forward between help topics. Click the Previous or Next button on the right side of the Help web page.

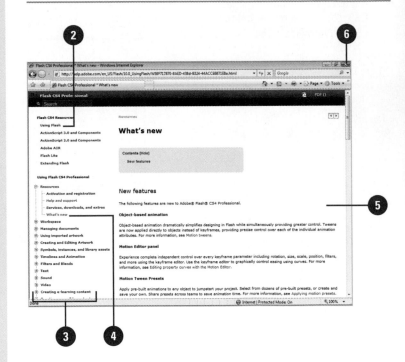

Search for Help Information

1 In Flash, on the menu bar (Win) or title bar (Mac), type one or more keywords in the Search box, and then press Enter (Win) or Return (Mac). You can also press F1 to open Help and use the Search box at the top of the screen.

Your browser opens, displaying an Adobe web site with a list of topics that match the keywords you entered in the Search box. An Internet connected is required.

2 Click the topic you want.

3 Read the topic, and then if you want, click any hyperlinks to get information on related topics or definitions.

4 When you're done, close your browser.

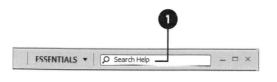

Search results

Did You Know?

You can find out what's new in Flash. Click the Help menu, click Flash Help, click Using Flash, click Using Adobe Flash Professional, click Resources, and then click What's New.

You can print out the selected Help topic. Open the Help screen in your browser, select the Help topic you want to print, select the Print command, specify print options, and then click Print (Win) or OK (Mac).

You can participate in the Adobe Product Improvement Program. **(New!)** Click the Help menu, click Adobe Product Improvement Program, and then follow the on-screen instructions. This is an opt-in program that allows you to test Adobe products and make suggestions for future products. This program enables Adobe to collect product usage data from customers while maintaining their privacy.

Flash Help Commands

Help Commands	Description
Flash Help	Access Flash Help window
Adobe Product Improvement Program **(New!)**	Participate in the direction of future versions of Adobe products
Flash Exchange	Access Flash downloadable applications
Manage Extensions	Access Flash extension information
Flash Support Center	Access Flash support on the Web
Adobe Online Forums	Access user conversations on the Web
Adobe Training	Access training information on the Web

Getting Online Updates and Support

Adobe offers a quick and easy way to update Flash CS4 and other CS4 related programs with any new software downloads directly from Flash using the Help menu. If you need more detailed information about a Flash task or feature, you can find out the latest information on the Web from the Adobe Flash Support Center and Flash Exchange Web sites. The Adobe Flash Support Center provides technical notes, documentation updates, and links to additional resources in the Flash community, while the Adobe Flash Exchange allows you to download additional applications and commands that other Flash users have developed and posted to extend the functionality of Flash. Some of the posted items are free while other charge a fee. You can access the Flash Support Center and the Flash Exchange from within Flash using commands on the Help menu.

Get Product Updates Online

1. Click the **Help** menu, and then click **Updates**.

   Flash checks your software with the latest available version and automatically updates it.

2. Click **Download and Install Updates**.

3. To change preferences, click **Preferences**, select the update options you want, and then click **OK**.

4. Click **Quit**.

Did You Know?

You can register to receive notices about upgrades and new products. If you haven't already registered during installation, click the Help menu, click Registration, and then follow the online instructions.

You can deactivate and activate Flash using the Help menu. If you have Flash installed on two computers, yet only have one license, you can use the Deactivate and Activate commands on the Help menu to go between the computers.

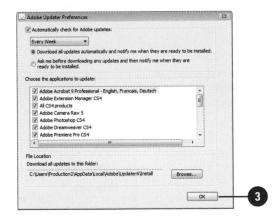

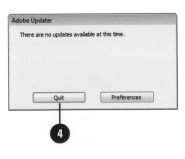

Get Online Support Information

1 Click the **Help** menu, and then click **Flash Support Center**.

Your Web browser opens, displaying the Adobe support Web site.

2 Search on the Web site for the help information you need.

3 When you're done, close your Web browser.

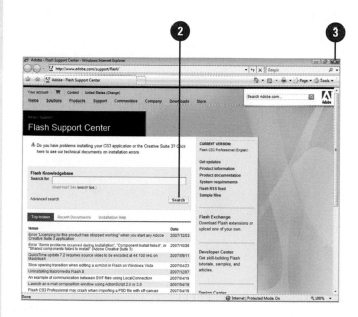

Get Resources from the Flash Exchange

1 Click the **Help** menu, and then click **Flash Exchange**.

Your Web browser opens, displaying the Adobe support Web site.

2 Search on the Web site for the help information you need, or click the **Product** popup, and then select a product to display the resource types you need.

3 Scroll through the list, and then follow the on-screen instructions to download and purchase (if necessary) the resources you want.

4 When you're done, close your Web browser.

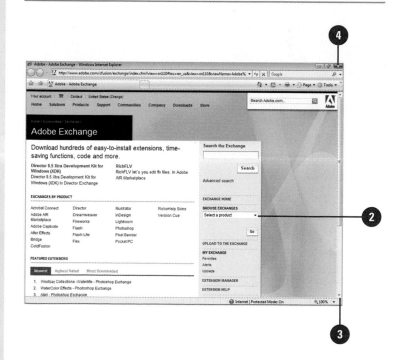

Finishing Up

After you work on a document, you can close the document by closing the document or by exiting Flash. You should save the document before closing it. Exiting Flash closes the current document and the Flash program and returns you to the desktop. You can use the Exit command on the File menu (Win) or Quit Flash command on the Flash menu (Mac) to close a document and exit Flash, or you can use the Close button on the Flash Document tab (**New!**). If you try to close a document without saving your final changes, a dialog box opens, asking if you want to do so.

Close a Document

1 Click the **Close** button on the Document tab, or click the **File** menu, and then click **Close**.

> **TIMESAVER** *Press ⌘+W (Mac) or Ctrl+W (Win) to close a document. Click the File menu, and then click Close All to close all open documents.*

2 If necessary, click **Yes** to save any changes you made to your open documents before the program quits.

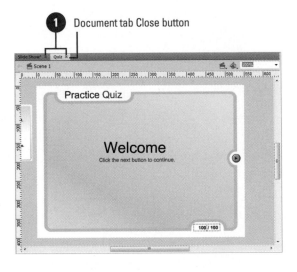

Document tab Close button

Exit Flash

1 Choose one of the following:

◆ Click the **Flash** menu, and then click **Quit Flash** (Mac).

◆ Click the **Close** button, or click the **File** menu, and then click **Exit** (Win).

2 If necessary, click **Yes** to save any changes you made to your open documents before the program quits.

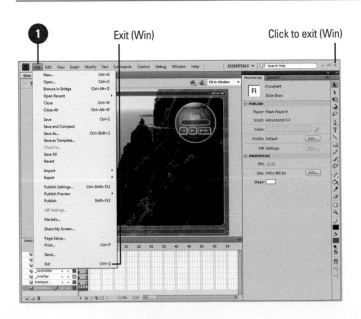

Exit (Win)   Click to exit (Win)

Working Within the Flash Environment

Introduction

Getting to know the Flash authoring environment makes you more effective and efficient as you create movies. You'll get to know the parts of the Flash window, which include the Timeline, Stage, panels, and Property Inspector.

The Tools panel, also known as the Toolbox, contains tools that you can use to draw, paint, select, and modify artwork. The Timeline represents the overall structure of a Flash document and controls the content. The Timeline consists of layers, frames, and scenes that make up a Flash document. Layers are like transparent sheets stacked on top of one another. Each layer can contain different images that appear on the Stage. A frame displays content at a specific moment on the Stage. The order in which frames appear in the Timeline determines the order in which they appear in the document. As you play a document, the playhead moves through the Timeline displaying the current frame with each layer on the Stage. If a project requires many animation sequences with hundreds of frames, you can organize the animations into scenes to make them easier to work with and manage. Below the Timeline is the Stage, which provides a place to compose the content for individual frames. Panels are windows that allow you to view, organize, and change elements and related options in a document. The Property Inspector is a specialized panel that allows you to change object-specific attributes and options.

Flash uses built-in keyboard shortcuts designed specifically for Flash. The built-in keyboard shortcuts are organized into sets, which you can duplicate and customize to create your own personalized set. Flash allows to you set preferences to customize the way you work in the program. As you design and develop a movie, you can print frames to review your work.

What You'll Do

Examining the Flash Window

When you start Flash, the program window displays several windows of varying sizes you can use to create a movie. These windows include the Timeline/Stage, various panels, and the Property Inspector. Depending on your installation and previous program usage, not all of these windows may appear, or additional ones may be visible. You'll do the bulk of your work in Flash with these windows.

In Flash, windows appear in the workspace with a title bar, such as the Timeline window, or in a panel. A **panel** is a window you can collapse, expand, and group with other panels, known as a panel group, to improve accessibility and workflow. A panel appears with a shaded header bar, which includes the window title and additional options. A panel group consists of either individual panels stacked one on top of the other

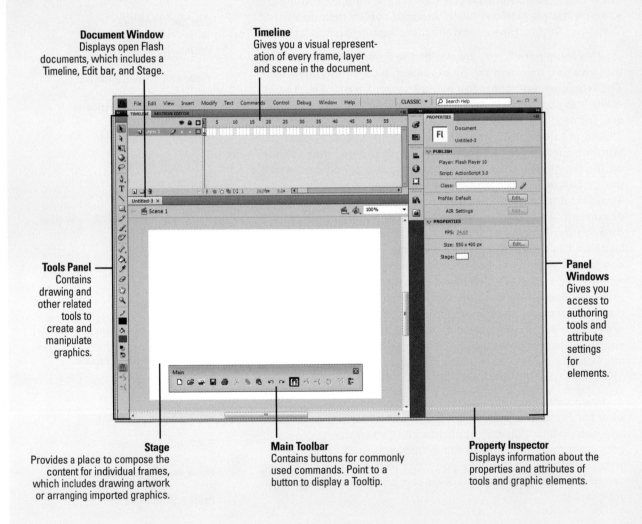

Document Window
Displays open Flash documents, which includes a Timeline, Edit bar, and Stage.

Timeline
Gives you a visual representation of every frame, layer and scene in the document.

Tools Panel
Contains drawing and other related tools to create and manipulate graphics.

Panel Windows
Gives you access to authoring tools and attribute settings for elements.

Stage
Provides a place to compose the content for individual frames, which includes drawing artwork or arranging imported graphics.

Main Toolbar
Contains buttons for commonly used commands. Point to a button to display a Tooltip.

Property Inspector
Displays information about the properties and attributes of tools and graphic elements.

or related panels organized together with tabs, such as the Components panel, to navigate from one panel to another. The Flash window Title bar displays the filename of the open file, and the program name Adobe Flash CS4. The Title bar also contains a Close button and resizing buttons.

A **menu** is a list of commands that you use to accomplish specific tasks. A **command** is a directive that accesses a feature of a program. Flash has its own set of menus, which are located on the menu bar along the top of the Flash window. On a menu, a check mark identifies a feature that is currently selected (that is, the feature is enabled or on). To disable (turn off) the feature, you click the command again to remove the check mark. A menu can contain several check-marked features. A bullet (Win) or diamond (Mac) also indicates that an option is enabled, but a menu can contain only one bullet-or diamond-marked feature per menu section. To disable a command with a bullet or diamond next to it, you must select a different option in the section on the menu.

When you perform a command frequently, it's faster, and sometimes more convenient, to use a shortcut key, which is a keyboard alternative to using the mouse. When a shortcut key is available, it is listed beside the command on the menu, such as ⌘+F3 (Mac) or Ctrl+F3 (Win) for the Properties command on the Window menu.

Flash (for Windows) also includes a Main toolbar. The **Main toolbar** contains buttons for the most frequently used commands. Clicking a button on a toolbar is often faster than clicking a menu and then clicking a command. When you position the pointer over a button, a tooltip appears, displaying the button name.

The **Tools panel** contains a set of tools you can use to create shapes, such as lines, rectangles, rounded rectangles, and ellipses. You can fill shapes with a color, pattern, or custom tile. The shapes and buttons you create in Flash are saved as media elements in the layers.

The **Document window** displays open Flash documents, which include a Timeline, Edit bar, and Stage. Flash (for Windows) also includes tabs to make it easier to switch back and forth between documents. At the top of the Document window is the Edit bar. The Edit bar displays what editing mode you are working in, and allows you to switch scenes.

The **Timeline** organizes and controls media elements over a linear timeline in rows called channels and in columns called frames. The Timeline displays a movie's Timeline and monitors the playback frame-by-frame. A frame represents a single point in a movie. The Timeline includes layers that control different parts of the movie.

The **Stage** is the visible portion of a movie, on which you determine where your media elements appear. The Stage is the rectangle area below the Timeline where you place graphic content, including vector art, text boxes, buttons, imported bitmap graphics, or audio and video clips. You can define the properties of your Stage, such as its size and color.

The **Property Inspector** provides a convenient way to view and change attributes of any selected object or multiple objects on the Stage in your movie. After you select an object, relevant commands and associated fields for it appear in the Property Inspector. You can apply filters (**New!**), such as gradient controls to text, buttons, and movie clips. In addition, you can display the Property Inspector horizontally (like previous versions of Flash) or vertically (**New!**).

Using the Timeline

The Timeline represents the overall structure of a Flash document and controls the content. The Timeline consists of layers, frames, and scenes that make up a Flash document. Layers appear on the left side of the Timeline and frames contained in each layer appear in a row to the right of the layer. The Timeline header above the frames displays the frame numbers. At the bottom of the Timeline, a Status bar appears, displaying the current frame indicator, the current rate indicator, and the elapsed time indicator. Sometimes it is hard to work with frames in a small view in the Timeline. You can change the size of frames and display frames with tinted cells. In addition, you can display thumbnail previews of frame content, which is useful for viewing animations.

Change the Timeline Display

◆ To lengthen or shorten layer name fields, drag the bar separating the layer names and the frames in the Timeline.

◆ To heighten or shorten the Timeline, drag the bar separating the Timeline and the Stage.

◆ To hide or show the Timeline panel, click the gray bar to the right of the Timeline tab.

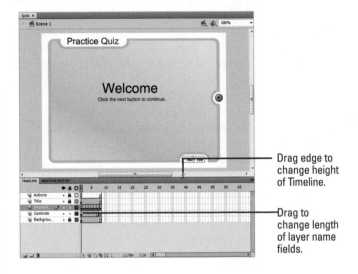

Drag edge to change height of Timeline.

Drag to change length of layer name fields.

Resize the Timeline Display

① Do one of the following:

◆ If the Timeline is docked to the program window, drag the bar separating the Timeline from the program window.

◆ If the Timeline is not docked to the program window, drag the size box in the lower right corner.

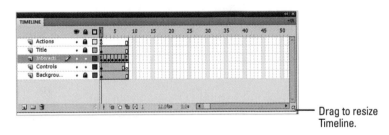

Drag to resize Timeline.

Change the Display of Frames in the Timeline

1. Click the **Frame View** button in the Timeline.

2. Select one of the following options from the list:

   ◆ To change the width of frame cells, click **Tiny**, **Small**, **Normal**, **Medium**, or **Large**.

   ◆ To decrease the height of frame cell rows, click **Short**.

   ◆ To turn frame sequence tinting on and off, click **Tinted Frames**.

   ◆ To display thumbnails of the content of each frame scaled to fit the Timeline frames, click **Preview**.

   ◆ To display thumbnails of each full frame, click **Preview In Context**.

   This is useful for viewing animation movement within their frames.

   ◆ To close the current tab, click **Close**. To close all the tabs, click **Close Group**. (**New!**)

See Also

See "Working with Panels" on page 52 for information on using the Timeline panel.

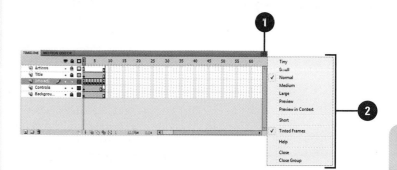

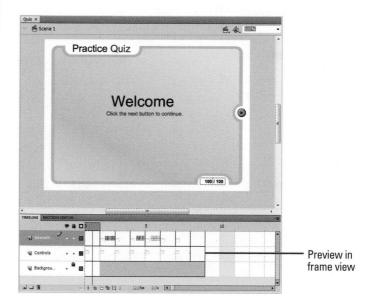

Preview in frame view

Working with Layers

Layers are like transparent sheets stacked on top of one another. Each layer can contain different images that appear on the Stage. You can draw and edit objects on one layer without affecting objects on another layer. Layers in a document are listed in the left column of the Timeline. Before you can work with a layer, you need to select it, or make it active. A pencil icon next to a layer or layer folder indicates it is active. Only one layer can be active at a time, even though you can select more than one layer. A new document comes with one layer, but you can add more to organize content on the Stage. As you create multiple layers of related content, you can create layer folders to make it easier to manage the layers.

Create a New Layer

1. Click the layer or folder above which you want to insert a layer.

2. Click the **New Layer** button at the bottom of the Timeline.

   The new layer appears above the selected layer.

Did You Know?

Flash names layers in order based on the highest number. If you add Layers 2 and 3, and then delete Layer 2. The next time you add a layer, Flash names it Layer 4.

Create a New Layer Folder

1. Click the layer or folder above which you want to insert a layer folder.

2. Click the **New Folder** button at the bottom of the Timeline

   The new layer folder appears above the selected layer.

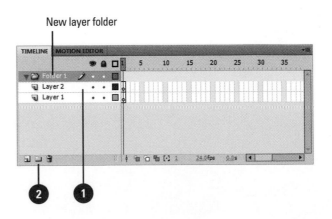

New layer folder

Rename a Layer or Folder

1. Double-click the name of a layer or folder.

2. Type a name.

3. Press Return (Mac) or Enter (Win).

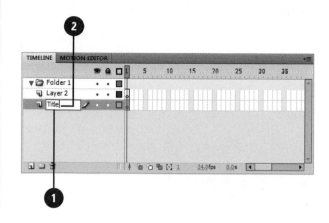

Delete a Layer or Folder

1. Select the layer or folder you want to delete.

2. Click the **Delete** button at the bottom of the Timeline.

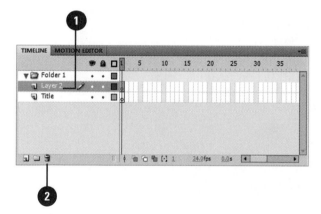

Did You Know?

There are several ways to select a layer. You can click the name of a layer or folder in the Timeline, click a frame in the Timeline of the layer you want to select, or select an object on the Stage that is located on the layer you want to select.

You can select multiple layers. To select contiguous layers or folders, click the first layer or folder, and then Shift+click the last layer or folder. To select noncontiguous layers or folders, ⌘+click (Mac) or Ctrl+click (Win) the layers or folders you want to select.

Viewing Layers

Flash includes controls (Eye, Lock, and Outline icons) in the layers section of the Timeline that allow you to quickly hide, show, lock, or unlock layers and layer folders, and display objects on a layer as colored outlines. Using colored outlines makes it easier to distinguish in which layer an object appears. When you hide a layer or folder with the Eye icon, a red X appears next to the name. When you lock a layer or folder with the Lock icon, a padlock appears next to the name. When you display layers as colored outlines with the Outline icon, a frame appears next to the name. When you change a folder, the controls affect all layers within a folder.

Show or Hide a Layer or Folder

1 Do one of the following:

◆ Click the Eye column to the right of the layer or folder to show or hide it.

◆ Click the **Eye** icon to show or hide all layers or folders.

◆ Option+click (Mac) or Alt+click (Win) in the Eye column to the right of a layer or folder to show or hide all other layers or folders.

Eye icon

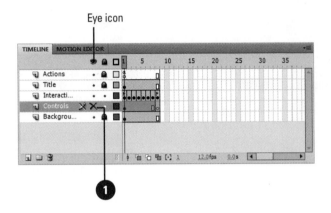

Lock or Unlock Layers or Folders

1 Do one of the following:

◆ Click in the Lock column to the right of the layer or folder to lock or unlock it.

◆ Click the **Lock** icon to lock or unlock all layers or folders.

◆ Option+click (Mac) or Alt+click (Win) in the Lock column to the right of a layer or folder to lock or unlock all other layers or folders.

Lock icon

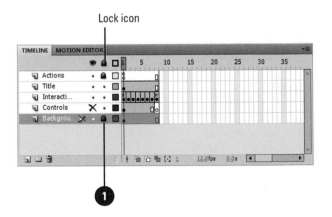

View the Contents of a Layer as Outlines

1. Do one of the following:

   ◆ Click the Outline column to the right of the layer's name to display its objects as outlines.

   ◆ Click the **Outline** icon to display objects on all layers as outlines.

   ◆ Option+click (Mac) or Alt+click (Win) in the Outline column to the right of a layer to display objects on all other layers as outlines.

Did You Know?

Hidden layers are visible when you publish a document. When you publish a Flash document as a .swf movie, hidden layers are visible in the Flash movie file.

See Also

See "Changing Layer Properties" on page 40 for information on changing the outline color.

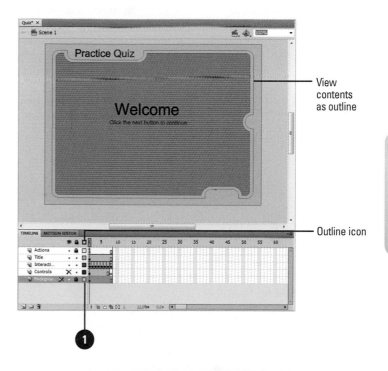

View contents as outline

Outline icon

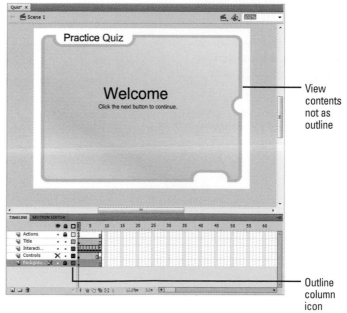

View contents not as outline

Outline column icon

Organizing Layers

In much the same way you organize files on your computer, you can use similar concepts to organize layers and layer folders in a document. You can expand or collapse a layer folder to show or hide its contents. You can also move a layer or folder into a layer folder or to another place in the layers list. Layer folders can contain layers and other layer folders. In addition, you can copy a layer or copy the contents of a layer folder.

Expand or Collapse a Layer Folder

1 Do one of the following:

◆ Click the triangle to the left of the folder name to expand or collapse the folder.

◆ Control+click (Mac) or right-click (Win) any layer, and then click **Expand All Folders** or **Collapse All Folders**.

Collapsed layer folder

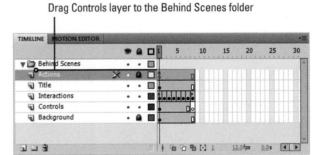

Move a Layer or Layer Folder

◆ To move a layer or folder into a layer folder, drag the layer or folder to the destination layer folder name in the Timeline.

◆ To move a layer or folder to another location, drag the layer or folder to a new position in the Timeline.

Drag Controls layer to the Behind Scenes folder

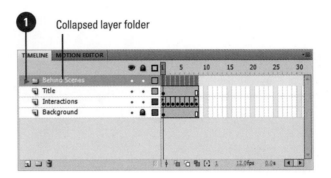

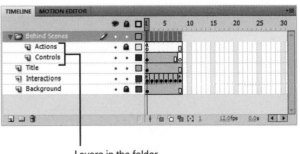

Layers in the folder

Copy a Layer

1. Click the layer you want to select.

2. Click the **Edit** menu, point to **Timclinc**, and then click **Copy Frames**.

3. Click the **New Layer** button.

4. Click the new layer to select it.

5. Click the **Edit** menu, point to **Timeline**, and then click **Paste Frames**.

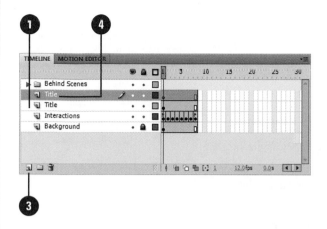

Copy the Contents of a Layer Folder

1. If necessary, click the triangle to the left of the folder name to collapse it.

2. Click the folder layer to select the entire folder.

3. Click the **Edit** menu, point to **Timeline**, and then click **Copy Frames**.

4. Select the layer below where you want to copy the layer folder.

5. Click the **New Folder** hutton.

6. Click the new layer folder to select it.

7. Click the **Edit** menu, point to **Timeline**, and then click **Paste Frames**.

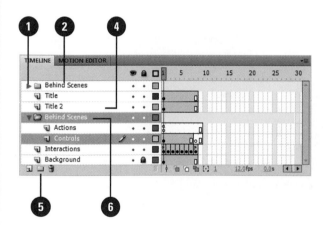

Changing Layer Properties

The Layer Properties dialog box makes it easy to changes several layer options at once. You can change a layer name, show or lock a layer, change a layer type or outline color, and modify the layer height to show more information in the Timeline. Setting layer properties of a folder automatically sets the properties for all the layers within that folder.

Change Layer Properties

1. Select the layer in the Timeline.

2. Click the **Modify** menu, point to **Timeline**, and then click **Layer Properties**.

3. Select from the following options:

    ◆ **Name.** Enter a new name.

    ◆ **Show.** Select this check box to show the layer.

    ◆ **Lock.** Select this check box to lock the layer or clear it to unlock the layer.

    ◆ **Type.** Select a layer option: Normal, Mask, Masked, Folder, or Guide.

    ◆ **Outline Color.** Click the Color box, and then select a color.

    ◆ **View Layer As Outlines.** Select this check box to view the layer as outlines.

    ◆ **Layer Height.** Click the popup, and then select a percentage to display more information in the Timeline.

4. Click **OK**.

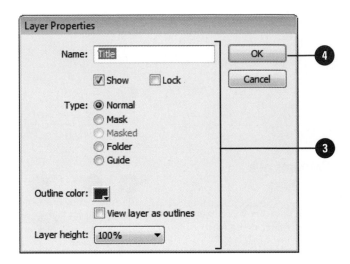

Layer Types	
Layer	**Description**
Normal	The default layer type.
Mask	Mask layers hide and reveal portions of linked layers that lie directly beneath the mask layer.
Masked	Masked layers contain elements that can be hidden or revealed by a mask layer.
Folder	Folder layers allow you to organize layers.
Guide	There are two types of guide layers: guides and motion guides. Guides help you place and align objects on the Stage, motion guides designate a path that an animated object follows. Guided layers contain objects that follow an animation path. You need to link the guided layer to the motion guide.

Using Guide Layers

Guide layers help you draw and align objects on layers that appear on the Stage. After you create a guide layer, you can align objects on other layers to objects you create on the guide layer. You can make any layer a guide layer. You can also create a motion guide layer to control the movement of objects in a motion tweened animation.

Create a Guide Layer

① Click the layer you want to convert to a guide layer.

② Control+click (Mac) or right-click (Win) the selected layer, and then click **Guide**.

Did You Know?

You can change a guide layer back to a normal layer. Control (Mac) or right-click (Win) the selected layer, and then click Guide.

You can convert a guide layer to a motion guide layer. Drag a normal layer onto a guide layer.

See Also

See "Using Snap Align" on page 94 for information on snapping items you draw or drag to snap to lines or shapes.

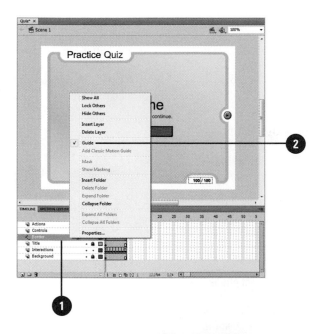

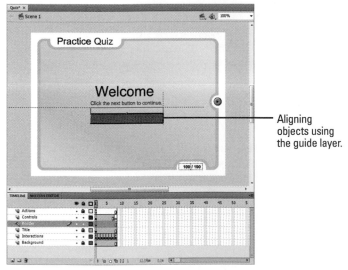

Aligning objects using the guide layer.

Working with Frames

A **frame** displays content at a specific moment on the Stage. The order in which frames appear in the Timeline determines the order in which they appear in the document. The Timeline displays each frame in sequential order from 1 to the end of the document. As you play a document, the **playhead** moves through the Timeline displaying the current frame with each layer on the Stage. When you work with frames, you can select, insert, delete, and move frames in the Timeline. When you move frames in the Timeline, you can place them on the same layer or a different layer. If you want to display a specific frame in a document, you can move the playhead to the frame in the Timeline to display the frame content on the Stage. Another type of frame is called a keyframe. A keyframe defines a change in an animation or uses actions to modify a document.

Select One or More Frames

◆ To select one frame, click on the frame.

   IMPORTANT *If the Span Based Selection preference is turned on, clicking a frame selects the entire frame sequence between two keyframes.*

◆ To select multiple contiguous frames, click the first frame in the sequence, hold down Shift, and then click the last frame in the sequence.

◆ To select multiple noncontiguous frames, ⌘+click (Mac) or Ctrl+click (Win) the frames you want to select.

Did You Know?

You can center the Timeline on the current frame. Click the Center Frame button at the bottom of the Timeline.

See Also

See "Using the Timeline" on page 32 for information on changing the view size of frames in the Timeline.

Playhead   Select one frame

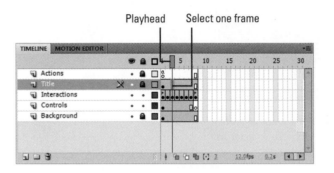

Select multiple contiguous frames

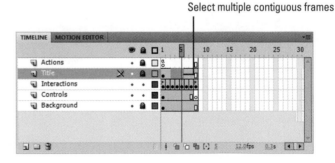

Select multiple noncontiguous frames

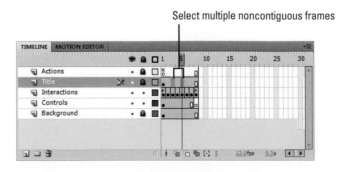

Insert a Frame

1. Click the frame's location in the Timeline header, or drag the playhead to the frame where you want to insert a frame.

2. Click the **Insert** menu, point to **Timeline**, and then click **Frame**.

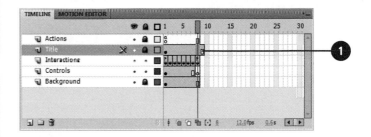

Did You Know?

You can add labels to frames to reference in ActionScripts. In the Timeline, select the frame you want. In the Property Inspector, enter a name in the Name box under Label.

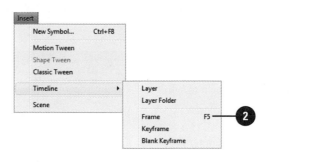

Delete Frames

1. Select the frame, keyframe, or sequence you want to delete.

2. Click the **Edit** menu, point to **Timeline**, and then click **Remove Frames**.

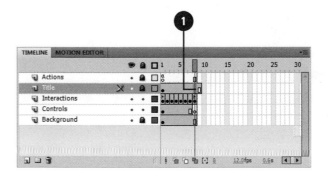

Did You Know?

You can move a frame sequence or keyframe. Drag the frame sequence or keyframe to another location in the Timeline.

You can copy a frame sequence or keyframe. Option+drag (Mac) or Alt+drag (Win) the frame sequence or keyframe to another location in the Timeline.

Working with Scenes

If a project requires a lot of animations with hundreds of frames, you can organize the animations into scenes to make them easier to work with and manage. The Scene panel makes it easy to display the number of scenes in the document, select current scenes for editing, create new scenes, duplicate scenes, delete scenes, and reorder them. You can also use the Edit bar to select a scene to edit. When you select a scene, Flash displays it on the Stage. When you publish a document as a movie, the scenes play in order unless you add interactivity to play them differently. Be aware that scenes are treated like self-contained movies, so transitions between scenes with interactivity may not be seamless.

Open the Scene Panel and Select a Scene

1. Click the **Window** menu, point to **Other Panels**, and then click **Scene**.

   A list of scenes appears in order in the panel. In a new document, the Scene panel displays only the default Scene 1.

2. Click the scene you want to display.

Add a Scene

1. If necessary, open the Scene panel.

2. Click the **Add Scene** button in the Scene panel.

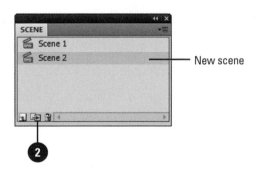

New scene

Did You Know?

Flash names scenes in order based on the highest number. If you add Scenes 2 and 3, and then delete Scene 2, the next time you add a scene, Flash names it Scene 4.

Rename a Scene

1. If necessary, open the Scene panel.

2. Double-click the scene you want to rename.

3. Type a new name.

4. Press Return (Mac) or Enter (Win).

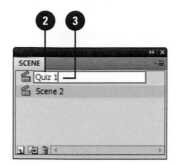

Delete a Scene

1. If necessary, open the Scene panel.

2. Click the scene you want to delete.

3. Click the **Delete Scene** button in the Scene panel.

4. Click **OK** to confirm the deletion.

   TIMESAVER *If you don't want to display the Confirmation dialog box, press ⌘+click (Mac) or Ctrl+click (Win) the Delete Scene button.*

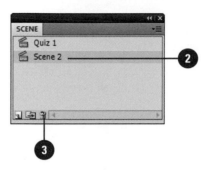

Did You Know?

You can undo the deletion of a scene. If you mistakenly delete a scene, you can undo; press ⌘+Z (Mac) or Ctrl+Z (Win).

You can reorder scenes in the Scene panel. In the Scene panel, drag a selected scene up or down in the list.

Using the Edit Bar

The Edit bar contains controls and information for editing scenes and symbols, and for changing the view size of the Stage. The Edit bar lets you know what editing mode you are working in and allows you to switch scenes. The Scene button allows you to edit a scene in document-editing mode, while the Symbol button allows you to edit symbols in the symbol-editing mode. The Back button on the Edit bar returns you to document-editing mode.

Show and Hide the Edit Bar

◆ To display the Edit bar, click the **Window** menu, point to **Toolbars**, and then click **Edit Bar** to select the check mark.

◆ To hide the Edit bar, click the **Window** menu, point to **Toolbars**, and then click **Edit Bar** to deselect the check mark.

Click to select (show) or deselect (hide) the check mark.

Back button

Current scene or symbol being edited

Edit bar

Change View Size of the Stage

1. Click the **View Size** popup in the Edit bar, and then select a view size percentage or an option:

   ◆ **Fit To Window**

   ◆ **Show Frame**

   ◆ **Show All**

Did You Know?

You can use the Hand tool to move the Stage to change the view. Click the Hand tool (H) on the Tools panel, and then drag the Stage to change the view.

Select and type a view percentage

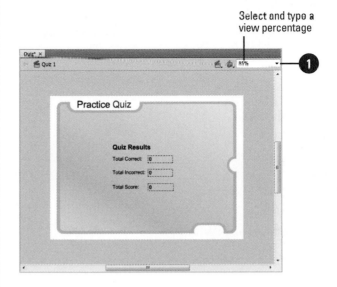

Select a Scene or Symbol to Edit

◆ To select a scene, click the **Edit Scene** button in the Edit bar, and then select a scene from the list.

◆ To select a symbol, click the **Edit Symbol** button in the Edit bar, and then select a symbol from the list.

Edit Scene button   Edit Symbol button

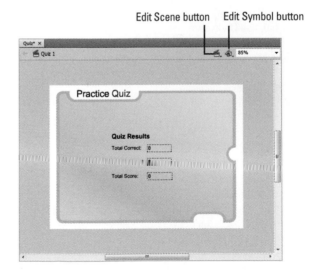

Using the Main Toolbar

If you use Windows, you can display and use the Main toolbar above the Document menu window to quickly access common document and object-related commands, such as New, Open, Save, Print, Cut, Copy, Paste, Redo, Undo, Snap To Objects, Smooth, Straighten, Rotate And Skew, Scale, and Align. When you're finished working with the Main toolbar, you can hide it to create more workspace.

Show and Hide the Main Toolbar in Windows

◆ To display the Main toolbar, click the **Window** menu, point to **Toolbars**, and then click **Main** to select the check mark.

◆ To hide the Main toolbar, click the **Window** menu, point to **Toolbars**, and then click **Main** to deselect the check mark.

Did You Know?

You can use Undo and Redo commands on the menu bar. The Undo and Redo commands on the Edit menu undo (returns you to a previous point) and redo (re-performs commands you undid) actions you've taken in a document. The names of the Undo and Redo commands change to reflect the current action.

Flash supports 100 undo and redo levels. To change the number of undo levels, click the Edit (Win) or Flash (Mac) menu, click the General tab, specify a number in the Undo Levels box, and then click OK. The lower the number of levels, the less amount of memory the program needs to run.

Click to select (show) or deselect (hide) the check mark.

Main toolbar

Resizing Panels

If you need more workspace, you can use the double-arrow button (at the top of a panel group) to quickly minimize a panel group, such as the Tools panel or Property Inspector. When you click the double-arrow button, the panel group collapses to icons, which increases the size of the workspace. You can click the icons to display the panel. When you click the double-arrow button again, the panel group reopens. If you need to increase or decrease the size of a docking panel, you can drag the resize bar at the top-left side of the panel group to resize it as you would any window.

Minimize and Maximize Panels

1 To minimize or maximize a docking channel, click the **Double-arrow** button at the top of the panel group.

The double-arrow direction indicates whether the panel minimizes or maximizes.

For example, if the double-arrow points to the left of the Tools panel that means when you click it the Tools panel minimizes. If the double-arrow points to the right that means when you click it the Tools panel maximizes.

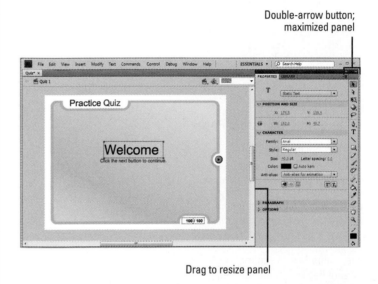

Double-arrow button; maximized panel

Drag to resize panel

Double-arrow button; minimized panel

Using the Tools Panel

The **Tools panel**, also known as the Toolbox, contains tools that you can use to draw, paint, select, and modify artwork. The Tools panel is divided into 4 main sections: (1) the first section at the top contains selection and transform tools; (2) the next section contains tools for drawing, painting, and adding text; (3) the next selection contains tools for changing, modifying, drawing and painting; and (4) the last section contains additional tool options for zooming and panning in the program window, changing stroke and fill colors, and selecting other options. You can show or hide the Tools panel as necessary and customize the Tools panel to display the tools you use most often. You can now expand and collapse the Tools panel to switch between one and two columns of tools. When you customize the Tools panel, you can display more than one tool in a location. The top tool in the group appears with an arrow in the lower right corner of its icon. When you click and hold the pointer on the top tool, the other tools in the group appear in a pop-up menu. When you select a tool from the group, it appears in the Tools panel as the top tool.

Show and Hide the Tools Panel

◆ To display the Tools panel, click the **Window** menu, and then click **Tools** to select the check mark.

◆ To hide the Tools panel, click the **Window** menu, and then click **Tools** to deselect the check mark.

◆ To collapse and expand the Tools panel between one and two columns, click the double-arrows at the top of the Tools panel.

Did You Know?

You can move the Tools panel. Drag the title bar or textured area at the top of the Tools panel to the desired location.

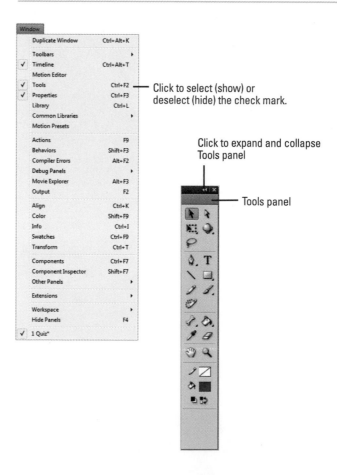

Click to select (show) or deselect (hide) the check mark.

Click to expand and collapse Tools panel

Tools panel

Customize the Tools Panel

① Click the **Flash** (Mac) or **Edit** menu (Win), and then click **Customize Tools Panel**.

② Click a tool in the Tools panel graphic.

③ To add a tool, select the tool in the Available Tools list, and then click **Add**.

   TIMESAVER *You can add more than one tool to a location.*

④ To remove a tool, select the tool in the Current Selection list, and then click **Remove**.

⑤ Click **OK**.

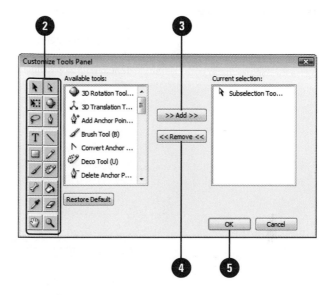

Did You Know?

You can restore the Tools panel to the default layout. Click the Flash (Mac) or Edit menu (Win), click Customize Tools Panel, click Restore Defaults, and then click OK.

You can identify keyboard shortcuts for the Tools panel. In the Customize Tools Panel dialog box, the letter in parenthesis indicates the keyboard shortcut.

For Your Information

Creating Tools

Flash lets you design your own Tools, using the JSFL language. In addition you can download tools created by other authors at the Adobe Exchange at http://www.adobe.com/cfusion/exchange /index.cfm. Although Adobe has yet to properly document the JSFL language, point your browser to *http://www.dynamicflash.co.uk/jsfl/* for a look at how JSFL is implemented in the Flash environment.

Working with Panels

Panels are windows that allow you to view, organize, and change elements and related options in a document. In Flash, you work with several panel windows at one time. Instead of continually moving, resizing, or opening and closing windows, you can collapse or expand individual panels within a window with a single click to save space. A panel appears with a header, which includes the tab titles and three accessibility options: the Minimize/Maximize button, the Close button, and an Options menu. The entire set of panels includes a double arrow you can use the collapse and expand the entire panel between icons with text and full panels. You use the Minimize/Maximize button to collapse or expand panels. The Options menu provides you with panel specific commands, including group, rename, maximize, close a panel, and use the Help system.

Open and Close a Panel

1. Click the **Window** menu.

2. Do one of the following:

   ◆ Click a panel name, such as Properties, Timeline, Tools, and Library.

   ◆ Point to a panel category, such as Other Panels, and then click a panel name.

   TIMESAVER *To close a panel, click the Close button on the panel or the tab you want.*

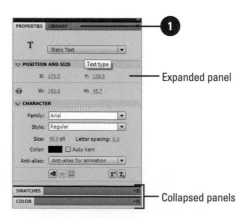

Panels on Window menu

More panels on Window submenu

Collapse and Expand a Panel

1. To collapse or expand an open panel, click the header bar or double-click the title tab on the header bar of the panel.

   TIMESAVER *To hide and show all panels, click the Window menu, and then click Hide Panels.*

   TIMESAVER *To Auto-Collapse Icon Panels or Auto-Show Hidden Panels, right-click (Win) or option-click (Mac), and then select a command.*

Expanded panel

Collapsed panels

Collapse and Expand the Panel Set Between Icons and Panels

◆ To collapse the panel set to icons with text, click the double arrow pointing right (Collapse to Icons) at the top of the panels.

◆ To expand the panel set from icons with text to full panels, click the double arrow pointing left (Expand Dock) at the top of the panels.

◆ To have an expanded panel icon automatically collapse or hide when you click away, right-click (Win) or control-click (Mac) a panel, and then click **Auto-Collapse Icon Panels** or **Auto-Show Hidden Panels**. (**New!**)

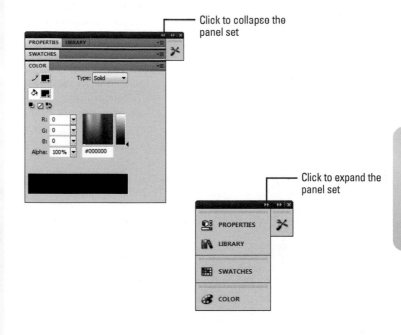

Click to collapse the panel set

Click to expand the panel set

Use the Panel Options Menu

1 Open or expand a panel.

2 Click the **Options** button on the right side of the panel header bar.

3 Click a command from the list (commands vary). Common commands include:

◆ **Help.** Accesses Flash Help.

◆ **Close.** Closes the currently displayed tab in the panel.

◆ **Close Group.** Closes all the tabs in the panel.

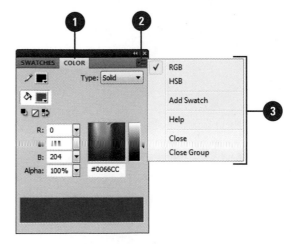

Docking and Undocking Panels

You can dock and undock, or temporarily attach and detach, panels or panel groups. You can display panels using the Window menu, and then drag them around the program window to dock or undock them to other panels. You can even drag the Property Inspector panel to display it horizontally or vertically (**New!**). However, document panels and the Stage cannot be docked. When you drag a panel over a dockable area, an outline around the target dock appears. When you release the mouse button, the panel snaps to the dockable area and stays there until you move it. You can even drag a panel tab to a new position. If you attempt to dock a panel over an undockable area, no outline appears.

Dock a Panel

1. Position the pointer on the panel tab or panel set header bar.

2. Drag the window away from the panel to a panel.

   ◆ **Add to Panel.** Drag to a panel until a blue rectangle appears around the panel.

   ◆ **Append to Panel.** Drag to a panel until a blue line appears along the side of the panel.

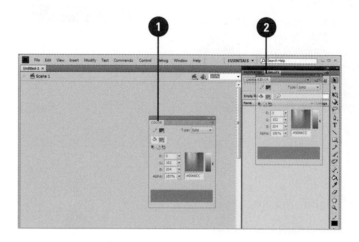

Undock a Panel

1. Position the pointer on the panel tab or panel set header bar.

2. Drag the window away from the panel to an empty area of the Flash window.

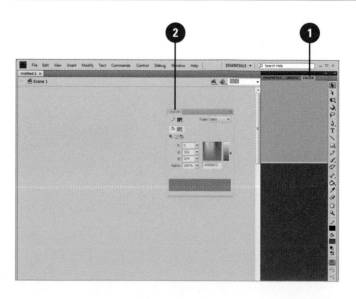

Grouping and Ungrouping Panels

You can group panels together to improve organization and workflow. When you group panels together, you can stack one on top of the other, or group related panels together as a tabbed panel group, such as the Component Inspector panel. You can add a panel to an existing panel group or you can create a new panel group. If you no longer need panels grouped together, you can ungroup them. You can use the panel tab to group or ungroup as well as dock or undock panel windows.

Group Panels Together

1. Position the pointer on the panel tab or panel set header bar.

2. Drag the window away from the panel to another panel window.

   ◆ **Add to Panel.** Drag to a panel until a blue rectangle appears around the panel.

   ◆ **Append to Panel.** Drag to a panel until a blue line appears along the side of the panel.

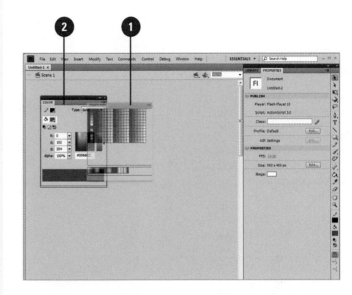

Ungroup Panels

1. Position the pointer on the panel tab or panel set header bar.

2. Drag the window away from the panel to an empty area of the Flash window.

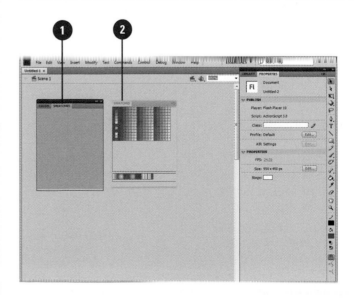

Creating a Workspace

As you work with Flash, you'll open, close, and move around windows and panels to meet your individual needs. After you customize the Flash workspace, you can save the location of windows and panels as a workspace, or custom panel set, which you can display by using the Workspace menu on the Applications bar (**New!**) or the Workspaces submenu on the Window menu. You can create custom workspaces, or use a workspace provided by Flash, which are designed for space and workflow efficiency. The built-in workspaces include Classic, Debug, Designer, Developer, or Essential. (**New!**) If you no longer use a custom workspace, you can remove it at any time. You can also rename a custom workspace to improve recognition.

Create a Workspace

1. Open and position the panels you want to include in a panel set.

2. Click the **Workspace** menu (**New!**) (the menu name displays the current workspace), and then click **New Workspace**.

   ◆ You can also click the **Window** menu, point to **Workspace**, and then click **New Workspace**.

   The New Workspace dialog box opens.

3. Type a name in the Name box.

4. Click **OK**.

   The panel set is now saved.

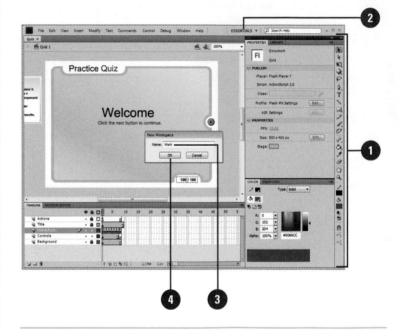

Display a Workspace

1. Click the **Workspace** menu (**New!**) (the menu name displays the current workspace), and then select a panel option:

   ◆ **Custom panel name.** Displays a custom panel layout that you created.

   ◆ **Classic**, **Debug**, **Designer**, **Developer**, or **Essential.** Displays panel layouts created by Adobe for specific purposes in Flash. (**New!**)

Workspace menu

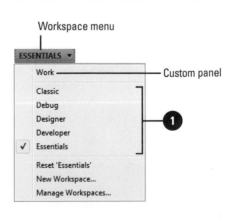

Custom panel

Delete a Workspace

1. Click the **Window** menu, point to **Workspace**, and then click **Manage Workspaces**.

   The Manage Workspaces dialog box opens.

2. Select the panel set you want to delete.

3. Click **Delete**.

4. Click **Yes** to confirm the deletion.

5. Click **OK**.

   The panel set is now deleted.

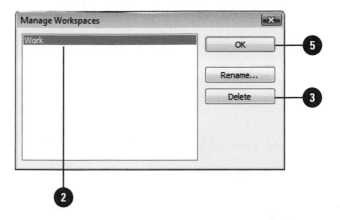

Did You Know?

You can hide all panels. Click the Window menu, and then click Hide Panels to select the check mark.

Rename a Workspace

1. Click the **Window** menu, point to **Workspace**, and then click **Manage Workspaces**.

   The Manage Workspaces dialog box opens.

2. Select the panel set you want to rename.

3. Click **Rename**.

4. Type a new name, and then click **OK**.

   The panel set is now renamed.

5. Click **OK**.

Creating Keyboard Shortcuts

Flash uses built-in keyboard shortcuts designed specifically for Flash. A complete list of the keyboard shortcuts is available in the back of this book. The built-in keyboard shortcuts are organized into sets, which you can duplicate and customize to create your own personalized set. If you use other programs, such as Adobe Illustrator or Adobe Photoshop, and you are more comfortable using their keyboard shortcuts for common commands, you can select a built-in keyboard shortcut set from any of the graphics programs to use in Flash.

Create a Keyboard Shortcut Set

1. Click the **Flash** (Mac) or **Edit** (Win) menu, and then click **Keyboard Shortcuts**.

2. Click the **Current Set** popup, and then select a set.

3. Click the **Duplicate Set** button.

4. Type a name for the new shortcut set.

5. Click **OK**.

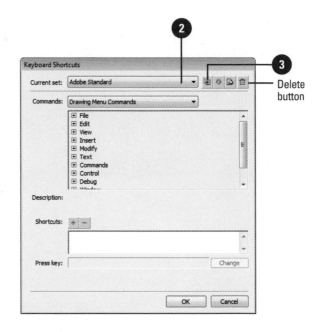

Delete button

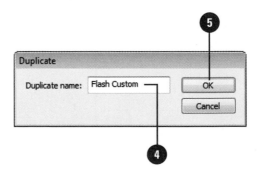

Did You Know?

You can delete a custom keyboard shortcut set. Click the Flash (Mac) or Edit (Win) menu, click Keyboard Shortcuts, select a shortcut set from the Current Set popup, and then click the Delete button. You cannot delete a built-in keyboard shortcut set that comes with Flash.

You can rename a custom keyboard shortcut set. Click the Flash (Mac) or Edit (Win) menu, click Keyboard Shortcuts, select a shortcut set from the Current Set popup, click the Rename Set button, enter a new name, and then click OK. You cannot rename a built-in keyboard shortcut set that comes with Flash.

Add or Remove a Keyboard Shortcut

1 Click the **Flash** (Mac) or **Edit** (Win) menu, and then click **Keyboard Shortcuts**.

2 Click the **Current Set** popup, and then select the set in which you want to change.

3 Click the **Commands** popup, and then select a shortcut category, such as Drawing Menu Commands, Drawing Tools, Test Movie Menu Commands, and Workplace Accessibility Commands.

4 Select the command for which you want to add or remove a shortcut in the Commands list.

5 Do the following:

◆ To add a shortcut, click the **Add Shortcut** (+) button, and then press the key combination to enter the new shortcut key in the Press Key box.

◆ To remove a shortcut, click the **Remove Shortcut** (-) button.

6 Click **Change**.

7 To add or remove additional shortcuts, repeat Steps 2 0.

8 Click **OK**.

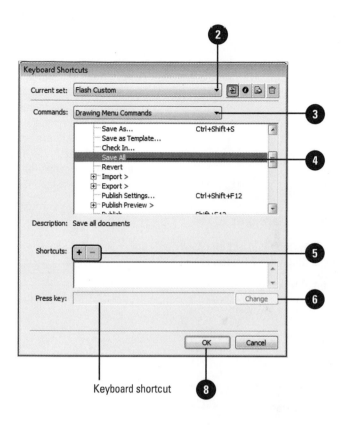

Keyboard shortcut

For Your Information

Export keyboard shortcuts as HTML

You can now export Flash keyboard shortcuts as an HTML file that you can view and print using a standard Web browser. To export the keyboard shortcuts, click the Flash (Mac) or Edit (Win) menu, click Keyboard Shortcuts, click the Current Set popup, select the set you want, click the Export Set As HTML button, enter a file name, specify a location, and then click Save.

Setting General Preferences

Flash allows you to set general preferences to customize the way you work in the program. You can specify what you want to display or open when you launch Flash. Some of the preferences allow you to specify the number of undo levels, enable multiple selection, show tooltips, open documents and test movies in tabs, enable span-based selection in the Timeline, make the first frame of each scene in a document a named anchor, and select a specific selection highlight color for different element types, such as drawings, groups, and symbols. You can also set Project preferences for closing and saving project files. In Flash CS4, the Preferences dialog box is reorganized with new categories and options for ease of use, such as having have Flash open a new document tab instead of opening in its own window.

Set General Preferences

1. Click the **Flash** (Mac) or **Edit** (Win) menu, and then click **Preferences**.

2. Click the **General** category.

3. Select from the following options:

   ◆ **On Launch.** Select an option to specify which document opens when you start the program.

      ◆ **Welcome Screen.**

      ◆ **New Document.**

      ◆ **Last Documents Open.**

      ◆ **No Document.**

   ◆ **Undo Levels.** Select Document or Object-level Undo, and then enter a value from 2 to 300 to set the number of undo/redo levels. The default level is 100.

   ◆ **Test Movie.** Select the Open Test Movie In Tabs check box to have Flash open a new document tab.

   ◆ **Auto-Collapse Icon Panels.** Select this check box to automatically collapse the panel set to Icons only.

   ◆ **Shift Select.** Select or clear this check box to control the selection of multiple elements.

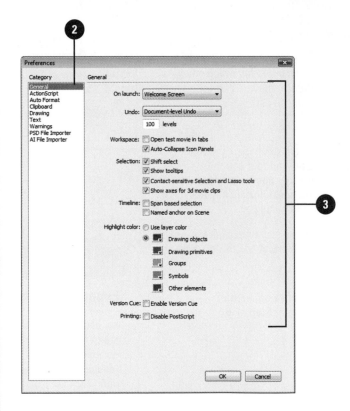

- **Show Tooltips.** Select to display tooltips when the pointer points to a button or control.

- **Contact-Sensitive Selection and Lasso Tools.** For the object drawing model, select to select objects when any part of the marquee touches it. Clear it to select objects that are completely enclosed by the marquee. Points within the selection will be selected.

- **Show Axes For 3D Movie Clips.** Select to show axes for 3d movie clips. (**New!**)

- **Span Based Selection.** Select to use span-based selection instead of frame-based selection.

- **Named Anchor On Scene.** Select to make the first frame of each scene in a document a named anchor.

- **Highlight Color.** Select the Use Layer Color option to use the current layer's outline color, or select the option, and then select a color for Drawing objects, Drawing primitives, groups, symbols, and other elements.

- **Version Cue.** Select this check box to enable Version Cue, a file version manager.

- **Printing (Win).** Select the Disable PostScript check box if you have problems printing to a postscript printer.

4 Click **OK**.

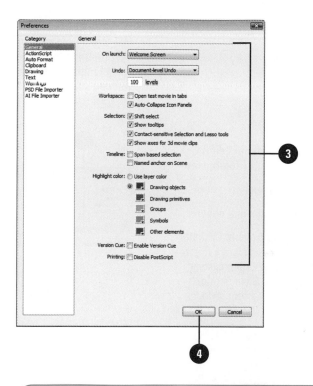

For Your Information

Setting Drawing Model Options

You can draw shapes in Flash using two main drawing models: Merge Drawing and Object Drawing. **Merge Drawing** model automatically merges shapes that you draw when you overlap them. If you select a shape that has been merged with another, and move it, the shape below it is moved too. For example, if you draw a square and overlay a circle on top of it, and then select the circle and move it, the portion of the square that overlaid the circle is removed. **Object Drawing** model allows you to draw shapes as separate objects that do not automatically merge together when overlaid. This lets you overlap shapes without altering their appearance should you choose to move them apart, or rearrange their appearance. Flash creates each shape as a separate object that you can individually manipulate. When you select a shape created using the Object Drawing model, Flash surrounds the shape with a rectangular bounding box. You can use the Pointer tool to move the object by clicking the bounding box and dragging the shape anywhere you'd like to position it on the Stage. You can now extend the Object Drawing mode by creating primitive rectangles and ovals in **Primitive mode**, which allows you to edit properties in the Property Inspector and specify the corner radius of rectangles and inner radius of ovals. This makes it easy to create pie wedges, round off corners, and other shapes.

Setting Text Preferences

When you edit or work with text in a Flash document, you can specify text related preferences. You can select a font to use when substituting missing fonts, or select text orientation options, which is useful when using English (horizontal) or Asian (vertical) language fonts. In addition, you can select a language as an input method.

Set Text Preferences

1. Click the **Flash** (Mac) or **Edit** (Win) menu, and then click **Preferences**.

2. Click the **Text** category.

3. Select from the following options:

   ◆ **Font Mapping Default.** Click the popup, and then select a font to use when substituting missing fonts. Click the **Style** popup, and then select a font style. (**New!**)

   ◆ **Show For Missing Fonts.** Select to show the Font Mapping dialog box. (**New!**)

   ◆ **Vertical Text options.**

      ◆ **Default Text Orientation.** Select to make default orientation vertical, which is useful for Asian fonts.

      ◆ **Right To Left Text Flow.** Select to reverse the default text display direction.

      ◆ **No Kerning.** Select to turn off kerning for vertical text.

   ◆ **Input Method.** Select the Text Input Window check box (Mac) or language option to select a language type.

   ◆ **ActionScript Editing.** Select the check box to use a key to insert the \ character. (**New!**)

   ◆ **Font Menus.** Select check boxes and option to show fonts in menus. (**New!**)

4. Click **OK**.

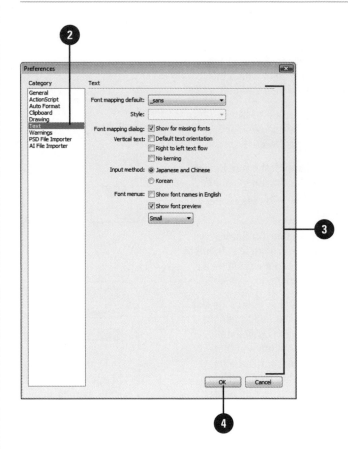

Setting Clipboard Preferences

When you copy or cut graphics to the Clipboard, you can set preferences to determine how you want to paste the graphic into a Flash document. The preference options give you control over the size and quality of the graphics you insert in a document. If you are using Windows, the Clipboard preferences include options for bitmaps and gradients in the Windows Metafile format. If you are using a Macintosh, the Clipboard preferences include options for the PICT format.

Set Clipboard Preferences

1. Click the **Flash** (Mac) or **Edit** (Win) menu, and then click **Preferences**.

2. Click the **Clipboard** category.

3. Select from the following options:

   ◆ **Bitmaps (Win).** Select options for Color Depth and Resolution to specify these parameters for bitmaps copied to the Clipboard. Select Smooth to apply anti-aliasing. Enter a value in the Size Limit box to specify the amount of RAM that is used when placing a bitmap on the Clipboard.

   ◆ **PICT Settings (Mac).** Select Objects to preserve data copied to the Clipboard as a vector graphic, or select one of the bitmap formats to convert the image. Enter a value for Resolution. Select the Include Postscript check box to include Postscript data. For gradients, select an option to specify quality in the PICT.

   ◆ **Gradient quality.** Select an option to specify the quality of gradient fills placed in the Windows Metafile.

   ◆ **FreeHand text.** Select the Maintain As Blocks check box to keep text editable in a pasted FreeHand file.

4. Click **OK**.

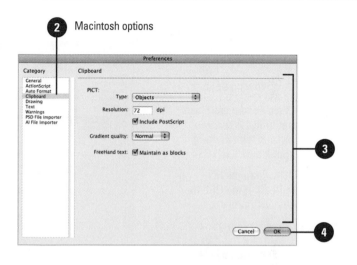

Macintosh options

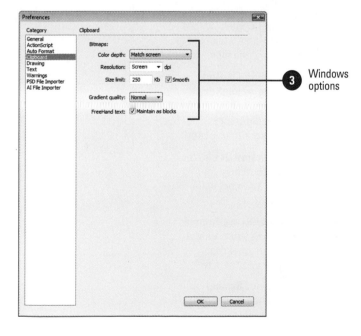

Windows options

Setting Warning Preferences

Flash provides warning messages when you perform actions that might create problems for your document or lose important data. The warnings help you avoid compatibility problems with Flash CS3 and character corruption from encoding, which lets you know about missing fonts, URL changes, and symbol conversion. Additional warnings let you know when importing audio and video content inserts frames and when motion frames or target objects contain ActionScript.

Set Warning Preferences

1. Click the **Flash** (Mac) or **Edit** (Win) menu, and then click **Preferences**.

2. Click the **Warnings** category.

3. Select from the following options:

   ◆ **Warn On Save For Adobe Flash CS3 Compatibility.** When you save documents with content features specific to Flash CS4.

   ◆ **Warn On URL Changes In Launch And Edit.** If the URL for a document has changed.

   ◆ **Warn On Reading Generator Content.** Displays a red X over objects not supported by Flash.

   ◆ **Warn On Inserting Frames When Importing Content.** When Flash inserts frames while you import audio or video files.

   ◆ **Warn On Encoding Conflicts When Exporting ActionScript Files.** When you create a document with different language characters for export.

   ◆ **Warn On Conversion Of Effect Graphic Objects.** When you attempt to edit a symbol with effects applied to it.

   ◆ **Warn on sites with overlapped root folder.** When you create a site in which the local root folder overlaps another site.

   ◆ **Warn On Behavior Symbol Conversion.** When you convert a symbol with a behavior attached to a symbol of a different type.

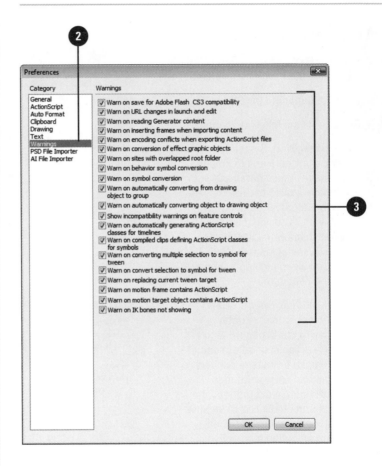

- **Warn On Symbol Conversion.** When you convert a symbol to a symbol of a different type.

- **Warn On Automatically Converting From Drawing Object To Group.** When you convert an object drawn in Object Drawing mode to a group.

- **Warn On Automatically Converting Objects To Drawing Objects.** When you change objects to drawing objects.

- **Show Incompatibility Warnings On Feature Controls.** When controls are not supported by the Flash Player version specified in Publish Settings.

- **Warn On Automatically Generating ActionScript Classes For Timelines.** When you don't create a class, Flash does.

- **Warn On Compiled Clips Defining ActionScript Classes For Symbols.** When you try to create ActionScript classes for symbols.

- **Warn On Converting Multiple Selection To Symbol For Tween.** (**New!**) When you don't have a symbol to create a tween.

- **Warn On Replacing Current Tween Target.** (**New!**) When you try to replace the current tween target

- **Warn On Motion Frame Contains ActionScript.** (**New!**) When a motion frame contains ActionScript.

- **Warn On Motion Target Object Contains ActionScript.** (**New!**) When the motion target contains ActionScript.

- **Warn On IK Bones Not Showing.** (**New!**) When the IK Bones are not showing.

4 Click **OK**.

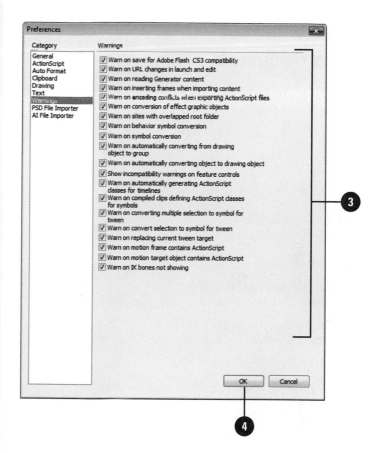

Working with Page Setup in Macintosh

You can use the Page Setup dialog box in Macintosh to select the size and location in the printer of the paper you want to use. You can also select the page orientation (portrait or landscape) that best fits the entire document or any selection. **Portrait** orients the page vertically (taller than it is wide) and **landscape** orients the page horizontally (wider than it is tall). When you shift between the two, the margin settings automatically change. **Margins** are the blank spaces between the edges of a page and the image. The printer only prints within these margins. You can use the Print Margins dialog box to change margins and layout. The layout options allow you to specify the frames you want to print, and the frame size and display on the page.

Work with Page Setup in Macintosh

1. Open a document.

2. Click the **File** menu, and then click **Page Setup**.

3. Click the **Settings** popup, and then click **Page Attributes**.

4. Select from the various Page Attributes options:

   ◆ **Format For.** Click the Format For popup, and then select a printer from the available options. If your printer is not accessible from the list, click the Edit Printer List, and then add your printer (you may need the printer CD, or access to the Internet, to load the latest drivers).

   ◆ **Paper Size.** Click the Paper Size popup, and then select from the available options. The default printer will determine the available paper sizes.

   ◆ **Orientation.** Click the Portrait, Landscape Left, or Landscape Right button.

   ◆ **Scale.** Enter a percentage value to increase (over 100) or decrease (under 100) the size of the printed document.

5. Click **OK**.

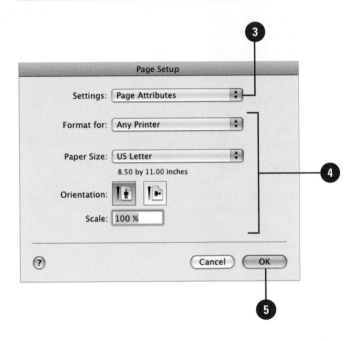

Change Print Margins and Layout in Macintosh

1. Open a document.

2. Click the **File** menu, and then click **Print Margins**.

3. Enter Left, Right, Top, and Bottom page margins, and then select the Center check boxes to center material on the page.

4. Select from the Layout options:

   ◆ Frames. Click the **Frames** popup, and then click **First Frame Only** or **All Frames**.

   ◆ Layout. Click the **Layout** popup, and then select a layout option: **Actual Size**, **Fit On One Page**, or one of the Storyboard options.

   ◆ Scale. Enter a scale percentage value.

5. Click **OK**.

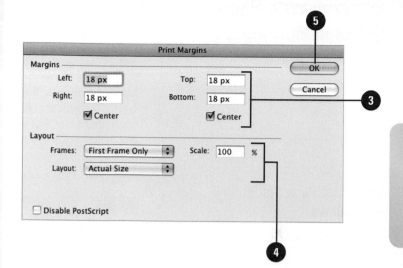

Working with Page Setup in Windows

You can use the Page Setup dialog box in Windows to select the size and location in the printer of the paper you want to use. You can also select the page orientation (portrait or landscape) that best fits the entire document or any selection. When you shift between the two, the margin settings automatically change. Margins are the blank spaces between the edges of a page and the image. You can also change page layout options, which allow you to specify the frames you want to print, and the frame size and display on the page. The printer only prints within these margins. Different printer models support different options and features; the available options depend on your printer and printer drivers.

Work with Page Setup in Windows

1. Open a document.

2. Click the **File** menu, and then click **Page Setup**.

3. Select from the various Page Setup options:

    ◆ **Margins.** Enter Left, Right, Top, and Bottom page margins, and then select the check boxes to center material on the page.

    ◆ **Size.** Click the Size list arrow, and then select from the available options.

    ◆ **Source.** Click the Source list arrow, and then select from the available options.

    ◆ **Orientation.** Click the Portrait or Landscape option.

4. Select from the Layout options:

    ◆ **Frames.** Click the Frames list arrow, and then click First Frame Only or All Frames.

    ◆ **Layout.** Click the Layout list arrow, and then select a layout option.

    ◆ **Scale.** Enter a scale percentage value.

5. Click **OK**.

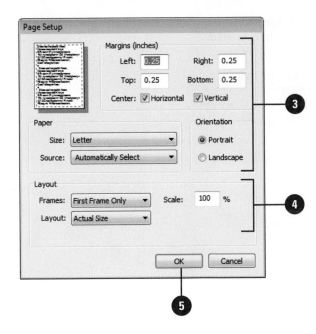

Set Printer Properties in Page Setup

1. Open a document.

2. Click the **File** menu, and then click **Print**.

3. Click the **Name** list arrow, and then select the printer you want to use.

4. Click **Properties**.

5. Select the printer options you want; each printer displays different options.

6. Click **OK** to close the Properties dialog box.

7. Click **OK** to close the Print dialog box.

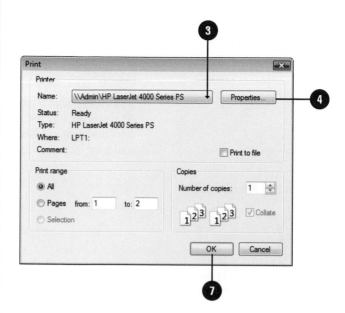

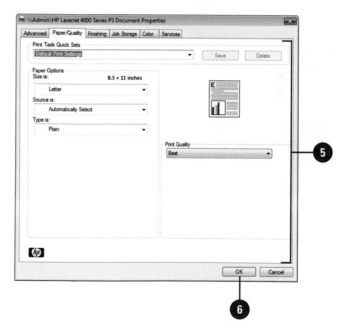

Printing a Document in Macintosh

The Print command is probably the most used of all Flash's print options. In addition to normal printing functions, such as Copies and Pages, the Print command gives you other menus that let you control specific printing functions, such as output ink and color management. Understand that the options available for the Print command will be partially determined by the default printer. For example, if your default printer uses more than one paper tray, you will see options for selecting a specific tray for the current print job. In spite of the differences, there are some universal options to all print jobs, and these are covered here.

Print a Document in Macintosh

1. Open a document.

2. Click the **File** menu, and then click **Print**.

3. Click the **Printer** popup, and then select from the available printer descriptions.

    IMPORTANT *Changes made here override any changes made in the Page Setup dialog box.*

4. Click the **Presets** popup, and then select from the available preset options.

5. Select the various Copies & Pages options: **Number Of Copies**, **Collated**, **Print All** or **Range Of Pages**.

6. Click the **Print Options** popup, click **Layout**, and then select the various options: Pages Per Sheet, Layout Direction, and if you want a Border.

7. Click the **Print Options** popup, click **Color Matching**, and then select the option you want to match color using ColorSync (on your computer) or the printer.

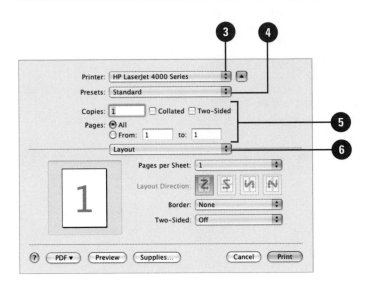

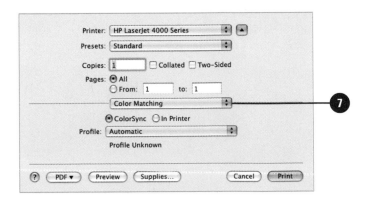

8 Click the **Print Options** popup, click **Paper Handling**, and then select your options.

9 Click the **Print Options** popup, click **Scheduler**, and then select the option you want to specify when you want to print the document.

10 Click the **Print Options** popup, click **Summary**, and then view the summary of settings.

11 Click the following options to finalize your print:

♦ **PDF.** Displays a menu to save a Flash document as a PDF with the option you want. The options include Fax PDF, Mail PDF, and Compress PDF.

♦ **Preview.** Displays a preview of the printed document

♦ **Supplies.** Displays an Apple Store Web site for printer supplies.

♦ **Cancel.** Stops a print job.

♦ **Print.** Prints the current document.

12 If you need additional help along the way, click the **Help** button.

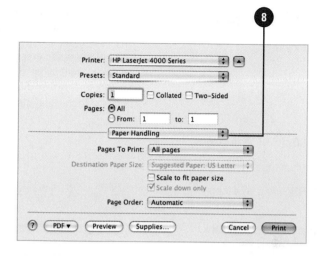

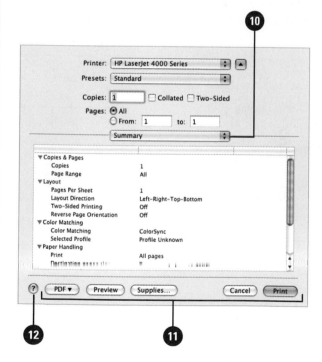

Printing a Document in Windows

Printing a paper copy is the most common way to preview and share your documents. You can use the Print dialog box to set how many copies to print, specify a range of pages to print, and print your document. Understand that the options available for the Print command will be determined by the default printer, and operating system. Different printers will display different options; there are some options that are fairly universal, and these options are covered here.

Print a Document in Windows

1. Open a document.

2. Click the **File** menu, and then click **Print**.

3. If necessary, click the **Name** list arrow, and then click the printer you want.

4. Type the number of copies you want to print.

5. Specify the pages to print:

   ◆ **All.** Prints the entire document.

   ◆ **Pages.** Prints the specified pages.

   ◆ **Selection.** Prints the selected item.

6. Click **OK**.

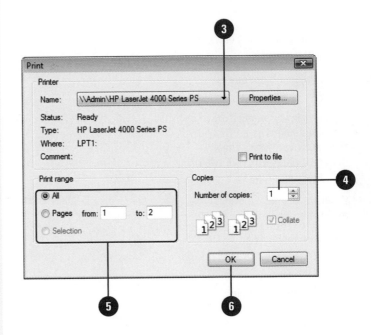

Creating Graphics

3

Introduction

Flash offers a full suite of tools for creating and editing graphics. When you draw in Flash, you create vector art. **Vectors** are mathematical descriptions of lines and points that, when connected, form shapes and objects. Vector-defined art is not limited by resolution like bitmaps are, so they can be scaled to any size without a loss in quality or increase in file size. This is the basis of Flash; and the main reason Flash files are so small and why they can be deployed on so many platforms. Vector graphics are also fully editable after they are created so you can continue to adjust their properties. Included in Flash are many of the drawing tools and procedures familiar to the seasoned user of vector drawing programs. It is also a good place for the beginner to learn. Sketch naturally with the Pencil and Brush tools or use vector-based objects, such as the Rectangle or Oval tools or the Polystar tool. Use the Pen tool to create lines and shapes with Bézier curves. Whatever is drawn can be edited and modified with a variety of tools and palettes. When you select an object or graphic on the Stage, the Property Inspector displays the attributes of that object that are modifiable, such as fill and stroke color, position, and scale.

You can draw shapes in Flash using two drawing models: Merge Drawing and Object Drawing. The **Merge Drawing** model, the default (like previous versions of Flash), automatically merges shapes that you draw when you overlap them. If you select a shape that has been merged with another, and move it, the shape below it is moved too. The **Object Drawing** model allows you to draw shapes as separate objects that do not automatically merge together when you overlap them. You can now extend the Object Drawing mode by creating primitive rectangles and ovals in **Primitive mode**, which allows you to edit properties in the Property Inspector and specify the corner radius of rectangles and inner radius of ovals. This makes it easy to create pie wedges, round off corners, and other curved shapes.

What You'll Do

Work with Object Drawing

Draw Lines and Shapes

Use the Selection Tools

Zoom In and Out

Move Around with the Hand Tool

Use Rulers, Grids, and Guides

Modify Grid and Guide Settings

Use Snap Align

Change Stroke and Fill Colors

Create Custom Colors

Add Colors Using the Kuler Panel

Edit Strokes with the Ink Bottle

Edit Fills with the Paint Bucket

Use the Spray Brush and Deco Tools

Edit Strokes and Fills with the Eyedropper

Create Gradients

Use the Fill Lock

Use Paint Brush Modes

Draw with the Pen Tool

Modify Shapes

Use the Free Transform Tool

Use Transform Options for Shapes

Change Drawing Settings

Working With Object Drawing

Previously in Flash, all shapes in the same layer on the Stage could change other overlapping shapes, known as Merge Drawing. In Flash, you can create shapes directly on the Stage that do not affect other overlapping shapes, known as Object Drawing. By default, Flash uses Merge Drawing. To draw shapes using Object Drawing, you use the Object Drawing button on the Tools panel. When you select a shape created using Object Drawing, Flash selects the shape with a rectangular bounding box, which you can use with the Pointer tool to move the shape on the Stage. You can use General preferences to set selection options for contact-sensitivity when selecting shapes created using Object Drawing.

Enable and Use Object Drawing

1. Select a drawing tool on the Tools panel that supports Object Drawing (Pencil, Line, Pen, Brush, Oval, Rectangle, and Polygon).

2. Select the **Object Drawing** button on the Tools panel.

   TIMESAVER *Press the J key to toggle between Merge and Object Drawing.*

3. With the **Pointer** tool, click to select an object, and then drag the bounding box to move it.

4. To switch back Merge Drawing, click the **Object Drawing** button again.

Did You Know?

You can convert a Merge Drawing shape to an Object Drawing shape. Select the shape on the Stage, click the Modify menu, point to Combine Object, and then click Union.

See Also

See "Setting General Preferences" on page 60 for information on options for contact-sensitivity when selecting shapes created using Object Drawing.

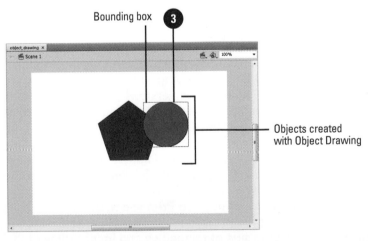

Bounding box ③

Objects created with Object Drawing

Drawing with the Line Tool

The Line tool draws perfectly straight lines in any direction you drag your mouse. In Flash, a line is called a stroke and there is a variety of thicknesses (0-200 pixels), styles, colors, and gradient fills that can be applied to it. You can also create your own line style for specific types of dashed, dotted or artistic lines. You can constrain the path a line draws to 45-degree angles or create closed shapes by intersecting the lines you draw. In Merge Drawing when a line overlaps another line on the same layer, it essentially cuts it into two pieces that can be edited as separate objects. You can also specify a line cap and join type. A **join** is the place where two strokes meet (Miter, Round, or Bevel). A **cap** is the end point of a stroke that does not join with another stroke. Select Stroke hinting to make stroke intersections easier to view.

Use the Line Tool

1. Click the **Line** tool on the Tools panel.

   The pointer becomes a crosshair that you can drag on the Stage.

   TIMESAVER *Press N to select the Line tool.*

2. Click and drag on the Stage, and then release the mouse when the line is the length you need.

   TIMESAVER *Hold down the Shift key, and then drag to draw a 45, 90, or 180 degree line.*

3. To change line properties, click to select the stroke, and then specify the options (Color, Weight (0-200), Style, Width and Height, Cap, Join, or Miter) you want in the Property Inspector.

   TROUBLE? *To display the Property Inspector, click the Window menu, point to Properties, and then click Properties.*

See Also

See "Changing Stroke and Fill Colors" on page 96 for information on using color.

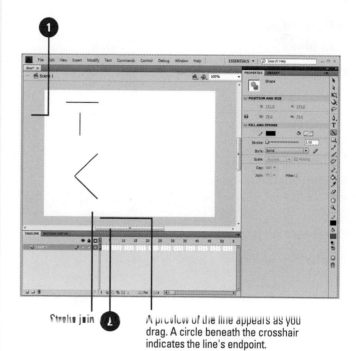

Stroke join

A preview of the line appears as you drag. A circle beneath the crosshair indicates the line's endpoint.

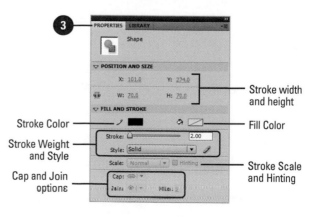

Stroke width and height

Stroke Color — Fill Color

Stroke Weight and Style

Scale — Stroke Scale and Hinting

Cap and Join options

Drawing with the Pencil Tool

FL 2.2

Use the Pencil tool for freeform drawing. When you draw with the Pencil tool you are creating strokes. It works the same way as a real pencil with options for smoothing and straightening. Depending upon which mode you choose, Flash makes corrections to the drawn line. Smooth mode softens the curve of the line you draw while Straighten mode transforms the line into a series of straight-line segments and standard curves. If you are using the Pencil or Brush tools with Smooth mode, you can specify the degree of smoothness. Additionally, Flash performs shape recognition to the lines you draw so that if it detects something approximating a simple geometric shape such as a rectangle, oval, or triangle, it converts your drawing into whichever shape it detects. To bypass these modifications, select Ink mode. This mode allows for the most freeform drawing with minimal correction by Flash.

Use the Pencil Tool in Straighten Mode

1 Click the **Pencil** tool on the Tools panel.

The pointer becomes a pencil. The Pencil tool options appear at the bottom of the Tools panel. The default mode is Straighten.

TIMESAVER *Press Y to select the Pencil tool.*

2 Draw on the Stage with the Pencil, and then release the mouse.

A rough preview of the line appears as you draw. In Straighten mode, Flash transforms the line into a series of straight-line segments and standard curves.

3 To change the straighten rate (**New!**), select the object, click the **Modify** menu, point to **Shape**, click **Straighten**, enter a value, and then click **OK**.

Did You Know?

Flash converts rough shapes into clean, geometric shapes. Set the tolerance level of shape recognition in the Drawing preferences.

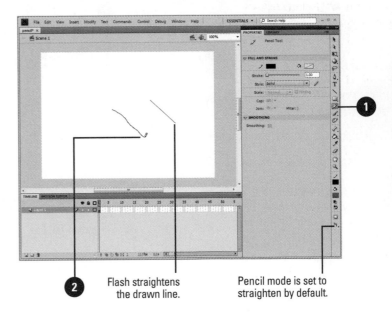

Flash straightens the drawn line.

Pencil mode is set to straighten by default.

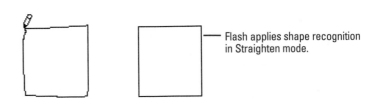

Flash applies shape recognition in Straighten mode.

Use the Pencil Tool in Smooth Mode

1 Click the **Pencil** tool on the Tools panel.

The pointer becomes a pencil. The Pencil tool options appear at the bottom of the Tools panel.

2 Click the **Pencil mode** popup in the Options area of the Tools panel, and then click **Smooth**.

3 In the Property Inspector, click the **Smoothing** popup, and then click a value from 1 to 100.

The default value is set to 50. The greater the smoothing value, the smoother the resulting line.

TROUBLE? *To display the Property Inspector, click the Window menu, point to Properties, and then click Properties.*

4 Draw on the Stage with the Pencil, and then release the mouse.

A rough preview of the line appears as you draw. In Smooth mode, Flash smoothes the line you draw into curved line segments.

5 To change the smooth rate and angles (above and below) (**New!**), select the object, click the **Modify** menu, point to **Shape**, click **Smooth**, enter a value, and then click **OK**.

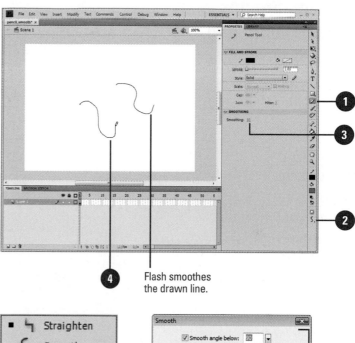

Flash smoothes the drawn line.

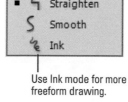

Use Ink mode for more freeform drawing.

Select to display a live preview of your changes

For Your Information

Smoothing Curves Another Way

You can also smooth curves by optimizing the shape. Optimizing a shape refines curved lines and fill outlines by reducing the number of curves used to define the shape. To optimize a shape, click it, click the Modify menu, point to Shape, click Optimize, specify a smoothing level, select additional options (select Use Multiple Passes to repeat the smoothing process until you can't anymore, and select Show Totals Message to display an alert when smoothing is complete), and then click OK.

Drawing Shapes with the Rectangle and Oval Tools

 FL 2.2

The Flash Tools panel includes several tools for quickly creating simple geometric vector shapes. They are easy to use; you just click and drag on the Stage to create the shapes. The Rectangle tool creates rectangles with square or rounded corners. The Oval tool creates circular shapes such as ovals and circles. These shapes can be comprised of Strokes, which are lines that surround and define the shape, Fills, which are a color or texture inside the shape, or both. You can create two types of shapes: Drawing or Primitive. Drawing, or standard, shapes are self contained; the stroke and fill of a shape are not separate elements, while for Primitive shapes they are separate elements.

Draw with the Oval Tool

1. Click the **Oval** or **Oval Primitive** tool on the Tools panel.

   TIMESAVER *Press O to select an Oval tool.*

2. Select a **Stroke** and **Fill Color** from the Colors area of the Tools panel.

3. Click and drag on the Stage, and then release the mouse.

   TIMESAVER *Press and hold Shift while you drag to create a circle.*

4. In the Properties Inspector, change the values you want.

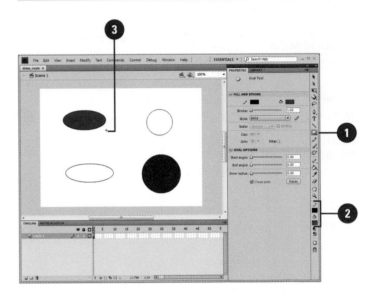

Draw with the Rectangle Tool

1. Click the **Rectangle** or **Rectangle Primitive** tool on the Tools panel.

   TIMESAVER *Press R to select a Rectangle tool.*

2. Select a **Stroke** and **Fill** color from the Colors area of the Tools panel.

3. Click and drag on the Stage, and then release the mouse.

   TIMESAVER *Press and hold Shift while you drag to create a square.*

4. In the Properties Inspector, change the values you want.

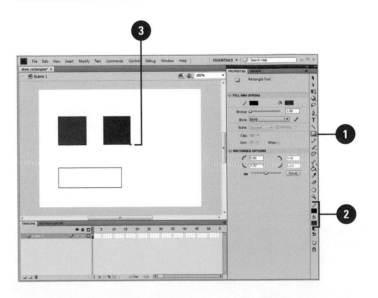

Draw a Rounded Rectangle

1. Click the **Rectangle** or **Rectangle Primitive** tool on the Tools panel.

2. Enter a value for the corner radius in the Properties Inspector.

3. To create an exact size rectangle shape, select the shape, enter the width and height values in the Properties Inspector.

4. Click and drag on the Stage, and then release the mouse.

Did You Know?

You can enter values ranging from 0 to 100 points in the Rectangle Settings dialog box. A value of zero gives you a straight-sided-square. Higher numbers produce squares with more rounded sides.

You can hold down the Shift key while dragging to produce a perfect square with equal sides or a perfect circle. If you want to draw an oval or a rectangle without a stroke or fill, you can set either of these options to No Fill in the Colors area of the Tools panel or in the Color Mixer.

You can draw shapes without a stroke or a fill. Set either of these properties to No Fill in the Colors section of the Tools panel or in the Color Mixer.

You can set specific sizes with a dialog box. Alt+click (Win) or Option+click (Mac) a rectangle or oval, set the values you want, and then click OK.

See Also

See "Changing Stroke and Fill Colors" on page 96 for information on changing shapes.

5 points   20 points   35 points

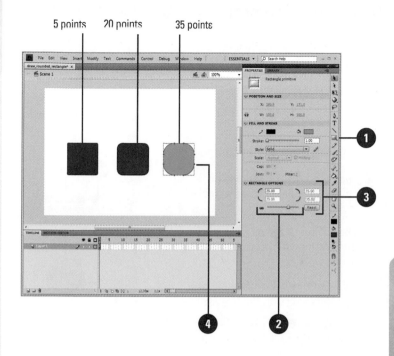

For Your Information

Creating Primitive Rectangles and Ovals

In addition to creating standard rectangles and ovals, you can now create Primitive rectangles and ovals. A Primitive shape allows you to change its attributes in the Property Inspector. The Primitive shape tools allow you to specify the corner radius of rectangles, and the start and end angle and the inner radius of ovals using controls in the Property Inspector, which makes it easy to create pie wedges, rounded corners, and other curved shapes. When either of the Primitive shape tools is selected, the Property Inspector retains the values of the last primitive object that you edited.

Using the Polystar Tool

FL 2.2

Working in much the same way as the Oval and Rectangle tools, the new Polystar tool allows you to easily create complex vector shapes. You can use this tool to create polygons and stars with up to 32 sides. Choose between creating a polygon or a star. Both styles have characteristics that can be adjusted in the Property Inspector before you draw the shape. Both the polygon and star style can have up to 32 sides, with the star style having an additional star point size that can be set. Experiment with several options to get the kind of shape you want.

Draw a Polygon or Star Shape

① Click and hold the **Rectangle** tool on the Tools panel, and then point to **PolyStar Tool**.

The pointer becomes a crosshair that you can drag anywhere on the Stage.

② Click **Options** in the Property Inspector.

TIMESAVER *Press ⌘+F3 (Mac) or Ctrl+3 (Win) to open the Property Inspector.*

③ Click the **Style** popup, and then select **Polygon** or **Star**.

④ Enter a value for the number of sides. You can create an object with up to 32 sides.

⑤ For the Star style, you can specify an additional option for your point size. You can enter a value ranging from .10 to 1.0 points.

⑥ Click **OK**.

⑦ Click and drag on the Stage, and then release the mouse.

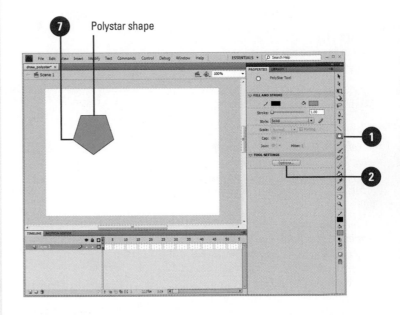

Polystar shape

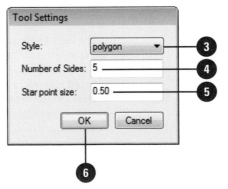

See Also

See "Editing Strokes with the Ink Bottle" on page 102 for information on editing an object.

Understanding Selections

When you create vector graphics in Flash, they are comprised of distinct elements that can be selected separately or as a whole with a variety of selection tools. The type of editing you need to perform determines which tool you use. For example, a simple rectangle drawn is comprised of four line segments that surround the contour of the shape and one fill in the center. Each of these five parts can be selected in tandem or individually with the Selection tool. Likewise, any stroke that intersects another stroke or fill splits them into distinct elements that can be selected separately.

In Normal selection mode, holding down the Shift key adds to the selection any additional elements you click on. You can change this option in the General tab of the Preferences window so that it isn't necessary to use the Shift key to perform this function. Double-click any stroke to select other strokes connected to it or double-click a fill to select it and any strokes that touch or intersect it. To select an entire shape (strokes and fills) or just a portion of it, you can drag a selection rectangle with the Selection tool or draw a freeform selection area with the Lasso tool. These methods work best for very complex shapes with many intersecting strokes and fills, or if there is only a portion of the shape you need to edit.

The Sub-Selection and Pen tools allow you to select the entire shape (strokes and fills) simultaneously, making its anchor points and Bézier handles visible for editing. Use this method when you need to edit the contours of the shape with precision.

For information on making selections using the Object Drawing model, see "Working with Object Drawing", on page 74.

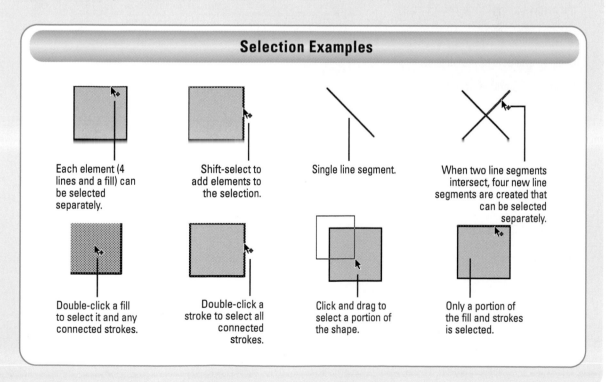

Selection Examples

Each element (4 lines and a fill) can be selected separately.

Shift-select to add elements to the selection.

Single line segment.

When two line segments intersect, four new line segments are created that can be selected separately.

Double-click a fill to select it and any connected strokes.

Double-click a stroke to select all connected strokes.

Click and drag to select a portion of the shape.

Only a portion of the fill and strokes is selected.

Selecting Strokes with the Selection Tool

There are several ways to select objects in Flash. You can select an object's stroke or fill or both. You can use the Selection tool to select parts of the object or drag over a portion of it to create a selection rectangle. The Property Inspector displays the properties of what is selected including Stroke line weight and style, Fill color, pixel dimensions, and X and Y coordinates. When a stroke or fill is selected, a dotted pattern appears over it indicating it has been selected. This makes editing and modifying graphics simple and illustrates the versatility of the vector-based graphics model used in Flash.

Select a Stroke with the Selection Tool

1 Click the **Selection** tool on the Tools panel.

The pointer becomes an arrow.

TIMESAVER *Press V to select the Selection tool.*

2 Position the arrow on the edge of the shape.

Notice that Flash displays a small curved line icon when you position the arrow over a Curve point and a corner line icon when over a Corner point.

3 Click on any part of the stroke.

Flash only selects a portion of it. This is because what appears to be one whole shape is actually a series of lines connected by points and each can be selected separately.

> ### See Also
>
> *See "Working with Object Drawing" on page 74 for information on selecting overlapping objects on the same layer.*

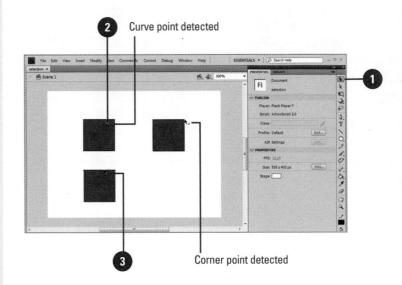

2 Curve point detected

3 Corner point detected

Select Multiple Stroke Segments

1. Click the **Selection** tool on the Tools panel.

   The pointer becomes an arrow.

   TIMESAVER *Press V to select the Selection tool. You can temporarily switch to the Selection tool from any other tool by pressing ⌘ (Mac) or Ctrl (Win).*

2. Click on any part of the stroke to select one segment.

3. Hold down the Shift key, and then click other strokes to add them to the selection.

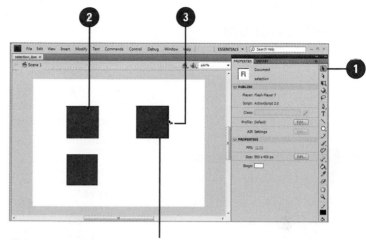

Shift-select to add stroke segments to the selection.

Did You Know?

You can turn off the Shift-select feature in the General tab of the Preferences dialog box. When this feature is disabled, you can add to the selected segments by clicking them without the need to hold down the Shift key. In this mode, holding the Shift key and clicking a selected stroke segment deselects that segment.

Select Connected Stroke Segments

1. Click the **Selection** tool on the Tools panel.

   The pointer becomes an arrow.

2. Double-click any part of the segment or stroke to select all connected strokes.

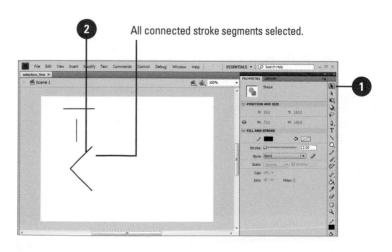

All connected stroke segments selected.

Selecting Strokes and Fills with the Selection Tool

The Selection tool provides the most simple and versatile procedures for selecting objects in Flash. The Selection tool selects anything you click on (provided it isn't on a locked layer). Double-clicking shapes with the Selection tool selects all fills and strokes that are connected. Shift-selecting allows you to add to the selection only what you need. Alternately, dragging a selection rectangle on the Stage with the Selection tool creates a bounding box that selects anything you drag it over. This bounding box method is the most reliable technique for selecting very complex objects with many intersecting strokes and fills.

Select Fills with the Selection Tool

1 Click the **Selection** tool on the Tools panel.

The pointer becomes an arrow.

2 Position the arrow in the Fill area or the center of the shape and click.

The fill becomes highlighted with a dotted pattern to indicate it has been selected. Hold down the Shift key to add other strokes and fills to the selection.

Double-clicking the shape selects both the fill and the stroke.

Selected fill

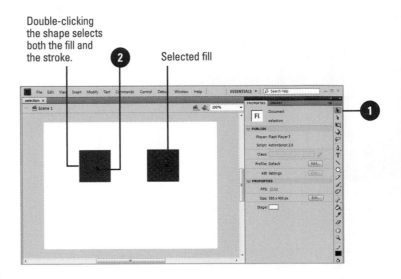

Select with a Selection Rectangle

1 Click the **Selection** tool on the Tools panel.

The pointer becomes an arrow.

2 Click on the Stage above and to the left of the shape you want to select and drag to create a Selection Rectangle, and then release the mouse when the bounding box fully encloses the shape.

Both fill and strokes are selected.

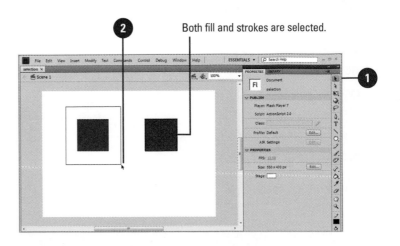

Making Selections with the Lasso Tool

Use the Lasso tool when you want to select shapes that are too close to shapes you don't want to select. This tool allows you to draw around the shape, selecting everything contained in the shape you draw. In the default mode, you can draw a freeform lasso around the object you want to select. You can also choose the Polygon mode for defining the selected area with a series of straight-line segments.

Select with the Lasso Tool

① Click the **Lasso** tool on the Tools panel.

   TIMESAVER Press L to select the Lasso tool.

② Draw around the shapes you want to select.

③ To complete the selection, return to the point where you started.

Did You Know?

You can select single or multiple objects. Holding the Shift key adds line segments and fills them. Shift-clicking selected items deselects them.

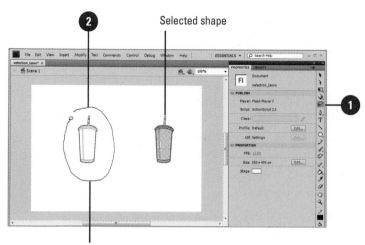

Selected shape

Flash draws a preview of the selection lasso as you draw.

Select with the Lasso Tool in Polygon Mode

① Click the **Lasso** tool on the Tools panel.

② Click the **Polygon Mode** button in the Options area of the Tools panel.

③ Click near the area you want to select. Move the pointer and click again. Keep clicking until the object or portion you want to select is surrounded.

④ Double-click to complete the selection.

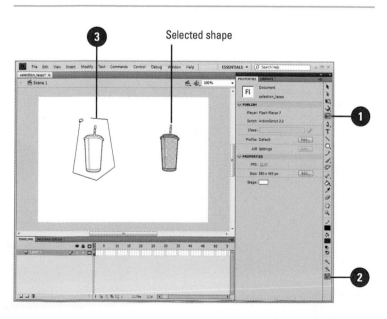

Selected shape

Zooming In and Out with the Magnifying Glass

Because the Stage and Work Area in Flash share the same space with a variety of panels, palettes and windows, it is often necessary to change the magnification level. You can use the Magnifying Glass to zoom out and see the entire piece or zoom in to do more detailed work on a small portion. The tool is made up of two modifiers: a plus (+) symbol in the circle indicates enlargement of the Stage and a minus (-) indicates reduction. Flash allows magnification levels from 8 percent to 2000 percent.

Zoom In

1. Click the **Zoom** tool on the Tools panel.

2. Click the **Enlarge** button in the Options area of the Tools panel.

   The pointer becomes a magnifying glass with a plus (+) symbol in it.

3. Click on the area of the Stage you want to zoom into.

   TIMESAVER *Press Z to select the Zoom tool. To temporarily toggle between the Enlarge and Reduce Modifiers buttons in the Options area of the Tools panel, press Option (Mac) or Alt (Win).*

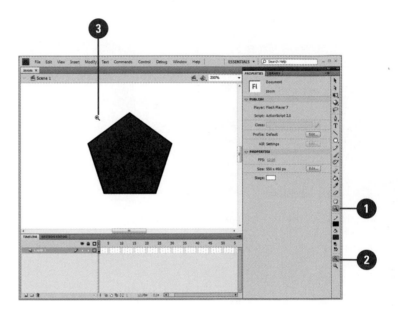

Zoom Out

1. Click the **Zoom** tool on the Tools panel.

2. Click the **Reduce** button in the Options area of the Tools panel.

   The pointer becomes a magnifying glass with a minus (-) symbol in it.

3. Click on the area of the Stage you want to zoom out from.

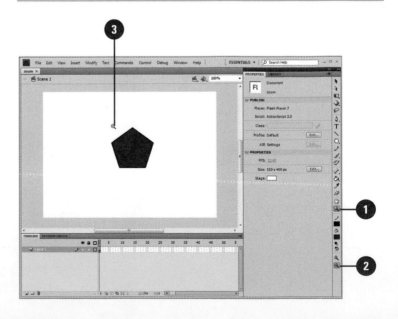

Zoom Into a Specific Area by Dragging on the Stage

① Click the **Zoom** tool on the Tools panel.

② Click the **Reduce** or **Enlarge** button in the Options area of the Tools panel.

③ Click on the area of the Stage you want to magnify and drag the pointer.

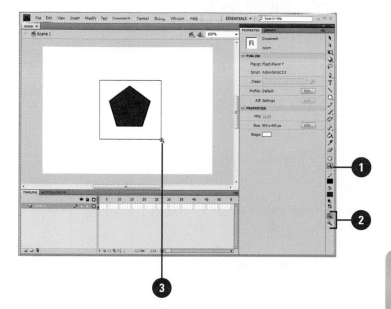

Did You Know?

You can change the magnification level in several places. The Zoom Control field in the top right hand corner of the Stage allows you to enter a value or access a popup with various magnification levels. You can also change the magnification submenu in the View menu or use the keyboard shortcuts ⌘+ - (Mac) or Ctrl+ - (Win) to zoom out, and ⌘+ + (Mac) or Ctrl+ + (Win) to zoom in. Quickly switch to 100 percent magnification by pressing ⌘+1 (Mac) or Ctrl+1 (Win).

Moving Around with the Hand Tool

At certain magnifications, parts of the Stage may not be viewable. Use the Hand tool to quickly move to different parts of the Stage without having to change the magnification level. The Stage is the active area of your movie, the only area that will be visible in the exported Flash movie. The gray area around the Stage is the Work Area. The Hand tool allows you to easily access artwork or other objects contained in this space if you are doing detailed work at high levels of magnification.

Move the Stage View

1. Click the **Hand** tool on the Tools panel.

   The pointer becomes a small hand that moves the entire Stage revealing other parts of the Stage as you drag.

   TIMESAVER *Pressing the space bar temporarily changes the active tool to the Hand tool. Continue holding as you drag.*

2. Click and drag the Stage to move the view.

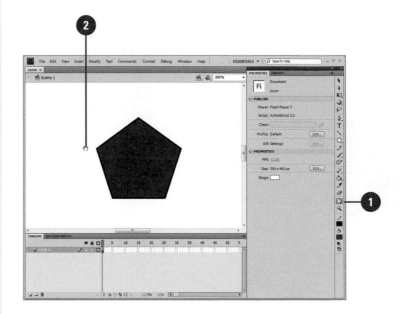

Did You Know?

You can turn off the visibility of the Work Area (the gray space around the Stage) and quickly change the View scale to 100 percent. Toggle the Work Area option in the View menu or use the keyboard shortcut ⌘+Shift+W (Mac) or Ctrl+Shift+W (Win). This is a great way to temporarily see what is viewable in the exported Flash file (SWF) when you are working with large images that extend past the Stage boundaries.

For Your Information

Using the Pasteboard Work Area

You can use the work area (called the **Pasteboard**) around the Stage to store artwork and other objects, such as components, without having them be visible in the published movie. The objects might not be visible on the Stage, but they contribute to the overall file size. It is a good idea to clean up your files before exporting the final movie. You can clean up by removing any artwork outside the boundaries of the Stage or by putting them on a guide layer.

Displaying Rulers

Ruler bars are located on the top and left sides of the Stage and serve several purposes. They let you measure the width and height of Flash elements and they let you place guides on the screen to control placement of objects on the Stage. In all, Rulers serve a very important role. When you display rulers, you can use guides to help you correctly align objects with other objects. By using guides, you have access to precise alignment systems. To use the guides, the ruler bars must first be visible. When you no longer need the rulers, you can hide the rulers to free up more workspace.

Show and Hide Rulers

1. Click the **View** menu, and then click **Rulers**.

   A check mark next to the option means its visibility is enabled.

2. To hide rulers, click the View menu, and then click Rulers to remove the check mark and hide the rulers.

   TIMESAVER *Press ⌘+Option+Shift+R (Mac) or Ctrl+Alt+Shift+R (Win) to turn the ruler on and off.*

Did You Know?

You can change the unit of measure displayed on the Rulers. Click the Modify menu, click Document, click the Ruler Units popup, select a unit of measure, and then click OK.

Horizontal ruler

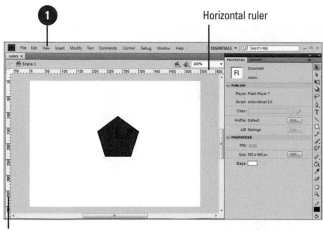

Vertical ruler

Using Grids and Guides

Flash comes with guides, grids, and rulers to help you lay out artwork and objects with precision. A grid is a series of crisscrossed lines that aid in aligning objects to each other on the Stage. Guides and grids are modifiable. You can change their visibility, position, color, and frequency. These items are invisible by default, but they can be easily turned on and adjusted. Though you see them in the Flash development environment, they are invisible on export. Use guides to align art and objects to each other on vertical or horizontal paths, or turn on the grid for use in designing a layout that is proportional and balanced.

Show and Hide Grids

1. Click the **View** menu, point to **Grid**, and then click **Show Grid**.

   ◆ You can also right-click (Win) or control-click (Mac) the **Stage**, point to **Grid**, and then click **Show Grid**.

   A check mark next to the option means its visibility is enabled.

2. To hide the grid, click the **View** menu, point to **Grid**, and then click **Show Grid** to remove the check mark and hide the grid.

   TIMESAVER Press
   ⌘+apostrophe (') (Mac) or
   Ctrl+apostrophe (') (Win) to toggle
   Grid visibility on and off.

See Also

See "Modifying Grid and Guide Settings" on page 92 for information on changing settings.

Grid when visible

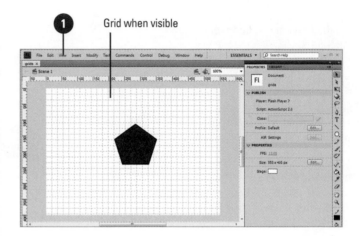

Create Guides

① Click the **View** menu, and then click **Rulers** to display rulers.

② Click on the vertical ruler on the left side of the work area with the Arrow pointer and drag to the right, and then release the mouse where you want to place the vertical guide.

A small directional triangle and line appears next to the pointer as you drag indicating that you are dragging the guide.

③ Click on the horizontal ruler at the top of the work area with the Arrow pointer and drag down, and then release the mouse where you want to place the horizontal guide.

④ Reposition the guides by selecting them with the pointer.

Did You Know?

You can turn guide visibility on and off, lock guides, and enable or disable snapping to guides. Click the View menu, and then click Guides to access these options or use the following keyboard shortcuts: ⌘+; (Mac) or Ctrl+; (Win) toggles between showing and hiding guides. Option+⌘+; (Mac) or Ctrl+Alt+; (Win) locks and unlocks guides. Shift+⌘+; (Mac) or Ctrl+Shift+; (Win) turns Snapping on and off.

See Also

See "Displaying Rulers" on page 89 for information on showing and hiding rulers.

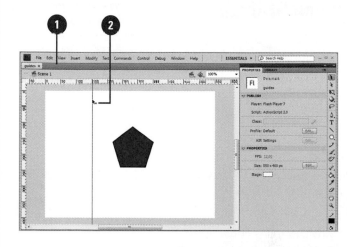

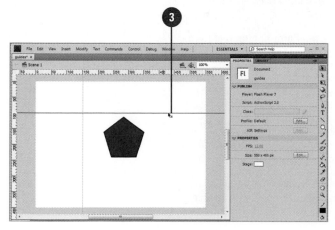

Modifying Grid and Guide Settings

The need for grids and guides varies depending upon the type of document you are working on. They are useful for aligning text and graphics to interface elements and are an invaluable tool for creating a well composed and proportioned layout. Every project is different and has different requirements, so Flash allows the display, behavior, and characteristics of guides and grids to be altered to fit your needs. They are only visible in the Flash development environment, and are not exported in the Flash movie.

Modify Grid

1. Click the **View** menu, point to **Grid**, and then click **Edit Grid**.

    TIMESAVER *Press Option+⌘+G (Mac) or Ctrl+Alt+G (Win) to quickly access the Grid dialog box.*

2. Click the **Color** popup, and then click a grid line color.

3. Select or clear the **Show Grid** check box to show or hide the grid.

4. Select or clear the **Show Over Objects** check box (**New!**) to show or hide the grid over objects.

5. Select or clear the **Snap To Grid** check box to enable or disable snapping.

6. Enter values for horizontal and vertical dimensions for the grid lines.

7. Click the **Snap Accuracy** popup, and then select a level of sensitivity for snapping to the grid. Select from Must Be Close, Normal, Can Be Distant, and Always Snap.

8. To make the current grid settings the default for new Flash files, click the **Save Default** button.

9. Click **OK**.

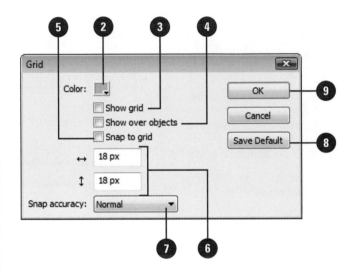

Modify Guides

1 Click the **View** menu, point to **Guides**, and then click **Edit Guides**.

> **TIMESAVER** *Press Option+Shift+⌘+G (Mac) or Ctrl+Alt+Shift+G (Win) to quickly access the Guides dialog box.*

2 Click the **Color** popup, and then click a guide line color.

3 Select or clear the **Show Guides** check box to show or hide guides.

4 Select or clear the **Snap To Guides** check box to enable or disable snapping.

5 Select or clear the **Lock Guides** check box to enable or disable movement of guides.

6 Click the **Snap Accuracy** popup, and then select a level of sensitivity for snapping to the guides. Select from Must Be Close, Normal, Can Be Distant.

7 To remove all guides from the active scene, click **Clear All**.

8 To make the current guides the default guides for new Flash files, click **Save Default**.

9 Click **OK**.

> **TIMESAVER** *Press ⌘+; (Mac) or Ctrl+; (Win) to toggle between showing and hiding guides; press Option+⌘+; (Mac) or Ctrl+Alt+; (Win) to lock and unlock guides; or press Shift+⌘+; (Mac) or Ctrl+Shift+; (Win) to turn Snapping on and off.*

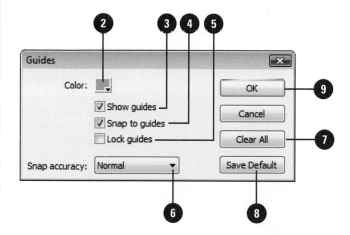

Using Snap Align

Snap Align is a new feature that enables dynamic alignment of art and objects on the Stage. Simply drag an object on the Stage and dashed lines appear that aid you in aligning to the edge or center vertices of other objects on the Stage. In the Edit Snapping dialog box you can enable and disable snap options, set the distance objects are to be from the movie borders and from each other before they snap, and save the settings as default. Additionally, you can choose to snap objects to edges or vertical and horizontal centers. Using the Snap Align feature enables you to lay out artwork more precisely and dynamically.

Enable Snap Align

① Click the **View** menu, point to **Snapping**, and then click **Snap Align**.

A check mark appears next to the menu item when Snap Align is enabled.

② Drag an object on the Stage.

Depending on the behaviors set in the Snap Align Settings dialog box, gray dashed lines appear when the edges or center vertices of objects move to within a certain pixel distance.

> ### Did You Know?
>
> ***You can change snapping tolerances.***
> Click the Flash (Mac) or Edit (Win) menu, and then click Preferences. Click the Drawing category, use the Connect Line popup to select an option, and then click OK.

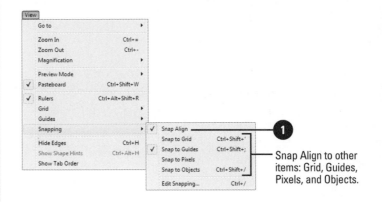

Snap Align to other items: Grid, Guides, Pixels, and Objects.

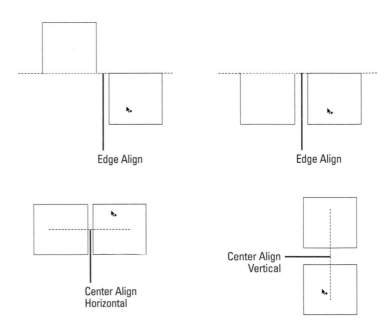

Edge Align

Edge Align

Center Align Horizontal

Center Align Vertical

Configure Snap Align and Save Defaults

1. Click the **View** menu, point to **Snapping**, and then click **Edit Snapping**.

2. Select the snap check box options you want to turn on.

3. Click **Advanced**.

4. Select from the following options:

   ◆ **Snap align settings.** Enter a value for the distance an object needs to be before it will snap to the boundaries of the stage movie (in pixels).

   ◆ **Object spacing.** Enter a value for horizontal and vertical edge tolerance (in pixels).

   ◆ **Center alignment.** Select the check boxes to center alignment on horizontal or vertical vertices or both.

5. To make the snap align setting the default for future use, click **Save Default**.

6. Click **OK**.

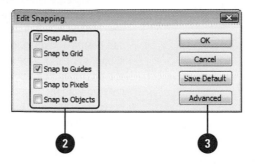

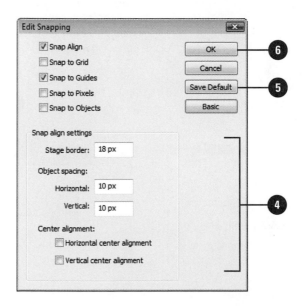

For Your Information

Snapping to an Object

You can use the Snap to Object command in the View menu or use the Snap option for the Selection tool on the Tools panel. If the Snap option is enabled, a small black ring appears under the pointer when you drag an object. The small ring changes to a larger ring when the object is within snapping distance of another object.

Changing Stroke and Fill Colors

Artwork created in Flash can have strokes and fills. Strokes and fills behave differently and are edited in different ways. A stroke is an outline. It describes the edges of a shape or it can be a simple line. You can create strokes with the Line tool or the Pencil tool. A fill is a solid shape, often contained or surrounded by a stroke. It is the surface area of a shape and can be a color, gradient, texture, or bitmap. Fills can be created with the Paintbrush tool and the Paint Bucket tool. The Oval, Rectangle, and Pen tool can create shapes with either a stroke or a fill, or both. You can edit the characteristics of strokes and fills, such as color, in several ways. If the shape is selected on the Stage, a color change to a stroke or fill can be made in any of the color palettes. Because Flash uses vectors to describe shapes, you can change their properties as much as you want without any loss in quality. It is important to grasp the concept behind them because they are the basis for drawing in Flash.

Change the Stroke Color

1. Click the **Selection** tool on the Tools panel.

2. Select the stroke of the shape by double-clicking it.

3. Click the **Stroke** color box on the Tools panel or Property Inspector.

4. Select a new color from the palette.

Did You Know?

You can change the stroke color in three other places. Stroke color boxes are also located in the Property Inspector, the Color Mixer panel, and the Swatches panel. In all cases, select the stroke you want to change and choose a new color from any of the palettes.

You can change the line width and style of a stroke or set the stroke color to None in the Property Inspector. Click the stroke you want to change to select it, and then select any of the options in the Property Inspector. Setting the stroke color to None removes the stroke from the shape.

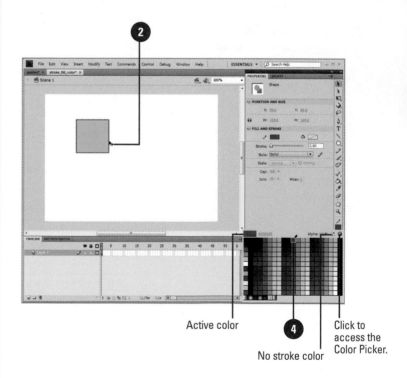

Active color

No stroke color

Click to access the Color Picker.

Change the Fill Color

1. Click the **Selection** tool on the Tools panel.

   The pointer becomes an arrow.

2. Click the fill of the shape to select it.

   This is the area inside the stroke.

3. Click the **Fill** color box on the Tools panel or Property Inspector.

4. Select a new color from the palette.

Did You Know?

You can change the fill color in three other places. Fill color boxes are also located in the Property Inspector, the Color Mixer, and the Swatches panel. Just select the fill and choose a new color from one of the palettes by clicking on a new color box.

See Also

See "Editing Fills with the Paint Bucket" on page 103 for information on changing the fill color.

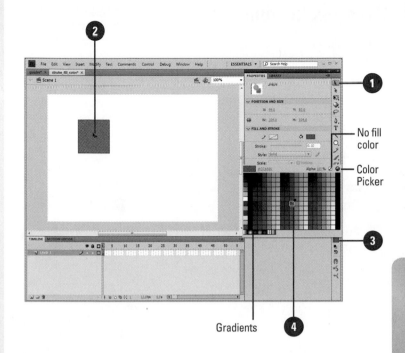

No fill color

Color Picker

Gradients

Creating Custom Colors

Each Flash document has its own color palette. The color palette displays as swatches when you access a color box or panel. The default color palette is the Web-safe palette of 216 colors. Flash allows you to edit and create new colors for strokes and fills in several ways in the Color Mixer panel. You can alter a color's RGB values (assigning it different levels of Red, Green or Blue), Hue, Saturation, Brightness, and Alpha (transparency). You can accomplish this by using sliders, dragging on a color-space, or entering a numeric value that corresponds to a specific color. In each case, you can save your color into the palette for easy access.

Create a Custom Color by Entering a Value

1. Open or expand the Color Mixer panel.

2. Enter values between 0 and 255 in the RGB numeric entry boxes.

3. Enter an alpha value between 0 and 100.

4. Click the **Options** button in the panel, and then click **Add Swatch**.

Did You Know?

You can alter the RGB values with the sliders located to the right of the numeric entry boxes. Click the small triangles, and then drag the sliders that appear. Additionally, you can drag the cursor over the Color space bar at the bottom of the Color Mixer panel to change the color interactively.

You can also specify a color using a hexadecimal number in the Color Mixer. A hexadecimal number is an internal computer numbering scheme that is used to identify colors in a color palette.

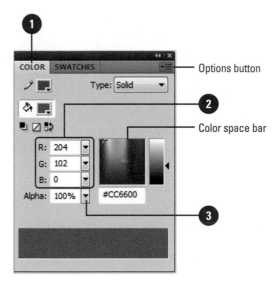

Options button

Color space bar

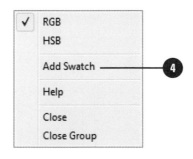

Create a Custom Color with the Color Picker

1 Click a **Stroke** or **Fill** color box on the Tools panel or the Property Inspector.

2 Click the **Color Wheel** button to the far right of the palette.

3 Click a color from one of the available pickers (Mac) or from the **Color Window** (Win).

4 Click **OK**.

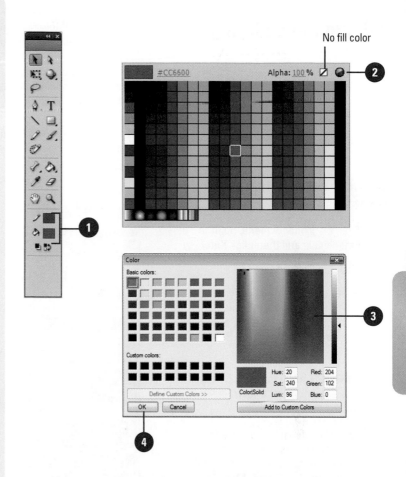

No fill color

Did You Know?

You can import and export solid and gradient color palettes between Flash files and other applications. You can share color palettes between applications, such as Adobe Fireworks and Adobe Photoshop. Click the Window menu, and then click Color Swatches. Click the Options button on the panel, and then click Add Colors or Replace Colors to import colors from a color palette, or click Save Colors to export as a color palette.

For Your Information

Working with Color Palettes

Each Flash file stores its own color palette, Web safe 216 by default. If you change colors in the default color palette, you can save the new palette as the default or change back to the Web safe 216 default. To view the color palette, click the Window menu, and then click Color Swatches. To load or save the default palette, click the Options button in the Color Swatches panel, and then click Load Default Colors or Save As Default. To reload the Web-safe color palette, click the Options button, and then click Web 216.

Adding Colors Using the Kuler Panel

The Kuler panel (**New!**) is an extension to Flash that allows you to use groups of color, or themes in your projects. You can use the panel to browse thousands of color themes, create your own using the complementary harmony rules, and share them with others in the Kuler community. After you find or create the theme you want, you can add it to the Swatches panel for use in your project. You can access the Kuler panel by using the Extensions submenu on the Window menu. The Kuler panel is also available in the CS4 version of Photoshop, InDesign, Illustrator, and Fireworks.

Browse Themes and Add to the Swatches Panel

1. Click the **Window** menu, point to **Extensions**, and then click **Kuler**.

2. Click the **Browse** tab.

3. To search for a theme, click in the Search box, enter the name of the theme, a tag, or a creator, and then press Enter (Win) or Return (Mac).

   IMPORTANT *In a search, use only alphanumerical characters (Aa-Zz, 0-9).*

4. To narrow down the browse list, click the popups, and then select the filter options you want. Some include Highest Rated, Most Popular, Newest.

   ◆ To save a search, click the first popup, click **Custom**, enter your search criteria, and then click **Save**.

5. To browse for a theme, click the **View previous set of themes** or **View next set of themes** button.

6. Select a theme in the panel.

7. To add the theme to the Swatches panel, click the **Add Selected Theme To Swatches** button.

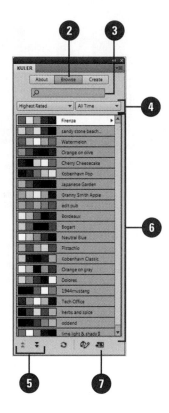

Create or Edit a Theme

1. Click the **Window** menu, point to **Extensions**, and then click **Kuler**.

2. To create or edit a theme, do either of the following:

   ◆ **Create a theme.** Click the **Create** tab.

   ◆ **Edit a theme.** Click the **Browse** tab, select the theme you want to edit, and then click **Edit Theme in Create Panel**.

3. Click the **Select Rule** popup, and then select a harmony rule or **Custom**.

   The harmony rule uses the base color as the basis for generating the colors in the color group, so you can create a theme with complementary colors.

4. Select a color box, and then use the sliders and the color wheel to display the color you want.

5. Use the buttons below the color boxes to add/remove the theme color, add the current stroke/fill color as the base color, or adjust the other colors.

   ◆ Double-click a color box to set the active color in Flash.

6. Upon completion, do any of the following:

   ◆ **Save theme.** Click **Save Theme**, name the theme, and then click **Save** to create a new one.

   ◆ **Add to Swatches Panel.** Click the **Add This Theme to Swatches** button.

   ◆ **Upload to Kuler.** Click the **Upload Theme to Kuler** button.

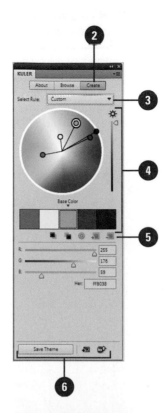

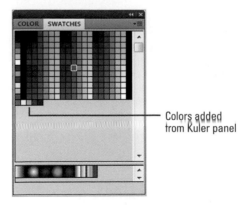

Colors added from Kuler panel

Editing Strokes with the Ink Bottle

There are a number of ways to change the stroke of an object. You can select the stroke and change its characteristics in the Property Inspector, the Swatch palettes, and the Color Mixer. If you need to apply the stroke properties of one object to that of another, use the Ink Bottle tool. The Ink Bottle tool holds the properties you've set for strokes in any of the palettes. You can click any object on the Stage to change the properties of its stroke (color, line weight and style) or add a stroke to an object that doesn't have one.

Use the Ink Bottle

1. Select a stroke on the Stage, and then change Stroke attributes in the Property Inspector.

2. Click the **Ink Bottle** tool on the Tools panel.

   The pointer becomes a small ink bottle.

   TIMESAVER *Press S to select the Ink Bottle tool.*

3. Click on the stroke of the shape to update it with the new attributes.

   The stroke updates to the new color.

Did You Know?

You can click anywhere on the shape with the Ink Bottle to change the stroke. If the object on the Stage is selected (stroke and fill), click down with the Ink Bottle tool to update its stroke.

Stroke Color

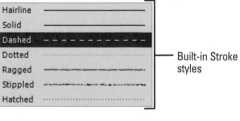

Stroke Weight

Stroke Style

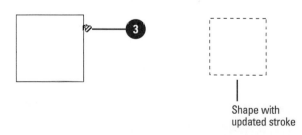

Built-in Stroke styles

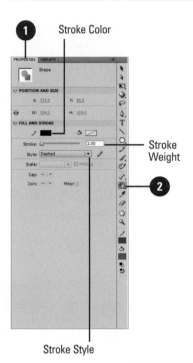

Shape with updated stroke

Editing Fills with the Paint Bucket

You can change the fill of an object with the Paint Bucket tool. The Paint Bucket stores the fill color you've set on the Tools panel or in the Property Inspector. You can change the fill color of any existing shape on the Stage by touching down on the shape with this tool. You can also add a fill to any shape that has a closed stroke. After you select the Paint Bucket tool, you can select Paint Bucket sensitivity options located at the bottom of the Tools panel.

Use the Paint Bucket

1 Change the **Fill** color box in either the Property Inspector, the Colors area of the Tools panel, or the Color Mixer.

2 Click the **Paint Bucket** tool on the Tools panel.

The pointer becomes a small paint bucket.

TIMESAVER *Press K to select the Paint Bucket tool.*

3 Click in the fill of a shape on the Stage.

The fill updates to the new color.

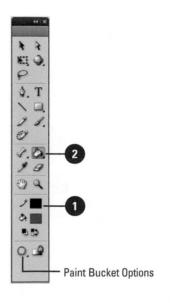
— Paint Bucket Options

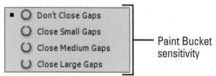
Paint Bucket sensitivity

Shape with updated fill

Did You Know?

You can set the sensitivity of the Paint Bucket tool in the Options areas of the Toolbox. These settings allow the Paint Bucket tool to close gaps in a shape (such as a break in the stroke line) and adjust how large or small a gap needs to be before Flash will close it.

Editing Strokes and Fills with the Eyedropper

The Eyedropper tool allows you to select the attributes of a shape such as fill and stroke color, and line weight and style, and then transfer them to other shapes. This tool detects whether you are selecting a stroke or a fill, and then changes into the Ink Bottle (when selecting strokes) or the Paint Bucket (when selecting fills). Instead of taking several steps to copy attributes from one shape to another, the Eyedropper provides a quick means for storing and transferring attributes between editable shapes.

Use the Eyedropper Tool to Edit Strokes and Fills

1 Click the **Eyedropper** tool on the Tools panel.

The pointer becomes an eyedropper.

TIMESAVER *Press I to select the Eyedropper tool.*

2 Position the eyedropper over the stroke or fill of a shape on the Stage.

◆ **Strokes.** When you are positioned over a stroke, a tiny pencil appears next to the tool. When you click on the stroke the Eyedropper becomes an Ink Bottle.

◆ **Fills.** When you are positioned over a fill, a tiny paint brush appears next to the tool. When you click on the fill the Eyedropper becomes a Paint Bucket.

3 Click on another shape's stroke or fill to transfer the selected attributes.

The stroke or fill updates to the new color.

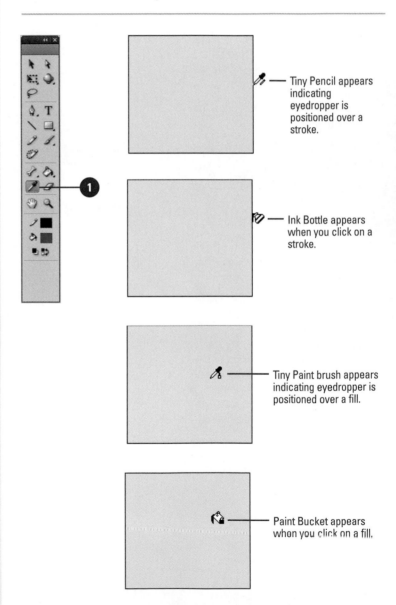

Tiny Pencil appears indicating eyedropper is positioned over a stroke.

Ink Bottle appears when you click on a stroke.

Tiny Paint brush appears indicating eyedropper is positioned over a fill.

Paint Bucket appears when you click on a fill.

Creating Gradients

Flash can create a number of paint effects in addition to solid colors. Gradients are made up of two or more colors that gradually fade into each other. They can be used to give depth to an object or create realistic shadows. Two gradient modes are available: linear and radial. Linear gradients are made up of parallel bands of color. Radial gradients radiate from a center focal point. Both can be edited for color, alpha, and position within a fill or stroke. You can add up to 16 colors to a gradient, precisely control the location of the gradient focal point, and apply other parameters. A gradient behaves like any other fill or stroke. It can be saved to the palette as a swatch using the Color Mixer panel Options button, and added to other shapes with the Paint Bucket tool.

Create a Multi-Color Gradient

1 With the **Selection** tool, select the fill or stroke of a shape on the Stage.

2 In the Color Mixer panel, click the **Fill Style Type** popup, and then click **Linear** or **Radial**.

3 Click the **Overflow** popup, and then select the gradient overflow style you want to control colors past the limits of the gradient when publishing for Flash Player 8 or later.

4 Position the pointer on the Color Picker box to display a plus (+) sign next to the pointer.

5 Click in the Gradient bar to create a color proxy indicated by a little box with a triangle on top.

TIMESAVER *To remove a proxy color indicator, drag it down.*

6 Click one of the color proxy indicators to select it.

7 Click a new color from the Color Picker box above.

8 Drag the color proxy indicator along the Gradient bar to adjust the color placement.

9 Repeat steps 4-8 to add up to 15 more gradient colors.

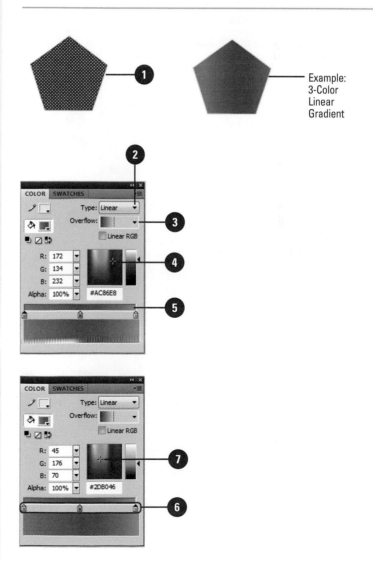

Example: 3-Color Linear Gradient

Using the Fill Lock

As you increase the complexity and number of shapes in your movie, it can become tricky to edit each object separately. When using gradient fills on several objects you can choose to span a gradient across several of these objects or give each object its own discreet gradient. The Lock Fill feature allows you to control how a fill is applied, essentially locking its position so that depending on where the shapes are positioned relative to the gradient, the one gradient spans all of the shapes. If you apply the same gradient to multiple shapes with the Fill Lock off, the gradient is applied to each shape independently.

Lock Gradients

1. Create two simple shapes using the **Rectangle** or **Oval** tool.

2. Select the first shape on the Stage with the Selection tool.

3. Click the **Paint Bucket** tool on the Tools panel.

    TIMESAVER *Press K to select the Paint Bucket tool.*

4. Click the **Lock Fill** button in the Options area of the Tools panel.

5. Select a Gradient from the Colors area of the Tools panel or use the Color Mixer or Property Inspector.

6. Click the **Eyedropper** tool on the Tools panel, and then click on the gradient fill in the first shape.

7. Click down on the second shape to add the gradient fill.

Did You Know?

You can quickly add a gradient that spans all of your shapes. Select all of the objects you want to fill, and then choose a gradient. Click the Paint Bucket tool and make sure Fill Lock is not selected. With your shapes still selected, click them with the Paint Bucket.

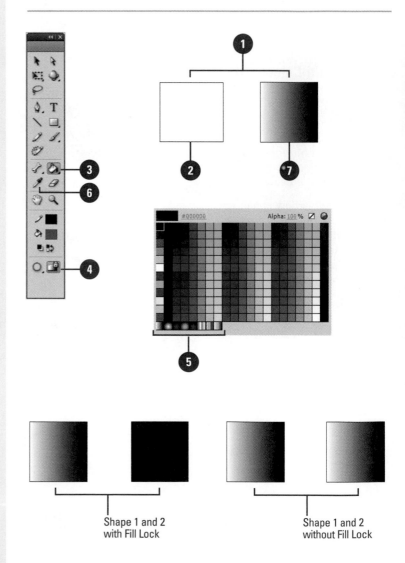

Shape 1 and 2
with Fill Lock

Shape 1 and 2
without Fill Lock

Using Paint Brush Modes

In addition to size, shape, and color settings for the Paint Brush tool, you can control how the brush behaves when painting on existing shapes and objects on the Stage. Paint Brush modes can restrict the area affected by the tool to fills or selections, empty areas of the Stage or specific shapes. When the Paint Brush tool is selected, a popup menu appears on the Tools panel. Select from the following modes: Paint Normal, Paint Fills, Paint Behind, Paint Selection, and Paint Inside. Each performs a specific operation providing you with varying levels of control as you paint. Flash previews your paint path as you paint, but it only affects the areas you've specified in the Paint modes. When you release the mouse, these previews disappear.

Use Paint Brush Modes

1. Click the **Brush** tool on the Tools panel.

2. Click the **Brush Mode** popup in the Options area on the Tools panel, and then select from the following:

    ◆ **Paint Normal.** The brush paints over everything including strokes and other fills.

    ◆ **Paint Fills.** Painting only affects existing fills and empty areas of the Stage. Strokes are ignored.

    ◆ **Paint Behind.** The Paint Brush only affects empty areas of the Stage keeping existing lines and fills intact.

    ◆ **Paint Selection.** Painting only affects the selected areas you define with any of the selection tools.

    ◆ **Paint Inside.** The Paint Brush only affects the fill of the shape you started in, ignoring other shapes and empty areas on the Stage.

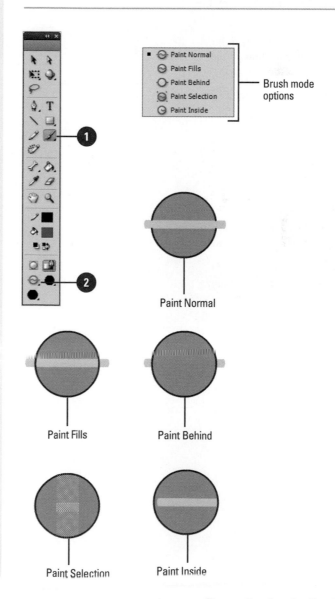

Brush mode options

Paint Normal

Paint Fills

Paint Behind

Paint Selection

Paint Inside

Using the Spray Brush Tool

 FL 2.2

The Spray Brush tool (**New!**) allows you to spray particles onto the Stage using the current fill color. If you want to create a more complex pattern, you can also use a movie clip or graphic symbol from the library as a particle. You can adjust the spray pattern by selecting Symbol and Brush options in the Property Inspector. The Symbol options include Scale, Random scaling, Rotate symbol, and Random rotation, while the Brush options include Width, Height, and Brush angle.

Use the Spray Brush Tool

1. Click the **Spray Brush** tool on the Tools panel.

2. Select a fill color for the default spray of dots and other options in the Property Inspector.

   ◆ **Color Selector.** Select a fill color for the default spray particle.

   ◆ **Edit.** Select a custom symbol from the library. You can use any movie clip or graphic symbol in the library as the spray particle.

   ◆ **Scale.** Scale the width and height of a symbol used as a spray particle.

   ◆ **Random Scaling.** Randomly spray particles on the Stage with different sizes.

   ◆ **Rotate Symbol.** Rotates the symbol spray particle around a center point.

   ◆ **Random Rotation.** Randomly rotate spray particles on the Stage.

   ◆ **Width and Height.** Specifies the brush width and height.

   ◆ **Brush Angle.** Specifies the spray angle of the particles.

3. Click or drag on the Stage where you want the pattern to appear.

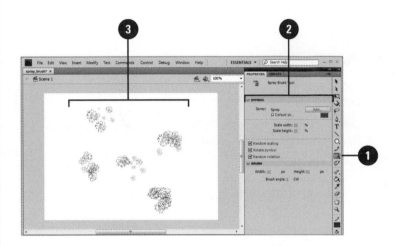

Using the Deco Tool

FL 2.2

The Deco tool (**New!**) allows you to apply a kaleidoscopic drawing effect to the Stage or a selected object on the Stage. You can apply several effects: Vine, Grid, or Symmetry. The Vine effect fills the Stage, symbol, object, or closed area with a vine pattern. You can also use your own artwork (symbols) for the leaves and flowers. The Grid effect fills the Stage, symbol, object, or closed area with a symbol from the library. You can create grid patterns, such as a tiled background or checkerboard. The Symmetry effect arranges symbols symmetrically around a central point, which you can control with a set of handles. You can create circular elements, such as a planet. The default symbol for the Symmetry effect is a 25 x 25 pixel black rectangle with no stroke.

Use the Deco Tool

1. Click the **Deco** tool on the Tools panel.

2. In the Property Inspector, click the **Drawing Effect** list arrow, and then select **Vine Fill**, **Grid Fill**, or **Symmetry Brush**.

3. Select a fill color for the default shape, or select a symbol.

    ◆ **Color Selector.** Select a fill color for the default pattern.

    ◆ **Edit.** Select a custom symbol from the library. You can use any movie clip or graphic symbol in the library as the pattern.

4. Specify the advanced options you want for the different effects; options vary depending on the selected effect.

5. Click the Stage or within the shape or symbol (Grid Fill and Vine Fill) where you want the pattern to appear.

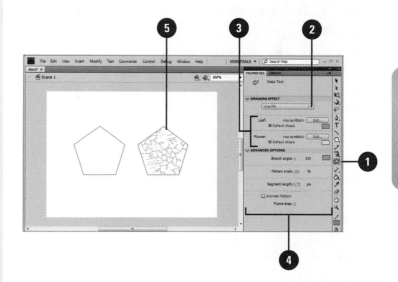

Drawing with the Pen Tool

The Pen tool is the basis for vector drawing. The Pen tool now behaves similarly to the Illustrator Pen tool to provide consistency across Adobe software. Flash provides a number of ways to draw and edit objects that are unique to Flash, but the Pen tool utilizes procedures that will be familiar to those who have used other vector drawing programs. The Pen tool utilizes anchor points and Bézier handles to create lines and shapes and behaves in a way that is familiar to those who have used other programs such as Adobe Illustrator and Adobe FreeHand. You can use the Pen tool arrow to select a different pen to add, delete, or convert anchor points. You can edit the anchor points and vectors to create the drawings you want.

Use the Pen Tool to Create an Open Path

1. Click the **Pen** tool on the Tools panel.

   TIMESAVER *Press P to quickly select the Pen tool.*

2. Click on the Stage.

   An anchor point is created.

3. Move your pointer to another position, and then click again.

   Flash connects the two anchor points.

4. Double-click to end the path.

   TIMESAVER *Ctrl+click (Win) or Command+click a blank area to leave the path open.*

Did You Know?

You can end an open path using a keyboard shortcut. Press ⌘+click (Mac) or Ctrl+click (Win).

See Also

See "Modifying Shapes with the Sub-Selection Tool" on page 116 for information on using tools.

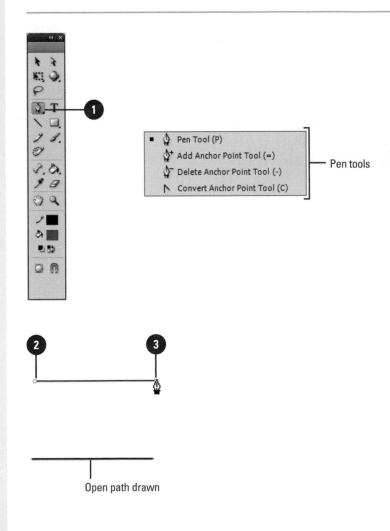

Pen tools

- Pen Tool (P)
- Add Anchor Point Tool (=)
- Delete Anchor Point Tool (-)
- Convert Anchor Point Tool (C)

Open path drawn

Use the Pen Tool to Create a Closed Path

1. Click the **Pen** tool on the Tools panel.

   TIMESAVER *Press P to quickly select the Pen tool.*

2. Click on the Stage.

   An anchor point is created.

3. Move your pointer to another position, and then click again.

   Flash connects the two anchor points.

4. Move the pointer to a third position, and then click again.

   Flash connects the second and third anchor points.

5. Move the pointer back to the first anchor point.

   A small circle appears next to the pen pointer indicating you can close the path of the shape.

6. Click to close the shape.

Did You Know?

You can delete an anchor point with the Pen tool. Click the Pen tool arrow, click Delete Anchor Point tool, and then click the point you want to delete.

You can add an anchor point with the Pen tool. Click the Pen tool arrow, click Add Anchor Point tool, and then click where you want to add a point.

You can create horizontal, vertical, and 45 degree lines while you draw. Hold the Shift key while you draw to constrain a line to horizontal, vertical, and 45 degree angles.

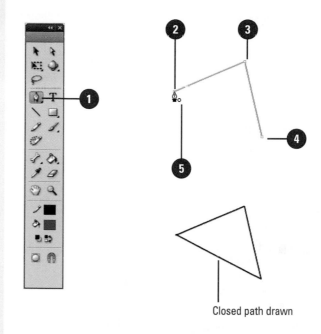

Closed path drawn

Understanding Pen Pointers

Pointer	Description
Initial Anchor Point ♠ₓ	First pointer to create the beginning of a new path.
Sequential Anchor Point ♠	Creates an anchor point with a line connecting the previous anchor point.
Add Anchor Point ♠₊	Adds an anchor point to existing path.
Delete Anchor Point ♠	Deletes an anchor point within a path.
Continue Path ♠	Extends a new path from an existing anchor point.
Close Path ♠ₒ	Closes the path of a drawing on the starting anchor point.
Join Paths ♠ₒ	Closes the path except not over the starting anchor point.
Retract Bézier Handle ♠	Displays Bézier handles when you point to an anchor. Click to retract the handles and revert to straight segments.
Convert Anchor Point Λ	Converts a corner point without direction lines to a corner point with independent direction lines. Use Shift+C modifier keys to toggle the pen.

Drawing Curves with the Pen Tool

The Pen tool can be used to draw precise and complex curves by simply clicking and dragging it on the Stage. These curves can be modified with precision by adjusting the Bézier handles that extend from the anchor points, or you can move the anchor points themselves. In this way, you can create any number of shape variations. For best results, make the grid visible so aligning anchor points isn't such a mystery.

Create Curved Line Segments

1. Click the **Pen** tool on the Tools panel.

2. Click on the Stage without releasing the mouse, drag up, and then release the mouse.

3. Position the pointer to the right of the original point, drag in the opposite direction of the curve, and then release the mouse when the curve is where you want it.

4. Continue adding points as needed. To end the path, double-click or point to the last anchor point drawn and click on it.

Did You Know?

You can select to Show Precise Cursors instead of the tool icons in the General tab of the Preferences dialog box. When this option is selected, drawing tools, such as the Pen tool, appear as crosshairs for better precision and alignment to grids and guides.

You can convert a curve point to a corner point. Click the Pen tool arrow, click Convert Anchor Point tool, and then click the curve point you want to covert to a corner point.

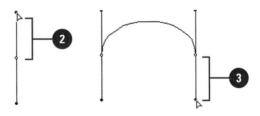

Curved line segment drawn

Create S-Curves

1. Click the **Pen** tool on the Tools panel.

2. Click on the Stage without releasing the mouse, drag down, and then release the mouse.

3. Position the pointer to the right of the original point, drag in the same direction as the first drag, and then release the mouse when the curve is where you want it.

4. Continue adding points as needed. To end the path, double-click or return to the last anchor point drawn and click on it.

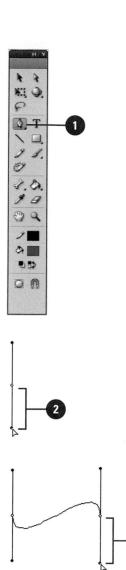

S-Curve drawn

Modifying Shapes with the Selection Tool

In Flash, unlike other vector drawing programs, you can edit shapes and lines in a unique, freeform way by simply dragging with the Arrow Selection tool. You can quickly adjust the curve or corner of a shape or line without having to select anchor points or use any other tools. This way of editing shapes is also useful for creating shape tweens where amorphous, organic movement is desired. This is what sets Flash apart from other animation tools and gives it its distinctive style. Additionally, you can convert curved line segments into corner points with this simple drag technique.

Use the Selection Tool to Modify a Shape

① Click the **Oval** tool on the Tools panel and then create a simple oval shape.

② Click the **Selection** tool on the Tools panel.

The pointer becomes an arrow.

③ Make sure the shape you want to modify is not selected.

④ Position the pointer on the edge of the shape, and then drag to modify the shape.

You can pull the curve to any position.

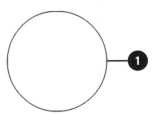

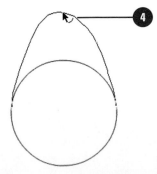

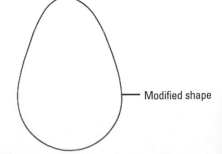

Modified shape

Convert Line Segments with the Selection Tool

1. Create a simple oval shape using the **Oval** tool.

2. Click the **Selection** tool on the Tools panel.

   The pointer becomes an arrow.

3. Make sure the shape you want to modify is not selected.

4. Position the pointer on the edge of the shape.

5. Press Option+drag (Mac) or Alt+drag (Win) to create a corner point.

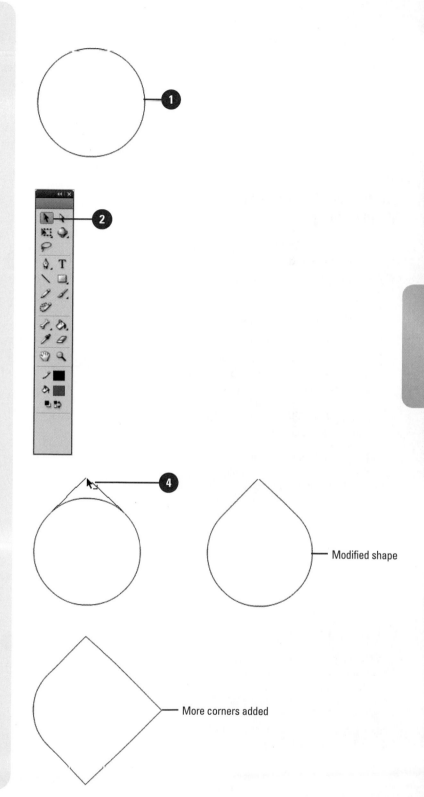

Modified shape

More corners added

Modifying Shapes with the Sub-Selection Tool

Vector shapes are made up of anchor points connected by line segments. There are two types of anchor points: corner points and curve points. Corner points connect two line segments in a sharp angle such as the corner of a square. Curve points define a curve or positions along a straight line and can be modified with Bézier handles. These handles extend out from the curve point and allow for very precise modification of the shape of the curve. The Sub-Selection tool works hand-in-hand with the Pen tool to create and modify shapes and lines in this way.

Use the Sub-Selection Tool to Modify a Shape

1 Create a simple oval shape using the **Oval** tool.

2 Click the **Sub-Selection** tool on the Tools panel.

   The pointer becomes an empty (or white) arrow.

3 Click on the edge of the shape to reveal the anchor points, and then click on an anchor point to select it or drag a selection rectangle to select multiple anchor points.

   The anchor points are the little white squares around the edge of the shape. When selected, Bézier handles appear on either side of the anchor point.

4 Grab one of the handles or the anchor points themselves and drag it, and then release the mouse.

Did You Know?

You can also use the arrow keys on the keyboard to move selected anchor points. Select one or more anchor points with the Sub-Selection tool, and then press the arrow keys to move the anchor point and its connected lines in the direction of the key you press.

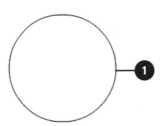

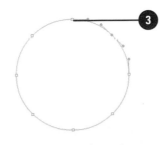

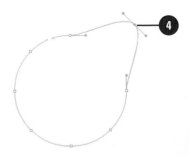

Convert Corner Points to Curve Points

1. Create a simple rectangle shape using the **Rectangle** tool.

2. Click the **Sub-Selection** tool on the Tools panel.

   The pointer becomes an empty (or white) arrow.

3. Click on the edge of the shape to select it and then click on one of the corner points to select it.

4. Press Option+drag (Mac) or Alt+drag (Win) the point to convert it to a curve point and create Bézier handles.

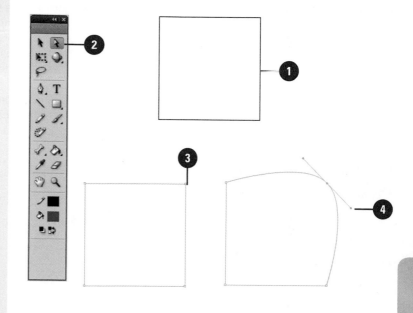

Convert Curve Points to Corner Points

1. Create a simple oval shape using the **Oval** tool.

2. Click the **Pen** tool on the Tools panel.

   The pointer becomes a small pen.

3. Click on the edge of the shape to reveal the anchor points.

4. Position the pointer over one of the curve points.

   A small corner icon appears.

5. Click on the point to convert it to a corner point.

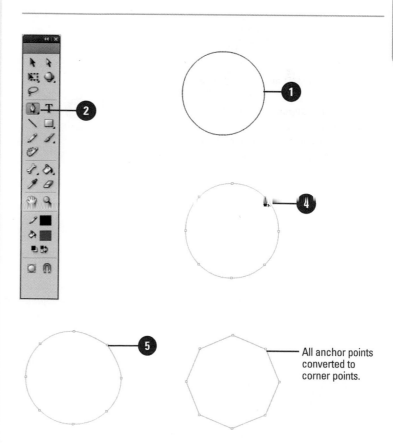

All anchor points converted to corner points.

Using the Free Transform Tool

FL 2.3

There are a number of ways to change the scale or size of graphics in Flash. The Free Transform tool on Tools panel allows you to interactively scale and rotate any selected object or shape on the Stage. Nearly every object in Flash can be transformed with these two functions of the Free Transform tool including groups, symbols, text, bitmaps, and editable shapes. The Free Transform tool allows you to select an object on the Stage and then interactively change its size or rotate it freely. Both options are available at once depending on where you place your mouse on the bounding box that appears.

Change the Scale of an Object

1. Select the object by clicking on it or by dragging a selection marquee around it with the **Selection** tool.

2. Click the **Free Transform** tool on the Tools panel.

   TIMESAVER *Press Q to select the Free Transform tool.*

3. Click the **Scale Modifier** button in the Options area of the Tools panel.

4. Drag any of the small handles on the bounding box to change the size of the shape. The corner handles resize proportionally while the handles along the sides resize either horizontally or vertically.

5. To change the transformation point, drag the circle handle.

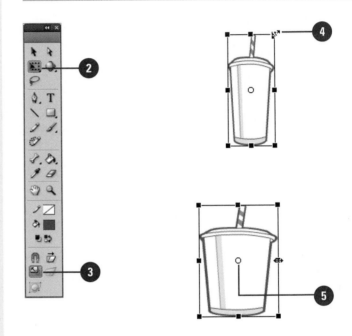

Did You Know?

You can restore a transformed object. Select the transformed object, click the Modify menu, point to Transform, and then click Remove Transform.

You can reset a transformed object. If you want to redo a transformation, select the object, and then click the Reset button in the Transform panel (available on the Window menu).

For Your Information

Working with the Transformation Point

When you transform an object, a transformation point appears at the center of the object. The point is initially placed in the center of the object, but you can move it at any time. To move the transformation point during a transformation, drag the point. To set it back to the center, double-click the point. To switch the point of origin for a scale or skew, Alt+drag (Win) or Option+drag (Mac) the point. To monitor the location of the transformation point (X and Y positions), click the center square in the grid in the Info panel (available on the Windows menu).

Rotate and Skew an Object

① Select the object by clicking on it or by dragging a selection marquee around it.

② Click the **Free Transform** tool on the Tools panel.

TIMESAVER *Press Q to select the Free Transform tool.*

③ Click the **Rotate/Skew Modifier** button in the Options area of the Tools panel.

④ Drag any of the corner handles on the bounding box to rotate the shape. Drag the handles along the side to skew the object.

⑤ To change the transformation point, drag the circle handle.

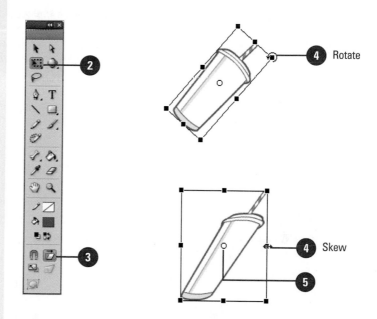

④ Rotate

④ Skew

Did You Know?

You can hold down the Shift key to constrain the rotation scale proportionally. When rotating, it constrains the rotation to 45-degree turns.

For Your Information

Working with Scale and Rotate

In the Default mode, both Scale and Rotate are enabled. Move the pointer to any of the four corner handles in the bounding box to enable the Rotate function. Scale and Rotate work relative to a center transformation point on the shape, which becomes visible when the shape is selected with the Free Transform tool. Move this point if you want to scale or rotate a shape from a different part of the shape. This is especially important when tweening and animating. You can change the scale and rotate objects by entering values in the Transform panel or in the Property Inspector. You can also access all of the Transform modes and some additional effects, such as Flip Horizontal and Vertical from the Transform submenu in the Modify menu.

Using Transform Options for Shapes

In addition to the scale and rotation changes that can be applied to groups, symbols, bitmaps, text and editable shapes, there are two additional transforms available only to editable shapes. Distort and Envelope are two modes available in the Free Transform tool options that enable you to transform the vectors of editable shapes to varying degrees. Distort transformations work on adjoining edges, tapering them down to vanishing points, similar to perspective. Envelope transformations allow you to warp the edges of a shape by splitting it up into smaller portions each controlled by their own vectors and anchor points.

Distort a Shape

1. Select the object.

2. Click the **Free Transform** tool on the Tools panel.

   TIMESAVER *Press Q to select the Free Transform tool.*

3. Click the **Distort Modifier** button in the Options area of the Tools panel.

4. Drag any of the corner handles on the bounding box to distort the shape.

5. Drag any of the side handles on the bounding box to skew or stretch the shape.

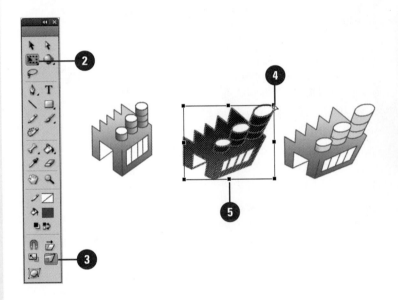

Change the Envelope of a Shape

1. Select the object.

2. Click the **Free Transform** tool on the Tools panel.

   TIMESAVER *Press Q to select the Free Transform tool.*

3. Click the **Envelope Modifier** button in the Options area of the Tools panel.

4. Drag any of the handles on the bounding box to pull the shape in any direction or use the Bézier handles to fine tune the curves.

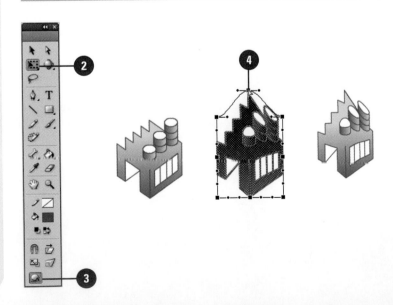

Transforming Gradient Fills

After you create a gradient fill, you can transform it by adjusting the size, rotation, width, or center of the fill with the Gradient Transform tool (formerly called the Fill Transform tool). For a radial gradient, you can now adjust the focal point (center) of a gradient fill applied to an object. You can also use the Gradient Transform tool to modify a bitmap fill.

Adjust a Gradient Fill

1. Click the **Gradient Transform** tool on the Tools panel.

2. Click the gradient fill to select it.

   A bounding box appears around it.

3. Position the pointer over an editing handle on the bounding box to identify its function.

   ◆ **Center point.** Four-way arrow.

   ◆ **Focal point.** Inverted triangle.

   ◆ **Size.** Circle with an arrow.

   ◆ **Rotation.** Four arrows in the shape of a circle.

   ◆ **Width.** Double-ended arrow.

4. Click and drag an editing handle to adjust the gradient fill.

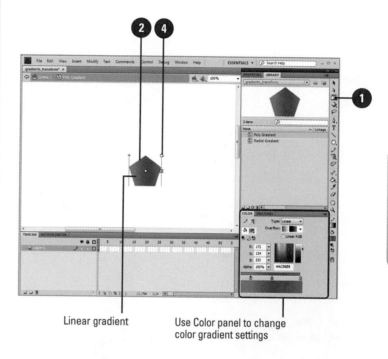

Linear gradient   Use Color panel to change color gradient settings

See Also

See "Modifying a Bitmap Fill" on page 200 for information on using the Gradient Transform tool with bitmaps.

Radial gradient

Moving and Rotating Objects in 3D Space

FL 2.3

In Flash, you can add 3D perspective effects (**New!**) to a movie clip by moving and rotating it in 3D space on the Stage. When you move or rotate a movie clip by the z axis, it becomes a 3D movie clip. Moving an object in 3D space is called **translation**, and rotating an object in 3D space is called **transformation**. Flash provides two different 3D space: global and local. Global 3D space is the Stage space, while local 3D space is the movie clip space. The default mode is global. You can move a movie clip in 3D space with the 3D Translation tool. When you do, three axes appear in the 3D object: the x axis is read, the y axis is green, and the z axis is blue. In addition, you can rotate a movie clip in 3D space with the 3D Transformation tool. When you do, you can rotate around an individual axis or use the orange free rotate control to rotate around the x and y axes at the same time. If you want to change the effect of the rotation, move the center point. When you select a 3D object, it appears with a 3D axis overlay.

Move Objects in 3D Space

1 Click the **3D Translation** tool on the Tools panel.

   TIMESAVER *Press G to select the 3D Translation tool.*

2 Click the **Global Transform** button on the Tools panel to select it for global mode or deselect it for local mode. The default is global.

   TIMESAVER *Press D to toggle between global and local mode.*

3 Select one or more movie clip objects.

   ◆ When you select multiple movie clips, and move one of them, the others move in the same way. Shift double-click one of the selected objects to move the axis controls to that object.

4 Drag the arrow tips (x- and y-axis) in the direction of the arrow or the black dot (z-axis) up or down.

   ◆ You can also move the object manually by using the Property Inspector.

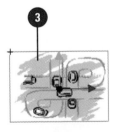

Rotate Objects in 3D Space

① Click the **3D Rotation** tool on the Tools panel.

TIMESAVER *Press W to select the 3D Rotation tool.*

② Click the **Global Transform** button on the Tools panel to select it for global mode or deselect it for local mode. The default is global.

③ Select one or more movie clip objects.

- ◆ When you select multiple movie clips, and move one of them, the others move in the same way. Shift double-click one of the selected objects to move the axis controls to that object.

④ Drag one of the four axis controls to rotate around that axis, or the free rotate control to rotate x and y axis at the same time.

⑤ To move the rotation control center point relative to the movie clip, drag the center point.

- ◆ Double-click the center point to move it back to the center of the movie clip.

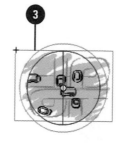

Did You Know?

You can turn the overlay on and off. Click the Edit (Win) or Flash (Mac), click Preferences, click General, select or clear the Show axes for 3d movie clips check box, and then click OK.

Changing the Perspective Angle in 3D Space

Change Perspective Angle in 3D Space

1. Select the 3D movie clip instance on the Stage that you want to change.

2. Click the **Window** menu, and then click **Properties** to open the Property Inspector.

3. Enter a new value in the Perspective Angle box or drag the hot text to change the value in the Property Inspector.

Did You Know?

You can automatically change the appearance 3D objects when you change the size of the Stage. Click the Modify menu, click Document, select or clear the Adjust 3D Perspective Angle to preserve current stage projection check box, and then click OK.

The Perspective Angle (**New!**) affects the size and view of 3D movie clips on the Stage. It's like zooming in and out with a camera lens, which changes the angle of view through the lens. When you increase the angle, 3D objects appear closer to the viewer. When you decrease the angle, 3D objects appear further away. The default angle is 55 degrees of view, which is like a normal camera lens. You can adjust the value from 1 degree to 180 degrees. You can control only one viewpoint, or camera. Each Flash file has only one Perspective Angle.

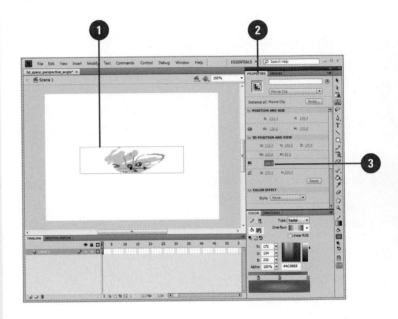

Adjusting the Vanishing Point in 3D Space

Adjust the Vanishing Point in 3D Space

1 Select the 3D movie clip instance on the Stage that you want to change.

2 Click the **Window** menu, and then click **Properties** to open the Property Inspector.

3 Enter an x- and y-axis value in the Vanishing Point boxes or drag the hot text to change the value in the Property Inspector.

As you drag the hot text, guides indicating the location of the Vanishing Point appears on the Stage.

4 To move the Vanishing Point back to the center of the Stage, click the **Reset** button in the Property Inspector.

Vanishing Point (**New!**) gives you the ability to move 3D movie clips and still maintain the same visual perspective of the original. Vanishing Point controls the orientation of the z-axis of 3D movie clips on the Stage. As you move the z-axis, 3D movie clips recede towards the Vanishing Point, which you can adjust to create the appearance you want. Each Flash file has only one Vanishing Point. If you move the Vanishing Point back to the default position in center of the Stage, you can use the Reset button in the Property Inspector.

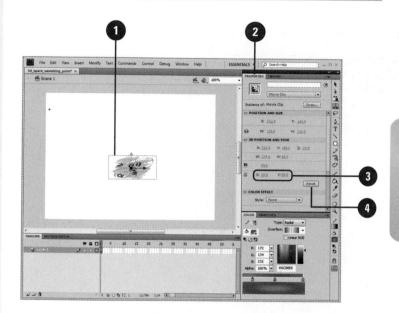

Cutting and Pasting Graphics Between Layers

Unless you lock or hide layers, or lock objects, the graphics on all layers are available for editing. You can select objects on one or more layers, cut or copy them, and then paste them all into a single layer. Flash can have only one layer active at a time. When you create and paste graphics, Flash places them on the active layer of a document. You can paste objects in two different ways: Paste In Center and Paste In Place. Paste In Center puts objects in the center of the open Flash window, which might not be the Stage. If you want to paste to the center of the Stage, you need to center the Stage in the open window. Paste In Place puts objects at the same location it had been when you cut or copied it.

Paste Objects Between Layers

1. Create or open a document with several layers.

2. Select one or more objects on the Stage.

   Flash selects the object's layer in the Timeline.

3. Click the **Edit** menu, and then click **Cut** or **Copy**.

4. Select a destination layer in the Timeline.

5. Click the **Edit** menu, and then click **Paste In Center**.

   Flash pastes the objects on the Stage in the middle of the active layer.

Did You Know?

You can use the area around the Stage to store graphics and other objects. Flash allows you to use the area around the Stage, called the Pasteboard, to store items for use later without having them appear on the Stage when you play the movie (SWF) file.

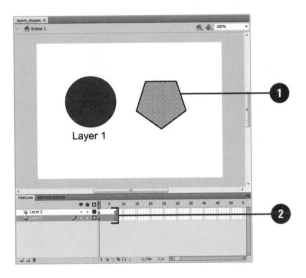

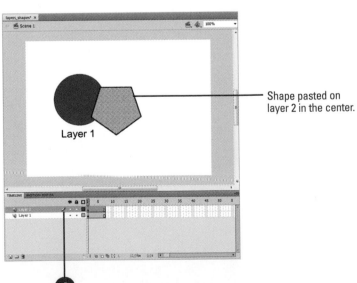

Shape pasted on layer 2 in the center.

Use the Paste In Place Command Between Layers

① Create or open a document with several layers.

② Select one or more objects on the Stage.

Flash selects the object's layer in the Timeline.

③ Click the **Edit** menu, and then click **Cut** or **Copy**.

④ Select a destination layer in the Timeline.

⑤ Click the **Edit** menu, and then click **Paste In Place**.

Flash pastes the objects into their original locations on the Stage.

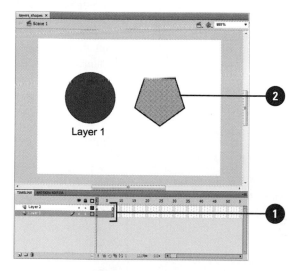

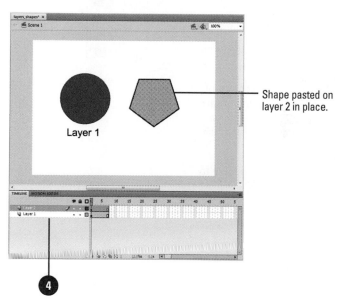

Shape pasted on layer 2 in place.

Working with Graphics on Different Layers

When you select an object on the Stage, Flash selects the object's layer in the Timeline. The reverse is also true. When you select a layer in the Timeline, Flash selects all the objects for that layer on the Stage. As you work with objects on different layers, it helps to know how selections work. Unless you lock or hide layers, or lock objects, the objects on all layers, either active or inactive, are available for editing. You can activate a layer and edit objects on inactive layers.

Edit Object on Inactive Layers

1. Create or open a document with several layers.

2. Click the **Selection** tool on the Tools panel.

3. Select an object on the Stage.

   Flash selects the object's layer in the Timeline.

4. Click a blank area of the Stage.

   Flash deselects the object but keeps the active layer.

5. Make changes to another object in another layer (inactive layer) without actually selecting the object. You can do any of the following:

   ◆ Drag an object's outline to reshape it.

   ◆ Select a tool on the Tools panel, such as the Paint Bucket tool, and use it to modify the object.

   Flash modifies the object in the inactive layer. The active layer didn't change. Flash changes active layers only if you select an object.

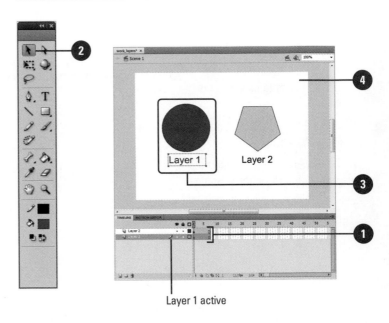

Layer 1 active

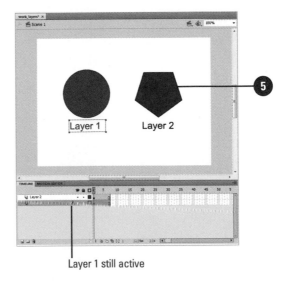

Layer 1 still active

Distributing Graphics to Layers

If you have several objects on a single layer, and need to move them onto separate layers, you can use Cut and Paste in place for each object or you can save time by using the Distribute to Layers command. The Distribute to Layers commands puts each object (shapes, groups, and symbols) in a selection on a separate layer; any unselected objects remain on their original layer. This command comes in handy when you want to create a motion tweening animation, which requires objects to be on individual layers.

Place Selected Objects on Separate Layers

1. Create or open a document with several objects on a single layer.

2. Select all the objects on a single layer you want to distribute to separate layers.

   TIMESAVER *Click the Edit menu, and then click Select All or press ⌘+A (Mac) or Ctrl+A (Win).*

3. Click the **Modify** menu, point to **Timeline**, and then click **Distribute To Layers**.

   TIMESAVER *Press ⌘+Shift+D (Mac) or Ctrl+Shift+D (Win) to distribute to layers.*

   Flash creates a layer for each object. New layers appear at the bottom of the Timeline in the order in which you originally placed them on the Stage. Each object is placed in the same location on the Stage (like the Paste In Place command).

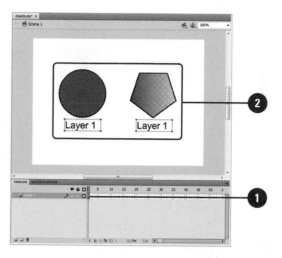

See Also

See Chapter 8, "Animating with Motion Tweening" on page 231 for information on using motion tweening.

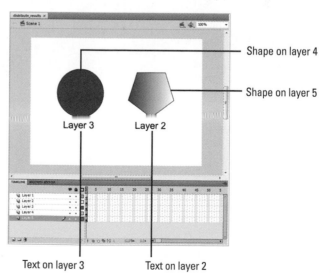

Shape on layer 4

Shape on layer 5

Text on layer 3

Text on layer 2

Changing Drawing Settings

The Drawing category on the Preferences dialog box contains a number of drawing settings that control the sensitivity and behavior of Flash's drawing tools. Make changes to the tolerance levels for smoothing or straightening, set the sensitivity for line and shape recognition, or fine-tune snapping. You can exercise greater control over your drawing or allow Flash to perform corrections and adjustments as you draw. You can customize the way you use Pen tools, draw connecting lines and smooth curves, and recognize lines and shapes.

Change the Drawing Settings

1. Click the **Flash** (Mac) or **Edit** (Win) menu, and then click **Preferences**.

2. Click the **Drawing** category.

3. Specify the drawing option you want:

   ◆ **Pen Tool options.** Select check boxes to show pen preview, solid points, and precise cursors.

   ◆ **Connect Lines.** Determines how close the ends of any two lines need to be before Flash connects them. It controls when a line is converted into a perfectly straight line.

   ◆ **Smooth Curves.** Determines the amount of smoothing applied to a drawn line. The lower the smoothing applied, the closer the line appears to what you have drawn.

   ◆ **Recognize Lines.** Defines how straight a line drawn with the Pencil tool must be before it's converted into a perfectly straight line.

   ◆ **Recognize Shapes.** Sets how precise simple geometric shapes must be drawn before they are detected as shapes.

   ◆ **Click Accuracy.** Determines how near to a shape the pointer must be before it's recognized.

   ◆ **IK Bone Tool.** Automatically sets the transformation point. (**New!**)

4. Click **OK**.

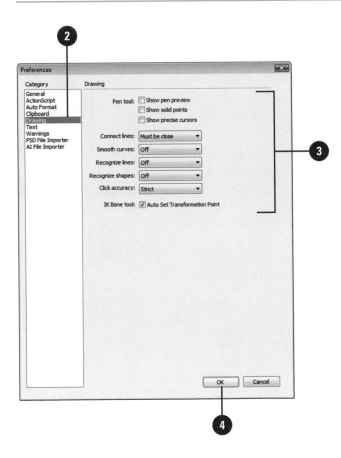

Working with Groups, Symbols, and Instances

Introduction

All vector objects are editable. As the complexity of your document increases, you can protect artwork from being inadvertently changed by storing it in special modes called groups and symbols. Groups provide a quick way to seal a shape by storing it in a bounding box that can only be edited by entering a group editing mode. Groups are created on the Stage and are not stored anywhere else. For items that are more global to your movie, you can convert them into symbols. The basis for interactivity and animation in Flash resides in its use of these reusable objects.

You can create artwork and then save that artwork as a symbol that is stored in the Library of your Flash document. Symbols are an efficient way to build your movies because you can reuse these assets as instances on the Timeline, and Flash will only store it in your file once. Apply ActionScript to control a movie clip symbol instance and to add interactivity, place art inside of button symbols to create hit states, or apply a variety of transparency and color effects to instances on the Stage. The Library stores all of the reusable art and objects in your movie including symbols, sounds, video clips, bitmaps, and components. It can be organized and sorted for easy access to your movie's assets. A Library can also be shared with other Flash documents.

What You'll Do

Create Groups

Arrange Multiple Groups

Use the Library

Create Symbols

Edit in Symbol Mode

Create Instances

Change Symbol and Instance Behaviors

Swap Symbol Instances

Use Graphic and Button Symbols

Enable and Disable Buttons

Create Invisible Buttons

Use Movie Clip Symbols

Break Symbols Apart

Modify Instance Properties

Modify Instance Color Styles and Blends

Use Advanced Color Options

Use 9-Slice Scaling on a Movie Clip Symbol

Set Highlight Color Preferences

Creating Groups

When you group artwork on the Stage, you prevent it from interacting with other artwork on the same layer. **Grouping** essentially stores the artwork in a bounding box that can only be edited by entering a special group editing mode, which you can easily do by double-clicking the group. For example, if you draw a shape over another shape on the same layer, the strokes and fills of the second shape will cut through or replace the strokes and fills of the shape directly beneath it. Grouping your artwork prevents this from happening. You can also use grouping to combine several shapes into one group so you can manipulate them simultaneously. You can ungroup artwork or objects that have been grouped by using the ungroup option or by breaking them apart. Doing so removes the bounding box and the artwork can be freely edited.

Group Artwork on the Same Layer

1. Select the artwork on the Stage that you want to group with any of Flash's selection tools or methods.

2. Click the **Modify** menu, and then click **Group**.

   TIMESAVER *Press* ⌘*+G (Mac) or Ctrl+G (Win) to quickly group selected objects or artwork.*

Ungroup Artwork

1. Select the artwork on the Stage that you want to ungroup.

2. Click the **Modify** menu, and then click **Ungroup**.

   TIMESAVER *Press Shift+* ⌘*+G (Mac) or Shift+Ctrl+G (Win) to quickly ungroup selected objects or artwork.*

See Also

See "Breaking Symbols Apart" on page 155 for information on taking apart elements.

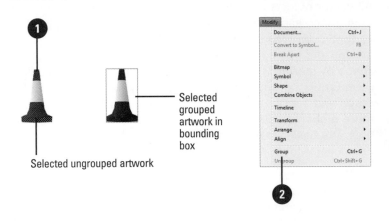

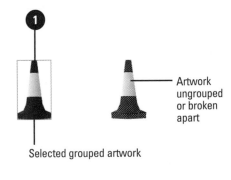

Selected grouped artwork in bounding box

Selected ungrouped artwork

Artwork ungrouped or broken apart

Selected grouped artwork

Arranging Multiple Groups

When objects are grouped they appear on top of shapes that aren't grouped on the same layer. Each subsequent group that is created will appear on top of the last. This is called the stacking order. Flash allows you to change this order with the Arrange command. You can send a group or symbol to the bottom of this stack or bring one at the bottom to the top. Additionally, you can change the order incrementally.

Change the Stacking Order

① Select the group whose stacking order you want to change.

② Click the **Modify** menu, point to **Arrange**, and then click:

◆ **Bring To Front**. The selected object is brought to the top of the stack.

   TIMESAVER *Press Option+Shift+Up (Mac) or Ctrl+Shift+Up (Win).*

◆ **Bring Forward**. The selected object is brought up one level in the stacking order.

   TIMESAVER *Press ⌘+Up (Mac) or Ctrl+Up (Win).*

◆ **Send Backward**. The selected object is brought down one level in the stacking order.

   TIMESAVER *Press ⌘+Down (Mac) or Ctrl+Down (Win).*

◆ **Send To Back**. The selected object is brought to the bottom of the stack.

   TIMESAVER *Press Option+Shift+Down (Mac) or Ctrl+Shift+Down (Win).*

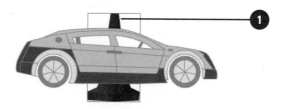

①

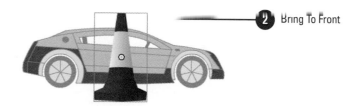

② Bring To Front

Opening the Library Panel

The **Library** panel is where all of the reusable assets in your Flash movie are stored. An **asset** is any artwork or object you have made into symbols, such as fonts, graphic symbols, movie clips, and buttons. Flash also stores bitmaps, sounds, video clips, and components in the Library. You can also open libraries from other Flash files to quickly transfer assets from one project to another. In Flash, you can use a single Library panel to view the library items of multiple Flash files at the same time.

Open the Library

1. Click the **Window** menu, and then click **Library**.

   TIMESAVER *Press ⌘+L (Mac) or Ctrl+L (Win) to open the Library panel.*

2. Click the **Document** popup, and then select a library from a currently opened document.

3. If you want one library selected regardless of what document is active, simply select the library from the Document popup menu, and click the **Pin** button.

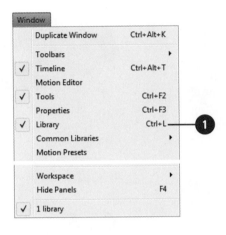

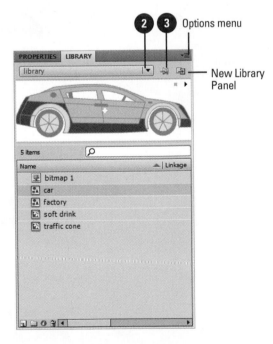

Open Other Libraries

1. Click the **File** menu, point to **Import**, and then click **Open External Library**.

   TIMESAVER *Press ⌘+Shift+O (Mac) or Ctrl+Shift+O (Win) to open the Open As Library dialog box.*

2. Navigate to the drive or folder where the Flash movie containing the Library is located.

3. Select the library file.

4. Click **Open**.

   The Library appears docked underneath the Library of the active project.

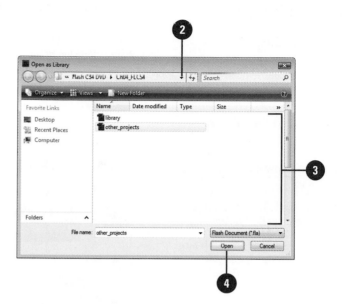

Did You Know?

You can use sample common libraries included with Flash and create your own. To use a common library, click the Window menu, point to Common Libraries, select the library type you want from the submenu, and then drag items from the library to your document. To create a common library, create a Flash file (.fla) with a library containing the symbols you want, and then save the file to the Libraries folder located in the Flash application folder on your hard disk.

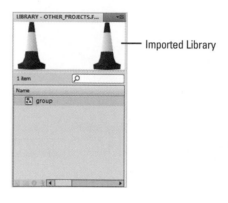

Imported Library

Working with the Library Panel

Organize Items in the Library Panel

1 Click the **Window** menu, and then click **Library**.

2 Use any of the following options to organize items in the Library panel:

◆ **Search.** Click in the Search box, start to type the name of the item you want to find. As you type, the list of Library items narrows to display the items that match what you typed.

Click **X** in the Search box to display all the items in the Library panel.

◆ **Sort.** Click the name header to sort the Library items from A-Z or Z-A.

◆ **New Folder.** Click the **New Folder** button, type a name, and then press Enter (Win) or Return (Mac).

◆ **Use Folders.** Select a Library item from the list and drag it to the folder where you want to store it. Click the triangle to expand/collapse the folder.

◆ **Delete Item.** Select the items you want to delete, and then click the **Delete** button.

◆ **Rename Item.** Double-click the item you want to rename, type a new name, and then press Enter (Win) or Return (Mac).

You can organize your Library assets into folders, sort the items, duplicate symbols or change their behavior. You can sort items (**New!**) by name, type, date, use count, or ActionScript linkage identifier. If you have a long list of items in your Library, you can search (**New!**) for the ones you want. The improved Library panel also allows you to set properties on most multiple Library items at once (**New!**).

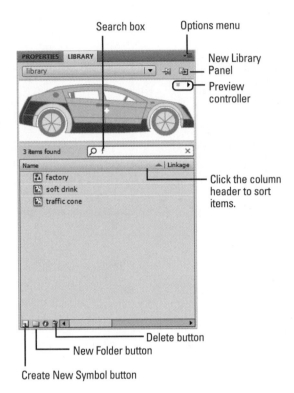

Search box

Options menu

New Library Panel

Preview controller

Click the column header to sort items.

Delete button

New Folder button

Create New Symbol button

Access Library Options

1. Click the **Options** menu on the Library panel.

   A menu of options for adding, deleting, organizing, and configuring Library items appears, such as:

   - **New Font.** Create a font symbol to embed a font in a movie.

   - **New Symbol.** Create a symbol.

   - **Duplicate.** Make a copy of the selected items.

   - **Edit or Edit With.** Edit items in a library. Select the item first.

   - **Linkage.** Define properties to share library assets for runtime or author development time.

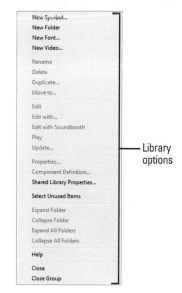

Library options

Change Library Item Properties

1. Click the **Window** menu, and then click **Library**.

2. Select the Library items you want to change.

   To select multiple items, hold down Ctrl (Win) or ⌘ (Win), and the click the items you want to select.

3. Click the **Properties** button.

4. Make the changes you want for the Library items.

5. Click **OK**.

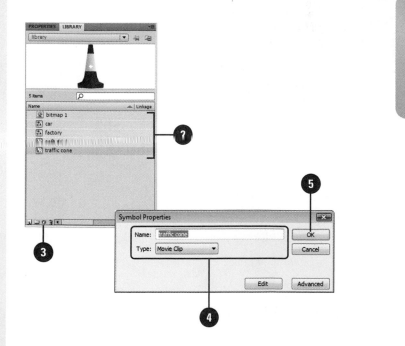

Creating Symbols

 FL 2.7

Using symbols is an efficient way to add artwork or elements to your Flash movie. When you create a symbol, it is stored in the Library where it can be reused as an instance in the Timeline. You can turn graphics or animations you've made into symbols or create a new one from scratch. There are three default symbol types you can choose from: graphic, movie clips, and buttons. How you use the symbol will determine which of these three types to use. Symbols have their own discrete Timelines. Think of a symbol as a package containing artwork that you can open and close. You enter a symbol editing mode to make changes and when you leave this mode the artwork is protected.

Create New Symbols

1. Click the **Insert** menu, and then click **New Symbol**.

   TIMESAVER Press ⌘+F8 (Mac) or Ctrl+F8 (Win) to create a new symbol.

2. Type a name for the symbol.

3. Select a symbol type option.

4. Click **OK**.

   Flash enters a special Symbol editing mode.

5. Create or insert a symbol item, and then click the **Back** button.

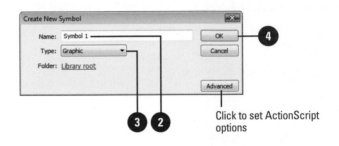

Click to set ActionScript options

Symbol editing mode indicator

Convert Existing Artwork into Symbols

1. Select the artwork on the Stage you want to make into a symbol.

2. Click the **Modify** menu, and then click **Convert To Symbol**.

   TIMESAVER Press F8 to convert the artwork into a symbol.

3. Type a name for the symbol.

4. Select a symbol type option.

5. Select a registration point.

6. Click **OK**.

   Symbol appears in the Library.

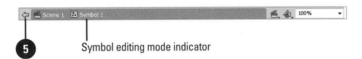

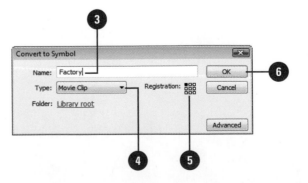

Convert Animations into Symbols

1. In the Timeline, select every frame in the animation that you want to make into a symbol.

2. Click the **Edit** menu, point to **Timeline**, and then click **Copy Frames**.

   TIMESAVER *Press Option+⌘+C (Mac) or Ctrl+Alt+C (Win) to copy frames.*

3. Click the **Insert** menu, and then click **New Symbol**.

4. Type a name for the symbol.

5. Select a movie clip or graphic symbol.

6. Click **OK**.

   Flash enters a special symbol editing mode.

7. Select the first frame of the Timeline.

8. Click the **Edit** menu, point to **Timeline**, and then click **Paste Frames**.

   TIMESAVER *Press Option+⌘+V (Mac) or Ctrl+Alt+V (Win) to paste frames.*

See Also

See "Editing in Symbol Mode" on page 140 for information on editing symbols in symbol editing mode.

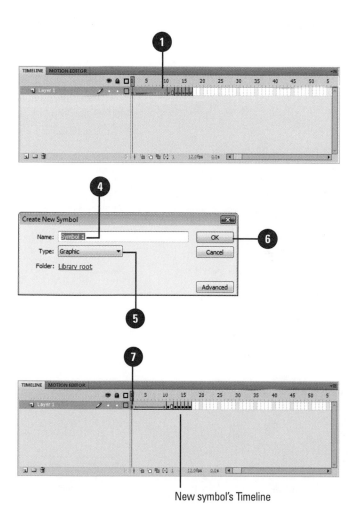

New symbol's Timeline

For Your Information

Selecting a Registration Point

In the Convert to Symbol dialog box, there is a registration grid. The grid represents the symbol's bounding box. It displays a small black square to indicate the registration point for the graphic. A **registration point** is the axis from which a symbol rotates or aligns to other objects. You can view the registration point for a symbol by selecting it, and then opening the Property Inspector or the Info panel.

Editing in Symbol Mode

When you need to change or modify a symbol, you must enter a special symbol editing mode. Entering this mode allows you to view and edit the symbol's Timeline. Any changes you make are stored in the Library, and all other instances of the symbol are updated with these changes. You can choose to enter the symbol mode, entirely replacing the view of the main Timeline, or view the symbol in context to the main Timeline. Additionally, you can open the symbol mode in a new window.

Enter Symbol Editing Mode

1. Select the symbol you want to modify.

2. Click the **Edit** menu, and then click **Edit Symbols**.

    Selecting Edit Symbols centers the symbol based on its registration point in the symbol editing work area. The Timeline is not visible.

    TIMESAVER *Double-click the symbol, or press ⌘+E (Mac) or Ctrl+E (Win) to enter symbol editing mode.*

3. Modify the symbol or its Timeline.

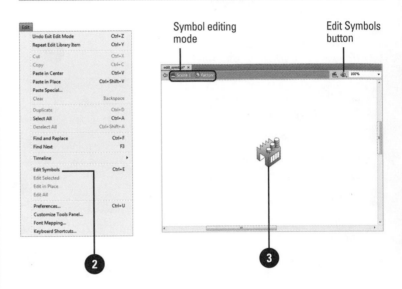

Symbol editing mode

Edit Symbols button

Did You Know?

You can use the Edit Symbols button to access any symbol stored in the Library. When you click the Edit Symbols button in the Edit bar, a list of symbols stored in the Library appears from which you can select.

For Your Information

Entering and Viewing a Symbol's Editing Mode

There are two additional modes for viewing a symbol's editing mode: Edit In Place and Edit In New Window. You can access these options from the Edit menu or from the context-sensitive menus by Control-clicking (Mac) or right-clicking (Win) the instance on the Stage.

Edit In Place. Preserves the view of the symbol's position in the main Timeline, dimming everything else in the main Timeline. This feature is useful when you need to see a symbol's placement relative to other elements in the main Timeline as you edit it. To quickly Edit in Place, double-click the instance on the Stage.

Edit In New Window. Opens the symbol's Timeline in a new window.

Additionally, you can select the symbol from the Edit Symbol popup on the right side of the Information bar above the Timeline.

Exit Symbol Editing Mode

1. When you are finished making changes to a symbol, you can return to the main Timeline in several ways:

   ◆ Click the **Back** button or the **Scene name** on the Edit bar to return to the parent scene.

   ◆ Click the **Edit Scene** button on the Edit bar, and then click another Scene name.

   ◆ Click the **Edit** menu, and then click **Edit Document** to return to the main Timeline.

   ◆ Press ⌘+E (Mac) or Ctrl+E (Win).

Back button and Scene name   Edit Scene button

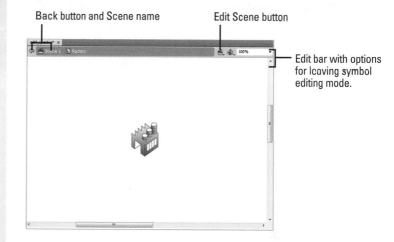

Edit bar with options for leaving symbol editing mode.

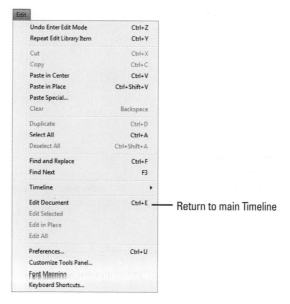

Return to main Timeline

Creating Instances

An **instance** is a copy of a symbol. When you use a symbol in your Timeline you are using an instance of it. You can animate an instance of a symbol and apply a variety of effects to it without affecting the original symbol in the Library. You can also use multiple instances of the same symbol. When you change the properties of an instance in the Timeline, you are only applying these changes to that copy, or instance, of the symbol. In this way, you keep the file size down because Flash only keeps track of the changes you've made while preserving the symbol in the form you created. If you have several instances of a symbol in your movie and you want to edit the artwork, you can make changes to the master symbol. When you do this, all of the instances of that symbol will be updated with these changes.

Place Instances on the Stage

1. Open or expand the Library panel.

   TIMESAVER *Press F11 or ⌘+L (Mac) or Ctrl+L (Win) to quickly open and close the Library panel.*

2. Select the symbol from the list of assets and drag it to the Stage to create an instance of that symbol.

   TIMESAVER *Drag the preview image of a symbol selected in the Library item list to create an instance of that symbol on the Stage.*

Instance of the symbol on the Stage ❶

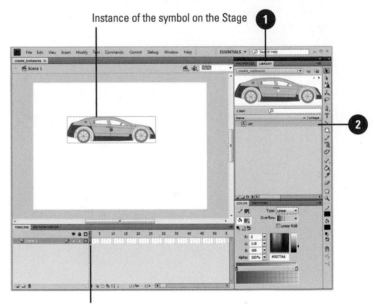

❷

Filled keyframe indicates instance is placed on the Stage.

Edit Master Symbols

1. Double-click any instance of a symbol you want to edit.

2. Make changes to the symbol artwork or animation.

3. Click the **Back** button or **Scene name** on the Edit bar to return to the main Timeline.

   All of the instances reflect these changes.

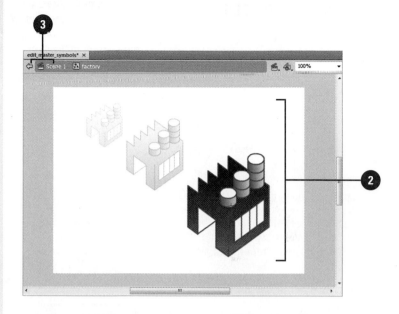

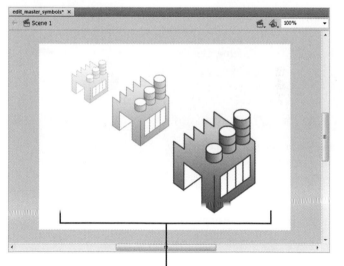

All other instances update with new changes.

Changing Symbol and Instance Type

Symbols have three specific types that are set when you first create the symbol: graphic, movie clip, and button. You can change these types for a symbol's instance by selecting it and then selecting a new type option in the Property Inspector. Do this when you need the instance to display a behavior different than its parent symbol. Alternately, you can change the behavior of the parent symbol itself in the Library. All subsequent instances that you create from this symbol will exhibit the new behavior.

Change a Symbol's Behavior

1. Open or expand the Library panel.

2. Select the symbol from the list.

3. Click the **Properties** button at the bottom of the Library window to open the Symbol Properties dialog box.

4. Select a different symbol type option.

5. Click **OK**.

   The symbol displays a new behavior. All subsequent instances will default to this behavior.

Did You Know?

If you are already using instances of a symbol in your movie, they will not be affected by a change in behavior. Flash allows you to change the types of instances separately from your symbol's default behavior. To update the instance to a new symbol, select it on the Stage, and then change the type in the Property Inspector.

See Also

See "Breaking Symbols Apart" on page 155 for information on taking apart elements.

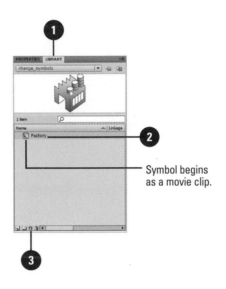

Symbol begins as a movie clip.

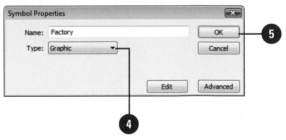

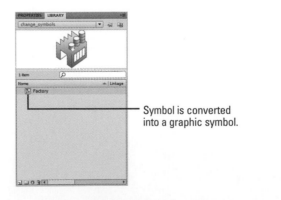

Symbol is converted into a graphic symbol.

Change the Symbol Behavior of an Instance

1. If necessary, open the Property Inspector.

2. Select the instance on the Stage.

3. Click the **Symbol** popup in the Property Inspector, and then select another behavior: **Movie Clip**, **Button**, or **Graphic**.

Did You Know?

You can use a method to change the symbol behavior of any instance. Select from any of the three options: graphic symbol, button, or movie clip. In this way, you can get graphic symbols to behave as movie clips, movie clips to behave like buttons, etc.

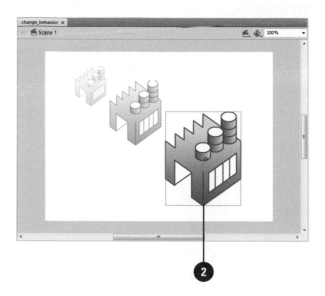

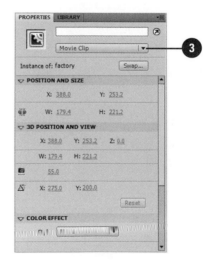

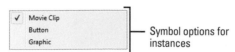

Symbol options for instances

Swapping Symbol Instances

Symbols are used in the Timeline as instances. If you apply motion or color effects to an instance, you only affect that instance, not its parent symbol. If you would like to swap the parent symbol for another symbol, while retaining any effects and/or animation that have been applied to the instance, you can use the Swap Symbol feature. All of the effects are preserved but are instead applied to and referencing the new chosen symbol. Alternately, if you are using several instances of a symbol and want to change the content (the master symbol itself) of one of these instances without affecting the other instances, you can duplicate and swap that symbol in the Swap dialog box. Essentially you create a new master symbol linked to your instance that is no longer related to the original master symbol and all its instances.

Swap Instances

1. If necessary, open the Property Inspector.

2. Select the instance on the Stage.

3. Click **Swap** in the Property Inspector to open the Swap Symbol dialog box.

   TIMESAVER *Control+click (Mac) or right-click (Win) the instance on the Stage, and then click Swap Symbol.*

4. Click a symbol from the list.

5. Click **OK**.

   The instance is now linked to a new symbol.

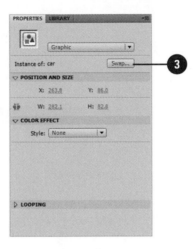

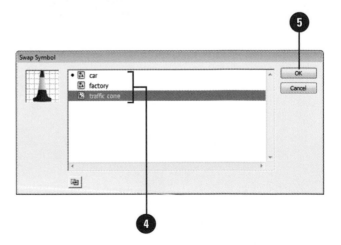

Duplicate Symbols During Swap

① Select the instance on the Stage.

② Click **Swap** in the Property Inspector.

③ Click the **Duplicate Symbol** icon in the bottom left-hand corner of the dialog box.

④ Enter a new name.

⑤ Click **OK**.

The instance is now linked to a new symbol, copied from the original master symbol.

⑥ Click **OK**.

See Also

See "Breaking Symbols Apart" on page 155 for information on breaking symbols apart in symbol editing mode.

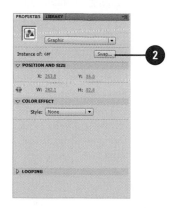

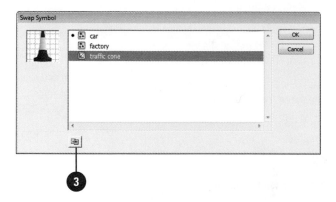

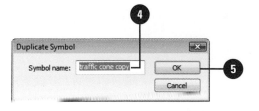

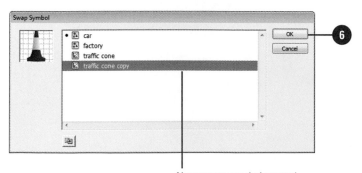

New master symbol created

Using Graphic Symbols

Graphic symbols can be used for static images and for animations that are in sync with the main Timeline. There are three instance options available to them: Loop, Play Once, and Single Frame. Set the instance to Loop if you want the symbol's Timeline to play continuously. Play Once plays the Timeline of a graphic symbol once and then stops. Single frame sets the instance to display as a single frame contained in the graphic symbol's Timeline. Unlike movie clip symbols, an animation contained in a graphic symbol can be seen in the main Timeline without having to export the Flash movie. However, any ActionScript and sounds that have been included in a graphic symbol's Timeline will not work.

Create a Graphic Symbol

1. Click the **Insert** menu, and then click **New Symbol**.

   TIMESAVER *Press ⌘+F8 (Mac) or Ctrl+F8 (Win) to create a new symbol.*

2. Type in a name for the symbol.

3. Click the **Type** popup, and then click **Graphic**.

4. Click **OK**.

   Flash enters a symbol editing mode that contains an empty Timeline for that symbol.

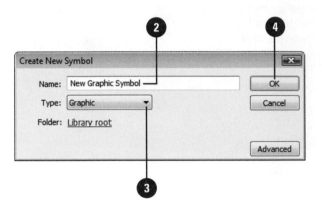

Did You Know?

Graphic symbol animations are synced up to the main Timeline. For example, if the animation in the graphic symbol spans 10 frames, the instance in the main Timeline must also span 10 frames if the entire animation is to be seen.

Change the Options for Graphic Symbol Instances

1. Select a graphic symbol instance on the Stage.

2. Click the popup in the Property Inspector, and then select from the following graphic options:

   ◆ **Loop.** The Timeline in the graphic symbol will loop continuously.

   ◆ **Play Once**. The Timeline in the graphic symbol will play once and stop. If there is no animation in the symbol or if there is only artwork on one frame, it will be treated as a static graphic.

   ◆ **Single Frame**. Sets the instance to a single frame in the Timeline of the master symbol. When this is selected, the graphic symbol is treated as a static graphic.

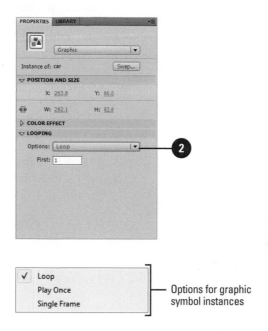

Options for graphic symbol instances

For Your Information

Converting a Graphic to a Symbol

In addition to creating a new symbol and adding a graphic, you can also convert an existing graphic to a symbol. Select the vector graphic on the Stage, click the Modify menu, and then click Convert To Symbol. In the Convert to Symbol dialog box, enter a name (that you'll refer to in an ActionScript), and then click the Graphic option as the type. The registration grid within the symbol bounding box displays a small black square to indicate the registration point for the graphic.

Using Button Symbols

Use buttons to add interactivity to your movie. Button symbols have their own four-frame Timeline. The first three frames define the states of the button: up, over, and down. The first frame is the Up state, which is the appearance of the button when in its normal, non-active state. The second frame is the Over state, which is triggered when the user places their mouse over the button. The third frame is the Down state, which appears when the user presses the button with their mouse. The fourth frame—which is invisible outside of the symbol editing mode—defines the active area. This is the area that the user must place their mouse over to activate the other states of the button. You can assign actions, such as sound or animation, to instances of buttons that tell Flash what to do when the button is clicked.

Create a Button

1. Click the **Insert** menu, and then click **New Symbol**.

   TIMESAVER *Press ⌘+F8 (Mac) or Ctrl+F8 (Win) to create a new symbol.*

2. Type in a name for the symbol.

3. Click the **Type** popup, and then click **Button**.

4. Click **OK**.

5. Place artwork in the keyframe of the first frame.

   This represents the button's Up state, its normal, inactive state.

6. Click the **Insert** menu, point to **Timeline**, and then click **Keyframe** to add a keyframe in the second frame (the Over state).

   TIMESAVER *Press F6 to quickly add a keyframe and press F7 to add a blank keyframe.*

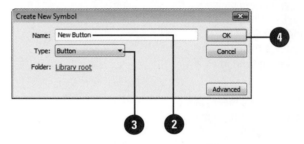

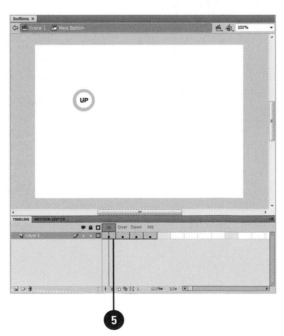

7 Change the artwork or add new artwork in this frame.

8 Click the **Insert** menu, point to **Timeline**, and then click **Keyframe** to add a keyframe in the third frame (the Down state).

9 Alter the artwork or add new artwork in this frame.

10 Click the **Insert** menu, point to **Timeline**, and then click **Keyframe** to add a keyframe in the fourth frame (the active area).

11 Add a simple graphic (a rectangle or oval, for example) to define the active area.

12 To assign a sound to a state of the button, select the state's frame in the Timeline, open the Property Inspector, and then:

◆ Select a sound from the Sound popup menu.

◆ Select an event from the Synchronization popup menu.

13 Click the **Control** menu, and then click **Test Movie** to test your button by exporting the movie.

TIMESAVER *Press ⌘+Return (Mac) or Ctrl+Enter (Win) to test your button.*

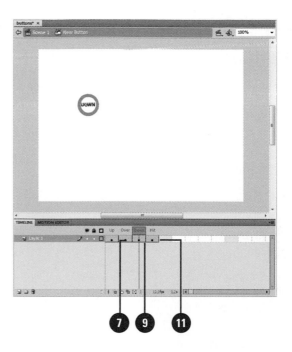

See Also

See "Enabling and Disabling Buttons" on page 152 for information on turning buttons on and off.

For Your Information

Adding Animation to a Button

There are several ways to add animation to a button. First, you can place an instance of the button symbol on the Stage and assign actions to it, not to frames in the button's Timeline. Another way is to create a button using a movie clip symbol or a button component. You can create more complex animation with the movie clip button. The downside is that file size increases. The button component provides more pre-built button types, such as PushButton and RadioButton, and customizable features. See Chapter 16, "Adding Display Components" on page 389 for information on components and using button components.

Enabling and Disabling Buttons

Flash allows you to test your buttons within the development environment without having to export the movie. You can test the behavior of simple buttons by toggling the Enable Simple Buttons feature on and off. When buttons are enabled, you can't select them or enter their symbol editing mode normally. Disable this feature if you need to enter the symbol mode. You can quickly see how the different states of your button behave without having to export the whole flash movie. Any ActionScript applied to the button will be ignored.

Enable and Disable Buttons

① Place a button on the Stage.

② Click the **Control** menu, and then click **Enable Simple Buttons** to enable the button.

> **TIMESAVER** *Press Ctrl+Alt+B (Win) or Option+⌘+B (Mac) to toggle the enabling and disabling of simple buttons.*

③ Place the mouse over the button to test the Over state.

④ Press down on the button to test the Down state.

⑤ To disable the button, click the **Control** menu, and then click **Disable Simple Buttons**.

Did You Know?

Regardless of whether buttons are enabled or disabled, they will be functional when you export your movie. The Enable Simple Buttons command is only relevant to the Flash development environment.

See Also

See "Using Button Symbols" on page 150-151 for information on creating a button.

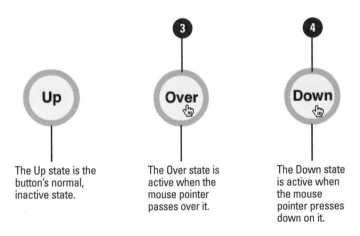

The Up state is the button's normal, inactive state.

The Over state is active when the mouse pointer passes over it.

The Down state is active when the mouse pointer presses down on it.

Creating Invisible Buttons

Buttons do not require graphics to be placed in the hit state frames (the first three frames). As long as the active area contains a shape, the button will be invisible but will be functional and ActionScript can be applied to it. The active area is the fourth frame in the button symbol Timeline. An instance of an invisible button appears as a transparent blue shape in the main Timeline, but it will not be visible in the exported movie.

Create an Invisible Button

1. Click the **Insert** menu, and then click **New Symbol**.

   TIMESAVER *Press ⌘+F8 (Mac) or Ctrl+F8 (Win) to create a new symbol.*

2. Click the **Type** popup, and then click **Button**.

3. Click **OK**.

4. Click the **Insert** menu, point to **Timeline**, and then click **Keyframe** to add a keyframe in the fourth frame (the active area).

   TIMESAVER *Press F6 to create a keyframe.*

5. Add a simple graphic (a rectangle or oval, for example) to define the active area.

6. Make sure the first three frames remain empty.

7. Return to the main Timeline.

8. Drag the invisible button from the Library to the Stage.

   Invisible buttons appear as transparent blue shapes but are invisible in the final export.

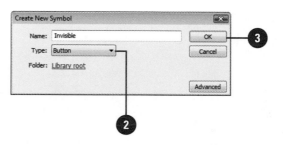

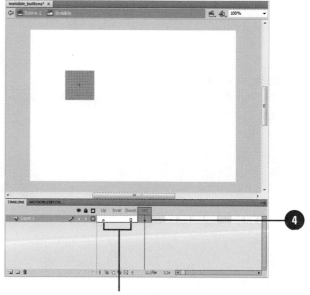

The first three frames of the button remain empty.

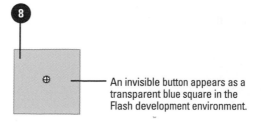

An invisible button appears as a transparent blue square in the Flash development environment.

Using Movie Clip Symbols

Movie clip symbols operate independently on the main Timeline. When you want an animation to loop on a single frame in the Timeline, you can store this animation in the Timeline of a movie clip that will sit on this frame. Movie clip instances can have actions applied to them and can be controlled from anywhere in the Flash movie through ActionScript. They can contain animations, interactive controls, sounds, and even other movie clips. Unlike graphic symbols, you can only see the first frame of the movie clip in the main Timeline. Export your movie to see the movie clip play.

Create and View Movie Clips Symbols

1. Click the **Insert** menu, and then click **New Symbol**.

2. Click the **Type** popup, and then click **Movie Clip**.

3. Click **OK**.

4. Add your content to the Movie Clip Timeline.

5. Return to the main Timeline by clicking the **Back** button or the **Scene name** on the Edit bar.

6. Drag the movie clip symbol to the Stage from the Library.

7. To change movie clip properties, select the clip on the Stage, and then change options in the Property Inspector.

   ◆ **Symbol.** Movie Clip, Graphic, or Button

   ◆ **X** and **Y position**

   ◆ **Width** and **Height**

   ◆ **Color.** Brightness, Tint, Alpha, and Advanced

8. Click the **Control** menu, and then click **Test Movie** to test the movie clip symbol by exporting the movie.

   TIMESAVER Press ⌘+Return (Mac) or Ctrl+Enter (Win) to quickly test your movie.

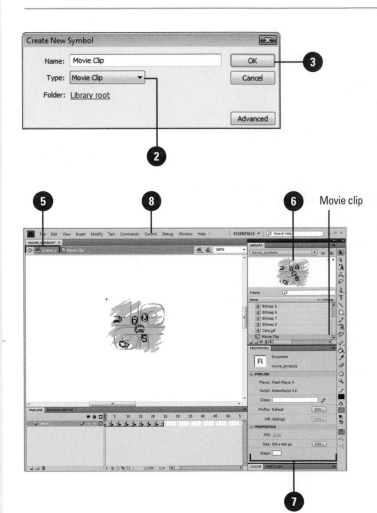

Movie clip

154

Breaking Symbols Apart

Sometimes you'll need to break a symbol instance so that it is no longer linked to the master symbol. You might do this if you want to add something to the symbol without affecting the other instances. In this way, the content inside the symbol will become a simple graphic that you can adjust without affecting the master symbol you made it from or any of its instances.

Break an Instance

1. Select an instance on the Stage you would like to break.

2. Click the **Modify** menu, and then click **Break Apart**.

   TIMESAVER *Press ⌘+B (Mac) or Ctrl+B (Win) to quickly break apart a symbol.*

See Also

See "Swapping Symbol Instances" on page 146 for information on swapping symbol instances.

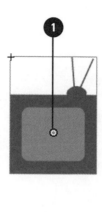

Symbol broken apart into an editable shape.

Modifying Instance Properties

You can alter the properties of an instance of a symbol without affecting the master symbol. Any transform applied to an instance can be animated with motion tweening. Flash will gradually draw the frames in between one transform to another. This is how you create movement in Flash. Change the scale of an instance or rotate and skew it. You can perform these functions interactively with the Free Transform tool. You can also add values in the Transform panel, or access additional Transform options in the program's Modify menu. Distort and Envelope cannot be applied to instances and are disabled on the Tools panel options when the Free Transform tool is selected.

Modify the Scale or Rotation

1. Select the instance on the Stage.

2. Click the **Free Transform** tool on the Tools panel.

   TIMESAVER *Press Q to quickly select the Free Transform tool.*

3. Click the **Scale** or **Rotate and Skew** button in the Options section of the Toolbar.

4. Drag the small handles around the bounding box to change the size of the instance or rotate it.

Did You Know?

You can select multiple instances and change their properties simultaneously. Press Shift+select each instance you would like to alter in tandem. A bounding box will appear around all selected instances.

The Transform panel allows you to enter values for various transforms.

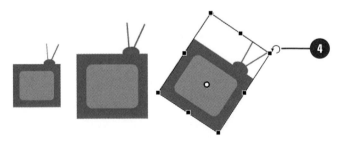

Use Additional Transform Commands

1 Select the instance on the Stage.

2 Click the **Modify** menu, point to **Transform**, and then click one of the following:

- ◆ **Free Transform.** Transforms the object freely.

- ◆ **Scale.** Constrains the transform to scale.

- ◆ **Rotate And Skew.** Constrains the transform to rotate and skew.

- ◆ **Scale And Rotate.** Constrains the transform to scale and rotation changes.

- ◆ **Rotate 90° CW.** Rotates the selected object 90° clockwise.

- ◆ **Rotate 90° CCW.** Rotates the selected object 90° counter-clockwise.

- ◆ **Flip Vertical.** Flips the object along a vertical axis.

- ◆ **Flip Horizontal.** Flips the object along a horizontal axis.

- ◆ **Remove Transform.** Removes any transform effects applied to the selected instance.

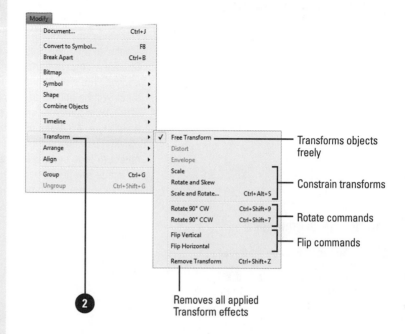

Transforms objects freely

Constrain transforms

Rotate commands

Flip commands

Removes all applied Transform effects

Did You Know?

Changing the scale or rotation of an instance can also be done in the Transform panel. Simply select the instance, and then access these panels. The Modify menu includes additional transform commands not available anywhere else.

Modifying Instance Color Styles and Blends

You can change the tint, brightness, or transparency of an instance in the Color popup located in the Property Inspector. This feature appears whenever an instance is selected on the Stage. If you would like to add a color to the instance, you can do so by selecting the Tint color style. Choose a color and then choose the amount of color that will be applied. You can adjust the Brightness (that is, how much white or black will be added) of an instance by choosing the Brightness color style. An instance can also be made transparent by altering the Alpha color style. An Alpha of zero will make the instance invisible, though it can still be selected and animated. This is useful when you want an object to fade on or off the Stage. You can also create unique composite image effects by varying color and transparency and applying a blend to two or more overlapping movie clips instances.

Modify the Brightness

1. Select the instance on the Stage.

2. Click the **Style** popup in the Property Inspector, and then click **Brightness**.

3. Enter a value between -100 and 100 (-100= no brightness, black; 100= maximum brightness, white).

   TIMESAVER *You can use the slider to the right of the field to interactively change the level of Brightness applied.*

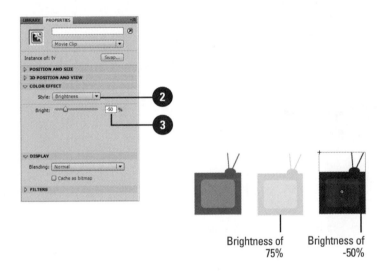

Brightness of 75%   Brightness of -50%

Modify the Tint Color

1. Select the instance on the Stage.

2. Click the **Color** popup in the Property Inspector, and then click **Tint**.

3. Click a color from the color box popup or enter an RGB value in the fields.

4. Enter a value between 0 and 100 (0= no color, 100= maximum saturation).

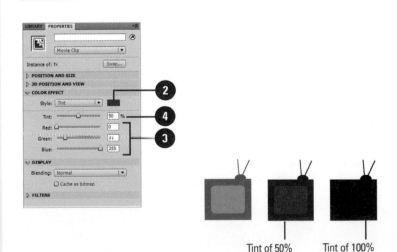

Tint of 50%   Tint of 100%

Modify the Transparency

1. Select the instance on the Stage.

2. Click the **Style** popup in the Property Inspector, and then click **Alpha**.

3. Enter a value between 0 and 100 (0= invisible, 100= fully visible).

   TIMESAVER *You can use the slider to the right of the field to interactively change the level of Alpha applied.*

   If you need to apply a color style with alpha you must use the Advanced option.

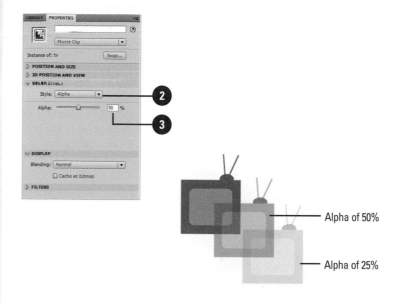

Alpha of 50%

Alpha of 25%

Modify the Blend

1. Select the movie instance on the Stage.

2. Click the **Style** popup and adjust the color and transparency.

3. Click the **Blending** popup, and then select a blend.

4. Position the movie clip with the blend over another symbol.

   To achieve the effect you want, you will need to experiment with the color and transparency of the movie clip and blend mode.

Did You Know?

A blending mode contains different elements. It contains a blend color, opacity (degree of transparency), base color (pixel colors under blend), and result color.

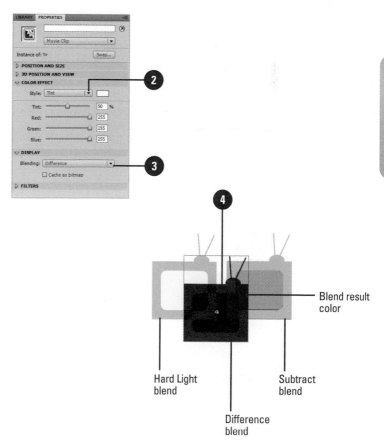

Blend result color

Hard Light blend

Subtract blend

Difference blend

Using Advanced Color Options

An instance can have only one color style (Brightness, Tint, or Alpha) applied. To apply multiple color styles, you must use the Advanced feature in the Property Inspector's Color popup menu. This option allows you to change the percentage of Red, Green, or Blue (0% -100%) added or subtracted as well as the constant values of RGB (-255 to +255). Additionally, there is an Alpha scale that can be applied to each of these options. Apply a color, brightness, or alpha style to an instance and then access the Advanced options to make adjustments. The applied color style is preserved. Experiment with this features until you get the effects that you need.

Modify the Color and Transparency Simultaneously

1. Select the instance on the Stage.

2. Click the **Style** popup in the Property Inspector, and then click **Tint**, **Brightness** or **Alpha** and apply an effect.

3. Click the **Style** popup again, and then click **Advanced**.

4. Add or subtract percentages or values of RGB and Alpha.

Did You Know?

You can go directly to the Advanced panel to add color effects without having applied any Brightness, Tint, or Alpha. If you have already chosen one of these options and then enter the Advanced settings, your previous applied effect will be preserved and the sliders in the Advanced Settings window will reflect this change. For example, if you have added a tint of red to your instance, the sliders in the Advanced setting will show that red has been added.

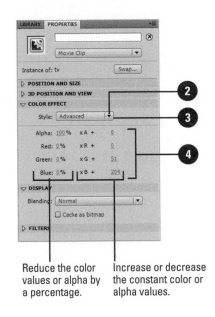

Reduce the color values or alpha by a percentage.

Increase or decrease the constant color or alpha values.

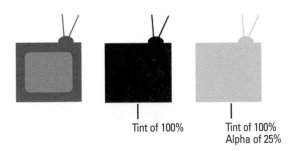

Tint of 100%

Tint of 100%
Alpha of 25%

Using 9-Slice Scaling on a Movie Clip Symbol

In previous versions, Flash scales movie clips equally in height and width. For many rectangular movie clips, this method of scaling doesn't work very well at the corners. In Flash, a method called **9-slice scaling** is used. A movie clip is visually divided into nine areas, or slices, with a grid overlay (dotted lines called slide guides). Each area of the grid is scaled separately, except the corners, which provides more accurate results. The slide guides are set at 25% of the symbol's height and width by default. Before you can scale a movie clip, you need to enable 9-slice scaling. To edit a movie clip, you need to use symbol-editing mode.

Enable 9-Slice Scaling

1. Select the movie clip symbol you want in the Library panel.

2. Click the **Options** menu, and then click **Properties**.

3. Click **Advanced**.

4. Select the **Enable guides for 9-slice scaling** check box.

5. Click **OK**.

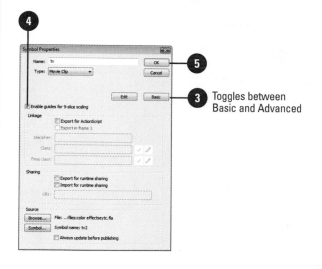

Toggles between Basic and Advanced

Scale a Movie Clip Symbol

1. Double-click the movie clip symbol in the Library to enter symbol-editing mode.

2. To see the scaling on the Stage, click the **Control** menu, and then click **Enable Live Preview**.

3. Drag the horizontal or vertical guides to scale the symbol.

   The new position of the guides provides the new scaling.

Drag any guide

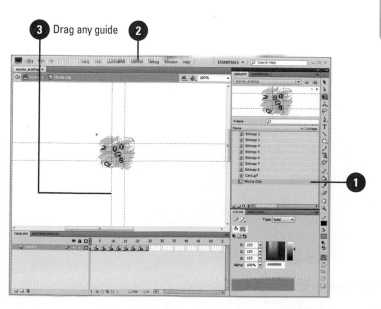

Setting Highlight Color Preferences

Flash allows you to set general preferences to customize the highlight, or selection, color of elements in Flash to make them easier to see. In the General category of the Preferences dialog box, you can select different colors for different types of elements, including drawing objects, drawing primitives, groups, symbols, and all other elements. If you don't want to set individual colors, you can use the layer color for all elements.

Set Highlight Color Preferences

1. Click the **Flash** (Mac) or **Edit** (Win) menu, and then click **Preferences**.

2. Click the **General** category.

3. Select the **Use Layer Color** option to use the current layer's outline color, or select the option, and then select the color you want for the following elements:

   ◆ **Drawing Objects.**

   ◆ **Drawing Primitives.**

   ◆ **Groups.**

   ◆ **Symbols.**

   ◆ **Other Elements.**

4. Click **OK**.

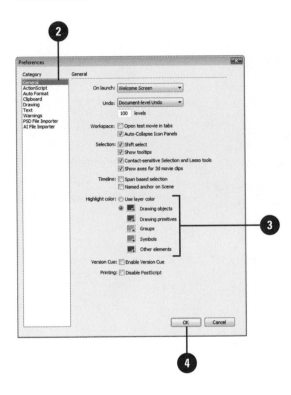

Working with Text

5

Introduction

In Flash, you can create three types of text: static, dynamic, and input. **Static** is text that doesn't change. **Dynamic** is text that updates, such as stock quotes, weather reports, or sports scores. **Input** is text entered by a user in forms or surveys. You can create editable text fields for use as static display text or to implement dynamic text objects with the Text tool. In the program's text menu, as well as the Property Inspector, there are a number of attributes to choose from such as Font type, size, color, indentation, and orientation. Also included are familiar letter form formatting procedures for kerning, tracking, and anti-aliasing. Because text fields are editable, you can change any text attribute—as well as the content in the text field—after it is created.

Use the Break Apart command to break editable text fields into shapes and edit them with any of the selection tools or pen modifiers. This is especially useful for creating new font forms, and it also allows you to implement shape tweening. Create dynamic text fields that can be updated from a text file on a server or some other source using ActionScript. In Flash, you can now configure the Find and Replace feature to target text contained in specific elements in your Flash document and swap these out with new entries from the built-in Adobe dictionaries or from a personal dictionary you create. Find and Replace makes navigating the text in large, complex files much simpler. Other new features include new implementation of Cascading Style Sheets for consistent HTML text formatting and the new built-in Spell Checker for enhanced productivity.

What You'll Do

Create Static Text

Change Font Type, Size, and Color

Modify Tracking and Kerning

Change Text Direction and Orientation

Change Text Alignment

Use Break Apart to Modify Characters

Use Anti-Alias Text

Use Font Mapping

Set Device Fonts Versus Embedded Fonts

Create Dynamic Text and Input Text

Set Dynamic Text and Input Text Options

Use Cascading Style Sheets with HTML Text

Check Spelling

Use Find and Replace

Creating Static Text

 FL 2.6

Static text refers to any text field that isn't dynamic or input text. It's generally used for displaying information or for animation. Text created in Flash is editable, which means that you can continue to change it after it is created. This includes changing its attributes as well as the textual content (the letters it contains). The Text tool creates an editable text box wherever you touch down on the Stage. Flash will keep the text on a single line until you hit the Return key. If you need a text box with a predefined width, you can create a text box before you start typing. The entered text will automatically wrap relative to the boundaries of the box and any formatting settings you've applied. To re-enter an existing text box to change the text, simply double-click any character in the Text box or click it with the Text tool to activate it and make it ready to edit.

Create Static Text

1 Click the **Text** tool on the Tools panel.

The pointer becomes a crosshair with a small "T" in the corner.

TIMESAVER *Press T to quickly select the Text tool.*

2 Click the Stage where you want your text box to begin.

Flash displays a handle on the corner of a text box to identify the type of text box.

3 Begin typing in the box that appears.

4 Click anywhere on the Stage outside the text field to deselect it.

5 To reselect a text box, click to select it.

A blue bounding box with square handles appears around a text box when it's selected.

See Also

See "Setting Text Preferences" on page 62 for information on setting preferences for Default Text Orientation, Right to Left Text Flow, and No Kerning.

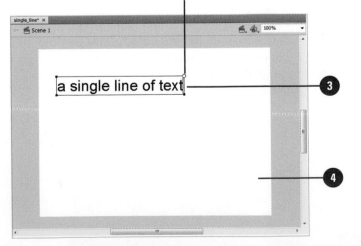

Small circle indicates single line of text.

a single line of text

Create a Text Box

1. Click the **Text** tool on the Tools panel.

   The pointer becomes a crosshair with a small "T" in the corner.

   TIMESAVER *Press T to quickly select the Text tool.*

2. Click the Stage where you want your text box to begin and drag until the box is the size you need.

3. Begin typing in the box that appears.

4. Click anywhere on the Stage outside the text field to deselect it.

5. To reselect a text box, click to select it.

   A blue bounding box appears around a text box when it's selected.

Did You Know?

You can change the size of an existing text box. Select the text box, drag any of the black resize handles, the white small circle (single line) or white square (text block) to resize. The text in the field wraps to accommodate to the new size.

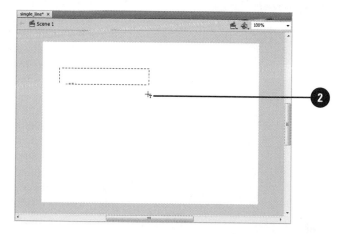

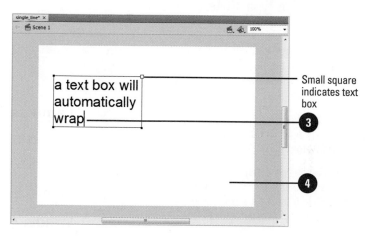

Small square indicates text box

For Your Information

Loading an External Text File

If you have a body of text that may change over time, you can use the ActionScript command LoadVars to load a text file (.txt). To load the text file headlines.txt (which contains headlines="sample text") into the headlines dynamic text box (instance is *headlines_text* and var is n*ews_lv*) using the LoadVars object, you can use a similar script:

```
var news_lv:LoadVars = new LoadVars();
news_lv.load("c:/yourfolderlocation/headlines.txt");
news_lv.onLoad = function () {
      headlines_txt.text = news_lv.headlines;
}
```

Changing Font Type, Size, and Color

 FL 2.4

Flash includes a number of text properties to choose from. These include a font type, style, size, and color. You can set these attributes before you create a text field or alter them on existing text. To make changes to the entire text field, select it with the Selection tool without entering the field (or making it active). Any changes made are applied to the whole field. A text box is considered "active" when the background of the field is an opaque white and text can be entered into it (as opposed to just being selected on the Stage, when it appears in a bounding box). If you only want to change a portion of the field, enter the text field and select only those characters or words you want to change. Attributes such as font type, style (**New!**), size, and color as well as more advanced text properties can be easily accessed in the Property Inspector. When the Text tool or any text field is selected, the Property Inspector displays all of the available attributes.

Change the Font Type, Style, and Size

1. Select the text field you want to change with the **Selection** tool or select text within the text field with the **Text** tool.

2. Click the **Family** popup in the Property Inspector, and then select a font name.

   The Family menu displays the font name and sample text for each font style to make it easier to decide what font you want to use. (**New!**)

3. Click the **Style** popup in the Property Inspector, and then select a font style: (**New!**) **Regular**, **Italic**, **Bold**, or **Bold Italic**.

4. Click the current point value in the Property Inspector, and then enter another point value in the Size entry box.

Did You Know?

You can change the font type, size, and style in the Text menu. Click the Text menu, point to Font, Size, or Style, and then select an option.

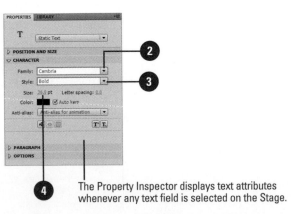

The Property Inspector displays text attributes whenever any text field is selected on the Stage.

Change the Font Color

1. Select the text field you want to change with the **Selection** tool, or select text within the text field with the **Text** tool.

2. Click the **Color** box in the Property Inspector, and then select a fill color or click the **Color Wheel** icon to create or select a custom color.

Did You Know?

You can change the text color in any of the color palettes. Change the fill color of any selected text field by clicking on any of the color palettes. They are located in the Tools panel, the Color Mixer panel, and the Color Swatches panel.

See Also

See "Setting Text Preferences" on page 62 for information on setting options for showing font previews on font menus.

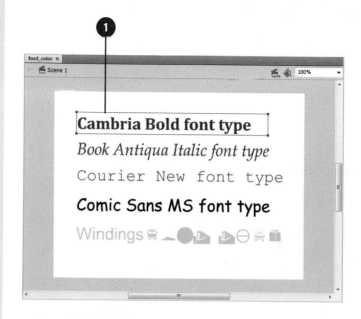

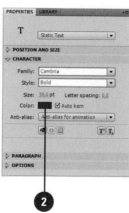

Modifying Tracking and Kerning

FL 2.4

Sometimes the space between text characters can appear awkward or where increasing the space is a creative solution. Flash provides methods for adjusting these spaces, called kerning and tracking. **Tracking** is the space between characters and words on a single line and adjusting tracking affects the entire line. **Kerning** deals with the space between any two characters and adjusting it will only affect that space. Many Fonts contain built-in information about problematic character pairs. Flash makes use of this information when you turn on Auto Kern in the Property Inspector.

Adjust Tracking

1. Select the text in a text field you want to track or you can select the entire text box with the **Selection** tool.

2. Click the **Text** menu, point to **Letter Spacing**, and then click **Increase** or **Decrease**.

   The Tracking increases or decreases in 0.5-point increments.

   TIMESAVER *You can adjust tracking in the Property Inspector with the Character Spacing entry field or slider.*

Did You Know?

You can quickly adjust kerning or tracking using the keyboard. Select the text or text field (to track) or place the cursor between two characters, and then press Option+⌘+right arrow (Mac) or Ctrl+Alt+right arrow (Win) to increase the space or Option+⌘+left arrow (Mac) or Ctrl+Alt+left arrow (Win) to decrease the space. Holding down the Shift key with this keyboard shortcut adjusts the space in larger increments.

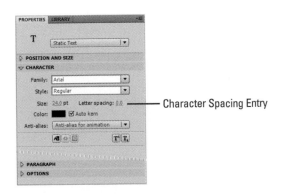

Increased tracking

Decreased tracking

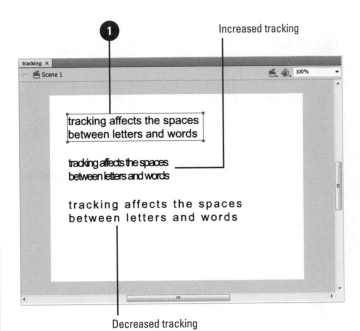

Character Spacing Entry

Adjust Kerning

1 Enter a text field on the Stage by double-clicking on it.

2 Place the cursor between the two characters you want to kern.

3 Click the **Text** menu, point to **Letter Spacing**, and then click **Increase** or **Decrease**.

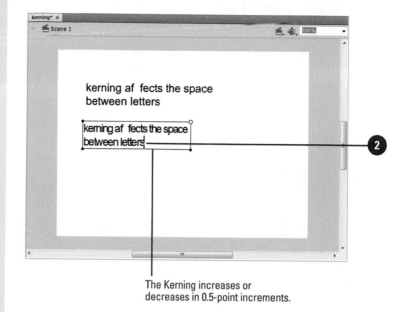

The Kerning increases or decreases in 0.5-point increments.

Set Auto Kerning

1 Select a text field with the **Selection** tool.

2 Select the **Auto Kern** check box in the Property Inspector.

Auto kern is enabled for that text field.

Auto Kerning can correct problematic character combinations.

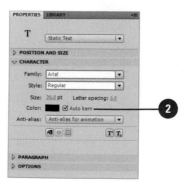

Changing Text Direction and Orientation

In addition to a variety of properties that can be applied to text in Flash, there are also procedures for changing the orientation and direction of text. Included is a formatting option for creating vertical text automatically without using any of the Transform commands. When text orientation is set to be vertical, the characters appear in columns though they remain in their normal horizontal orientation. If you need the text to rotate ninety degrees and follow the orientation of the line, you can set it to rotate automatically in the Property Inspector. This is useful if you are looking for something other than a column. The orientation of the text becomes vertical.

Create a Single Column of Vertical Text

1. Click the **Text** tool on the Tools panel.

2. Click the **Change Orientation** button in the Property Inspector, and then click **Vertical, Left To Right**, or **Vertical, Right To Left**.

3. Click the Stage where you want your text box to begin, and then start typing in the box that appears.

    TIMESAVER *Press Return (Mac) or Enter (Win) to create a new column.*

4. When you're finished, click on the Stage outside the text field.

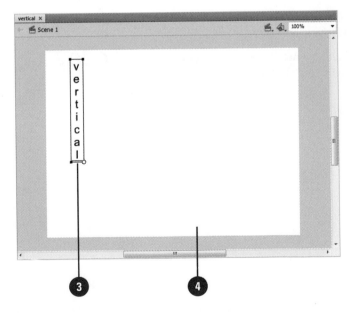

Did You Know?

You can convert an existing text field into a vertical text field. Select the text field on the Stage, click the Change Direction popup in the Property Inspector, and then select a vertical option.

You can make vertical text the default orientation. Select the Default Text Orientation check box in the Editing tab of the Preferences dialog box. This can be useful when working in some Asian languages.

Create a Vertical Text Block

1. Click the **Text** tool on the Tools panel.

2. Click the **Change Orientation** button in the Property Inspector, and then click **Vertical, Left To Right**, or **Vertical, Right To Left**.

3. Click the Stage where you want your text box to begin and drag until the box is the size you need.

4. Begin typing in the box that appears.

5. When you're finished, click anywhere on the Stage outside the text field.

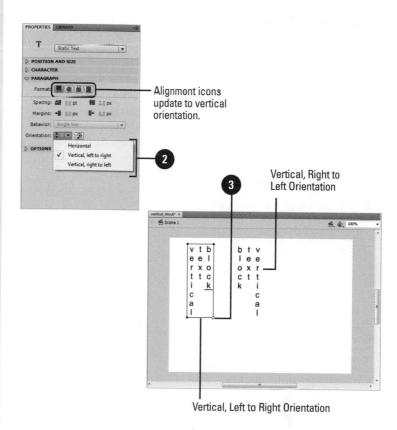

Alignmont icons update to vertical orientation.

Vertical, Right to Left Orientation

Vertical, Left to Right Orientation

Rotate Characters in a Vertical Text Field

1. Select a character or word in an active vertical text field or select the entire field with the **Selection** tool.

2. Click the **Rotate Text** button in the Property Inspector.

Did You Know?

The Rotate Text button is enabled only for vertical text fields. To rotate horizontal text fields, either convert them to vertical or use the Free Transform tool.

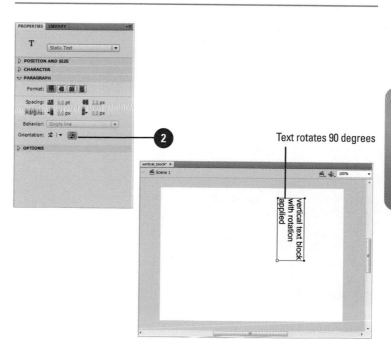

Text rotates 90 degrees

Changing Text Alignment

FL 2.4

Similar to other text editing tools or word processing programs, Flash includes features for formatting paragraphs with alignment, margins, and indentation. These features can be accessed through the Text menu and in the Property Inspector whenever any text field is selected on the Stage. Each text field can have its own individual properties assigned to it. Alignment governs the position of the text in a text box, margins are the space between the left and right side of the text and the boundaries of the text box, and indentation sets the amount of character spaces before the first line of text in a paragraph begins.

Align Paragraph Text

1. Select the text in a text field you want to align or you can select the entire text box with the **Selection** tool.

2. In the Property Inspector in the Paragraph section, click one of the following:

   ◆ **Align Left**. Aligns text to the left margin.

   ◆ **Align Center.** Text is centered between the boundaries of the text box.

   ◆ **Align Right.** Aligns text to the right margin.

   ◆ **Justify.** Each line of text fills the width of the text box boundary.

Did You Know?

You can quickly select all text in a text field. If you are inside an active text field, press ⌘+A (Mac) or Ctrl+A (Win) to select all of the text.

You can transform text just like other objects. You can scale, rotate, skew, and flip text boxes to create unique effects.

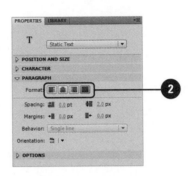

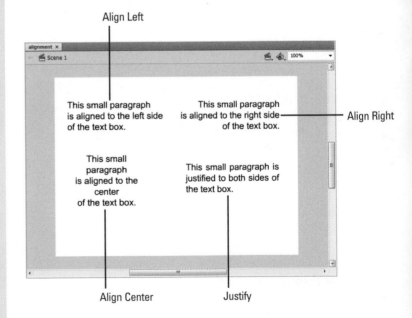

Align Left

Align Right

Align Center

Justify

Set Margins and Line Spacing

1 Select a text field with the **Selection** tool.

2 In the Property Inspector in the Paragraph section, enter values for any of the following:

TROUBLE? *Options differ depending on the orientation of the text box.*

- ◆ **Indent**. Indents the first line of the paragraph.

- ◆ **Line Spacing**. Adjusts the space between lines of text.

- ◆ **Left Margin**. Adjusts the amount of space between the left barrier of the text box and the left side of the paragraph.

- ◆ **Right Margin**. Adjusts the amount of space between the right barrier of the text box and the right side of the paragraph.

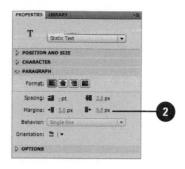

Indentation space affects the first line of text.

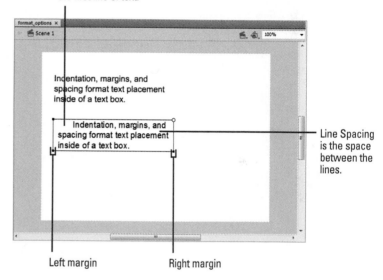

Indentation, margins, and spacing format text placement inside of a text box.

Indentation, margins, and spacing format text placement inside of a text box.

Line Spacing is the space between the lines.

Left margin

Right margin

Using Break Apart to Modify Characters

When a line of text is created in Flash, it appears in a bounding box that is editable. Sometimes you might need to adjust the characters separately or you might want to modify the shape of the characters themselves to create new character styles. The Break Apart command allows you to do this. There are two levels of breaking that you can utilize. The first break will separate the text field into singular, editable characters. This is useful if you want to reposition or align the letters of a word independently. The second break severs the text from its font reference: in essence it becomes a shape that you can edit with any of the drawing tools or pen modifiers.

Break a Text Field into Single Characters

1 Select the text field on the Stage with the **Selection** tool.

2 Click the **Modify** menu, and then click **Break Apart**.

Each character appears in its own editable box.

TIMESAVER *Press* ⌘+B *(Mac) or Ctrl+B (Win) to use the Break Apart command.*

Text fields can be broken.——**1**

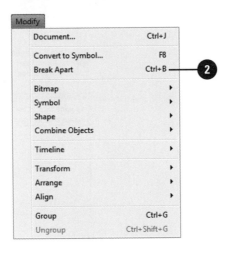

Text fields can be broken. — Broken text field

bro k e n .

The text field is broken into separate text fields that can be moved and edited separately.

Break a Text Field into Shapes

① Select the text field on the Stage.

② Click the **Modify** menu, and then click **Break Apart**.

③ Click the **Modify** menu again, and then click **Break Apart**.

The characters become simple shapes that you can adjust with Flash's drawing tools.

TIMESAVER *Press ⌘+B (Mac) or Ctrl+B (Win) twice to break text into editable shapes.*

See Also

See "Using the Free Transform Tool" on page 118 for information on transforming objects.

Text fields can be broken. —①

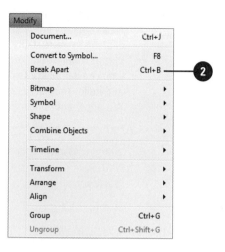

Text fields become editable shapes.

For Your Information

Transforming Text

You can use the Free Transform tool or the options on the Modify menu under Transform to transform text boxes in the same ways you transform other objects. You can scale, rotate, skew and flip text boxes, but the text might become hard to read. However, you can still edit it. Important: when you scale a text box as an object, the point size in the Property Inspector may not be accurate. To restore a transformed object, select the object, click the Modify menu, point to Transform, and then click Remove Transform.

Using Anti-Alias Text

Anti-aliasing affects the pixels on the edge of a shape by allowing them to blend in with the background. It is a crucial feature when working with some text as it makes it appear smoother and more integrated. Flash includes **FlashType**, a new text rendering feature that improves anti-aliasing and readability for fonts. FlashType is enabled whenever Flash Player 8 is the selected player, and anti-aliasing is set to anti-aliasing for readability or custom. The drawback with anti-aliasing is that at smaller font sizes the text can appear blurry. To avoid this problem, use sans serif text, such as Helvetica or Arial, and don't use bold and italic. You can use anti-aliasing with static, dynamic, and input text. You apply anti-aliasing to text boxes instead of characters.

Set a Text Field to Anti-Alias Text

1. Select the text field with the **Selection** tool.

2. Click the **Font Rendering Method** popup in the Property Inspector, and then select one of the following:

   ◆ **Use Device Fonts**. The SWF file uses fonts installed on the local computer to display fonts.

   ◆ **Bitmap Text (No Anti-Alias)**. No text smoothing.

   ◆ **Anti-Alias for Animation.** Smooths out animation (Flash Player 8 or earlier).

   ◆ **Anti-Alias for Readability.** Uses anti-aliasing (Flash Player 8 only).

   ◆ **Custom Anti-Alias**. Modify font properties.

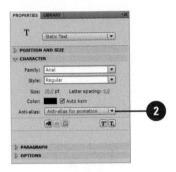

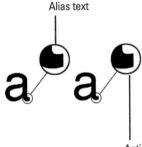

Alias text

Anti-aliasing blends the edge pixels with the background.

Anti-alias text at small sizes

Anti-Alias text can look blurry at small sizes

Anti-Alias text can look blurry at small sizes

Anti-Alias text can look blurry at small sizes

Anti-Alias text can look blurry at small sizes

Alias text produces crisp fonts at small sizes.

Using Font Mapping

FL 2.4

If you open a document with a missing font on a computer, a Missing Font alert appears, asking you to choose a substitute font. You can open and use the Font Mapping dialog box to map a substitute font to the missing font, view the mapped fonts in the document, and delete a font mapping. After you select a substitute font, text appears with the correct font (if available) or the substitute font (if missing). When you use a substitute font, the text box or attributes might need to be adjusted.

Select Substitute Fonts

1. Open a document.

   ◆ To view all the font mappings saved on your computer, close all documents.

2. Click the **Flash** (Mac) or **Edit** (Win) menu, and then click **Font Mapping**.

3. Click a font in the Missing Fonts column.

   TIMESAVER *Press Shift+click to select multiple missing fonts to map to the same substitute font.*

4. Click the **Substitute Font** popup, and then click a font, or click **System Default**.

5. Click **OK**.

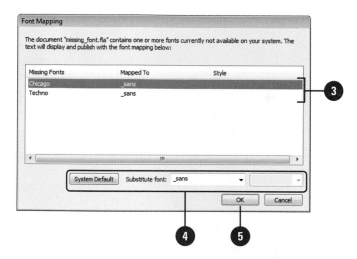

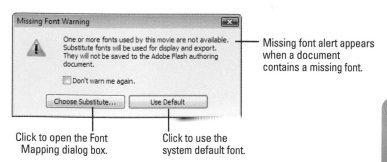

Missing font alert appears when a document contains a missing font.

Click to open the Font Mapping dialog box.

Click to use the system default font.

Did You Know?

You can delete the font mapping. Close all documents, click the Flash (Mac) or Edit (Win) menu, click Font Mapping, select a font mapping, click Delete, and then click OK.

You can turn off the Missing Font alert. Click the Flash (Mac) or Edit (Win) menu, click Font Mapping, select the Don't Show Again For This Document, Always Use Substitute Fonts check box, and then click OK.

Setting Device Fonts Versus Embedded Fonts

FL 2.4

When you include a font in your Flash document that is installed on your computer, the font outline information is embedded in the exported Flash movie. This is called an **embedded font** and it ensures that your fonts will look consistent when displayed on other computers. Of course this adds to the file size, as each character from the selected font family has to be included in the final .swf. If file size is an issue, and the exact character matching is not important, you can choose to use device fonts. When a font is set to device, Flash will not embed the font information in the exported file. Instead the Flash Player will substitute the closest resembling font by name on the computer playing the Flash movie. The drawback is that you won't be able to predict how the fonts will display on every computer. To combat this uncertainty, Flash includes three device fonts. Each is designed with characteristics of typical fonts usually found by default on most computers. You can also choose device fonts when using small font sizes because they are not anti-alias and display clearly.

Set a Text Field to Device Font

1. Select a text field you want to set to the device font.

2. Click the **Anti-Alias** popup in the Property Inspector, and then click **Use Device Fonts**.

    The Device Font has now been changed.

Set a text field to device font.

1

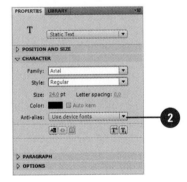

2

Choose a Built-In Flash Device Font

1 Select a text field you want to set to device font.

2 Click the **Family** popup in the Property Inspector or click the **Text** menu, point to **Font**, and then select one of the following fonts:

- ◆ **_sans**. Matches up with a sans-serif font, such as Helvetica or Arial.

- ◆ **_serif**. Matches up with a serif font, such as Times or Garamond.

- ◆ **_typewriter**. Matches up with a typewritten-looking font, such as Courier.

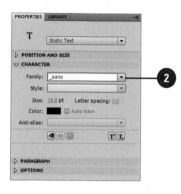

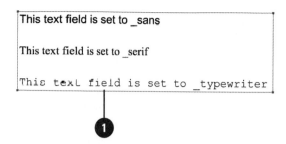

Creating Dynamic Text and Input Text

FL 2.6

When you create text fields in Flash, they default to static fields. A static field is for display only and is hard-coded in the .swf. One cannot be changed unless you return to the Flash development environment, edit it, and re-export the file. If you need your text to be updatable from an outside source, such as a text document on a server or if you need the user to input text for you to retrieve and process with ActionScript, you can set your text field to enable this functionality. Setting your text field to dynamic text turns it into an ActionScript object that can be given an instance name or turned into a variable that can be populated from some other source outside of the .swf. This is great when you need to update content on the fly and would rather not have to deal directly with Flash for each update. If you require the user to enter a string of text, such as in a form, you can set a text field to input text. This enables the user to enter information in the text field that can be retrieved and processed.

Set a Text Field to be Dynamic

1 Select the text field on the Stage you want to be a dynamic field.

2 Click the **Text Type** popup in the Property Inspector, and then click **Dynamic Text**.

3 Select from the following properties:

◆ **Instance Name**. Gives the text field an instance name so it can be controlled with ActionScript.

◆ **Letter Spacing**. Changes character position on a line.

◆ **Render Text As HTML**. Preserves Rich Text Formatting, allowing you to include hyperlinks and HTML tags.

◆ **Show Border**. Displays a border around the text field in the exported movie.

◆ **Variable Name**. Gives the text field a variable name for use with ActionScript.

◆ **Character Options**. Allows you to choose which characters you want to embed in the text.

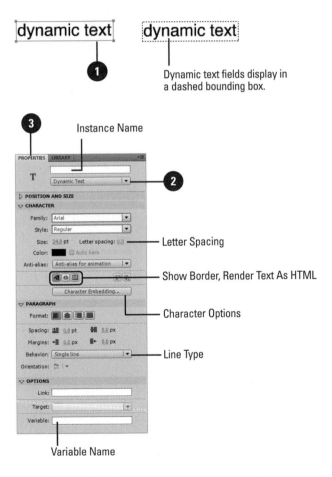

Dynamic text fields display in a dashed bounding box.

Instance Name

Letter Spacing

Show Border, Render Text As HTML

Character Options

Line Type

Variable Name

Set a Text Field to be an Input Field

1. Select the text field on the Stage you want to be an input field.

2. Click the **Text Type** popup in the Property Inspector, and then click **Input Text**.

3. Select from the following properties:

   ◆ **Instance Name**. Gives the text field an instance name so it can be controlled with ActionScript

   ◆ **Letter Spacing**. Changes character position on a line.

   ◆ **Line Type**. Choose from Single Line and Multi-Line with or without Wrap, and Password (available only for Input text).

   ◆ **Selectability**. Allows or denies the user the ability to select the text in the exported movie.

   ◆ **Show Border**. Displays a border around the text field in the exported movie.

   ◆ **Variable Name**. Gives the text field a variable name for use with ActionScript.

   ◆ **Maximum Characters**. Limit the amount of characters a user can enter into the field.

   ◆ **Character Options**. Allows you to choose which characters you want to embed in the text.

Did You Know?

You can create scrolling text. Shift-double-click the handle of dynamic and input text to create text boxes that don't expand when you enter text on the Stage.

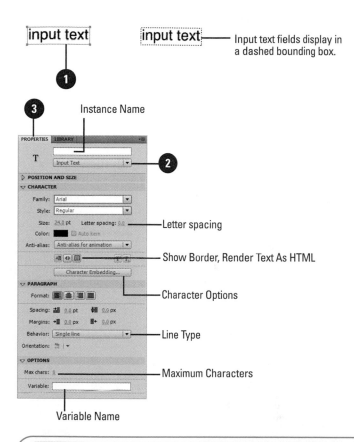

input text

input text — Input text fields display in a dashed bounding box.

Instance Name

Letter spacing

Show Border, Render Text As HTML

Character Options

Line Type

Maximum Characters

Variable Name

For Your Information

Using Multiple Languages in a Document

When you're working with text in a Flash document, don't forget the global community. Flash supports multi-language authoring. You could create a document that displays text in Spanish and English, using a variety of methods: The text can be written within an external file and called using the #include ActionScript within a dynamic or text input field, or the text can be inserted into the document at runtime using an external XML (Extensible Markup Language) file. This allows you to insert different languages that automatically appear to the visitor. When you're working with multi-language Flash documents, click the Window menu, point to Other Panels, and then click Strings. The Strings panel lets you streamline the process of localizing content into multiple languages, because it collects and tracks all character strings throughout the development process in a central place. In the Strings panel, you can select a language and assign each text string, either a dynamic or input text field, in the document with a unique ID. The Strings panel has been improved to include multi-line support in the String field and the language XML file.

Setting Dynamic Text and Input Text Options

FL 2.6

The Character Options that are available to dynamic and input text allow you to specify which, if any, font outlines you want embedded in the Flash movie for use in these fields. This is a great way to keep file size down because you can include only those characters you need. You can also limit the types of characters a user can enter. For example, if you are asking a user to enter a zip code, you can disable all characters except numbers from being entered.

Use the Character Options Dialog Box

1. Select a dynamic or input text field on the Stage.

2. Click the **Edit Character Options** button in the Property Inspector.

3. Select which character's outlines you want to embed in the exported movie.

   TIMESAVER *Use ⌘+select (Mac) or Ctrl+select (Win) to select multiple lines from the Character list.*

4. Type specific characters into the Include These Characters box to include those outlines.

5. Click **Auto Fill** to include each unique character from the selected text box on the Stage.

6. Click **OK**.

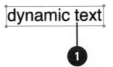

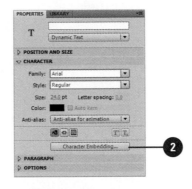

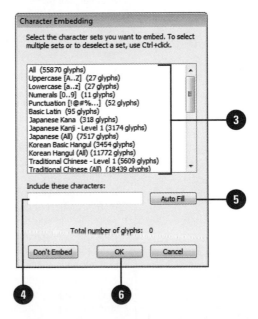

Using Cascading Style Sheets with HTML Text

Cascading Style Sheets (CSS) contain sets of formatting rules for HTML and XML text. CSS allow you to define certain text attributes and give them a style name. This style name, called a selector, can be applied to any implemented text. Each time you need to implement the defined style, you can refer back to the CSS. This allows for more control over the text displayed on your Web page. Load styles from an external CSS or create them within Flash using the Style Sheet Object. The ActionScript class for CSS is described as: TextField.StyleSheet. This is a new functionality and it is only available to SWFs in the Flash 7 Player or later.

Load an external CSS

In any text or HTML editor, place the following code:

```
// External CSS File: styles.css
headline {
        font-family: Arial, Helvetica, sans-serif;
    font-size: 12 px;
}
bodyText {
        font-family: Arial, Helvetica, sans-serif;
    font-size: 10 px;
}
```

This code is typically found in a CSS. This example defines two styles, one for a sans-serif headline at 12 pixels, the other a sans-serif body text at 10 pixels.

Select the first frame of your Flash movie. Place the following code in the Actions panel:

```
var css_styles = new TextField.StyleSheet();
css_styles.load("styles.css");
css_styles.onLoad = function(ok) {
  if(ok) {
    // display style names
    trace(this.getStyleNames());
  } else {
    trace("Error loading CSS file.");
  }
}
```

The CSS you created, "styles.css" is loaded into this object. A loader is created to ensure the CSS is loaded properly. Make sure the CSS and the swf are in the same directory.

Create a CSS in Flash

Select the first frame of your Flash movie. The following code creates a text style for headline text and body text. Place the following code in the Actions panel:

```
var styles = new TextField.StyleSheet();
styles.setStyle("headline",
    {fontFamily: 'Arial,Helvetica,sans-serif',
    fontSize: '12px'}
);
styles.setStyle("bodyText",
    {fontFamily: 'Arial,Helvetica,sans-serif',
    fontSize: '10px'}
);
```

This CSS code can now be placed in the Actions panel in Flash. This example defines two styles, one for a sans-serif headline at 12 pixels, the other a sans-serif body text at 10 pixels.

Checking Spelling

Flash includes a global spell-checker that is fully configurable. Search the entire Flash document or isolate specific elements to search in the Spelling Setup dialog box. You can choose from a variety of built-in dictionaries as sources including a personal dictionary you can edit. Additionally, you can choose which text characteristics to ignore, such as words with numbers and internet addresses, as well as choose what type of alternative suggestions you want Flash to provide.

Set Up Spell Checking

1. Click the **Text** menu, and then click **Spelling Setup**.

2. Select from the following options:

   ◆ **Document Options**. Specify which elements in the Flash document you want to spell check. You can also specify whether you want to live-edit the document during the Check Spelling process.

   ◆ **Dictionaries**. Select a built-in dictionary as a source. At least one dictionary must be selected to activate Check Spelling.

   ◆ **Personal Dictionary**. Specify an option to use a dictionary created and edited by you. Navigate to a text document on your hard drive or edit the default one included by clicking the Edit Personal Dictionary button. Each new entry in the personal dictionary must be on a separate line.

   ◆ **Checking Options**. Set word-level behaviors. You can have Internet addresses ignored, find duplicate words, or specify the types of suggestions you want displayed in the Check Spelling window.

3. Click **OK**.

Allow or deny on-the-fly editing during Spell Check

Set locations to Spell Check

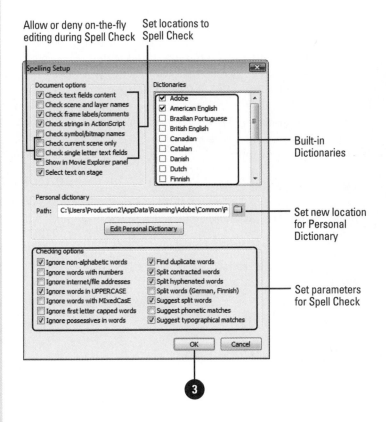

Built-in Dictionaries

Set new location for Personal Dictionary

Set parameters for Spell Check

Use Spell Checking

① Click the **Text** menu, and then click **Check Spelling**

② If Flash finds suspect words, the Check Spelling dialog box opens. Otherwise, Flash displays a message that the Spell Check is complete.

Word not found (*element*):

This identifies the suspect word and what type of element it was found in parenthesis.

③ Do one of the following:

◆ **Add To Personal.** Click to add the word to your personal dictionary.

◆ **Ignore.** Click the Ignore and Ignore All buttons to not flag this word again in this Check Spelling session.

◆ **Change.** Click Change or Change All. In the Change To and Suggestions fields, Flash displays the closest alternatives to the suspect word.

◆ **Delete.** Click to delete the word from the field that contains it.

④ Continue until Flash produces a message that Check Spelling is complete or click **Close** to stop the Check Spelling process before it is completed.

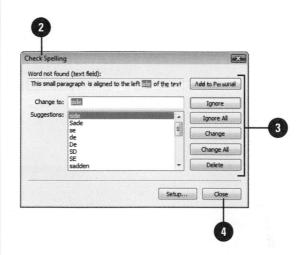

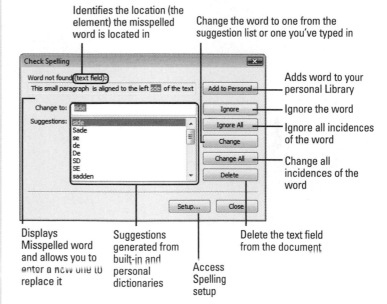

Identifies the location (the element) the misspelled word is located in

Change the word to one from the suggestion list or one you've typed in

Adds word to your personal Library

Ignore the word

Ignore all incidences of the word

Change all incidences of the word

Displays Misspelled word and allows you to enter a new one to replace it

Suggestions generated from built-in and personal dictionaries

Access Spelling setup

Delete the text field from the document

Did You Know?

You must access the Spelling Setup once to activate Check Spelling. You need to activate Check Spelling to select a dictionary. Click the Text menu, and then click Spelling Setup.

Using Find and Replace

Use Find and Replace to locate specific elements in your Flash document. You can specify where to look, what to look for, and what to replace it with. Choose to search the entire Flash document or the currently active scene. Each element you search for has its own configurable settings and options. Included is a log that shows the exact locations of the found element.

Locate Items with Find and Replace

1. Click the **Edit** menu, and then click **Find And Replace**.

   TIMESAVER *Press ⌘+F (Mac) or Ctrl+F (Win) to quickly open the Find and Replace window.*

2. Select where you want to search from the **Search In** popup menu.

3. Select which element from the **For** popup menu you want to search for in Flash:

   ◆ Text

   ◆ Font

   ◆ Color

   ◆ Symbol

   ◆ Sound

   ◆ Video

   ◆ Bitmap

4. Enter and/or select the parameters you want for your search.

5. To find the element with the characteristics you've entered, click **Find Next** or **Find All**.

6. To update the found element with the new characteristics, click **Replace** or **Replace All**.

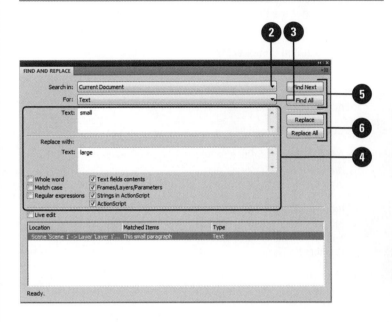

Importing Graphics

Introduction

In addition to the vector drawing tools that allow you to create graphics and animation in Flash, you can also import artwork in other formats to use in your Flash movie. Flash has full native support for Adobe Photoshop, Adobe Illustrator, Freehand, BMP, JPEG, GIF, and PNG files, the standard bitmapped graphics. However, you can also import EPS and PDF by using Adobe Illustrator. This allows you to import a variety of different graphic formats into your Flash production process.

Flash drawing tools create and edit vector objects, not pixels, so preparation is necessary for bitmapped graphics in a paint application outside of Flash, such as Adobe Photoshop. Fortunately, Flash allows you to convert a bitmapped graphic into a vector with the Trace Bitmap function. You can also use a bitmap as a fill for vector objects. An important thing to remember is that any bitmap used in your project can add considerable size to your Flash movie. Flash includes several procedures for optimizing these bitmaps on export, through compression settings applied globally, or specifically to each image.

What You'll Do

Understand Vector and Bitmap Graphics

Examine Import File Formats

Set Illustrator Import Preferences

Set Photoshop Import Preferences

Import Photoshop and Illustrator Files

Import Bitmaps

Import Fireworks PNG Files

Import Multiple Files

Copy Images from Other Programs

Edit Bitmaps in an Outside Editor

Set Bitmap Compression

Use Break Apart to Create Fill Patterns

Modify a Bitmap Fill

Edit a Bitmap with the Magic Wand

Use Trace Bitmap to Create Vector Shapes

Understanding Vector and Bitmap Graphics

 FL 1.1, 2.5

Vector graphics are comprised of anchor points connected to each other by lines and curves, called vectors. These anchor points and vectors describe the contour and surface of the graphic with some included information about color, alpha, and line width. Because they are general descriptions of the coordinates of a shape, they are resolution-independent; that is they can be resized without any loss to the quality of the graphic. Resolution represents the amount of information contained within a linear inch represented by a grid.

Bitmapped graphics are made up of small, colored squares, called pixels that form a grid. Each pixel is given a specific color and a grid of these pixels forms a mosaic, which is your image. Because of this, bitmaps are dependent on resolution (the number of pixels in the grid). Resizing up or down forces pixels to be created or removed to accommodate the new grid size, which can result in a loss of image quality. In Flash, bitmaps look much better on the Stage when severely enlarged or reduced. The smoothing process makes the appearance of these bitmaps in the Flash authoring tool and in Flash Player now consistent.

Both vector and bitmap graphics have their strengths and weaknesses. Vector shapes are simple and graphic in nature. They are a good choice for creating high-contrast, geometric art or art with limited color shifts. If you need to implement artwork with a richer surface texture, color depth, and shading, like those qualities found in a photograph, a bitmap better suits this purpose. The strength of Flash as a content creator is that you can combine the strengths of both vector art and bitmapped art.

Bitmap Image

Vector Image

Examining Import File Formats

 FL 1.1, 2.5

The following files can be imported into Flash:

File Formats

File Type	Extension	Windows	Macintosh
Adobe Illustrator	.ai	✓	✓
Adobe Photoshop	.psd	✓	✓
AutoCAD DXF	.dxf	✓	✓
Bitmap	.bmp	✓	✓ (Using QuickTime)
Enhanced Windows Metafile	.emf	✓	
FreeHand	.fh7-.fh11	✓	✓
Future SplashPlayer	.spi	✓	✓
GIF and animated GIF	.gif	✓	✓
JPEG	.jpg	✓	✓
PNG	.png	✓	✓
Flash Player	.swf	✓	✓
Windows Metafile	.wmf	✓	✓

File Formats

File Type	Extension	Windows	Macintosh
MacPaint	.pntg	✓	✓
PICT	.pct, .pic	✓ (as a Bitmap)	✓
QuickTime Image	.qtif	✓	✓
Silicon Graphics Image	.sgi	✓	✓
TGA	.tga	✓	✓
TIFF	.tiff	✓	✓

Setting Illustrator Import Preferences

Flash allows you to set preferences to customize the way you import Adobe Illustrator (.ai) files. You can specify general options to specify whether to use the import dialog box, import objects outside the Illustrator artboard or import hidden layers. After you set the general options, you can set options for specific element types you want to import, such as text, paths, images, groups, and layers. The options you set are applied to all Illustrator files when you import them into Flash. However, you can change options in the Illustrator import dialog box.

Set Illustrator File Import Preferences

1. Click the **Flash** (Mac) or **Edit** (Win) menu, and then click **Preferences**.

2. Click the **AI File Importer** category.

3. Select from the following options:

   ◆ **General.**

      ◆ **Show Import Dialog Box.** Select to show AI File Importer dialog box.

      ◆ **Excludes Objects Outside Art Board.** Select to exclude object outside the artboard or crop area.

      ◆ **Import Hidden Layers.** Select to import hidden layers.

   ◆ **Import Text As.**

      ◆ **Editable Text.** Imports Illustrator text as editable text in Flash.

      ◆ **Vector Outlines.** Converts text to vector paths; use to preserve appearance.

      ◆ **Bitmaps.** Converts text into a bitmap; not editable.

      ◆ **Create Movie Clips.** Imports text into a movie clip; use to maintain blends, AI effects, and transparency.

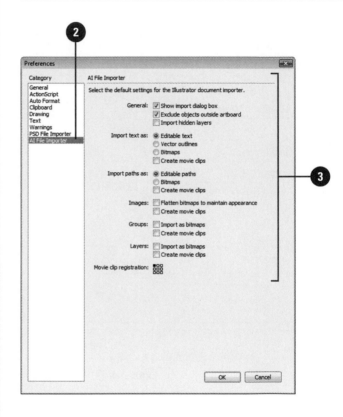

190

- **Import Paths As.**
  - **Editable Paths.** Imports Illustrator path as editable in Flash.
  - **Bitmaps.** Converts the path into a bitmap; use to preserve appearance of path; not editable.
  - **Create Movie Clips.** Imports path into a movie clip symbol in Flash.
- **Images.**
  - **Flatten Bitmaps To Maintain Appearance.** Converts an image into a bitmap; not editable.
  - **Create Movie Clips.** Imports an image into a movie clip symbol in Flash.
- **Groups.**
  - **Import As Bitmaps.** Converts all objects in the group into a bitmap; not editable.
  - **Create Movie Clips.** Imports all objects into a movie clip symbol in Flash.
- **Layers.**
  - **Import As Bitmaps.** Converts the layer into a bitmap; not editable.
  - **Create Movie Clips.** Imports the layer into a movie clip symbol in Flash.
- **Movie Clip Registration.** Select the global registration point for movies and all other object types.

4 Click **OK**.

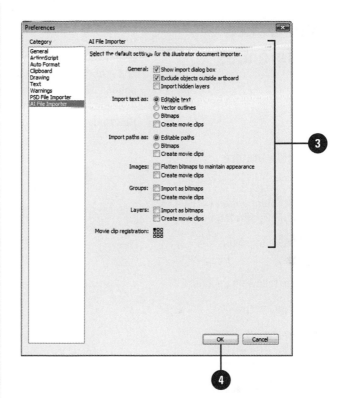

Setting Photoshop Import Preferences

Flash allows you to set preferences to customize the way you import Adobe Photoshop (.psd) files. You can set options for specific element layer types you want to import, such as images, text, paths, shapes, and groups. You can also set compression and quality publishing options for the imported Photoshop files. The options you set are applied to all Photoshop files when you import them into Flash. However, you can change options in the Photoshop import dialog box.

Set Photoshop File Import Preferences

1. Click the **Flash** (Mac) or **Edit** (Win) menu, and then click **Preferences**.

2. Click the **PSD File Importer** category.

3. Select from the following options:

   ◆ **Import Image Layers As.**

      ◆ **Bitmap Images With Editable Layer Styles.** Create a movie clip with a bitmap clipped inside.

      ◆ **Flatten Bitmap Images.** Convert an image into a bitmap; not editable.

      ◆ **Create Movie Clips.** Imports an image into a movie clip symbol in Flash.

   ◆ **Import Text Layers As.**

      ◆ **Editable Text.** Imports Photoshop text from the text layer as editable text in Flash.

      ◆ **Vector Outlines.** Converts text to vector paths; the object is also converted to a movie clip.

      ◆ **Flattened Bitmap Images.** Converts text into a bitmap; not editable.

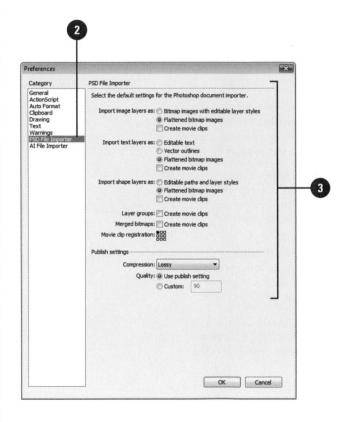

- **Create Movie Clips.** Imports the text layer into a movie clip symbol.

- **Import Shape Layers As.**

  - **Editable Paths And Layer Styles.** Creates an editable vector shape with a bitmap clipped inside the vector shape.

  - **Flatten Bitmap Images.** Converts an image into a bitmap; not editable.

  - **Create Movie Clips.** Imports an image into a movie clip symbol in Flash.

- **Layer Groups.** Select the Create Move Clips check box to convert all groups into a movie clip in Flash.

- **Merged Bitmaps.** Select the Create Movie Clips check box to convert the shape layers into a movie clip in Flash. This option is disabled if the Maintain Editable Paths And Layers check box is selected.

- **Movie Clip Registration.** Select the global registration point for movies and all other object types.

- **Publish Settings**

  - **Compression.** Select the Lossy (JPEG) or Lossless (PNG/GIF) compression mode you want.

  - **Quality.** For the Lossy compression, select the Use Publish Setting or Custom option; select the quality 1 to 100; the higher the setting, the greater quality, yet the larger the file size.

4 Click **OK**.

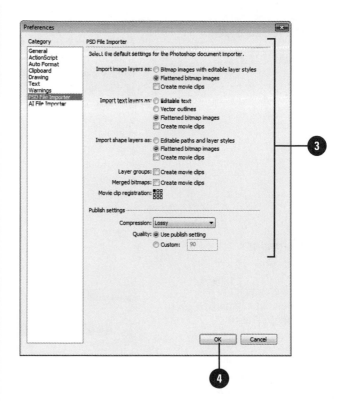

Importing Photoshop and Illustrator Files

Flash includes support for importing Adobe Photoshop (.psd) files and Adobe Illustrator files created in versions 6 through 10. When these files are imported, there are a number of options you can choose from. Before you import Photoshop and Illustrator files, you need to set import options in the Preferences dialog box. For Illustrator files, you can also specify whether you want to show an import dialog box where you can set import settings for specific parts of an Illustrator file. The options you set are applied to all Illustrator and Photoshop files when you import them into Flash. However, you can change options in the import dialog box. Some options in the Import dialog box are context-sensitive; that is, they only appear if they are relevant to the imported file. The import options are similar between Illustrator and Photoshop; when they differ, the options are noted.

Import a Photoshop or Illustrator File

1. Click the **File** menu, point to **Import**, and then click **Import To Stage** or **Import To Library**.

   ◆ Open and select the library where you want to import files.

2. Click the **Show** popup (Mac) or **Files Of Type** (Win), and then select **Photoshop**, **Adobe Illustrator** or **All Formats**.

3. Navigate to the drive or folder where the file is located.

4. Select the Photoshop or Illustrator file you want to import.

5. Click **Import** (Mac) or **Open** (Win).

   Flash inserts the image file or displays an import dialog box for files, where you can specify options for the specific files. If the Import dialog box opens, continue.

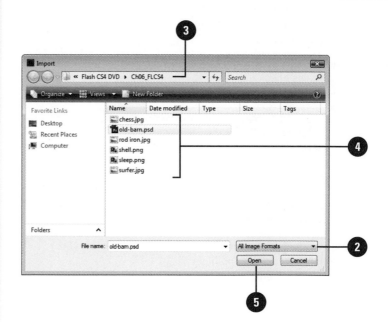

Did You Know?

You can import an Illustrator EPS or PDF using Illustrator CS4. Open the file in Adobe Illustrator CS4, save it as a CS4-compatible AI file, and then import into Flash as an AI file.

6 To generate a list of items from Illustrator now compatible with Flash, click **Incompatibility Report**.

7 Select the check boxes with the elements you want to import, select each element and set the related options you want; you may need to ungroup elements.

8 Click the **Convert Layers To** list arrow, and then click.

◆ **Flash Layers**. Click this option to convert the layers in the imported file into corresponding layers in the Flash Timeline.

◆ **Keyframes**. Click this option to convert the layers in the imported file into consecutive keyframes.

◆ **Single Flash Layer**. Click this option to flatten the layers in the imported file onto a single layer in Flash.

9 Select from the following options:

◆ **Place At Original Position**. Select to maintain the same positions from Illustrator or Photoshop to Flash.

◆ **Set Stage Size To Same Size As**. Select to set the Flash Stage to the same size as the Illustrator artboard or Photoshop canvas.

◆ **Import As Unused Symbols (AI)**. Select to import AI symbols not used as instances as unused symbols in Flash.

◆ **Import As A Single Bitmap Image (AI)**. Select to convert into a bitmap.

10 Specify the compression and quality settings you want (PSD).

11 Click **OK**.

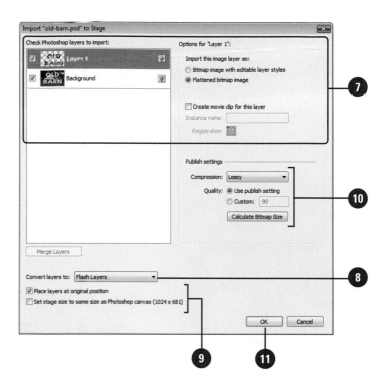

For Your Information

Importing Freehand Files

You can import Freehand 7 or later files into Flash. Freehand is a vector graphics application. When you import Freehand files, Flash retains Freehand layers, text blocks, library symbols, and pages. However, if you import a file with CMYK colors, Flash converts the file to RGB color. To import a Freehand file into Flash, follow the instructions (steps and options vary slightly) for importing Illustrator files.

Importing Bitmaps

You can import bitmaps of several file types directly into Flash to use in your Flash movie. It is important to remember that even though you can edit and resize bitmaps in Flash, the original bitmap will always be embedded in the exported Flash file. If file size is an issue, it is best to bring your bitmapped art in at the size you want to export it. For example, if your image is going to be 160 pixels by 160 pixels in the final movie, it is best to import it at this size and not resize it up or down in Flash. You will end up with higher-quality images and smaller files if you do this. You can import files using the Import To Stage or Import To Library methods. The Import To Stage method stores the bitmap in the Library and places a copy on the Stage, while the Import To Library method stores the bitmap in the Library and doesn't place a copy on the Stage.

Import a Bitmap to the Stage

1. Click the **File** menu, point to **Import**, and then click **Import To Stage**.

2. Click the **Show** popup (Mac) or **Files Of Types** list arrow (Win), and then select the format of the file you want to import.

3. Navigate to the drive or folder where the file is located.

4. Select the file you want to import.

5. Click **Import** (Mac) or **Open** (Win).

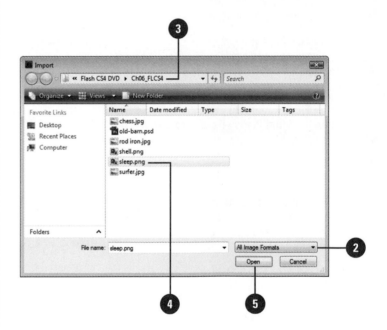

Did You Know?

You may not be able to see the images you've imported to the Stage at certain magnification levels. Flash aligns the top left-hand corner of the image at the 0,0 coordinate. If you are zoomed in, the image may have appeared outside the viewable area. Use the Hand tool to navigate around, zoom out, or press Shift+⌘+W (Mac) or Ctrl+Shift+W (Win) to toggle the Work Area off. This sets the zoom level to 100% and hides the Work Area.

For Your Information

Scaling Image Before Importing

Scaling bitmaps reduces the quality of the image, so it's best to import an image into Flash at the size you want it to be. If you need to scale an image in Flash, it's a good idea to import the image at a slightly larger size, so when you scale it down, loss of quality is minimized.

Import to the Library

1. Click the **File** menu, point to **Import**, and then click **Import To Library**.

2. Click the **Show** popup (Mac) or **Files Of Types** list arrow (Win), and then select the format of the file you want to import.

3. Navigate to the drive or folder where the file is located.

4. Select the file you want to import.

5. Click **Import To Library** (Mac) or **Open** (Win).

Did You Know?

You can quickly swap bitmaps. You can exchange an image on the Stage with another one from the Library. To swap one bitmap with another on the Stage, select the bitmap image on the Stage, open the Property Inspector, click Swap, select the image you want from the list of currently stored images in your document library, and then click OK.

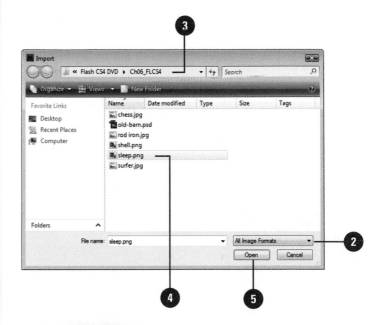

Image is placed in the Library.

Importing Fireworks PNG Files

 FL 1.1, 2.5

You can import Adobe Fireworks PNG files into Flash as editable objects or bitmap images. When you import a PNG file as a bitmap image, the file, including any vector data, is flattened, or rasterized, and converted to a bitmap. When you import a PNG file as an editable image, the file retains any vector data, bitmaps, text (with default anti-alias settings), filters (called effects in Fireworks) and guides. In Flash, you can retain Fireworks filters, blend modes, and text, and continue to modify them using Flash. When you import Fireworks files into Flash, PNG file graphic properties remain intact. You can also select multiple PNG files to import in a batch. When you batch PNG files, you select import settings one time. When you import a PNG as a flattened image, you can also edit the image in Fireworks directly from Flash. Flash updates the image with your changes from Fireworks creating easy round-trip edits.

Import and Edit Fireworks PNG Files

1. Click the **File** menu, point to **Import**, and then click **Import To Stage** or **Import To Library**.

2. Click the **Show** popup (Mac) or **Files Of Types** list arrow (Win), and then click **PNG File** or **All Formats**.

3. Navigate to the Fireworks PNG files you want to import, and then select one or more.

4. Click **Import** or **Import To Library** (Mac) or **Open** (Win).

5. To flatten the PNG file into a bitmap, select the **Import as a Single Flattened Bitmap** check box.

   IMPORTANT *To use round-trip editing, you need to flatten the PNG file into a bitmap. You cannot edit bitmaps from Fireworks PNG files imported as editable objects.*

6. Click the **Import** popup, and then click **Page** or other available option.

7. Click the **Into** popup, and then click **Current Frame As Movie Clip**, **New Layer** or other available options.

8 For objects and text, select one of the following:

◆ **Import As Bitmaps To Maintain Appearance**. Retains Fireworks fills, strokes, and effects in Flash.

◆ **Keep All Paths Editable**. Retains vector properties; however, some Fireworks fills, strokes, and effects are lost; places file and related files in a Fireworks Objects folder in the Library.

9 Click **OK**.

10 To edit a flattened PNG bitmap, right-click (Win) or control-click (Mac) the PNG/bitmap's icon in the Library, and then click **Edit with** and select an image editing program or click **Edit with Fireworks**.

◆ In the Edit Image dialog box, specify whether the PNG file or the bitmap file is to be opened.

◆ In Fireworks, edit the image, click **Done** or click the **File** menu, and then click **Update**.

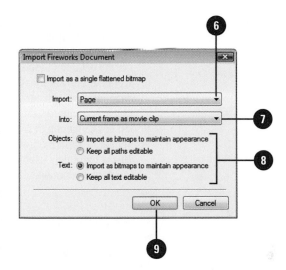

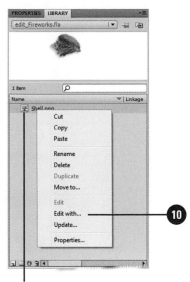

PNG file from Fireworks

Did You Know?

You can optimize PNG images in Fireworks for Flash. Images can increase the size of a movie so you want to optimize images to be as small as possible while still maintaining high quality. You can optimize bitmap and PNG images in Fireworks using round-trip editing from Flash. In Fireworks, specify options on the Optimize panel to optimize and compress images.

Importing Multiple Files

Flash allows you to import multiple files simultaneously to save time. This is useful if you have many files to import. You can select multiple, non-sequential files in the Import dialog box. Choose to import to the Library or to the Stage directly. When you import to the Stage, the file is stored in the Library and a copy is placed on the Stage so you can begin editing it immediately. If you attempt to import a series of files that are numbered sequentially, Flash detects this and produces a dialog box to handle this. When sequential images are imported, they will appear in separate frames by order of the number in their file name. This is extremely useful for image sequences where a series of images forms an animation.

Import Multiple Files or a Sequence of Files

1. Click the **File** menu, point to **Import**, and then click **Import To Stage** or **Import To Library**.

2. Click the **Show** popup (Mac) or **Files Of Types** list arrow (Win), and then select the format of the file you want to import.

3. Navigate to the drive or folder where the file is located.

4. Select the first file you want to import.

5. To import multiple files, hold down the ⌘ (Mac) or Ctrl (Win) key and click additional files to select them.

6. Click **Import** (Mac) or **Open** (Win).

   For a sequence of files, Flash detects that this image is part of a sequence and asks whether you want to import all of them at once.

7. Click **Yes**.

   The numbered files are imported and placed on separate sequential keyframes on the selected layer in the Timeline.

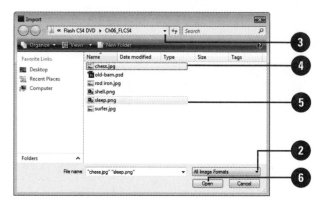

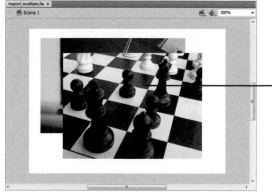

Multiple files imported appear stacked on top of each other. Press down and drag with your mouse to reveal images underneath.

Each imported image appears on a separate frame sequentially.

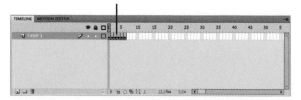

Copying Images from Other Programs

You can paste a bitmap image from other image editing programs, such as Adobe Photoshop or Adobe Fireworks. Simply use the standard copying procedure in the program of your choice to place the bitmap into the clipboard, which is where the operating system dynamically stores information you copy, and then paste it into Flash directly on the Stage. Copying images from other programs works well for bitmaps. However, results are unpredictable when pasting vector graphics from other programs. Often they become corrupted when they are copied to the clipboard, depending upon the origin program or the operating system. It is best to use the Import command to import vector graphics into Flash.

Paste from the Clipboard

1. Copy the image to the clipboard in an image-editing program.

2. Launch or switch to Flash, and then open the Flash document in which you want to paste an image from the clipboard.

3. Select an unlocked layer or keyframe.

4. Click the **Edit** menu, and then click **Paste in Center** or **Paste in Place**.

   TIMESAVER Press ⌘+V (Mac) or Ctrl+V (Win) to quickly paste in center from the clipboard; press ⌘+Shift+V (Mac) or Ctrl+Shift V (Win) to quickly paste in place from the clipboard.

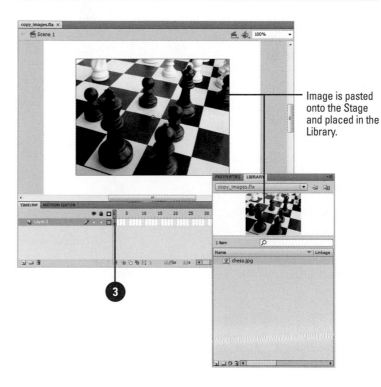

Image is pasted onto the Stage and placed in the Library.

Editing Bitmaps in an Outside Editor

You can edit a bitmap in its native program or some other image editing tool. Once it is re-saved to the hard drive, you can update the bitmap in Flash. You can also import another image to replace the bitmap in the Library. In either case, every copy of the bitmap used in the Flash movie (including bitmap fills) will update with these changes. This is a convenient way to make global changes to bitmap art included in your project.

Update an Image Edited Outside of Flash

1. Import a bitmap into Flash.

2. Edit this bitmap in an outside image-editing program of your choice (such as Adobe Photoshop), and then save to the hard drive.

3. In Flash, open the **Library** panel, and then select the bitmap from the item list.

4. Click the **Properties** icon in the bottom of the panel or double-click the bitmap file in the list.

5. Click **Update**.

6. Click **OK**.

   The bitmap updates to the new version saved to your drive.

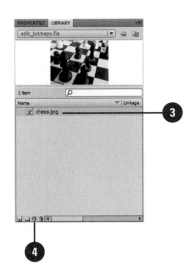

Did You Know?

Flash preserves the path when you import a bitmap. When you import a bitmap into Flash, the path to that image is preserved in the Bitmap Properties. If you have moved the image to another directory on your hard drive and you want to update the file in the Library with the new changes, navigate to it by using the Import button in the Bitmap Properties window.

Larger preview of the bitmap

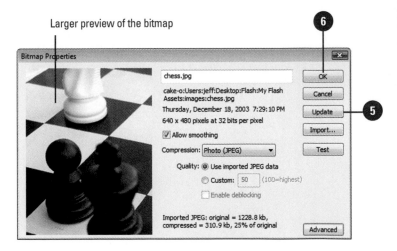

Replace a Bitmap

1. Open the **Library** panel, and then select the bitmap from the item list.

2. Click the **Properties** icon in the bottom of the panel or double-click the bitmap file in the list.

3. Click **Import**.

4. Navigate to the replacement file on your hard drive.

5. Select the replacement file.

6. Click **Import** (Mac) or **Open** (Win).

7. Change the name and any other options you want.

8. Click **OK**.

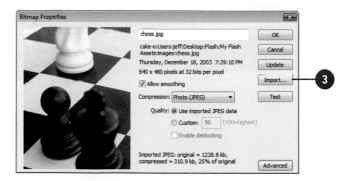

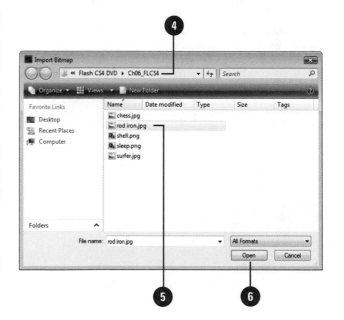

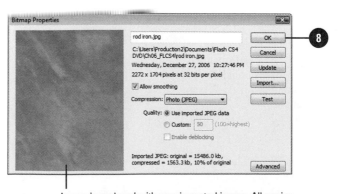

Image is replaced with new imported image. All copies used in the Flash movie update to this new image.

Setting Bitmap Compression

When you export a Flash movie, you can decide how much color information to include in each exported bitmap. This is called **compression**. The more compression you apply, the less color information is included and the lower the size and quality of the image. **Lossy** compression reduces the file size by removing color information, while **lossless** compression reduces the file size (not as much) without removing information. You can choose to set a global compression for all bitmap files used in a Flash movie or you can set a separate compression for each image. As with all image compression, file size needs to be weighed against image quality. It is always best to experiment until you get the results you want.

Set Compression for a Bitmap

1. Open the **Library** panel.

2. Select the bitmap from the Library item list in which you want to set compression.

3. Click the **Properties** icon in the bottom of the panel or double-click the bitmap file in the list.

4. Select the **Allow Smoothing** check box to anti-alias the edges of the image, making it appear smoother.

5. Click the **Compression** popup, and then select from the following options:

   ◆ **Lossless (PNG/GIF).** Compresses the image without losing any information; remains in its highest quality.

   ◆ **Photo (JPEG).** You can choose to use the compression information contained by selecting the **Use Document Default Quality** check box. By deselecting this feature you can set the level of JPEG compression applied to the bitmap. The values are 1-100. The higher the number, the less compression applied, producing a higher quality image.

6. Click **OK**.

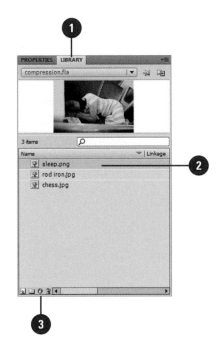

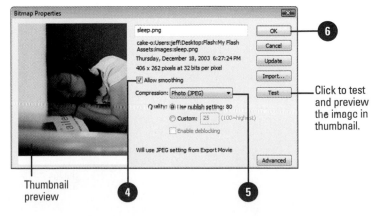

Thumbnail preview

Click to test and preview the image in thumbnail.

Using Break Apart to Create Fill Patterns

By default, when you import a bitmap into Flash and drag it to the Stage, you are limited in how you can edit it. Break Apart the image to remove the image from its bounding box and enable you to cut into the image, remove parts, select regions, and use it as a fill pattern. The bitmap is still linked to its parent in the Library. Any edit made to a bitmap only affects the copy on the Stage. For example, if you break an image and then edit it down to a tiny portion, in the exported movie the image appears exactly as you edited it. However, it will still have the same file size of the image you imported (less any compression you may have applied). It is always best to do your most severe editing in a bitmap or paint program outside of Flash.

Create a Bitmap Fill Pattern

1. Drag a copy of a bitmap to the Stage from the Library panel; make sure the bitmap is selected on the Stage.

2. Click the **Modify** menu, and then click **Break Apart**.

   TIMESAVER Press ⌘+B (Mac) and Ctrl+B (Win) to quickly break apart a bitmap on the Stage.

3. Click the **Eyedropper** tool on the Tools panel.

4. Position the eyedropper over the image, and then click to select it.

   The bitmap is a selected fill that you can use to fill vector shapes.

5. Click the **Rectangle** or **Oval** tool on the Tools panel.

6. Click and drag on the Stage to create a new shape with the bitmap fill.

Did You Know?

You can select the bitmap fill in the Color Mixer panel. In the panel, click Bitmap from the Fill Style popup, and then select a thumbnail fill (bitmaps from the Library appear).

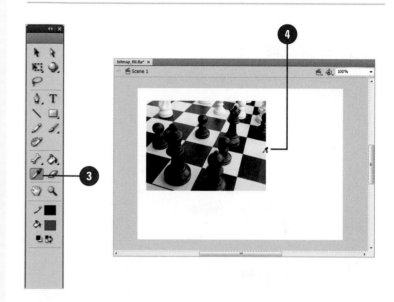

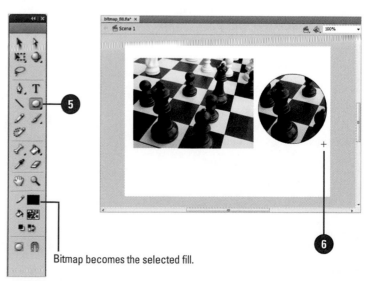

Bitmap becomes the selected fill.

Modifying a Bitmap Fill

Flash defaults to tiling a bitmap fill. Tiling is simply when an image is repeated in a grid until it fills the entire object. If you have applied a bitmap fill to a vector object, you can continue to edit its characteristics and placement. You can resize, skew, or rotate the fill or change its center point within the shape with the Gradient Transform tool. This tool allows you to dynamically make these changes when it is applied to any editable shape. As with most of the assets Flash stores in the Library, any change you make to the application of the fill does not affect the master object stored in the Library. In this way, bitmaps like video clips and sounds, behave similarly to symbols in that their master object is not affected. Although when you use a bitmap in your movie Flash refers to this as a copy, not an instance, because there are no built-in controls for bitmaps.

Change the Center Point

① Create a shape on the Stage with a bitmap fill.

② Click the **Gradient Transform** tool on the Tools panel.

The pointer changes to an arrow with a small gradient box in the right-hand corner.

TIMESAVER *Press F to quickly select the Gradient Transform tool.*

③ Click the shape to select it.

A bounding box appears on the tile.

④ Position the pointer over the white circle in the center of the bounding box.

The cursor becomes a Move icon.

⑤ Click and drag the center point to a new position.

The tile accommodates to the new position of the center point.

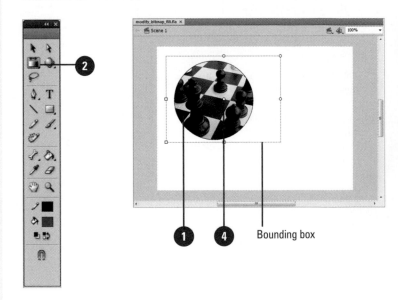

Bounding box

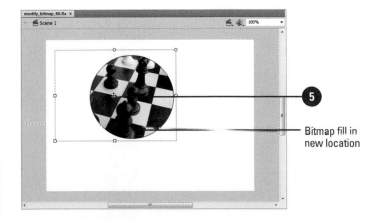

Bitmap fill in new location

206

Modify the Orientation and Size of a Bitmap Fill

1. Create a shape on the Stage with a bitmap fill.

2. Click the **Gradient Transform** tool on the Tools panel.

   The pointer changes to an arrow with a small gradient box in the right-hand corner.

3. Position the pointer over the shape, and then select it.

   A bounding box appears on the tile.

4. Do one of the following:

   - **Bottom-left-corner square.** Drag this to resize the fill proportionally.

   - **Left-center square.** Drag this to resize width of fill.

   - **Bottom-center square.** Drag this to resize height of fill.

   - **Top-right-corner circle.** Drag this to rotate fill.

   - **Top-center circle.** Drag this to skew fill horizontally.

   - **Right-center circle.** Drag this to skew fill vertically.

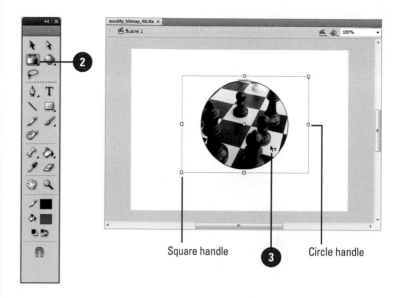

Square handle   Circle handle

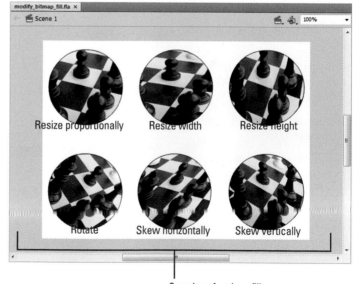

Resize proportionally   Resize width   Resize height

Rotate   Skew horizontally   Skew vertically

Samples of various fills

Editing a Bitmap with the Magic Wand

When you use Break Apart on a bitmap, the bitmap becomes a fill and its content is editable. You can select specific regions of it with any of Flash's selection tools and procedures. If you want to remove parts of the bitmap or replace them with different fills you can select those parts with the Magic Wand tool. The Magic Wand tool selects regions of similar colors. Clicking on other parts adds those parts to the selection. The color threshold (or sensitivity) for this tool can be set in the Magic Wand options popup menu.

Use the Magic Wand

1. Select a bitmap on the Stage.

2. Click the **Modify** menu, and then click **Break Apart**.

   TIMESAVER *Press ⌘+B (Mac) or Ctrl+B (Win) to quickly break apart a bitmap on the Stage.*

3. Click on the Stage to deselect the broken bitmap.

4. Click the **Lasso** tool on the Tools panel.

5. Click the **Magic Wand Mode** button in the Options section of the Tools panel.

   The pointer becomes a small magic wand.

6. Position the pointer over regions of the image you want to select.

   The color region you clicked on is selected. Subsequent clicks on other regions are added to the selection.

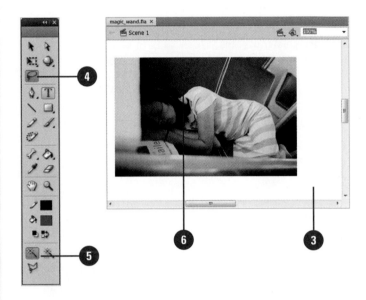

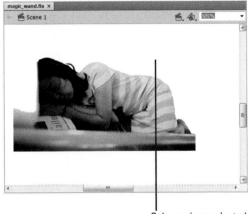

Color regions selected and deleted from bitmap fill.

Set the Magic Wand Options

① Click the **Lasso** tool on the Tools panel.

② Click the **Magic Wand Properties** button on the Tools panel.

③ Enter a color threshold between 0 and 200.

This number defines how close adjacent colors have to be to the selected color before they are added to the selection. A higher number selects a broader number of colors.

④ Click the **Smoothing** popup, and then select from the following options: **Pixels**, **Rough**, **Normal**, and **Smooth**.

This sets the smoothness of the edges of the selection.

⑤ Click **OK**.

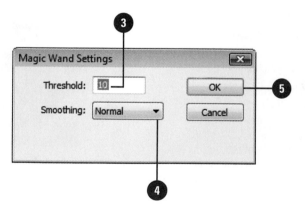

Using Trace Bitmap to Create Vector Shapes

Flash provides a procedure to convert bitmaps into vector art. When Trace Bitmap is used, Flash interprets the pixel information in the bitmap and converts it into vector shapes. The results can be unpredictable in quality and have unwieldy file sizes if the bitmaps are very complex. However, there are several parameters in the Trace Bitmap dialog box that can be modified to strike a balance between file size and quality.

Trace a Bitmap

1 Drag a copy of a bitmap to the Stage from the Library panel; make sure the bitmap is selected on the Stage.

2 Click the **Modify** menu, point to **Bitmap**, and then click **Trace Bitmap**.

> **TROUBLE?** *The Trace Bitmap command is disabled if you select a broken bitmap (a bitmap fill).*

3 Specify values and options to determine how close the vector shape resembles the bitmap:

- **Color Threshold.** If the difference in the RGB color value for two pixels is less than the color threshold, the pixel colors are considered the same. Enter a value between 1 and 500. The higher the value, the lower the number of colors.

- **Minimum Area.** Determines how many neighboring pixels to include in the threshold calculation. Enter a pixel value between 1 and 1000.

- **Curve Fit.** Determines how smoothly Flash creates vector outlines.

- **Corner Threshold.** Controls whether to preserve sharp edges or create more smooth contours.

4 Click **OK**.

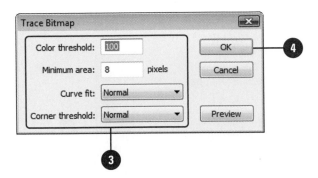

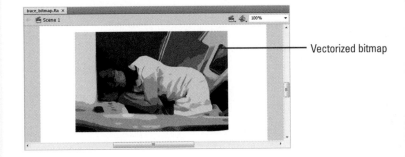

Vectorized bitmap

For Your Information

Creating Vectors Closest to the Original Bitmap

Adobe recommends using the following settings in the Trace Bitmap feature to produce a vector version that is closest to the original bitmap: Color Threshold = 10, Minimum Area = 1 pixel, Curve Fit = Pixels, and Corner Threshold = Many Corners. However, depending on the complexity of the bitmap, this can produce very large and unwieldy file sizes and, in some cases, take a long time for Flash to complete the operation.

Creating Frame-by-Frame Animation

7

Introduction

Flash provides several methods for creating animation. In addition to shape and motion tweening, you can create frame-by-frame animations. The frame-by-frame method is derived from the traditional animation process whereby the content is redrawn on each frame with slight differences from the last frame. When these frames are played in sequence, there is an illusion of movement. In Flash, you utilize keyframes in the Timeline to accomplish this. A **keyframe** defines a change to the artwork placed on the Stage. There are a number of ways to create and edit keyframes, as they are editable objects. Keyframes can be moved, copied, and pasted to and from any Timeline in your Flash movie or between different Flash documents. Frame-by-frame animations can be previewed in the Flash development environment so you can quickly see the results and check your work as you animate. They can also be viewed in the Flash Player using the Test Movie feature.

Additionally, there is an Onion Skin mode that allows you to see the active frame in context to the frames around it, making it easier to fine-tune keyframe changes. The versatility of the Timeline and the strength of the Flash Player allow you to implement animation in your movie and give it life.

What You'll Do

Understand Frame-by-Frame Animation

Create Keyframes

Convert Frames to Keyframes

Use Frame-Based Versus Span-Based Selection

Clear Keyframes Versus Removing Frames

Edit Keyframes

Create a Simple Frame-by-Frame Animation

Play an Animation

Use Onion Skinning

Modify Onion Skin Markers

Edit Multiple Frames

Understanding Frame-by-Frame Animation

Animation is the illusion of movement. It is comprised of a series of pictures, each slightly different from the last, that when played sequentially imply movement. Motion pictures work the same way. What you see when you view a film is a long strip of images played at specific intervals. In this way, the content in the pictures moves and seems to imitate real life.

Traditional cell animators draw a picture onto a frame of celluloid and then draw the same thing onto the next frame but with slight changes made to the drawing. Static parts of the scene (such as a background) are copied and only the objects that change are redrawn. In this way the process is more efficient.

The principles for animating in Flash have derived from this process. In Flash, you create frame-by-frame animations in the Timeline through the use of keyframes. Each keyframe defines a change on the Stage, and when played in succession, the content can seem to evolve, or move. When you export your movie, Flash will play these frames in succession at specific intervals depending on the frame rate you set. A good introduction to this concept, as well as the basics of animation, is the dissection a character walk cycle. When human beings walk, they are essentially repeating the same motion over and over again. In an animated walk cycle, the same thing occurs, though instead of drawing the cycle over and over again, the motion is spaced out so that the last frame (the last image drawn) meets up with the first frame. If this animation is looped, the character will seem to walk perpetually.

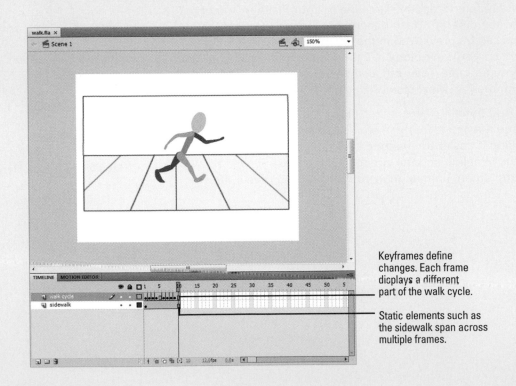

Keyframes define changes. Each frame displays a different part of the walk cycle.

Static elements such as the sidewalk span across multiple frames.

Frame-by-Frame Animation

Frame 1

Frame 2

Frame 3

Frame 4

Frame 5

Frame 6

Frame 7

Frame 8

Creating Keyframes

When art is placed on the Stage, it appears in a keyframe in the Timeline. A keyframe is represented as a black-bounded box with a small circle in it. By default, each layer in the Timeline has a keyframe on its first frame. An empty keyframe displays an empty or hollow circle, but when you place artwork or objects on the Stage, the bounding box becomes shaded and the small circle becomes a filled black dot. A keyframe can span multiple frames when there are no changes to the art. To make a change you create another keyframe. In this way, you can create animations or content that seems to move or change over time.

Create a Keyframe

1 Place art or an object on the Stage.

2 Click on a frame later in the Timeline.

3 Click the **Insert** menu, point to **Timeline**, and then click **Keyframe**.

A new keyframe appears.

TIMESAVER *Press F6 to add a keyframe or Control+click (Mac) or right-click (Win) the selected frame, and then click Add Keyframe.*

Did You Know?

You can remove content from a keyframe. Select a filled keyframe in the Timeline or the art on the Stage contained in that keyframe, and then press the Delete (Mac) or Backspace (Win) key.

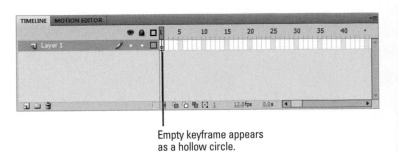

Empty keyframe appears as a hollow circle.

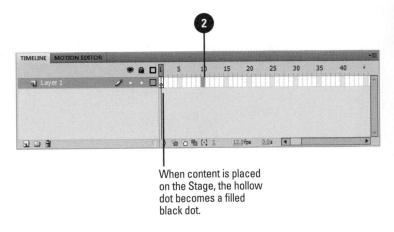

When content is placed on the Stage, the hollow dot becomes a filled black dot.

New keyframe appears

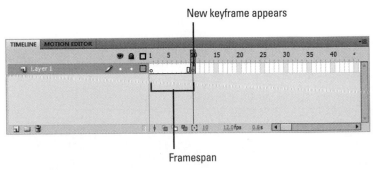

Framespan

Create a Blank Keyframe

1. Click on a frame in the Timeline where you want to add a blank keyframe.

   IMPORTANT *You can only add a blank keyframe to a frame without an existing keyframe (sometimes called an inactive frame or keyspan).*

2. Click the **Insert** menu, point to **Timeline**, and then click **Blank Keyframe**.

   TIMESAVER *Press F7 to add a keyframe or Control+click (Mac) or right-click (Win) the selected frame, and then click Add Blank Keyframe.*

Increase the Keyframe Span

1. Click anywhere in a keyframe span.

   ◆ To insert multiple keyframes, select the number of frames you want.

2. Click the **Insert** menu, point to **Timeline**, and then click **Frame**.

   Repeat until you've increased the framespan to the length you need.

   TIMESAVER *Press F5 to add a frame or Control+click (Mac) or right-click (Win) the selected frame, and then click Insert Frame.*

Did You Know?

You can decrease the keyframe span. Press Shift+F5 for each frame you want to remove.

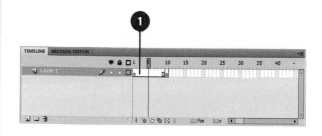

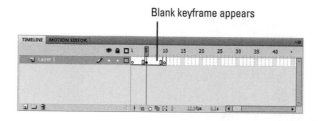

Blank keyframe appears

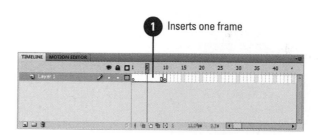

Inserts one frame

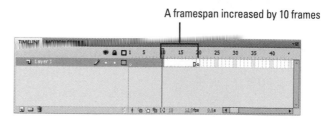

A framespan increased by 10 frames

Converting Frames to Keyframes

Any frame can be converted into a keyframe. As a time-saver, you can select a range of frames and convert them all into keyframes simultaneously. This is useful when you have many frames to convert. It is also a good technique for fine-tuning shape and motion tweens. After the tween has been applied, you can convert the frames in the tweened span into keyframes and edit them independently.

Convert Multiple Frames Into Keyframes

1 Click on a frame, and then drag to select a frame span.

2 Click the **Modify** menu, point to **Timeline**, and then click **Convert To Keyframes**.

TIMESAVER *Press Ctrl+click (Mac) or right-click (Win) the selected frames, and then click Convert To Keyframes or Press F6 after selecting all of the frames you want to convert.*

Did You Know?

You don't have to select a frame to add keyframes. If you place the playhead over a frame and add a keyframe or a blank keyframe, it appears without you having to select the actual frame. However, if you are working with multiple layers, Flash adds a keyframe to all layers at that frame if no frame is selected.

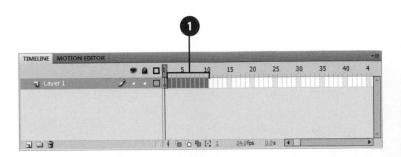

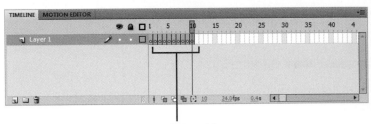

Selected frames are converted into keyframes.

Using Frame-Based Versus Span-Based Selection

Depending upon how you like to work, you can choose between two selection modes in Flash. The default mode is frame-based selection. In this mode, frames are treated as individual elements. When span-based selection is chosen, Flash treats frames as part of a frame span, which means all of the frames adjacent to a keyframe are selected as a unit. You can accomplish the same tasks in either mode and you can switch between the two depending upon the task at hand.

Set the Frame Selection Style

1. Click the **Flash** (Mac) or **Edit** (Win) menu, and then click **Preferences**.

2. If necessary, click the **General** category.

3. Select the **Span Based Selection** check box to enable span-based selection or clear it to enable frame-based selection.

4. Click **OK**.

Did You Know?

You can select a single frame in span-based mode. Press ⌘+click (Mac) or Ctrl+click (Win) the frame. Likewise, to select a span of frames in frame-based mode, click the first or last frame in the span, and then drag until you've selected the entire span.

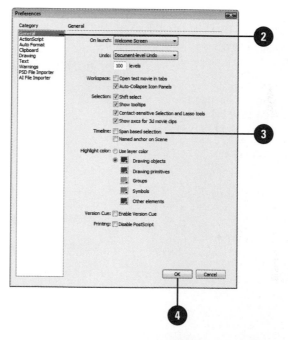

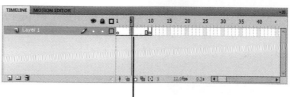

Frame-based selection:
Clicking once on a frame selects that frame

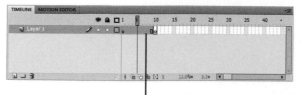

Span-based selection:
Clicking once on a frame selects the entire span

Clearing Keyframes Versus Removing Frames

Depending on what you are trying to accomplish, you can choose to remove a frame's status as a keyframe or remove the frame entirely. Clearing a keyframe preserves the length of the framespan and the overall duration of the animation on the layer. It simply turns the keyframe back into a regular frame and removes any changes the keyframe contained. Conversely, removing frames deletes the entire frame and shortens the framespan as well as the length of your animation in the Timeline.

Clear Keyframes

① Click on the frame to select it or click and drag to select a range of frames.

② Click the **Modify** menu, point to **Timeline**, and then click **Clear Keyframe**.

Flash converts the keyframe back into a regular frame.

TIMESAVER *Press Shift+F6 to clear keyframes.*

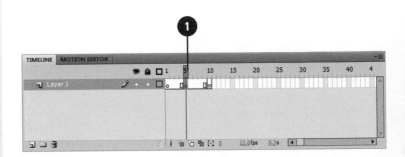

The keyframe is cleared

The duration is maintained

Remove Frames

1. Click on the frame to select it or click and drag to select a range of frames.

2. Click the **Edit** menu, point to **Timeline**, and then click **Remove Frames**.

Flash removes the selected frame(s) and shortens the length of the animation.

TIMESAVER *Press Shift+F5 to remove frames.*

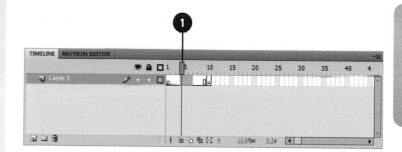

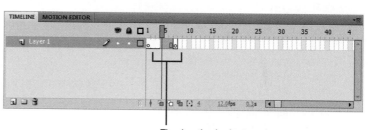

The duration is shortened

Editing Keyframes

Keyframes are editable elements. You can add or remove content from a keyframe, move keyframes around by simply dragging, or copy and paste keyframes in the same Timeline, across scenes and even other Flash documents. Because keyframes are so versatile, you can continue to fine-tune your animations after they are created. When the playhead is placed on a frame, the content of that frame is displayed on your Stage. Selecting the keyframe in the Timeline selects all of the content on that keyframe on the Stage. Likewise, selecting any of your content on the Stage will select its corresponding keyframe. In this way, you can interactively edit the content in a keyframe or the keyframe's position in the Timeline and know what you are affecting.

Copy and Paste Keyframes

① Click on the keyframe to select it or click and drag to select a keyframe and a range of frames.

② Click the **Edit** menu, point to **Timeline**, and then click **Copy Frames**.

TIMESAVER *Press Option+⌘+C (Mac) or Ctrl+Alt+C (Win) to copy frames.*

③ Click on the frame where you want to paste the frames.

④ Click the **Edit** menu, point to **Timeline**, and then click **Paste Frames**.

TIMESAVER *Press Option+⌘+V (Mac) or Ctrl+Alt+V (Win) to paste frames.*

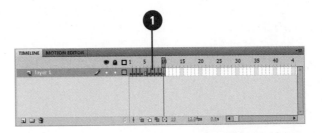

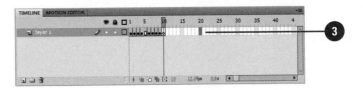

Frames are pasted starting on selected frame.

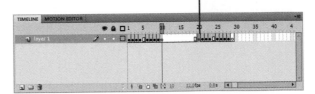

Drag and Drop Keyframes

① Click on the keyframe to select it or click and drag to select a keyframe and a range of frames.

② Click again on the selected frame(s), and then drag to a new area of the Timeline.

Did You Know?

It's important to understand the difference between the normal copy and Paste commands and the copy frames and Paste Frames commands. When you copy and paste frames you are copying the keyframes and in-between frames and the content contained in them. Pasting them preserves the structure and layout. If you select a keyframe and use the normal copy and paste commands ⌘+C and ⌘+V (Mac) or Ctrl+C and Ctrl+V (Win), you are only copying the content contained in that keyframe.

You can use drag and drop to copy frames. Press and hold down the Option (Mac) or Alt (Win) key as you drag frames, Flash copies them to a new location.

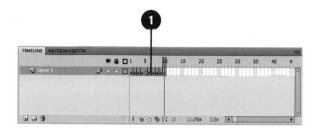

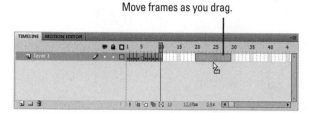

Move frames as you drag.

Frames are moved to the new location.

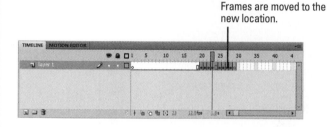

Press the Option key (Mac) or the Alt key (Win) to copy frames as you drag them.

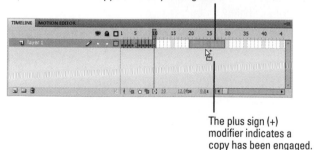

The plus sign (+) modifier indicates a copy has been engaged.

Frames copied to the new location.

Creating a Simple Frame-by-Frame Animation

Flash incorporates the traditional animation technique with its use of keyframe-based animation. Artwork is placed in a keyframe in the Timeline and subsequent keyframes are created to record changes to the artwork. When played consecutively, these minute changes mimic movement as each keyframe describes an altered position or transform effect. Static art that does not change is stored on separate layers and can span the entire animation. In this way, you don't have to redraw the entire frame and you can quickly create complex animations.

Create a Frame-by-Frame Animation

1. Create a new Flash document or open an empty Timeline.

2. Click the first frame to select it.

3. Click the **Oval** tool on the Tools panel.

4. Click on the Stage, and then drag to draw a circle.

5. Click the second frame to select it.

6. Click the **Insert** menu, point to **Timeline**, and then click **Keyframe**.

   TIMESAVER *Press F6 to insert a keyframe.*

7. Select the second keyframe or double-click the circle on the Stage and drag it slightly to the right.

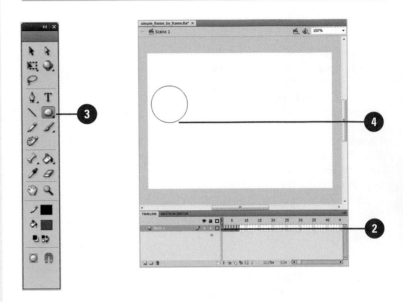

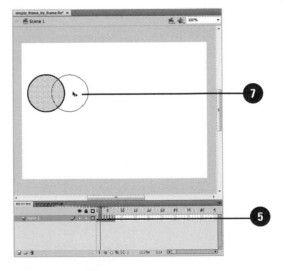

8 Click on the third frame to select it.

9 Repeat step 6.

10 Select the third keyframe or double-click the circle on the Stage and drag it slightly further to the right.

11 Continue to add keyframes and move the circle until it reaches the right edge of the Stage.

IMPORTANT *The more keyframes you add the smoother the animation is.*

12 Click the **Playhead** and move it across the frames to preview the movement of the circle.

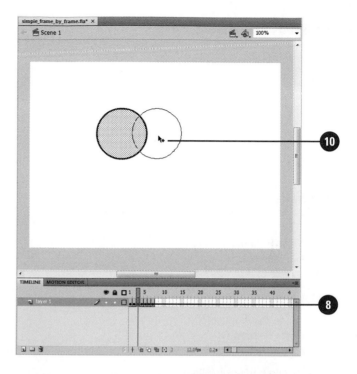

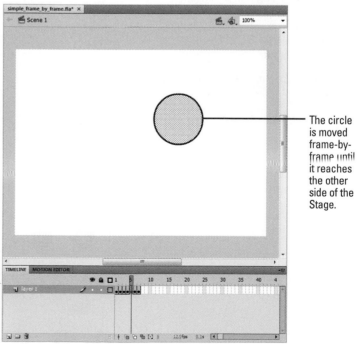

The circle is moved frame-by-frame until it reaches the other side of the Stage.

Playing an Animation

In addition to moving the playhead in the Timeline to view your animation, commonly called scrubbing, Flash provides a controller to navigate the Timeline. The Controller resembles the transport controls on a VCR and can be used in the same way. Additionally, you can export your Flash document into a Flash movie (a .swf file). You do this to see your Flash movie in its final state, as there are some elements that are not viewable in the Flash Development environment, such as animations contained in movie clip symbols and ActionScript functionality. To preview basic animations from their own Timeline, you can use the Controller to preview them.

Use the Controller to Play an Animation

1 Click the **Window** menu, point to **Toolbars**, and then click **Controller**.

2 To stop the animation, click **Stop**.

3 To rewind to the first frame of the animation, click **Rewind To Beginning**.

4 To step back one frame, click **Step Back**.

> **TIMESAVER** *Press the < key to step back a frame.*

5 To play or stop the animation, click **Play**.

> **TIMESAVER** *Press Return (Mac) or Enter (Win) to play if stopped or to stop if playing.*

6 To step forward one frame, click **Step Forward**.

> **TIMESAVER** *Press the > key to step forward a frame.*

7 To fast-forward to the end of the animation, click **Go To End**.

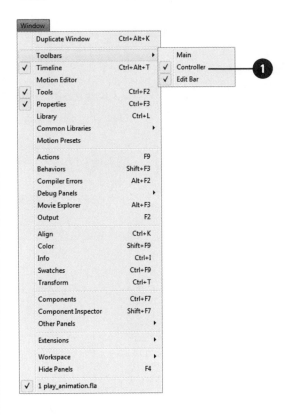

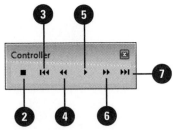

Test Animation in the Flash Player

1. Click the **Control** menu, and then click **Test Movie**.

   Flash exports the entire Timeline and any other scenes you've created into a .swf file that plays in the Flash Player.

   TIMESAVER *Press ⌘+Return (Mac) or Ctrl+Enter (Win) to Test Movie.*

Control	
Play	Enter
Rewind	Shift+,
Go To End	Shift+.
Step Forward One Frame	.
Step Backward One Frame	,
Test Movie	Ctrl+Enter
Test Scene	Ctrl+Alt+Enter
Delete ASO Files	
Delete ASO Files and Test Movie	
Loop Playback	
Play All Scenes	
Enable Simple Frame Actions	Ctrl+Alt+F
Enable Simple Buttons	Ctrl+Alt+B
✓ Enable Live Preview	
Mute Sounds	Ctrl+Alt+M

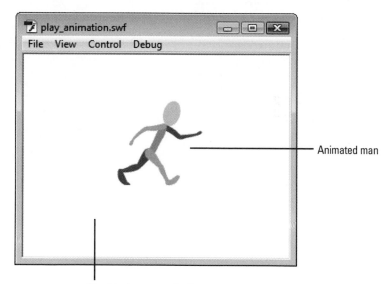

Animated man

Test Movie exports the Flash movie, which has a .swf extension. The Flash Player plays .swf files.

Using Onion Skinning

Normally, the playhead shows one frame at a time—the frame it's placed on. As you play the Timeline, the Stage displays the content of one frame at a time, forming your animation. Onion Skinning mode allows you to view multiple frames simultaneously. This is useful for fine-tuning your animation, because you can see the content on the frames immediately preceding and following the active frame.

Activate Onion Skinning

① Open a Timeline with a multiple frame animation.

② Click the **Onion Skin Mode** button in the Status bar.

Onion skin markers appear in the area above the frame numbers and the area of the range of frames selected dims. The frames that precede the active frame and the frames that follow appear in varying degrees of shading on the Stage, becoming lighter the further they are from the active frame.

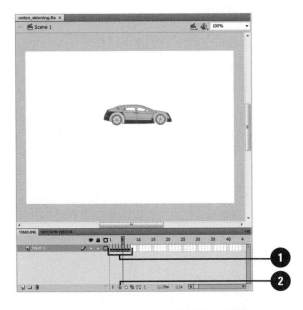

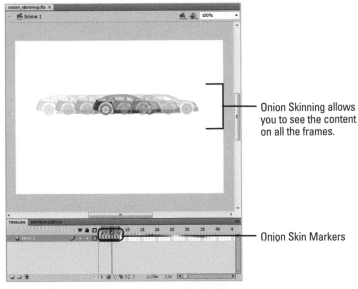

Onion Skinning allows you to see the content on all the frames.

Onion Skin Markers

Use Onion Skin Outlines

1. Open a Timeline with a multiple frame animation.

2. Click the **Onion Skin Outlines** button in the Status bar.

   The frames that precede the active frame and the frames that follow appear as outlines on the Stage.

Did You Know?

You can only edit the active frame. This is the frame the playhead is on. The art that appears when Onion Skin (regular and outline) is enabled is for preview only.

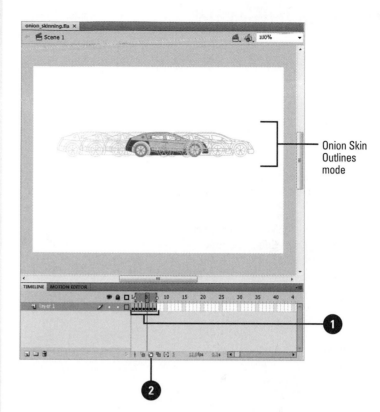

Onion Skin Outlines mode

Modifying Onion Skin Markers

You can adjust the number of frames previewed in the onion skin by manually dragging the onion skin markers. These markers have draggable handles that set the beginning and end of the onion skin. The handles appear as brackets with small dots. Alternately, you can set the range of the markers from the Modify Onion Markers popup menu.

Set Onion Skin Markers Manually

1. Click the **Onion Skin Mode** button in the Status bar, if necessary

2. Click on the small dot on either end of the onion skin markers and then drag to include or exclude any consecutive frames in the onion skin.

Did You Know?

You can only edit the active frame in the onion skin. To edit other frames and maintain the selected frames, select Anchor Onion in the Modify Markers popup menu.

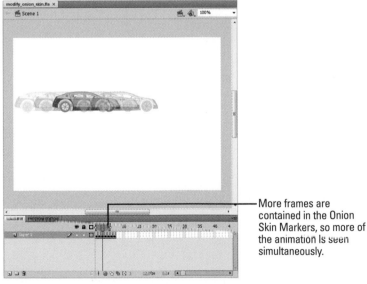

More frames are contained in the Onion Skin Markers, so more of the animation is seen simultaneously.

Set Onion Skin Markers in Modify Onion Markers Window

① Click the **Modify Onion Markers** button.

The Modify Onion Markers popup appears.

② Select from the following options:

◆ **Always Show Markers.** Keeps Onion Skin Markers visible in and out of Onion Skin mode.

◆ **Anchor Onion.** Maintains the selected frames even if you move the playhead.

◆ **Onion 2.** Shows two frames before and after the current frame.

◆ **Onion 5.** Shows five frames before and after the current frame.

◆ **Onion All.** Includes the entire duration of the Timeline in the markers.

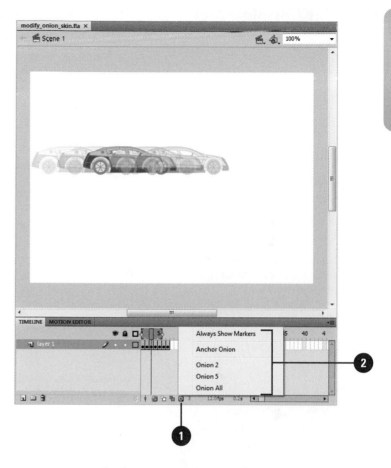

Onion Skin Markers

Command	Description
Always Show Markers	Keeps Onion Skin Markers visible in and out of Onion Skin mode.
Anchor Onion	Prevents the Markers from moving as you move your playhead.
Onion 2	Selects two frames before and after the active frame.
Onion 5	Selects five frames before and after the active frame.
Onion All	Selects all the frames in the Timeline.

Editing Multiple Frames

If you need to make changes to an entire animation or to a series of frames at once, you can select them in Edit Multiple Frames mode. When this feature is enabled, brackets appear similar to those in Onion Skinning mode. Drag them to select the range of frames you want to edit. This works well if you need to make global changes to your animation such as resizing it or changing its location. You can select an entire framespan or layer instead of moving or resizing the content on each individual frame separately.

Select Multiple Frames

1 Open a Timeline with a multiple frame animation.

2 Click the **Edit Multiple Frames** button in the Status bar.

3 Click and drag the markers until they include all the frames you want to select.

All of the content in the selected frames appears on the Stage.

4 Click the **Selection** tool on the Tools panel.

TIMESAVER *Press V to select the Selection tool.*

5 Drag a selection box around the content on the Stage.

You can make changes to location, scale, effects, etc. All the selected frames will be affected.

TIMESAVER *Press ⌘+A (Mac) or Ctrl+A (Win) to select all the content on all unlocked layers.*

Did You Know?

When Edit Multiple Frames is activated, it selects all of the frames on all layers contained in the markers. You must lock any layers you don't want included in the selection.

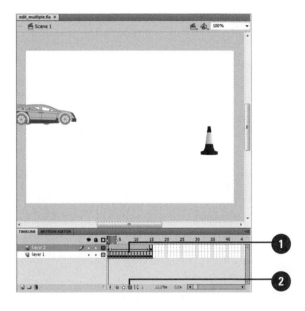

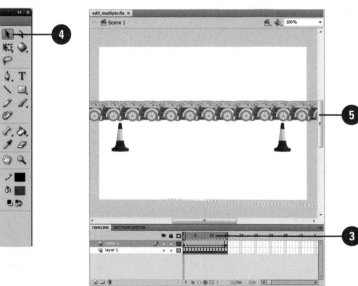

Animating with Motion Tweening

8

Introduction

In Flash, it's not necessary to draw every frame of an animation. You can set the position and attributes of your art in the beginning and ending frames, and Flash will create all of the frames in between. This is called **tweening**. A motion tween connects two keyframes, each with different effects or characteristics applied to them and then gradually "morphs" one into the other. Tweening allows you to quickly animate objects, apply fades, and gradually alter color, alpha, scale, and any other effect that can be applied to a symbol, group, or text object.

The span between the starting frame and ending frame of a motion tween is called the **tween span**. The tween span consists of a group of frames in a single layer with a blue background in the Timeline in which an object changes over time. Only one object, known as the **target object**, on the Stage can be animated in each tween span.

Once an animation is tweened, you can continue to edit it by adding or removing frames to make it move slower or faster, adjust effects, or control the inertia with ease-in and ease-out properties, adding further complexity. Motion tweening produces smaller files than frame-by-frame animation because Flash describes the motion mathematically, incrementally transforming the object in between the two keyframes.

Understanding Motion Tweening

Motion tweening allows you to apply smooth motion and transform effects, such as scale, position, rotation, and skew, to symbol instances (movie clip, graphic, and button) and text fields. Additionally, you can utilize Flash's advanced color effects to apply changes to color, alpha, and brightness.

Because these effects are applied to instances, they only affect the instance placed on the Stage. Its parent (original) symbol in the Library is not affected. Motion tweening produces the smallest file sizes of any of Flash's animation methods.

Flash use two different types of motion tweens: **classic tween** and **motion tween** (**New!**). A classic tween uses several instances in keyframes of an object along with property keyframes to create a tween, while a motion tween uses one object instance over the entire span along with property keyframes to create a tween. A property keyframe (**New!**) is a frame within the motion tween where you define a value for a property. A motion tween is known as object based animation. Motion tweens are easy to create and provide precise control, while classic tweens are more complex to create and provide more advanced control. All motion tweens from previous versions of Flash are classic tweens.

Tween Differences

There are several differences between classic and motion tweens.

Classic Tweens

◆ Use Keyframes and property keyframes to create tweens.

◆ Allow frame scripts.

◆ Allow only symbols (movie clip, graphic, and button) as a tweenable type. It converts all others (editable shapes, groups, and text objects) to a graphic symbol.

◆ Consist of groups of individually selectable frames in the Timeline.

◆ Apply eases to groups of frames between keyframes within the tween.

◆ Allow animation between two different color effects, such as tint and alpha transparency.

◆ Don't allow animation of 3D objects.

◆ Allow symbol swaps and setting the frame number of a graphic symbol to display in a property keyframe.

Motion Tweens

◆ Use one object instance and property keyframes instead of keyframes to create tweens.

◆ Don't allow frame scripts.

◆ Allow text as a tweenable type. It doesn't convert it to a symbol.

◆ Treat tween spans as a single object that you can stretch and resize in the Timeline.

◆ Apply eases across the entire length of a motion tween span.

◆ Apply only one color effect per tween.

◆ Allow animation of 3D objects.

◆ Don't allow symbol swaps and setting the frame number of a graphic symbol to display in a property keyframe.

◆ Convert all non-allowed object types (editable shapes and groups) to a movie clip symbol.

Motion Tweening of Scale and Alpha Changes

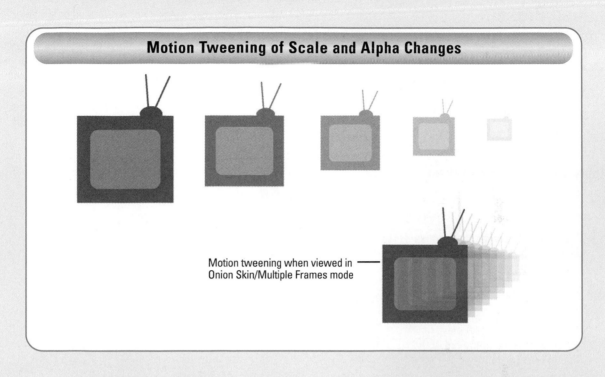

Motion tweening when viewed in Onion Skin/Multiple Frames mode

Motion Tweening of Scale, Alpha, and Rotation Changes

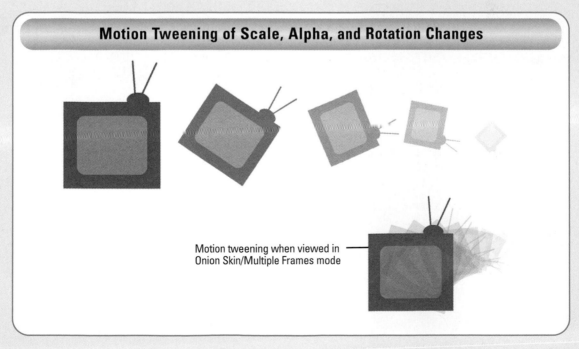

Motion tweening when viewed in Onion Skin/Multiple Frames mode

Applying Motion Tween Presets

FL 3.3

Motion Presets (**New!**) are ready-made motion tweens that you can apply to an object on the Stage. After you preview a motion tween in the Motion Presets panel, you can quickly apply it to a selected object. You can apply only one motion preset per object on the Stage. If you apply another preset to an object, it replaces the previous one. You can only apply a 3D motion preset to a movie clip instance, which is the only object type for 3D effects. Each motion preset contains a specific number of frames, which you can adjust later. In the Motion Presets panel, you can also create and save your own custom motion presets as well as import and export them (stored as XML files) to share with others.

Apply a Motion Tween Preset

1. Select a tweenable object (symbol instance or text field) on the Stage.

2. Click the **Window** menu, and then click **Motion Presets** to open the panel.

3. Select a preset in the Motion Presets panel.

   A preview of the preset plays in the Preview pane at the top of the Motion Presets panel.

   ◆ To stop the preview, click outside the Motion Presets panel.

4. Click **Apply**.

   ◆ If you apply a motion tween to a non-tweenable object, a dialog box appears, asking you to convert it to a symbol.

   The motion is set to start at the current position of the object on the Stage.

   ◆ To apply the preset so that the motion ends at the current position of the object on the Stage, hold down Shift, and then click **Apply**.

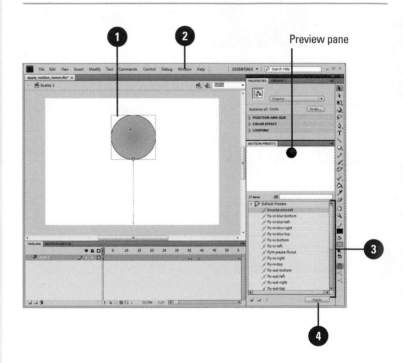

Preview pane

Save a Tween as a Custom Motion Preset

1. Select the tween span, object on the Stage, or the motion path on the Stage with the custom tween that you want to save as a preset.

2. Click the **Window** menu, and then click **Motion Presets** to open the panel.

3. Click the **Save Selection As Preset** button.

4. Type a name for the preset.

5. Click **OK**.

   The new preset appears in the Motion Presets panel under Custom Presets. The preset is saved as an XML file in the Motion Presets folder, which you can locate by performing a search using Instant Search (Win) or Spotlight (Mac).

   ◆ To create a preview for the new preset, publish a SWF of the motion tween with the same name in the Motion Presets folder.

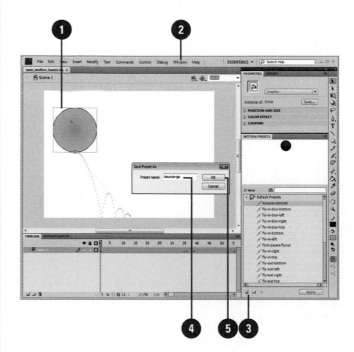

Did You Know?

You can import and export a motion preset. To import a motion preset, click the Options button on the Motion Presets panel, click Import, select the XML file, and then click Open. To export a motion preset, select the preset in the Motion Presets panel, click the Options button, click Export, specify a name and location, and then click Save.

You can delete a motion preset. Select the motion preset in the Motion Presets panel that you want to delete, and then click the Remove Item button.

Creating a Motion Tween

FL 3.1

You can tween position, scale, rotation and other transform effects applied to symbols instances and text fields (**New!**). A motion tween uses one instance over the entire span along with property keyframes, which you define with property values to modify the tween. You can change property keyframes on Stage, in the Property Inspector, or in the Motion Editor. You should have only one object when you apply the tween or the results will be unpredictable. Tweened frames must reside on the same layer in the Timeline. After you add a tween to a layer, Flash changes it to a tween layer, which you can no longer draw on. A tween layer can contain tween spans, static frames, and actions.

Create a Motion Tween

1. Select one or more objects to tween on the Stage.

   ◆ To create multiple tweens at once, place objects on multiple layers, and then select them all.

2. Click the **Insert** menu, and then click **Motion Tween**.

   ◆ If you apply a motion tween to a non-tweenable object, a dialog box appears, asking you to convert it to a symbol.

   Flash converts the layer containing the tweened object to a tween layer and creates a tween span in the layer.

3. To change the length of the tween span, drag either end of the tween span in the Timeline.

4. To add motion to the tween, click a frame within the tween span, and then drag the object on the Stage.

5. To tween 3D rotation or position, use the **3D Rotation** tool or **3D Translation** tool.

6. To remove a motion tween, select the tweened object, click the **Insert** menu, and then click **Remove Tween**.

7. To add another tween to an existing layer, drag a tween span from a different layer.

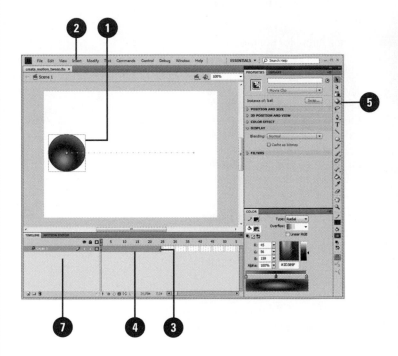

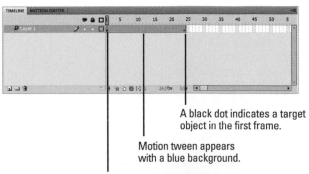

A black dot indicates a target object in the first frame.

Motion tween appears with a blue background.

Black diamonds indicate property keyframes and the last frame.

Adjusting Motion Tween Properties

Motion tweens can be fine-tuned in the Property Inspector or the Motion Editor. When a tweened object is selected, a number of options are enabled that you use to add complexity to your motion path. You can set motion tween properties to deal with position and size, set rotation direction and frequency, apply color and display blending effects, or control the easing in or out of the motion. The options you set in the Property Inspector are applied to the entire tween span.

Set Motion Tween Properties in the Property Inspector

① Click the **Window** menu, and then click **Properties** to open the Property Inspector.

② Select an object on the Stage with a tween applied.

③ Choose from the available settings; options vary depending on the selected tweened object:

- ◆ **Ease.** Sets the motion speed in and out.

- ◆ **Position and Size.** Sets the X and Y position, and the selection width and height.

- ◆ **3D Position and View.** Sets the 3D X, Y, and Z position, 3D perspective selection width and height, perspective angle, and vanishing point.

- ◆ **Rotation.** Sets the direction and frequency your object rotates. Select the **Orient To Path** check box to keep your object parallel to the guide relative to its center point.

- ◆ **Path.** Sets the X and Y position, and the selection width and height.

- ◆ **Color Effect.** Sets the color style effect: Brightness, Tint, Alpha, or Advanced.

- ◆ **Display.** Sets the display blending effect, which includes Darken, Overlay, and Invert.

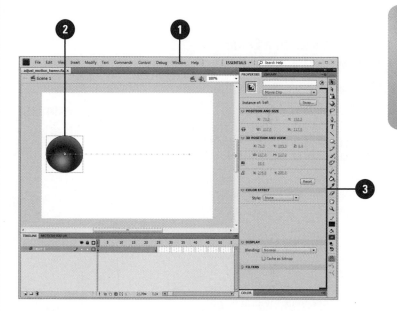

Editing Motion Tween Properties with the Motion Editor

 FL 3.2

The Motion Editor panel (**New!**) allows you to view and edit all tween properties and related keyframe properties. You can change the basic motion of the tween by changing the x-, y-, and z-axes, transform the skew and scale, apply color and filter effects, or add motion speed easing in or out. You can open the Motion Editor panel by using the Window menu. It appears next to the Timeline. When you select a tween space, a tweened object, or motion path, the Motion Editor panel displays tween property values in categories and a grid with a graph for each property.

Change the Motion Editor Display

① Select an object on the Stage with a tween applied.

② Click the **Window** menu, and then click **Motion Editor** to open the panel.

③ To change the display of the Motion Editor, do any of the following:

◆ **Display Properties.** Click the triangle next to a property category.

◆ **Expand/Collapse Property View.** Click the property name to toggle it.

◆ **Viewable Frames.** Sets the number of frame of a tween shown in the Motion Editor.

◆ **Graph Size.** Sets the size of the graph.

◆ **Expanded Graph Size.** Sets the expanded property view size of the graph.

◆ **Add Eases Options.** Adds an ease option to menus in the Motion Editor. Click the **Add** button on the Eases category, and then select an ease option.

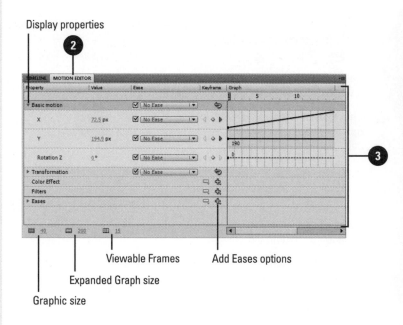

Display properties

Graphic size

Expanded Graph size

Viewable Frames

Add Eases options

Set Motion Tween Properties in the Motion Editor

① Select an object on the Stage with a tween applied.

② Click the **Window** menu, and then click **Motion Editor** to open the panel.

③ Click the triangle to expand a category, and then specify any of the following:

◆ **Basic Motion.** Specify values for the x-, y-, and z-axes, and other related options.

◆ **Transformation.** Specify skew and scale values, and other related options.

◆ **Color Effect.** Click the **Add** or **Remove** button on the Color Effect category, and then select an option. Specify the color effect options you want.

◆ **Filters.** Click the **Add** or **Remove** button on the Filters category, and then select an option. Specify the filter options you want.

④ Select or clear the **Ease** check box to enable or disable it for a property or category, and then set an ease value. Positive values increase the ease at the end of the curve, while negative values increase the ease at the beginning of the curve.

⑤ To reset values for an option, click the **Reset Values** button.

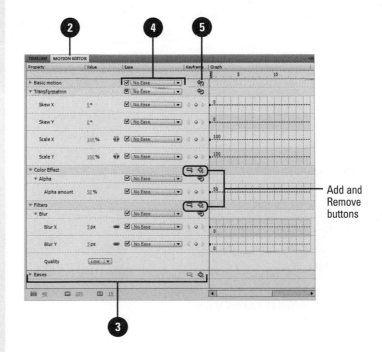

Add and Remove buttons

Adding Color Effects and Filters

FL 3.2, 3.5

Wondering where Timeline Effects have gone in Flash CS4. They are now a part of the Motion Editor. You can add many Timeline Effects by using filters in the Motion Editor. You can add filter effects (**New!**), such as Drop Shadow, Blur, Glow, Bevel, Gradient Glow, Gradient Bevel, and Adjust Color, to a motion tween. You can also add color effects, such as Alpha, Brightness, Tint and Advanced Color, to a motion tween. You can apply more than one effect or filter to an object to create a different effect. If an applied color effect or filter doesn't work for you, you can remove it.

Add Color Effects and Filters to a Motion Tween

1. Select an object on the Stage with a tween applied.

2. Click the **Window** menu, and then click **Motion Editor** to open the panel.

3. Click the triangle to expand the Color Effect or Filters category.

4. Use any of the following:

   ◆ **Color Effect.** Click the **Add** button on the Color Effect category, and then select an option.

     The options include Alpha, Brightness, Tint, and Advanced Color.

   ◆ **Filters.** Click the **Add** button on the Filters category, and then select an option.

     The options include Drop Shadow, Blue, Glow, Bevel, Gradient Glow, Gradient Bevel, and Adjust Color.

5. Specify the options you want for the category; options vary depending on the color effect or filter that you choose.

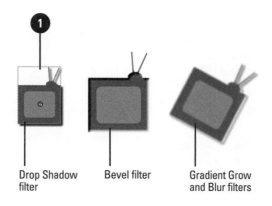

Drop Shadow filter   Bevel filter   Gradient Grow and Blur filters

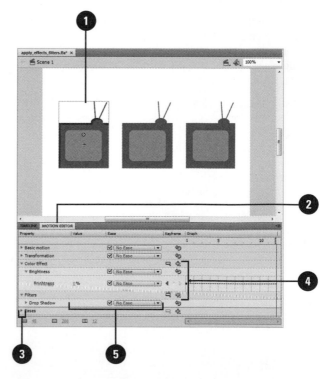

240

Work with Color Effects and Filters

1. Select an object on the Stage with a tween applied.

2. Click the **Window** menu, and then click **Motion Editor** to open the panel.

3. Click the triangle to expand the Color Effect or Filters category.

4. Specify the options you want for the category; options vary depending on the color effect or filter that you choose.

5. To remove a color effect or filter, click the **Remove** button on the Color Effect or Filter category, and then select the effect or filter that you want to remove.

6. To reset values back to the default, click the **Reset Values** button for the effect or filter.

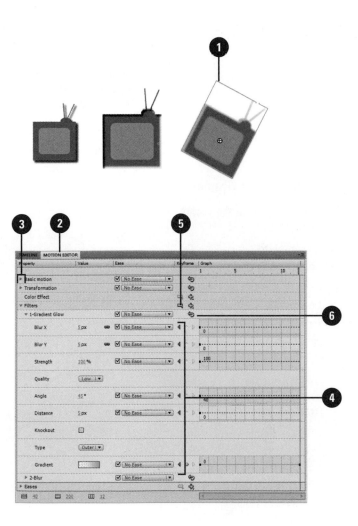

Working with Property Keyframes

FL 3.2

When you select a tween space, a tweened object, or motion path, the Motion Editor panel displays tween property values in categories and a grid with a graph for each property. Each keyframe property (**New!**) for a specific property appears as a control point on the graph. You can add or remove a property keyframe at any time. Control points can be either smooth or corner points. When a point is smooth, Bezier handles appear, which you can adjust. Some properties in the Motion Editor are associated with each other, such as Scale X and Scale Y. You can use the Link icon to constrain values to match to each other.

Work with Property Keyframes

1. Select an object on the Stage with a tween applied.

2. Click the **Window** menu, and then click **Motion Editor** to open the panel.

3. Click the triangle to expand a category.

4. To work with property keyframes, do any of the following:

   ◆ **View.** Click the **Go To Previous Keyframe** or **Go To Next Keyframe** arrows.

   ◆ **Add.** Place the playhead where you want to property keyframe, and then click the **Add or Remove Keyframe** button.

   ◆ **Remove.** Right-click (Win) or Control-click (Mac) the control point in the graph, and then click the **Remove Keyframe**.

   ◆ **Smooth or Corner.** Alt-click (Win) or Command-click (Mac) the control point to toggle between smooth and corner.

   ◆ **Link.** Click the **Link** icon to constrain values to match for associated pairs. Click the icon again to unlink a pair.

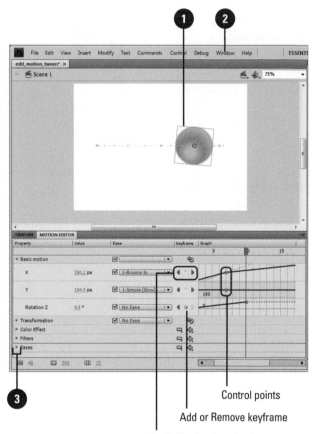

Control points

Add or Remove keyframe

Go To Preview/next keyframe

Editing the Path of a Motion Tween

FL 3.2

If you want to change the x-, y-, or z-axes, it's easier to make bigger adjustments in the motion path of a tween on the Stage and minor ones in the Motion Editor (**New!**). You can move the entire motion path to another location on the Stage or edit individual points on the path. If segments within the path become to fast or slow, you can use the roving property for the x-, y-, and z- axes to make the speed consistent throughout the tween.

Edit the Path of a Motion Tween

1. Select an object on the Stage with a tween applied.

2. To make changes directly on the Stage, do any of the following:

   ◆ **Object Position.** Place the playhead in the frame you want to move, click the **Selection** tool, and then drag the target object to a new location.

   ◆ **Motion Path Position.** Click the **Selection** tool, click the motion path, and then drag the path.

   ◆ **Motion Path Size.** Click the **Free Transform** tool, click the motion path, and then drag a resize handle.

   ◆ **Motion Path Shape.** Click the **Selection** tool, click away from the motion path, and then drag any line segment on the path.

   Click the **Subselection** tool, click the path, and then drag a control point to move it, or click a control point, and then drag the Bezier handles of the control point to reshape it.

   ◆ **Delete Motion Path.** Click the **Selection** tool, double-click the motion path, and then press Delete.

   ◆ **Roving.** Right-click (Win) or Control-click (Mac) the tween span or an individual control point in a Motion Editor graph, and then click **Roving** to toggle on and off.

Path

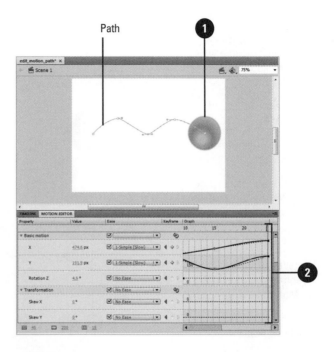

Selection tool

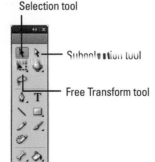

Subselection tool

Free Transform tool

Copying Motion as ActionScript

If you have a complex animation in the timeline that you want to convert into ActionScript 3.0 code, you can use the Copy Motion as ActionScript 3.0 command to get the job done. When you use the command, Flash copies the properties that define the motion tween on the timeline and writes the ActionScript 3.0 code for you to apply to a symbol. You can apply the code as timeline code or in class files for the Flash document file.

Copy Motion as ActionScript 3.0

1. Create the animation using a symbol on the timeline in a layer that you want to copy as ActionScript 3.0 code.

2. Create a new layer.

3. Create a new symbol or drag another instance of your existing symbol on the Stage.

4. Select the entire animation that you want to copy on the animation layer of the timeline. Click the first frame, press Shift, and then click click the last frame.

5. Right-click (Win) or Control-click (Mac) the animation, and then click **Copy Motion as ActionScript 3.0**.

6. Type an instance name to use in the ActionScript code. Enter the instance name of the instance that you want to apply the ActionScript code to.

7. Select your second instance that you added to layer 2 (from Step 2), and type the instance name you entered into the Properties panel.

8. Create a new layer (for the ActionScript), and select the first frame of that layer.

9. Open the Actions panel and paste the code into the Script pane.

   Before you test the animation, make sure layer 2 has the same number of frames as the animation layer.

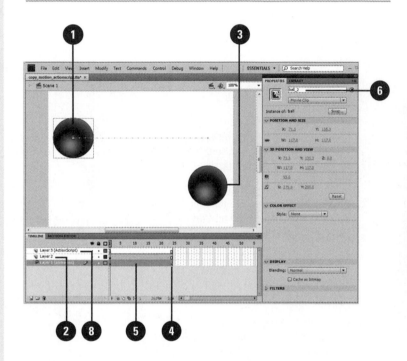

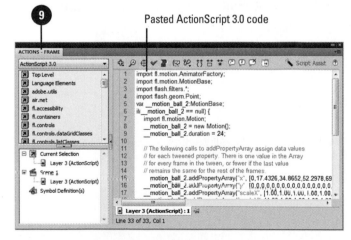

Pasted ActionScript 3.0 code

Animating with Classic Tweening

9

Introduction

In Flash, it's not necessary to draw every frame of an animation. You can set the position and attributes of your art in the beginning and ending frames, and Flash will create all of the frames in between. This is called **tweening**. A motion tween connects two keyframes, each with different effects or characteristics applied to them and then gradually "morphs" one into the other. Tweening allows you to quickly animate objects, apply fades, and gradually alter color, alpha, scale, and any other effect that can be applied to a symbol, group, or text object.

The span between the starting frame and ending frame of a motion tween is called the **tween span**. The tween span consists of a group of frames in a single layer with a blue background in the Timeline in which an object changes over time. Only one object, known as the **target object**, on the Stage can be animated in each tween span.

Once an animation is tweened, you can continue to edit it by adding or removing frames to make it move slower or faster, adjust effects, or control the inertia with ease-in and ease-out properties, adding further complexity. Motion tweening produces smaller files than frame-by-frame animation because Flash describes the motion mathematically, incrementally transforming the object in between the two keyframes.

Classic tweening can only be applied to symbols. For editable shapes, groups, and text objects, you must convert them into symbols or Flash will automatically convert them when you apply motion tweening.

What You'll Do

Work with Classic Tweening

Understand Frame and Instance Properties

Create a Classic Tween

Adjust Classic Tween Properties

Copy and Paste a Tween

Change the Length of a Tween

Change the Frame Rate

Reverse Frames

Add and Remove Keyframes from a Classic Tween

Scale and Rotation a Classic Tween

Add Color Effects to a Classic Tween

Create a Classic Motion Guide Layer

Animate Along a Classic Motion Guide

Orient Objects to a Classic Motion Path

Ease In and Out of a Classic Tween

Working with Classic Tweening

Classic tweening can only be applied to instances of symbols. When applying classic tweening to groups or text objects, Flash automatically converts them into symbols and stores them in the Library. When this happens, they appear in the Library named as Tween 1, Tween 2, etc. It is a good idea to convert them into symbols as the tweening is applied. When managing large projects with many assets it can become confusing to have assets named in this generic way. Of course you can always rename them by selecting the field in the Library and typing in a new name.

If your classic tweened animation doesn't behave as expected, there are a few things you can check. If the object disappears when you play the animation and only re-appears on the end keyframe, you may have more than one object on the keyframe. Make sure that only one object, or instance, is on each keyframe in the tweened span. Also, make sure that both instances are of the same object. Flash cannot motion tween two different objects. To "morph" different shapes into each other you must use shape tweening.

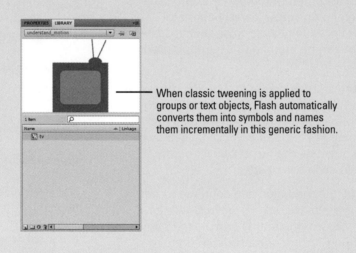

When classic tweening is applied to groups or text objects, Flash automatically converts them into symbols and names them incrementally in this generic fashion.

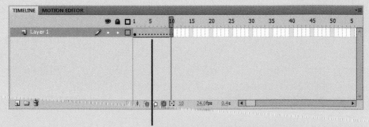

A dotted line in a tween span indicates that there is a problem with the tween. Makes sure there is only one instance (the same instance) on each keyframe.

Understanding Frame and Instance Properties

There is a difference between frame properties and instance properties. This is a source of initial confusion when dealing with animation tweens (both motion and shape). Because the Property Inspector is context-sensitive, it displays properties for many different objects in Flash, depending on which of these objects is selected.

Classic motion (and shape) tweens are applied to keyframes in the Timeline. Color and Transform effects are applied to instances on the Stage. To view the classic tween properties for a specific frame or keyframe, you must select that frame. It is here that you activate tweening and tell Flash what you are going to tween (such as scale or rotation). This needs to be differentiated from the effects you apply to the instances in the tweened keyframes. These are accessed in the Property Inspector and the Transform panel whenever any instance is selected on the Stage. For example, if you check scale as an option in the tween properties for a keyframe, a change in size only results if the size of one of the instances is changed. Conversely, if you want to tween a change in alpha, you can't do this by selecting either of the keyframes in a tween; you must select the instance on the Stage and apply the alpha change when the instance properties appear in the Property Inspector.

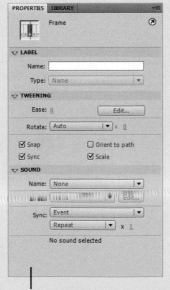

Frame Properties appear when a frame is selected in the Timeline.

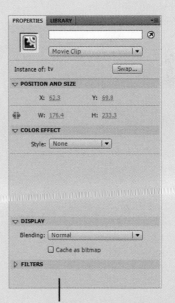

Instance Properties appear when the instance is selected on the Stage.

Creating a Classic Tween

FL 3.1

Create a Simple Classic Tween

1. Create a new Flash document, and then click on the first frame of the Timeline.

2. Do one of the following:

   ◆ Draw a shape on the Stage with any of Flash's drawing tools and convert into a symbol.

   ◆ Drag an instance of a symbol from the Library.

3. Select the first frame.

4. Click the **Insert** menu, and then click **Classic Tween**.

5. Click frame 10 in the Timeline.

6. Click the **Insert** menu, point to **Timeline**, and then click **Frame**.

   Flash displays a dashed line in the framespan to indicate an incomplete or broken motion tween. It also tints the framespan a pale, bluish-purple to indicate that a motion tween has been applied.

   TIMESAVER *Press F5 to add frames, or right-click the frame, and then click Insert Frame.*

You can tween position, scale, rotation and other transform effects applied to symbols, groups, and text. Additionally, you can apply classic tweening to color and alpha changes. A classic tween connects two keyframes. You should have only one object in the keyframe when you apply the tween or the results will be unpredictable. Tweened frames must reside on the same layer in the Timeline.

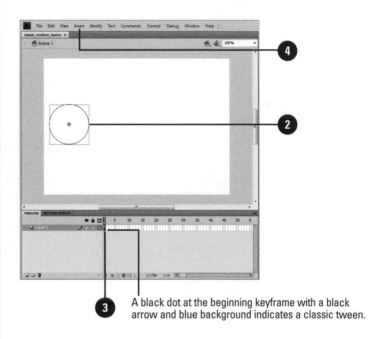

A black dot at the beginning keyframe with a black arrow and blue background indicates a classic tween.

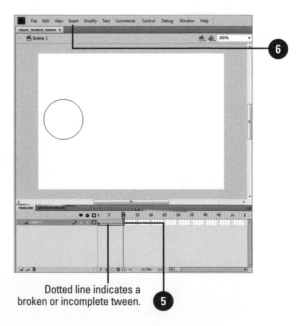

Dotted line indicates a broken or incomplete tween.

7 Click and drag the object on the Stage at frame 10 to a new location.

Flash creates a second keyframe that is connected to the first with an arrow. This indicates the motion tween is complete.

8 Click the **Control** menu, and then click **Test Movie** to test the animation.

Flash gradually moves the object.

Did You Know?

You can add keyframes and then alter the position of the object on the Stage. Tweening can be applied to any two existing keyframes on the same layer. Select the first keyframe, click the Tweening popup in the Property Inspector, and then click Motion.

You can move keyframes around in the Timeline. Simply click to select it, and then click it again and drag it to a new location.

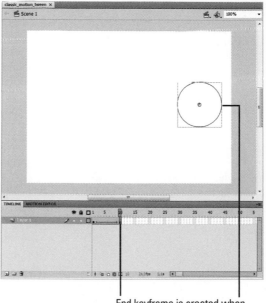

End keyframe is created when object is moved to a new position.

Motion tween viewed in Onion Skin mode.

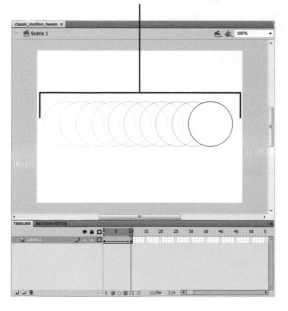

Adjusting Classic Tween Properties

Classic tweens can be fine-tuned in the Property Inspector. When a tweened frame is selected, a number of options are enabled that you use to add complexity to your motion path. It is also where you remove an applied classic tween. Set the tween to deal with scale, set rotation direction and frequency, or apply inertia by easing in or out of the motion. Additionally, you can set orientation and snapping when using a motion guide. In Flash, you can customize easing in or out of a motion using the Edit button in the Property Inspector.

Set Classic Tween Properties

1 Click the **Window** menu, and then click **Properties** to open the Property Inspector.

2 Select a keyframe with motion tween applied.

3 Choose from the following settings:

◆ **Scale.** Check this when you are tweening scale changes.

◆ **Rotate.** Sets the direction and frequency your object rotates.

◆ **Orient To Path.** Use this when you have applied a motion guide layer. This keeps your object parallel to the guide relative to its center point.

◆ **Sync.** This synchronizes the animation contained in the symbol with the Timeline that contains it. Use this when your symbol's Timeline is not an even number of frames.

◆ **Snap.** Check to snap the object's registration point to a motion guide.

◆ **Edit.** This button allows you to create custom ease in and ease out transitions.

4 To remove a classic tween, click the **Insert** menu, and then click **Remove Tween**.

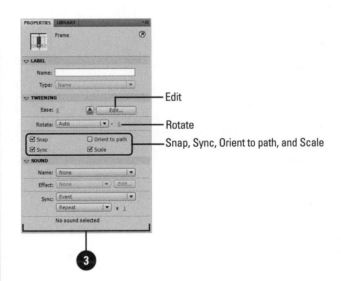

Edit

Rotate

Snap, Sync, Orient to path, and Scale

Set Ease Properties in a Classic Tween

1. Click the **Window** menu, and then click **Properties** to open the Property Inspector.

2. Select a keyframe with motion tween applied.

3. Click the **Ease** field, and then select the setting to set the speed at which your object eases in or out of its motion.

   A positive value eases in, a negative value eases out. A zero value evenly distributes motion across each frame.

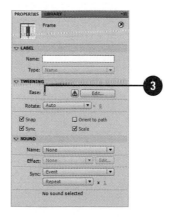

3

No Easing

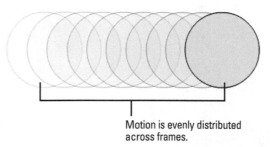

Motion is evenly distributed across frames.

Ease Out

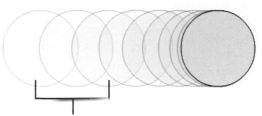

Most of the motion is applied to the beginning frames so the object appears to slow down as it stops.

Ease In

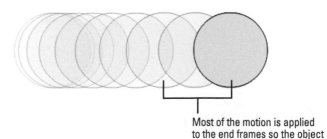

Most of the motion is applied to the end frames so the object appears to slowly accelerate.

Copying and Pasting a Tween

After you fine-tune a motion tween, you can copy and paste the frames, tween, and symbol information to another object. When you paste a motion tween, you can also specify the motion tween properties you want to apply, such as X and Y position, horizontal and vertical scale, color, filters, and blend. You can also override target scale, rotation, and skew properties. If you want to use a motion tween as ActionScript 3.0 in the Actions panel or other code-specific location, you can use the Copy As ActionScript command.

Copy and Paste a Motion Tween

1. Select the frames in the Timeline with the motion tween you want to copy. The frames you select need to be on the same layer. However, the selection can span a tween, empty frames, or two or more tweens.

2. Click the **Edit** menu, point to **Timeline**, and then click **Copy Motion**.

3. Select the symbol instance to receive the copied motion tween.

4. Click the **Edit** menu, point to **Timeline**, and then click **Paste Motion**.

   The frames, tween, and symbol information are inserted to match the original copied tween.

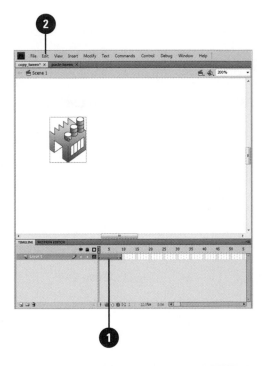

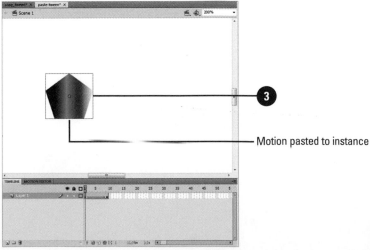

Motion pasted to instance

Paste Motion Tween Properties

1 Select the frames in the Timeline with the motion tween you want to copy.

2 Click the **Edit** menu, point to **Timeline**, and then click **Copy Motion**.

3 Select the symbol instance to receive the copied motion tween.

4 Click the **Edit** menu, point to **Timeline**, and then click **Paste Motion Special**.

5 Choose from the following settings:

◆ **X or Y Position.** Pastes how much to move in the X (horizontal) and Y (vertical) direction.

◆ **Horizontal or Vertical Scale.** Pastes the ratio between the current and the natural size in the horizontal (X) or vertical (Y) direction.

◆ **Rotation And Skew.** Pastes the rotation of the object.

◆ **Color.** Pastes the color values of the object.

◆ **Filters.** Pastes the filter properties of the object.

◆ **Blend Mode.** Pastes the blend properties of the object.

◆ **Override Target Scale or Rotation and Skew Properties.** Select to override the existing scale, or rotation and skew properties of the object. Clear to paste the properties relative to the target object.

6 Click **OK**.

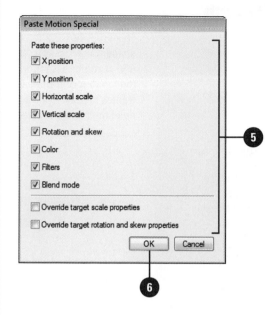

For Your Information

Copying Motion As ActionScript 3.0

In addition to copying motion tweens in the Timeline, you can also copy motion tweens to the Actions panel or use them as ActionScripts. To accomplish this task, you use the Copy Motion As ActionScript command. This command copies the properties that define a motion tween in the Timeline as ActionScript 3.0. These properties include Position, Scale, Skew, Rotation, Transformation Point, Color, Blend Mode, Orientation To Path, Cache As Bitmap Setting, Frame Labels, Motion Guides, Custom Easing, and Filters. After you copy the properties, you can apply them to another symbol in the Actions panel or in the source files for the Flash document that uses ActionScript 3.0. To copy a motion tween as ActionScript 3.0, select the frames in the Timeline with the motion tween you want to copy, click the Edit menu, point to Timeline, click Copy Motion As ActionScript 3.0, type the name of the instance to attach the motion tween to, and then click OK. Flash generates ActionScript for the specific instance name. The code appears on the Clipboard for use in the Actions Panel or other place.

Changing the Length of a Tween

Tweens in Flash are editable after they have been created. You can continue to change their properties and position in the Timeline, and Flash redraws the tweened frames. To change the length of a motion or shape tween (that is, the time it takes to complete the tween), you can add or remove frames in the framespan. Essentially you are adjusting the amount of frames Flash uses in its calculation of the tween. Adding frames means it takes longer for the transformation to happen, while deleting frames shortens the time.

Add Frames to a Tween

1. Click anywhere except the last keyframe on a motion or shape tweened framespan to place the playhead.

   ◆ To add multiple frames, select multiple frames in the Timeline.

2. Click the **Insert** menu, point to **Timeline**, and then click **Frame**.

   TIMESAVER *Press F5 to add frames.*

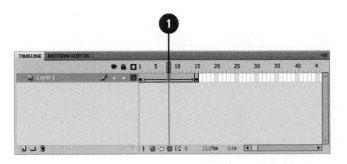

Frame is added to tween span.

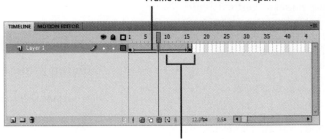

Duration of other tweens is maintained.

Remove Frames from a Tween

1. Click anywhere on a motion or shape tweened framespan to place the playhead.

   ◆ To remove multiple frames, select multiple frames in the Timeline.

2. Click the **Edit** menu, point to **Timeline**, and then click **Remove Frames**.

   TIMESAVER *Press Shift+F5 to subtract frames.*

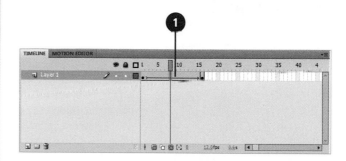

Tween span is reduced by one frame.

Did You Know?

If no layer is selected, the entire Timeline increases or decreases when you add or remove frames. To constrain this action to one target layer, lock all other layers you don't want to affect, or simply select the frame in the tween you want to adjust.

Tweens with more frames will be smoother. The more frames you add to a tween, the smoother the animation plays, because Flash has more frames to split the motion between. However, if you add too many frames the animation may move so slowly that the illusion of movement could be hampered. It is best to experiment with the length of a motion or shape tween and the frame rate of your Flash movie until you get the results you are looking for.

Changing the Frame Rate

The frame rate describes the amount of frames the Flash Player will play each second. The higher you set the frame rate, the smoother your animations will play. Traditional animations play at a rate of 24 frames per second, the same rate at which film plays, while NTSC video plays at 29.97 frames per second. It is important to keep your audience in mind and what the destination of the Flash movie will be. For delivery via the Web, you should consider the processor speeds of the destination computers. If you set the frame rate too high, the computer may not be powerful enough to play all of the frames. When this happens, Flash will drop frames in order to stay in sync. Try to avoid this scenario because it can make your animations play choppily. Consider where your Flash movie is going to be played and choose accordingly. Avoid frame rates over 30 fps, and, for slower computers, you can go as low as 12 fps, which is the default frame rate in Flash.

Change Frame Rate

① Click a blank area on the Stage.

② Click in the **Frame Rate** field in the Property Inspector or at the bottom of the Timeline, and then type in a frame rate.

Did You Know?

You can also change the frame rate in the Document options window. Access this window by clicking the Document button in the Property Inspector or in the Modify menu.

The frame rate is ignored for flv Flash video. You need to set its frame rate in the encoder or editing application.

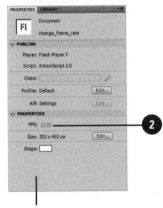

Document settings appear in the Property Inspector when nothing is selected on the Stage or the Timeline.

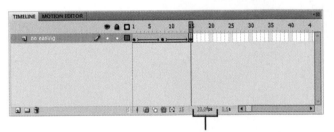

The frame rate is also available to change at the bottom of the Timeline.

Reversing Frames

With a classic tween, use the Reverse Frames command to reverse the frames in the Timeline. You can access this action in the Modify menu and it will be applied to all selected frames. This works for animations created frame-by-frame or with motion or shape tweening applied. Flash changes the order of the frames so your animation plays backwards.

Reverse Frames

1 Click and drag on the range of the frame span or tween you want to reverse.

2 Click the **Modify** menu, point to **Timeline**, and then click **Reverse Frames**.

> **TROUBLE?** *If the tween is not preserved when you use the reverse frames command, you might not have applied motion or shape tweening to the end keyframe in the tween. Flash only requires you to apply tweening to the starting keyframe in a tween. It is implied that it tweens into the next (or end) keyframe. To fix this, do one of the following: (1) Before you reverse frames, select the end keyframe and apply Motion (for motion tweening) or Shape (for shape tweening) to it from the Property Inspector. (2) After you reverse frames, select the beginning keyframe (which use to be the end keyframe) and apply Motion (for motion tweening) or Shape (for shape tweening) to it from the Property Inspector.*

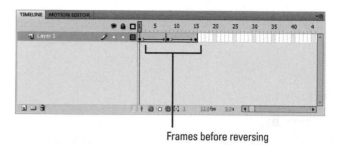

Frames before reversing

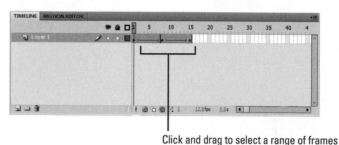

Click and drag to select a range of frames

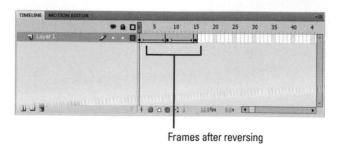

Frames after reversing

Adding and Removing Keyframes from a Classic Tween

With a classic tween, you can add keyframes to a motion tween by simply dragging the object on the Stage on the frame on which you want the change (or keyframe) to be created or by using the Add Keyframe function in the Insert menu. For example, if you want the object to move to another coordinate before it reaches the end position, you can set another keyframe between them. In this way, you can animate shapes in several directions in the same motion tween. Alternately, you can clear a keyframe from the tween by selecting it and using the Clear Keyframe function in the Modify menu. In either case, the length of the tween is preserved; the frame's status as a keyframe is removed and Flash redraws the animation, connecting the keyframes located before and after.

Add a Keyframe to a Classic Tween

1 Click on a frame in a tweened framespan you want to add a keyframe to.

2 Click the **Insert** menu, point to **Timeline**, and then click **Keyframe**.

TIMESAVER *Press F6 to insert a keyframe.*

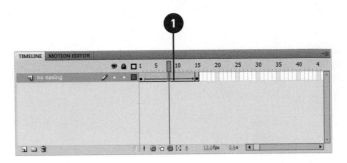

Did You Know?

You can click and drag the object on the Stage and move it to another coordinate. Flash automatically creates a keyframe on the active frame if the playhead is in a motion tweened framespan.

Keyframe is added

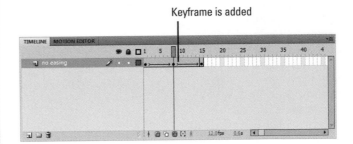

Remove a Keyframe from a Classic Tween

1. Click on the keyframe you want to remove in the motion tween.

2. Click the **Modify** menu, point to **Timeline**, and then click **Clear Keyframe**.

   The keyframe is cleared but the duration of the tween is preserved. The first and last keyframe are automatically reconnected and Flash redraws the tween.

   TIMESAVER Press Shift+F6 to remove the keyframe.

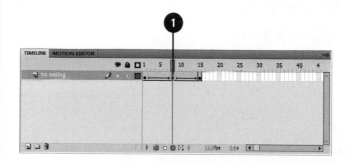

Keyframe is removed

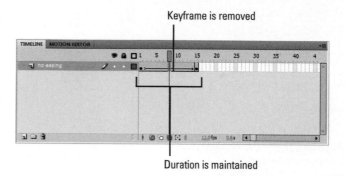

Duration is maintained

Scaling and Rotating a Classic Tween

With a classic tween, any change made to an object on either keyframe can be tweened. Included are any changes made to the scale or rotation of objects on either keyframes in a tweened span. Simply alter the size or rotation of the instance on either frame, and Flash gradually tweens these properties. To change scale, you must select the scale option in the Property Inspector, while rotation has several options to choose from, including clockwise and counter-clockwise rotation, and frequency of rotation.

Change Scale During a Classic Tween

1. Open a document with a tweened animation or create a new one.

2. Select the first keyframe in the tween to open the Motion settings in the Property Inspector.

3. Select the **Scale** check box in the Property Inspector.

4. Change the size of the object on either keyframe with any of Flash's transform methods including the Free Transform tool, the Transform panel or the transform options in the Modify menu.

5. To preview the animation, drag the playhead in the Timeline, or click the **Control** menu, and then click **Test Movie**.

   Flash gradually increases or decreases the size of the object.

   TIMESAVER Press ⌘+Return (Mac) or Ctrl+Enter (Win) to test your movie by viewing it in the Flash Player.

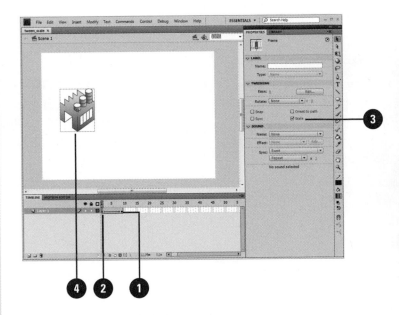

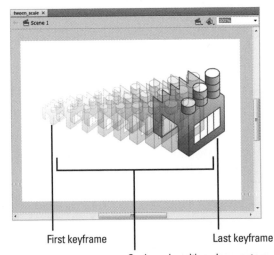

First keyframe

Last keyframe

Scale and position changes tweened

Change Rotation During Classic Tween

1. Open a document with a tweened animation or create a new one.

2. Change the rotation of the object on either keyframe with any of Flash's transform methods including the Free Transform tool, the Transform panel or the transform options in the Modify menu.

3. In the Property Inspector, click the **Rotation Options** popup, and then select a rotation property:

   ◆ **None.** This is the default setting. No rotation is applied.

   ◆ **Auto.** Rotates the object in the direction requiring the least motion.

   ◆ **CW.** Rotates the object clockwise. Enter the number of times you want the object to rotate.

   ◆ **CCW.** Rotates the object counter-clockwise. Enter the number of times you want the object to rotate.

4. To preview the animation, drag the playhead in the Timeline, or click the **Control** menu, and then click **Test Movie**.

   Flash gradually rotates the object in the direction indicated.

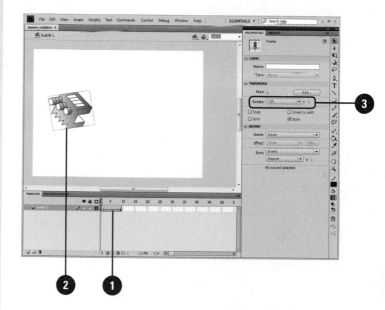

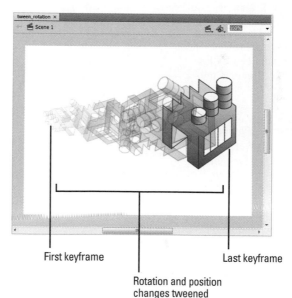

First keyframe

Last keyframe

Rotation and position changes tweened

Adding Color Effects to a Classic Tween

With a classic tween, any color effect that can be applied to an instance can be transformed in a motion tween. You can tween any color properties applied to either the starting or ending keyframe. For example, if the starting keyframe in a motion tween is tinted red and the ending keyframe is tinted yellow, Flash will gradually change the tint of the object from red, through shades of orange to the final tint of yellow. Use these properties to create any number of color effects in your animations. Additionally, you can tween the alpha of an object to make it appear to fade on and off the Stage.

Add Color Effects to a Classic Tween

1. Open a Timeline with a tweened animation or create a new one.

2. Select the object on the Stage on either keyframe in the tween.

3. Click the **Color Styles** popup in the Property Inspector, and then select an effect: **Brightness**, **Tint**, **Alpha**, or **Advanced**.

4. Drag the slider to set the percentage of the Color Styles applied or enter a value in the entry field.

    TROUBLE? *If the Color styles don't appear in the Property Inspector, you may have selected the keyframe in the Timeline and not the object on the Stage.*

5. To preview the animation, drag the playhead in the Timeline, or click the **Control** menu, and then click **Test Movie**.

    Flash applies the tint gradually between the two keyframes.

See Also

See "Creating a Motion Tween" on page 237 for information on creating a motion tween.

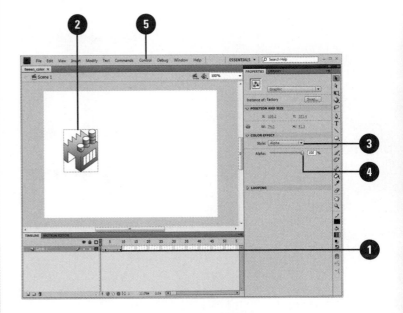

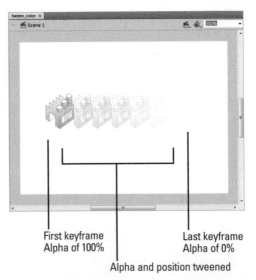

First keyframe
Alpha of 100%

Last keyframe
Alpha of 0%

Alpha and position tweened

Creating a Classic Motion Guide Layer

If you want to implement motion that is smoother, or that follows a curve or some specific path, you can create a motion guide. A motion guide has its own layer just above the layer containing the object. Flash allows you to draw a line that you want your object to follow with any of the built-in drawing tools. Because this layer is a guide, it will be invisible in the exported Flash movie.

Create a Classic Motion Guide

1. Select the layer containing the classic motion tween.

2. Right-click (Win) or Control-click the layer containing the classic tween, and then click **Add Classic Motion Guide**.

   Flash creates a new layer above the selected layer and indents the affected layer.

   TIMESAVER *Press Control+click (Mac) or right-click (Win) the layer you want to add a motion guide to, and then click Add Motion Guide.*

3. Click on the motion guide layer to select it.

4. Draw a line on the Stage with any of Flash's drawing tools to define the path your object will follow.

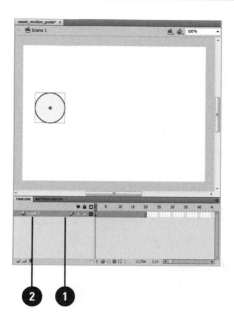

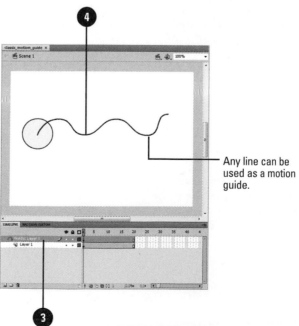

Any line can be used as a motion guide.

Animating Along a Classic Motion Guide

Turn snapping on to easily animate along a classic motion guide. The center point of the object must be on the classic motion guide path for it to work, and snapping ensures that this happens. Once the classic motion guide is created, all you have to do is drag the object in the first and last frames of the tween to the classic motion path you drew and Flash will draw the in-between frames along this path.

Animate Along a Classic Motion Path

1. Create a classic motion guide.

2. Click on the first keyframe of the motion tween, and then click and drag the object on the Stage onto the start of the motion path.

   The object snaps to the motion path.

   TROUBLE? *If the object doesn't snap to the motion path, verify that the Snap setting is turned on in the Property Inspector for this frame. The objects on both the beginning and ending keyframe must be snapped to the motion guide line for the motion to follow the guide line.*

3. Click on the last keyframe of the motion tween, and then click and drag the object on the Stage onto the end of the motion path.

   The object follows the line you drew located in the motion guide layer.

See Also

See "Creating a Classic Motion Guide Layer" on page 263 for information on creating a motion guide.

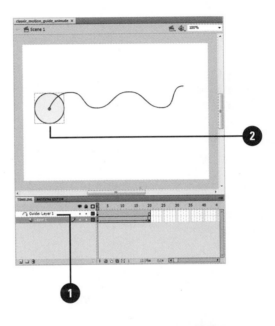

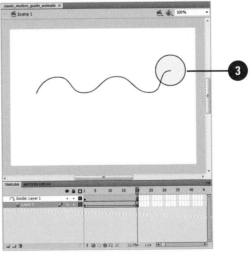

Orienting Objects to a Classic Motion Path

When objects are tweened along a classic motion path, they remain in their native orientation regardless of the path. For certain objects, such as a circle, this is ok. For more complex objects, you must rotate the object so that it follows the path in a more naturalistic way. A good example of this sort of orientation in motion is in the path a car takes while driving down a road-the car must rotate gradually as the road curves to remain parallel with the road, and so, avoid disaster. Flash can do this work for you when you set the Orient To Path option in the motion tween settings.

Animate Along a Classic Motion Path

1. Animate an object along a classic motion guide.

2. Click on the first keyframe of the motion tween to select it.

3. Select the **Orient To Path** check box in the Property Inspector.

   The object will automatically rotate to remain parallel with the motion guide.

See Also

See "Animating Along a Classic Motion Guide" on page ??? for information on creating animation using a motion guide.

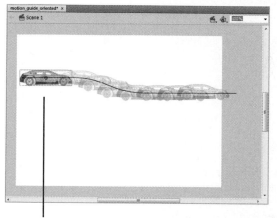

Tweening along a motion guide without orientation can seem unnatural.

Orient to Path makes sure the baseline is always parallel.

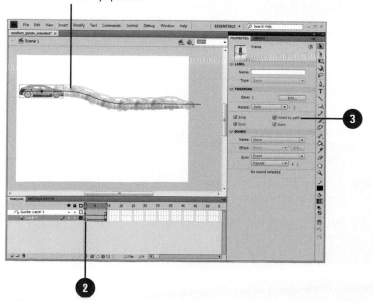

Easing In and Out of a Classic Tween

With a classic tween, you can customize easing in or out of a motion tween using the Edit button in the Property Inspector. The ease in and out of a motion tween is the rate at which the change of location is applied to an object. You can make an object move back and forth on the Stage within a single tween or create more complex tweens. Flash displays a graph representing the degree of motion in frames over time. The percentage of change is the vertical axis and the number of frames is the horizontal axis. The rate of change of the object is indicated by the slope of the graph's curve.

Set Ease In and Out Motion Tween Properties

1. Click the **Window** menu, and then click **Properties** to open the Property Inspector.

2. Select a keyframe with motion tween applied.

3. Click the **Edit** button in the Property Inspector.

4. Select or clear the **Use One Setting For All Properties** check box. Select it (default) to customize one curve, clear it to customize a curve for each curve property (Position, Rotation, Scale, Color, and Filters).

   If cleared, use the Property popup to select a curve.

5. Click a point on the ease line to add a control point, and then drag the control point to change ease in and out. You can add and change multiple points.

6. Drag a tangent point (hollow circles on the sides of a control point to further change ease in and out.

7. Click the **Play** or **Stop** buttons to try the customized ease settings.

8. To reset setting to the default, click **Reset**.

9. Click **OK**.

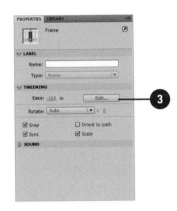

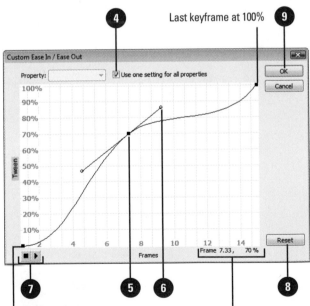

Last keyframe at 100%

First keyframe at 0%;
square handles (control points) represent frame indicators.

Click a control point (square handle) to display its keyframe and % of change.

Animating with Shape Tweening

10

Introduction

Shape tweening works similarly to motion tweening. It follows the same structure of keyframing in the Timeline. You can animate many of the same changes such as alpha, color, scale, and position, though its main purpose is to transform the shape of an object into another shape. Whereas motion tweening is applied to groups and symbols, shape tweening must be applied to an editable shape. You can determine whether an object is editable by selecting it with the Selection tool—if it doesn't have a bounding box when selected, shape tweening can be applied. The reason for this is that when you convert a shape into a symbol, you are essentially protecting it from editing by storing it in its own Timeline. To apply shape tweening to a symbol, you must enter symbol editing mode and apply it to the shape contained inside the symbol. Shapes are created with any of Flash's drawing tools, such as the Oval or Rectangle tools. By making changes to the shape with any of Flash's editing tools, you can change the contours of the shape (for example, turn a circle into a square) and then use shape tweening to make this change happen gradually over time. Because the results of a shape tween can be unpredictable, you can set shape hints to let Flash know how to proceed with the tween. This is useful when you are working with complex shapes such as letterforms. In all cases you should only tween one shape at a time in a tweened span for best results.

In addition to shape tweening, you can also animate shapes using Inverse Kinematics (IK), which allows you to stretch and bend shape objects and link groups of symbol instances to make them move together in naturalistic ways using an internal structure of bones to create character animation.

What You'll Do

Use Shape Tweening

Create a Shape Tween

Add and Remove Keyframes from a Shape Tween

Change Shape Positions with Shape Tweening

Change Shape Position and Form Simultaneously

Adjust Shape Tween Properties

Change Shape Tweening Color and Alpha Options

Use Shape Hints

Create Animation Using ActionScript

Use Inverse Kinematics

Add Bones to an Armature

Edit Armatures and Bones

Bind Bones

Using Shape Tweening

You can use shape tweening when you need to alter the form of any editable shape gradually. Place artwork in a keyframe and then use any of Flash's drawing and editing tools to adjust the contours of a shape on another keyframe. When you apply shape tweening, Flash draws the frames in-between the two keyframes so that the object appears to "morph" between the two states. To provide even more control, you can use shape hints.

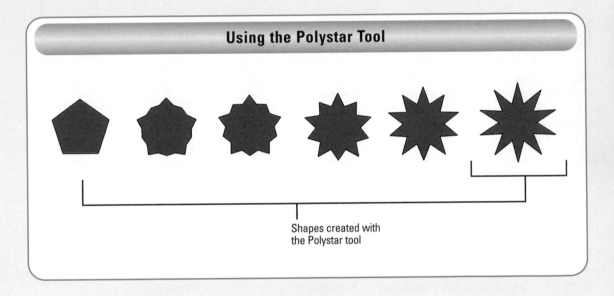

Using the Polystar Tool

Shapes created with
the Polystar tool

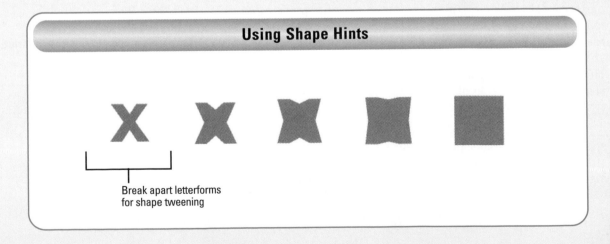

Using Shape Hints

Break apart letterforms
for shape tweening

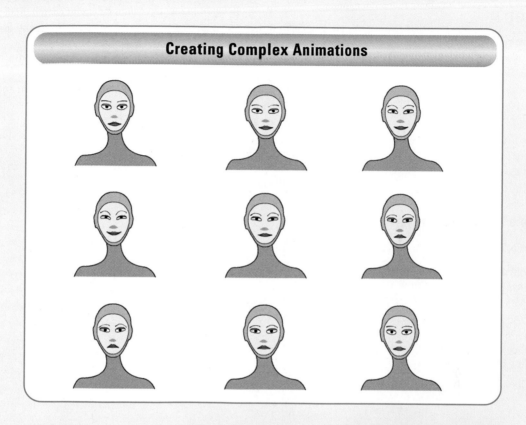

Creating Complex Animations

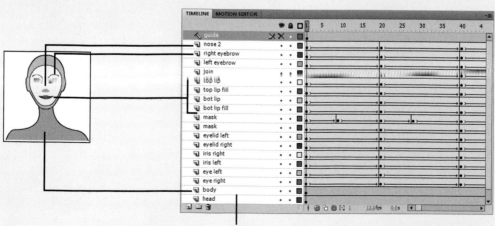

For best results, tween shapes separately on different layers

Creating a Shape Tween

In most cases, you can easily shape tween any two simple shapes. Geometric forms such as lines, rectangles and circles yield the best results. Because Flash draws the tweened frames mathematically, the simpler the shape, the more likely it will tween without any problems or without having to apply corrections such as shape hints. Experimentation is the key. As long as both keyframes contain an editable shape, Flash will attempt to morph one object into another. Use any of Flash's drawing tools or import a vector shape from another vector drawing program. If you want to apply a shape tween to grouped artwork or a symbol, you can break apart the group or enter symbol editing mode and apply the shape tween to any editable shape in the symbol's Timeline. You can quickly view your animation by exporting it with the Test Movie command. By default, Flash loops animations in the Flash Player.

Create a Shape Tween

1. Create a new Flash document.

2. With any of Flash's drawing tools, draw a shape on the Stage at frame 1.

3. Select the first frame.

4. Click the **Insert** menu, and then click **Shape Tween**.

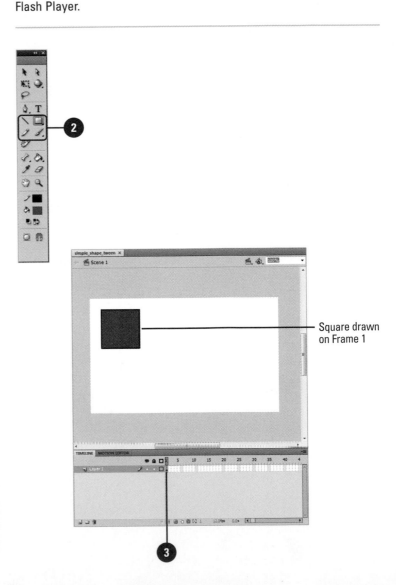

Square drawn on Frame 1

⑤ Select frame 10.

⑥ Click the **Insert** menu, point to **Timeline**, and then click **Blank Keyframe**.

Flash tints a shape-tweened span a pale green.

TIMESAVER *Press F7 to add a blank keyframe.*

⑦ With any of Flash's drawing tools, draw a different shape on the Stage at frame 10.

⑧ Click the **Control** menu, and then click **Test Movie** to test the animation.

The shape on frame 1 slowly transforms into the shape on frame 10.

TIMESAVER *Press ⌘+Return (Mac) or Ctrl+Enter (Win) to test your movie by viewing it in the Flash Player.*

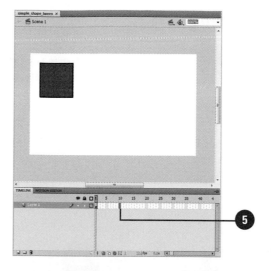

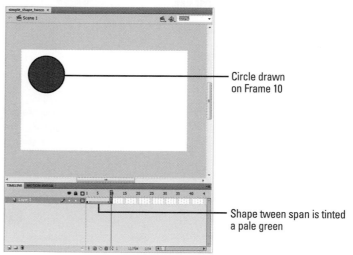

Circle drawn on Frame 10

Shape tween span is tinted a pale green

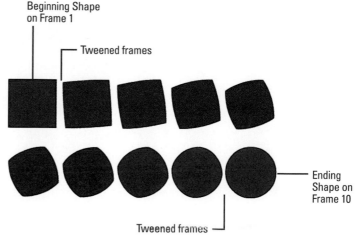

Beginning Shape on Frame 1

Tweened frames

Ending Shape on Frame 10

Tweened frames

Adding and Removing Keyframes from a Shape Tween

The procedure for adding or removing keyframes in a shape tween is similar to that of motion tweens except for one crucial difference. In a motion-tweened framespan you can drag the object on the Stage and a new keyframe is automatically created. In shape-tweened spans, the object is only selectable on a keyframe. To add additional locations or shape changes along a shape-tweened span, you must add the keyframe first and then edit the shape. You can do this by using the Add Keyframe function in the Insert menu. Once the keyframe is added, the shape at that point in the framespan becomes editable.

Add a Keyframe to a Shape Tween

1. Place the playhead between any two shape tweened keyframes.

2. Click the **Insert** menu, point to **Timeline**, and then click **Keyframe**.

   TIMESAVER *Press F6 to insert a keyframe.*

Keyframe is added

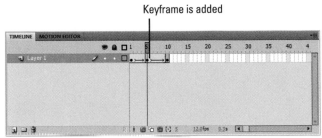

Remove a Keyframe from a Shape Tween

① Click on the keyframe you want to remove in the shape tween.

② Click the **Modify** menu, point to **Timeline**, and then click **Clear Keyframe**.

The keyframe is cleared but the duration of the tween is preserved. The first and last keyframes are automatically reconnected, and Flash redraws the tween.

TIMESAVER *Press Shift+F6 to remove the keyframe.*

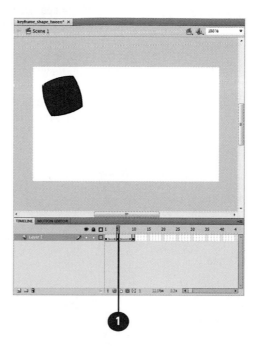

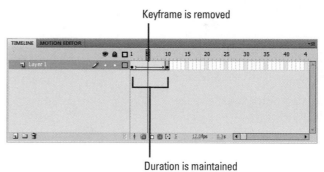

Keyframe is removed

Duration is maintained

Changing Shape Positions with Shape Tweening

To create a shape tween you need to draw or place an editable shape in a keyframe. Use any of Flash's drawing tools or import a vector shape from another vector drawing program. If you want to apply a shape tween to grouped artwork or a symbol, you can break apart the group or enter symbol editing mode and apply the shape tween to any editable shape in the symbol's Timeline. You can quickly view your animation by exporting it with the Test Movie command. By default, Flash loops animations in the Flash Player.

Animate a Ball with Shape Tweening

1. Create a new Flash document.

2. Select the **Oval** tool on the Tools panel.

3. Set the **Stroke Color** to None.

4. On the first frame, draw a circle on the left side of the Stage.

5. Select the first frame.

6. Click the **Insert** menu, and then click **Shape Tween**.

7. Click frame 20 in the Timeline.

8. Click the **Insert** menu, point to **Timeline**, and then click **Keyframe**.

    Flash tints a shape-tweened span a pale green.

    TIMESAVER Press F6 to add a keyframe.

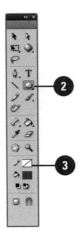

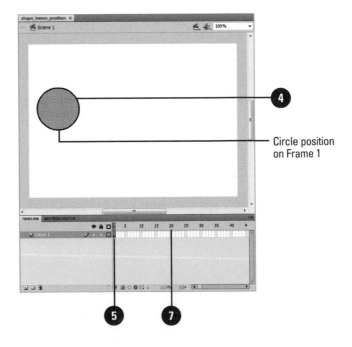

Circle position on Frame 1

9. Select the **Selection** tool on the Tools panel.

10. Select the circle on frame 20 and drag it to the right side of the Stage.

11. Click frame 40 in the Timeline, and then add another keyframe.

12. Select the circle shape on frame 40 and drag it back to the left side of the Stage.

13. Click the **Control** menu, and then click **Test Movie** to test the animation.

The ball animates back and forth across the screen.

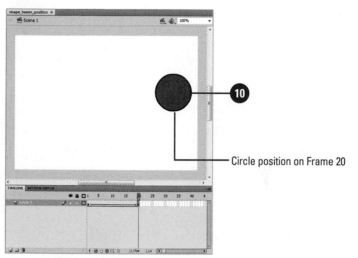

Circle position on Frame 20

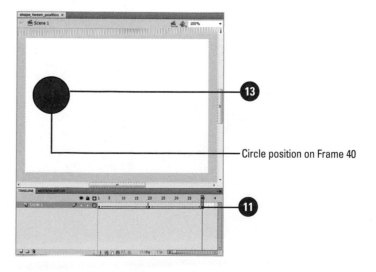

Circle position on Frame 40

Changing Shape Position and Form Simultaneously

Many of the same motion effects can be applied using either motion or shape tweening. What differentiates shape tweening from motion tweening is that shape tweening is applied to editable shapes. You can change the form of the shape on either keyframe and these changes will be applied gradually by Flash across the tween, slowly morphing one into the other. Additionally, you can combine movement with this tweening process, so your shape can change its shape as it changes its location.

Combine Shape Tweening and Movement in a Ball Animation

1. Create a shape tween of a moving ball that begins on the left side of the Stage, hits the right side of the Stage, and then returns to the left.

2. Click to place the playhead between the first and second keyframes in the shape tween.

3. Click the **Insert** menu, point to **Timeline**, and then click **Keyframe**.

4. Select the **Selection** tool on the Tools panel.

5. Place the pointer on the left edge of the shape and pull it to create a tail off the circle.

   The shape must be deselected on the Stage to pull the edges of the shape.

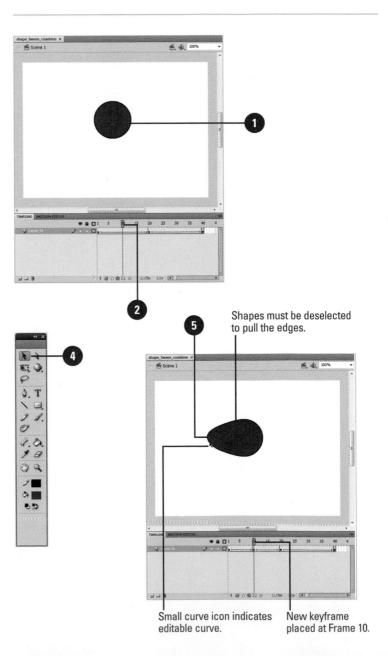

Shapes must be deselected to pull the edges.

Small curve icon indicates editable curve.

New keyframe placed at Frame 10.

6. Click to place the playhead between the second and third keyframes in the shape tween.

7. Click the **Insert** menu, point to **Timeline**, and then click **Keyframe**.

8. With the **Selection** tool still selected, place the pointer on the right edge of the shape and pull it to create a tail off the circle.

9. Click the **Control** menu, and then click **Test Movie** to test the animation.

The ball stretches as it animates back and forth across the screen.

See Also

See "Changing Shape Positions with Shape Tweening" on page 274 for information on animating a moving ball.

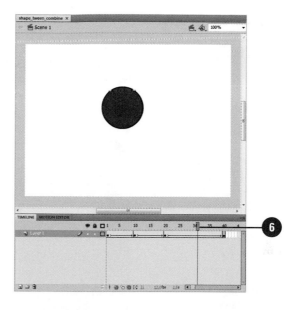

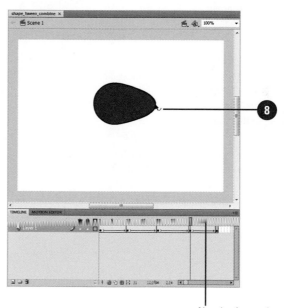

New keyframe placed at Frame 30.

Adjusting Shape Tween Properties

When shape tweens are applied to keyframes, the Property Inspector enables several options for controlling how Flash draws the tweened frames. Settings such as easing in and easing out enable you to control how the shape changes are distributed across the frames in the tween. Frame Blending allows you to set preferences to let Flash know which qualities to maintain during the tween.

Set Shape-Tween Properties

1. Click the **Window** menu, and then click **Properties** to open the Property Inspector.

2. Select a keyframe with shape tween applied.

3. Choose from the following settings:

   ◆ **Ease**. This sets the speed at which your object eases in or out of its motion. A positive value eases in, a negative value eases out.

   ◆ **Blend**. The Distributive option smoothes out the tweened shapes, while the Angular option preserves corners and straight lines in the shape tweens.

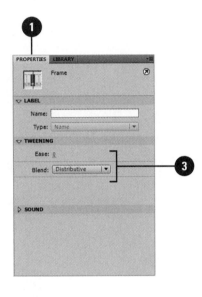

Changing Shape Tweening Color and Alpha Options

Because shape tweening can only be applied to editable shapes, you can't use the same color style effects that are available to instances. Instead, you must make these changes directly to the shape using the color palettes, the Color Mixer, or the Swatches Panel. When shape tweening is applied, differences in color and alpha are tweened along with any shape changes. This applies to strokes as well as fills.

Change Shape-Tween Color

1 Select the beginning or ending keyframe in a shape tween or select the shape on the Stage.

2 Click the **Window** menu, and then click **Color**, if necessary.

TIMESAVER *Press Shift+F9 to open the Color panel.*

3 Make changes to the shape's stroke and fill colors by entering values in the RGB and Alpha fields, or by using the list arrows to the right of these fields.

4 Click the **Control** menu, and then click **Test Movie** to test the color tween.

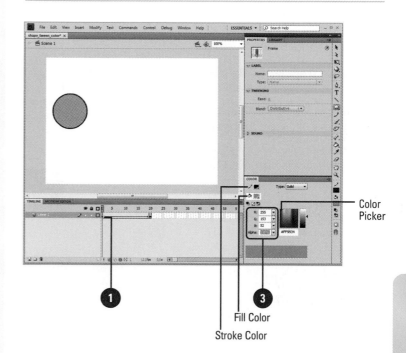

Color Picker

Fill Color

Stroke Color

Did You Know?

You can use any palette available to change the color of a shape in a tween. In addition to the Color Mixer, there are palettes located on the Tools panel, Property Inspector, and Swatches panel.

See Also

See "Modifying Instance Color Styles and Blends" on page 158-159 for more information on working with color and alpha options.

Using Shape Hints

Sometimes it isn't possible to predict how some, more complicated, shapes will tween. To exercise greater control over the tweening process, you can set shape hints to guide how Flash draws the in-between frames. You simply specify a beginning shape hint and then a corresponding end shape hint. In this way, Flash will know which parts of the shape in the first keyframe will transform into which parts in the end keyframe. Even with shape hints enabled, the results can be unpredictable, but you will have a greater control over the process.

Set Shape Hints

1. Create a shape tween of a simple shape into a complex shape.

2. Click to place the playhead on the first frame of the shape tween.

3. Click the **Modify** menu, point to **Shape**, and then click **Add Shape Hint**.

    A small red, circle with a small letter on it appears in the center of the shape. The first letter is "a". Shape hints appear in alphabetical order "a, b, c...". You can use up to 26 hints in one tween.

    TIMESAVER *Press Shift+⌘+H (Mac) or Ctrl+Shift+H (Win) to insert a shape hint.*

4. Drag the shape hint to an area of the shape you want to control.

5. Click to place the playhead on the last frame of the shape tween.

    The corresponding shape hint appears as a small green circle with a corresponding letter that matches the beginning hint.

Did You Know?

You can show all shape hints. Click the View menu, and then click Show Shape Hints.

Beginning shape hint "a"   Place start shape hints on problem areas.

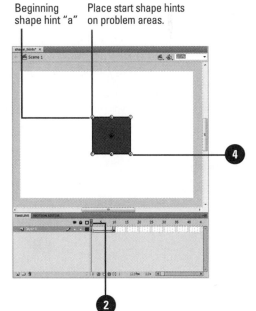

End shape hint "a"   Place end shape hints on corresponding areas.

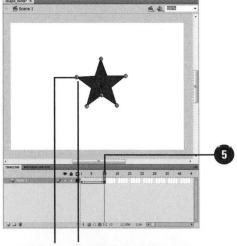

6 Drag the corresponding end shape hints to the part of the shape that corresponds to the placement of the beginning shape hint.

"a" should correspond with "a", "b" should correspond with "b", etc.

7 Move the playhead back to the first frame.

8 Repeat steps 3, 4, 5, 6, and 7 until you have set and placed shape hints on all areas of the shape you want to control.

9 Click the **Control** menu, and then click **Test Movie** to test the animation.

The shape hints help make complex shape tweens more predictable.

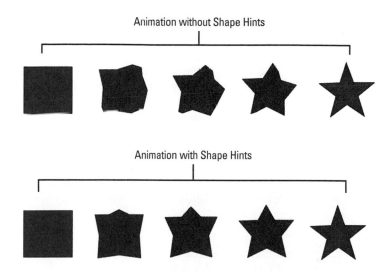

Animation without Shape Hints

Animation with Shape Hints

Did You Know?

You can remove shape hints. Drag shape hints off the Stage or click the Modify menu, point to Shape, and then click Remove All Hints.

You should place your shape hints consecutively in a clockwise or counter-clockwise direction. Placing shape hints out of order can confuse Flash and often produces unwanted results.

Creating Animation Using ActionScript

In addition to creating animation using the Timeline and Property Inspector, you can also use ActionScript to animate movie clips, buttons, text, and components. You can animate any instance name with ActionScript. For an ActionScript 3.0 example, see Project 4, "Modifying an Object with ActionScript on page 515. For ActionScript 2.0, you can animate an object over time and change any ActionScript property, such as scale, rotation, color, and transparency. ActionScript provides two events that work well for animation: onEnterFrame and setInterval. The onEnterFrame event is a continuously executing event based on the frame rate of your movie until you stop (delete) it. The setInterval event is a continuously executing event for only a certain period of time. The one disadvantage of these actions is the large use of memory and CPU, so you need to clear it.

◆ **onEnterFrame event.** The following example is a frame script that animates a movie clip to the right until it reaches the position it should be in:

```
myMovieClip.onEnterFrame=function()
{
        if(this._x<300)
          {
                  this._x+=10;
          }
        else
          {
delete this. onEnterFrame;
```

◆ **setInterval event.** This event requires two parameters: funtionName and an interval (amount of time in milliseconds between executions). If your interval is smaller than your frame rate, the screen cannot refresh. If your interval is greater than your frame rate, it executes as close as possible. The following example moves a TextArea component to the right every 10 milliseconds until it has reached its final location:

```
myInternval=setInterval(textAreaMove, 10);
function textAreamove()  {
        if (textAreaInstance._x<300)  {
                  textAreaInstance._x += 10;
        } else
        clearInterval(myInterval);
        }
}
```

Using Inverse Kinematics

 FL 2.3, 3.7

Inverse Kinematic (IK) (**New!**) allows you to stretch and bend shape objects and link groups of symbol instances to make them move together in naturalistic ways using an internal structure of bones to create character animation.

You can add bones to the interior of a shape or to separate symbol instances. When you move one bone, the other connected bones move in relation to the one that initially moved. A chain of bones is called an **armature**, which is either linear or branched in structure.

There are two types of Inverse Kinematic animation: those with symbols and those with shapes. For the symbol type, you link them together as a chain. For the shape type, you add bones inside the shape.

When you add bones to a shape or symbol instance, Flash creates a new layer called a **pose layer**. For a shape, Flash also converts the selected shapes and bones into an IK shape object. Each pose layer can contain only one armature. The first bone in an armature is the root bone. It appears with a circle around the head of the bone. Each bone has a head, the round end, and a tail, known as the pointed end.

After you add bones to an armature, you can change the position and length of a bone, delete bones, and edit objects containing bones.

When you're ready to animate an armature, all you need to do is add frames to the pose layer and reposition the armature on the Stage to create a keyframe. Keyframes in pose layers are called **poses**. To insert a frame in a pose layer, right-click (Win) or Option-click (Mac) a frame in a pose layer to the right of any existing frames, and then click Insert Frame. To add a pose to a frame, right-click (Win) or Option-click (Mac) the frame in the pose layer, and then click Insert Pose. After you insert a pose, you can use the Selection tool to change the configuration of the armature. If you want to change the length of the animation, drag the last frame of the pose layer to the right or left in the Timeline to add or remove frames.

You can adjust the speed of an armature animation in frame around each pose by applying an easing motion. To add easing to frames in a pose layer, click a frame in a pose layer, open the Property Inspector, click the Ease popup, select an ease option, and then enter an ease strength value (0-100, where 0 is no easing and 100 is the most easing).

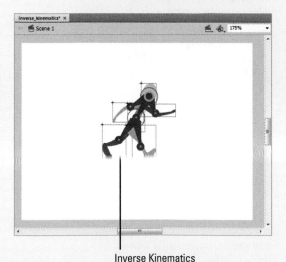

Inverse Kinematics

Adding Bones to an Armature

FL 2.3, 3.7

With Inverse Kinematic (IK) (**New!**), you can use bones to create two types of IK animations: those with symbols and those with shapes. For the symbol type, you link them together as a chain. For the shape type, you add bones inside the shape. When you add bones to a shape or symbol instance, Flash creates a new pose layer. For a shape, Flash also converts the selected shapes and bones into an IK shape object. The first bone in an armature is the root bone. It appears with a circle around the head of the bone. Each bone has a head, the round end, and a tail, known as the pointed end.

Add Bones to a Shape

1 Create one or more filled shapes and arrange them the configuration you want.

2 Select the entire shape on the Stage.

3 Click the **Bone** tool on the Tools panel.

4 Click inside the shape, and then drag to another location within the shape.

While you drag, a bone appears. When you connect the points, a solid bone appears between them. Flash converts the selected shape into an IK shape object and moves it to a new pose layer in the Timeline.

5 To add another bone, drag from the tail of the first bone to another location in the shape.

As you add bone instances, Flash moves each one to a new pose layer in the Timeline.

6 To create a branched armature, click the head of an existing bone, and then drag to create a new branch of the first bone.

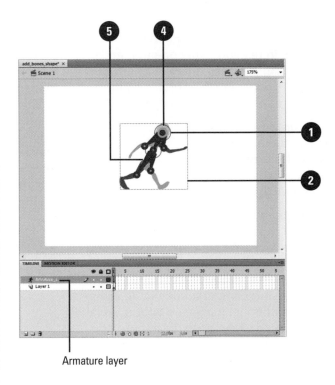

Armature layer

Add Bones to a Symbol

① Arrange the instances in the configuration you want.

② Click the **Bone** tool on the Tools panel.

③ Click the symbol instance that you want as the root or head of the armature.

④ Drag the symbol instance to another symbol instance to connect it.

While you drag, a bone appears. When you connect the symbols, a solid bone appears between the symbols. As you add bone instances, Flash moves each instance to a new pose layer in the Timeline.

⑤ To add another bone, drag from the tail of the first bone to the next symbol instance you want to add to the armature.

⑥ To create a branched armature, click the head of an existing bone, and then drag to create a new branch of the first bone.

You can add as many branches as you want.

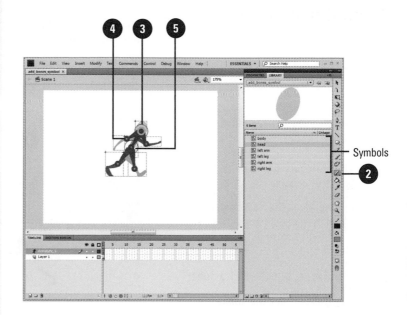

Symbols

Did You Know?

You can move an armature. Select the IK shape object with the Selection tool, and then drag any of the bones to move it.

Editing Armatures and Bones

FL 2.3, 3.7

Edit Armatures, Bones, and Related Objects

1. Select the bones and associated objects you want:

    ◆ **Bone.** Click the **Selection** tool, and then click a bone. You can Shift-click to select multiple bones.

    ◆ **Armature.** Double-click a bone.

    ◆ **IK Shape.** Click the shape.

    ◆ **Symbol Instance.** Click the instance.

2. To move bones, do any of the following:

    ◆ **Bone.** Drag a bone.

    ◆ **IK Shape.** Select the shape, and then change its X and Y position in the Property Inspector.

    ◆ **Bone End in IK Shape.** Click the **Subselection** tool, and then drag the end of the bone.

    ◆ **Bone Joint, Head, or Tail.** Use the Transform panel to move the transformation point of the symbol instance.

    ◆ **Rotate a Bone.** Shift-drag a bone to rotate it with its child bones with out moving the parent bone.

After you add bones to an armature, you can change the position and length of a bone, delete bones, and edit objects containing bones (**New!**). An armature can only be edited in pose layers that contain an initial pose in the first frame in which the armature appears in the Timeline. To edit the armature, you need to delete any additional poses after the first frame of the armature.

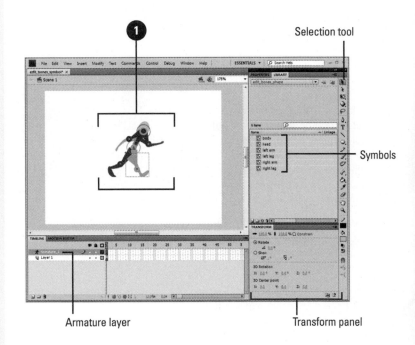

Selection tool

Symbols

Armature layer

Transform panel

3 To delete bones, do either of the following:

- ◆ **Bone.** Select the bones you want to delete, and then press Delete.

- ◆ **IK Shape or Symbol Instance.** Select the shape or symbol, click the **Modify** menu, and then click **Break Apart**.

4 To edit an IK shape, do any of the following:

- ◆ **Move the Position of a Bone.** Drag a bone endpoint to move the position of a bone without changing the IK shape.

- ◆ **Display Control Points of the Boundary.** Click the stroke of the IK shape.

- ◆ **Move Control Point.** Drag the control point.

- ◆ **Add Control Point.** Click a part of the stroke without any control points. You can also use the Add Anchor Point tool on the Tools panel.

- ◆ **Delete Control Points.** Click a control point to select it, and then press Delete. You can also use the Delete Anchor Point tool on the Tools panel.

10 To set motion constraints, open the Property Inspector, and then specify the options you want to move or constrain joints, disable bone rotation around joints, constrain the rotation of a bone, make a bone stationary, or limit the motion speed of a bone.

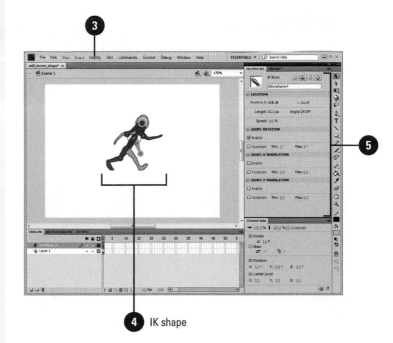

4 IK shape

Binding Bones

When the stroke of an IK shape doesn't distort in the way you want, you can use the Bind tool (**New!**) to edit the connections between individual bones and shape control points to create the appearance you desire. By default, the control points of an IK shape are connected to the bone that is nearest them. The Bind tool allows you to change it. You can bind multiple control points to a bone and multiple bones to a control point.

Bind Bones to Shape Points

◆ **Highlight Control Points Connected to a Bone.** Click the **Bind** tool, and then click a bone.

The connected points are highlighted in yellow while the selected bone is highlighted in red.

◆ **Add Control Points.** Select a bone, and then Shift-click an unhighlighted control point.

◆ **Remove Control Points.** Ctrl-click (Win) or Option-click (Mac) a control point that is highlighted in yellow.

◆ **Highlight Bones Connected to a Control Point.** Click the **Bind** tool, and then click the control point.

The connected bones are highlighted in yellow while the selected control point is highlighted in red.

◆ **Add Other Bones to a Control Point.** Select a control point, and then Shift-click a bone.

◆ **Remove a Bone from a Control Point.** Select a control point, and then Ctrl-click (Win) or Option-click (Mac) a bone that is highlighted in yellow.

Binded bones to shape points

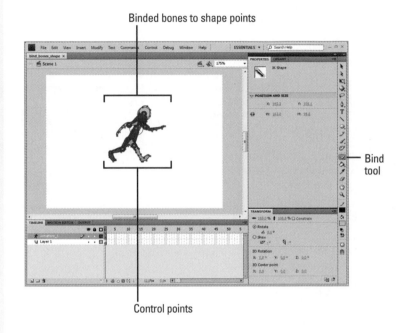

Bind tool

Control points

Creating Masks

11

Introduction

You can create mask layers to show and hide parts of your artwork on the Stage. A mask works like a window blocking out everything but a certain area that you define. Any shape, symbol or text object can be used as a mask. The shape you place in a mask layer defines the area that will be visible in the linked layers below it. You can animate a mask to reveal the content on a layer in stages or animate the art in the layer beneath the mask. It is useful for spotlighting and controlling the shape of the viewable area. Masks are great tools for keeping the boundaries of the art on your Stage neat and controlled. They are also useful for cropping and experimenting with different borders and layouts, because you don't have to edit your art, you simply edit the mask. When creating a mask layer, it is important not to mix elements. For example, don't use an editable shape and a group on the same mask layer group everything together or break the groups into editable shapes. For the most consistent results, use ungrouped, editable shapes in the mask layer.

What You'll Do

Understand Masks

Create a Mask Layer

Draw a Mask

Activate a Mask

Edit a Mask

Remove a Mask

Add Layers to a Mask

Animate a Mask Layer

Understanding Masks

You use a mask in Flash to control what is viewable on a layer. Whatever you paint or draw onto a mask layer defines the viewable area on any layer it is linked to. Essentially, the shape you place on the mask layer acts like a window to the layers linked beneath it.

To link a layer, you simply drag it into the linked set. When a layer is linked to a mask it displays a tinted icon and is indented underneath the mask layer. Masks are useful for cropping artwork on the Stage, and animated masks can create interesting visual effects.

Draw any shape or shapes on a mask layer to limit the visible area of any layer linked to it.

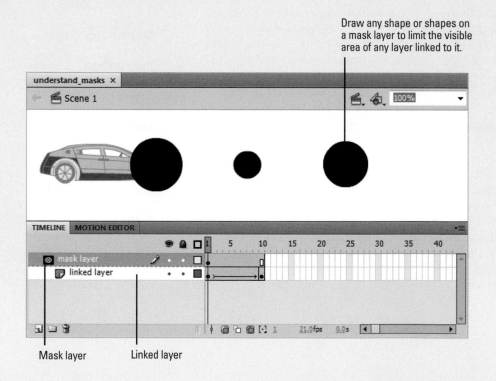

Mask layer   Linked layer

The mask layer and all linked layers
must be locked to activate the mask.

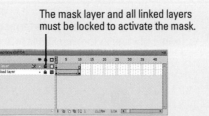

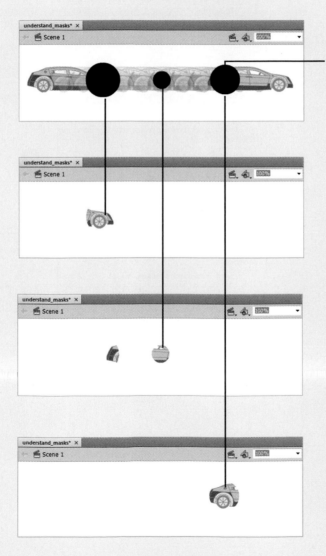

Shapes drawn on the
mask layer define the
visible area.

Creating a Mask Layer

Any layer can be converted into a mask layer. A **mask layer** only affects the linked layers beneath it, and there is no limit to the number of layers that can be included. Once a mask layer is created, you can drag other layers beneath it to link them. It is important to keep in mind that too much masking can affect performance in the Flash Player, especially when objects in the masked layers or the mask itself are animated.

Create a Mask Layer

1. Create a new Layer in the Timeline or select an existing one.

   The layer you select will be the one converted into a mask. If you want to mask the selected layer, create a new layer above this layer and select it.

2. Click the **Modify** menu, point to **Timeline**, and then click **Layer Properties**.

3. Click the **Mask** option from the Layer Type list.

4. Click **OK**.

   A blue masking icon appears on the layer.

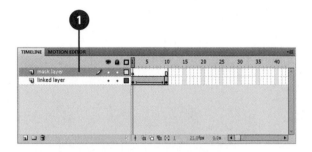

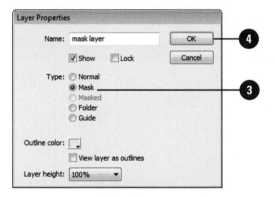

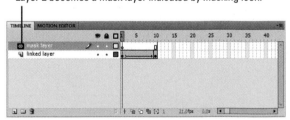

Layer 2 becomes a mask layer indicated by masking icon.

5 Click the layer name of the layer directly beneath the mask layer, and then drag the layer slightly up to link it to the mask.

TIMESAVER *Press Control+click (Mac) or right-click (Win) the Layer Name area of the layer you want to convert into a mask, and then click Mask. When you use this method, Flash converts the layer into a mask and then automatically links it to the layer directly beneath it.*

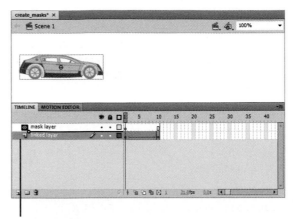

Drag layer 1 slightly up until the gray bar appears. This links it to the mask layer.

Mask layer

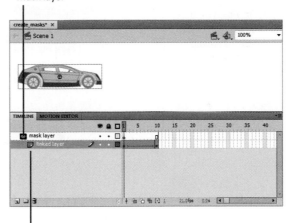

Layer is linked to the mask layer. It appears in the Timeline indented under the mask layer with a tinted icon.

Drawing a Mask

You can use any filled shape as a mask. Flash ignores gradients, lines, and the content in bitmaps—in all cases it just deals with the whole shape. Use any of Flash's drawing tools to create a shape that will define the viewable area of the linked layers below. Keep in mind that mixing elements at different levels (editable shapes and symbols, for example) can produce unexpected results. Try to use only one type of element in any one mask: editable shapes, symbols, or groups.

Create a Mask Layer

1 Click to select the mask layer.

2 If the mask layer is locked, click on the **lock** icon in the Lock Layer column to unlock it.

3 Draw a shape with any of Flash's drawing tools or drag a symbol from the Library.

The area of the shape drawn, or symbol used, is the area that will be the visible area of the linked layer(s) beneath the layer mask.

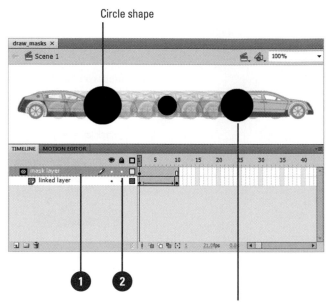

Circle shape

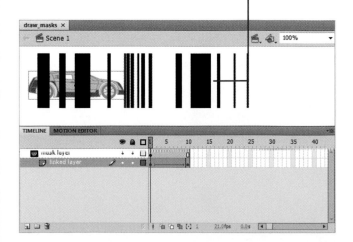

Any shape or shapes drawn on the mask layer defines what is visible in the linked layers beneath.

Activating a Mask

To activate a mask, you simply lock it and any of the linked layers beneath it. Linked layers are indented in the Layer Name region and have tinted blue icons. You can lock and unlock a mask and its layers to edit them and see the effects of the mask in the Flash development environment. You can also use the Test Movie command to view the masking effects in the Flash Player.

Activate a Mask

1. Open a document with a masked layer.

2. Click the **black dot** in the lock column of the mask layer to lock it.

3. Click this dot on each linked layer to lock all of them and see the masking effect.

   TIMESAVER *You can click the Lock icon at the top of the lock layers column to lock all the layers in your Timeline simultaneously.*

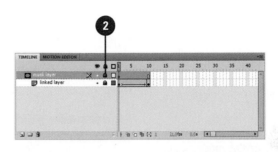

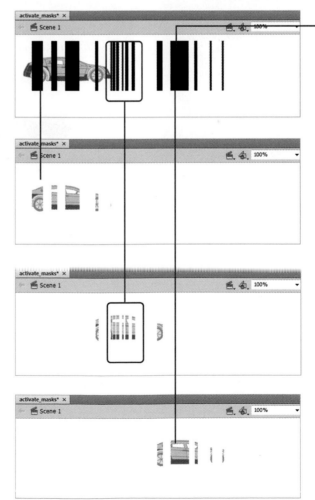

Shapes drawn on the mask layer define the visible area.

Editing a Mask

Masks are editable. Which type of element you are using in the mask layer defines the procedure for editing: editable shapes can be modified with Flash's drawing tools, while groups and symbols must be edited in their own editing modes. Regardless, Flash only concerns itself with the fill area. Changes to color, alpha, and other such attributes are ignored. To edit a mask, you must first unlock it. To view your changes, simply re-lock the mask layer and all of its linked layers.

Edit a Mask

1. If the mask layer is locked, click on the **lock** icon in the Lock Layer column to unlock the layer and enable it for editing.

2. Edit the shape of the mask or, if using a group or symbol, enter the group or symbol's editing mode.

3. Re-lock the mask layer and any linked layers to view changes.

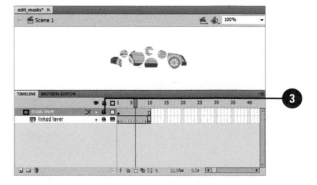

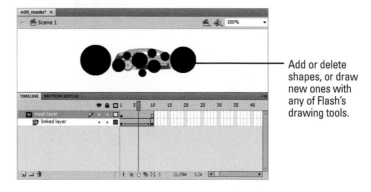

Add or delete shapes, or draw new ones with any of Flash's drawing tools.

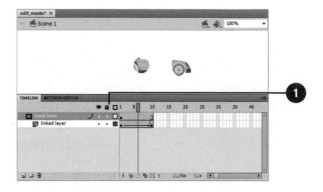

Removing a Mask

To remove a mask layer entirely, select it and then click the Delete Layer icon. You can also convert a mask layer back to a normal layer in the Layer Properties dialog box. Additionally, you can remove linked layers from a mask layer set by dragging them out of the indented set.

Remove a Mask

1. Click on the mask layer to select it.

2. Click the **Modify** menu, point to **Timeline**, and then click **Layer Properties**.

3. Click the **Normal** option from the Layer Type list.

4. Click **OK**.

   The mask layer is converted into a normal layer.

   TIMESAVER *Press Control+click (Mac) or right-click (Win) the Layer Name area of the mask layer you want to convert back into a normal layer, and then click Mask to deselect it.*

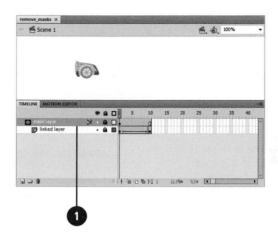

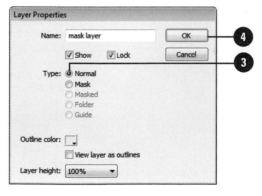

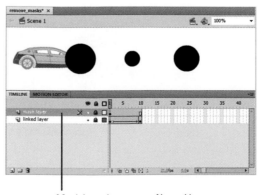

Mask layer becomes a Normal layer.

Adding Layers to a Mask

Add layers to an existing mask by dragging them to any region within the masked layer hierarchy. Simply drag it between layers already linked, drag it under the mask layer, or drag it slightly up toward the bottom of a masked layer set. There is no limit to the number of layers that can be contained in a mask. Additionally, you can remove linked layers by dragging them out and above the mask layer set.

Link Additional Layers to a Mask

① To add additional layers to a mask, do one of the following:

◆ Click and drag the layer below the mask.

◆ Click and drag the layer until it touches the bottom of a layer already linked to the mask.

Did You Know?

You can change the order of the linked layers. Masked layers behave the same as other layers. Click and drag the layers to reorder them in the indented set.

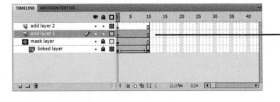

Any layer can be added to an existing mask layer set.

To add a layer to the bottom of the mask set, click and drag slightly below the set to link it.

To add a layer to the top of or between the linked layers of the mask set, click and drag the layer into the indented set.

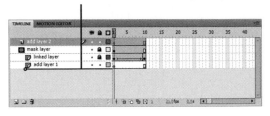

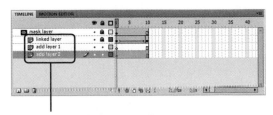

Layers linked to the mask.

Remove a Linked Layer from a Mask

① Click on the linked layer, and then drag it above the masked layer.

The layer will no longer be linked to the mask and the indentation disappears.

Select the layer you want to remove.

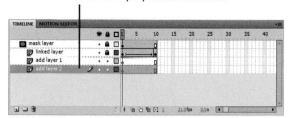

Select the layer you want to remove. Drag it above the mask layer until a gray bar appears.

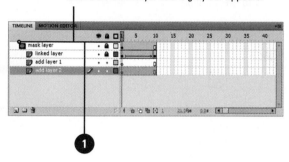

Layer is no longer linked to the mask.

Animating a Mask Layer

To create special effects such as a spotlighting effect or a gradual reveal of artwork on the Stage, you can animate a mask. Use any form of animation such as frame-by-frame animation or a shape or motion tween. The path of the shape or object on the mask layer will reveal the art below as it passes over it. Transforms to scale and position work well as well as shape tweens to editable objects. Other effects such as color and alpha will be ignored.

Animate a Mask

1. Place artwork in a linked layer.

2. Click on the first frame of the layer's mask layer in the Timeline.

3. Do one of the following:
   - Draw a shape on the Stage with any of Flash's drawing tools.
   - Drag an instance of a symbol from the Library.

4. Select the first frame with the shape or symbol.

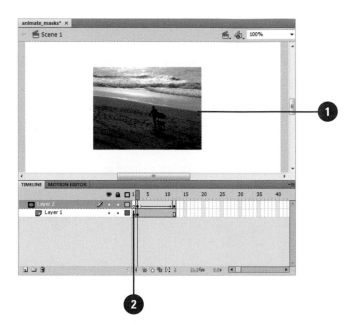

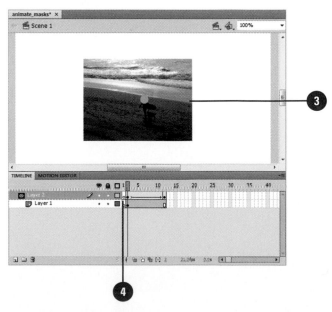

5. Click the Insert menu, and then click **Classic Tween** (when using symbols) or **Shape Tween** (when using editable shapes).

6. Click frame 12 in the Timeline.

7. Click the **Insert** menu, point to **Timeline**, and then click **Keyframe**.

   TIMESAVER *Press F6 to add a keyframe.*

8. Transform the object with any of Flash's editing procedures: scale, skew, position, or in the case of shape tweening, edit the shape of the object.

9. Lock the mask layer and linked layer to see the effect.

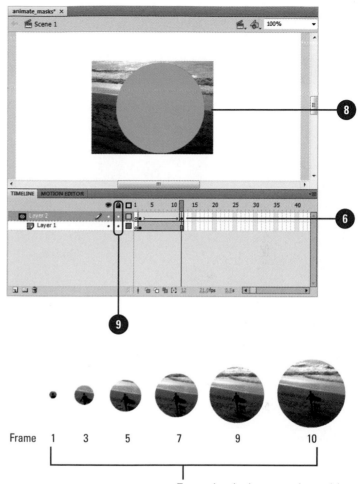

Frame   1   3   5   7   9   10

Tweened scale changes on the mask layer reveal the photograph located on the linked layer beneath the mask in stages.

Working with Sounds

12

Introduction

Incorporating audio can really bring life to a Flash movie; however, the effect is very subtle. For example, most people would not be able to tell you the background music playing behind their favorite movie, but try leaving the sound out and they'll immediately notice. This makes audio a powerful influence on the viewers of your Flash movies. Adobe understands the power of audio and gives you the ability to import audio in a variety of formats, including ASND, MP3, WAV, AIF, and AU. If you want more control over your audio, you can edit sounds in Adobe Soundbooth CS4 directly from Flash (**New!**). You can use on-clip controls to make fast edits and intuitive, task-based tools to clean up recordings, polish voice-overs, customize music, modify sound effects, apply high-quality filters, and much more.

There are two types of sounds: **event** sounds and **stream** sounds. An event sound needs to download completely before it starts to play, while a stream sound starts to play as soon as enough data downloads for the first few frames. Event sounds continue to play until they are done or you explicitly stop them. Steam sounds are synchronized to the Timeline for playing on a web site.

Flash audio can be controlled using Flash's version of JavaScript, called ActionScript, and it even gives you the ability to load streaming MP3 files. Add to that the ability to choose between mono and stereo, and you can further reduce the size of your audio files (mono audio files are half the size of stereo). The one drawback to using audio is that it produces a much larger file (even compressed audio files are relatively large), but even this can be reduced to a minimum by using shared audio libraries. Since audio files create large Flash movies, use sounds when they are necessary to the design of the Flash movie, and remember that sometimes silence is golden.

What You'll Do

Import Audio

Use Audio on the Timeline

Sync Sounds to the Timeline

Add Effects and Loop Sounds

Load a Sound from a Shared Library

Use Audio with ActionScript

Play and Stop Sounds

Load a Streaming MP3 File

Publish Documents Containing Audio

Edit Sounds

Importing Audio

 FL 3.4

When working with Flash, understand that Flash will let you import audio in a variety of formats. However, Flash has no way to record or create sounds; you can do it with Adobe Soundbooth. Therefore, audio must come from external sources. You can use the sample Sounds library that comes with Flash (**New!**) or conduct audio searches on the Internet using your favorite search engine to find a lot of audio files. One other consideration is creating your own audio, using your computer, an attached microphone, and a bit of imagination. Flash supports the following sound formats: ASND (from Adobe Soundbooth) (**New!**), WAV, AIFF, MP3, Sound Designer II (Mac), Sound Only QuickTime Movies, AU, and System 7 Sounds (Mac). When you import an audio file to Flash's Stage, you will first need to have a specific layer and keyframe selected. When you work on a Flash project, it might be beneficial to bring audio files directly into Flash's Library. That way you have easy access to them when needed. Any unused audio files are purged when you publish the Flash movie.

Import Audio Files to the Stage

1. Select a keyframe in the Timeline in which you want the audio file placed.

   IMPORTANT *You should always place audio files in a separate layer. This gives you easy access and control over the audio file once it's been placed on the Stage.*

2. Click the **File** menu, point to **Import**, and then click **Import To Stage**.

3. Navigate to the drive or folder location with the files you want.

4. Select one or more audio files to import.

   To select more than one file, click an audio file, then hold down the Shift key and click another file to select contiguous audio files, or hold down the ⌘ (Mac) or the Ctrl key (Win), and then click to select non-contiguous audio files.

5. Click **Import** (Mac) or **Open** (Win).

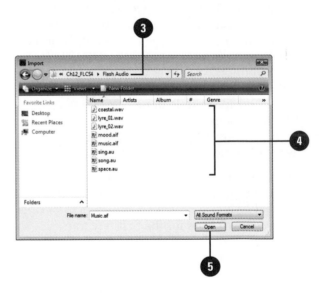

For Your Information

Using QuickTime for Sound

In addition, many formats that are not easy to import can be converted using the QuickTime plug-in. Point your browser to *www.quicktime.com* and download this free plug-in. You can also purchase QuickTime Pro to perform a wider range of conversions. In addition, you can perform limited conversions for free at *www.itunes.com*.

Import Audio Files to the Library

1. Open and select the library where you want to import your audio files.

2. Click the **File** menu, point to **Import**, and then click **Import To Library**.

3. Navigate to the drive or folder location with the files you want.

4. Select the audio file or files you want moved into the Library.

5. Click **Import To Library** (Mac) or **Open** (Win).

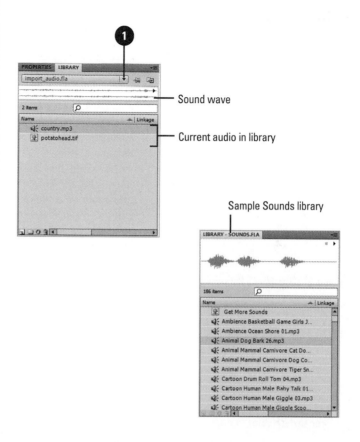

Sound wave

Current audio in library

Sample Sounds library

Did You Know?

You can sync sound to a Timeline animation. Select the sound on the Stage, and then change the Sync option on the Properties panel to Stream. Flash will force the animation to sync to the timing of the audio file even if it has to drop video frames to keep up.

See Also

See "Using Audio on the Timeline" on page 306-307 for information on importing audio using an external library.

For Your Information

Audio files

Audio files are embedded directly into the Flash movie. When you publish the Flash movie, by default, all audio files are embedded with the movie. Therefore, the Flash .swf file becomes a self-contained movie file without the need to access the original audio files.

Using Audio on the Timeline

 FL 3.4

Once you've imported audio files into the active document's Library, it's a simple matter to transfer the file to the Timeline. Flash's Timeline is actually a frame-by-frame representation of the Stage. For example, if you select frame 23 on the Timeline, the Stage displays the contents of the 23rd frame on the Stage. Audio, however, does not have a visible Stage object, so when you add an audio file to the Timeline, the effects are only apparent on the Timeline, not the Stage. Flash's Library holds all of the audio files that you've imported into the active Flash document. No matter how many times you use that audio file in the source document, Flash only needs to save it one time in the published Flash movie. In addition the main Library, you can also use audio from the Sounds library that comes built-in to Flash (**New!**). One of Flash's powerful features is the ability to use audio files from other Flash libraries. External Flash libraries are simply Flash source documents, which have an active Library. This gives you the ability to create libraries of audio files and use them over and over again.

Add Audio Using the Library or Sound Library

1. Open the library that you want to use:

   ◆ **Library.** Click the **Window** menu, and then click **Library**.

   TIMESAVER Press ⌘+L (Mac) or Ctrl+L (Win) to open the Library panel.

   ◆ **Sound Library.** Click the **Window** menu, point to **Common Libraries**, and then click **Sounds**.

2. Select a layer and keyframe in the Timeline in which you want the audio file placed.

3. Drag the audio file from the Library directly onto the Stage.

   Flash places the audio file in the selected keyframe.

Library

Sound library

Audio file placed on the keyframe.

Add Audio Using an External Library

1. Click the **File** menu, point to **Import**, and then click **Open External Library**.

2. Navigate to the drive or folder location with the files you want.

3. Select a Flash document that contains an active Library.

4. Click **Open**.

5. Drag items from the external Library directly to the Stage.

6. Drag items from the external Library to the active document's Library.

IMPORTANT When you drag an object from an external Library onto the Stage of the active Flash document, it is automatically added to the active document's Library.

Did You Know?

You can use a single Library panel for all open documents. When you open multiple documents, Flash now consolidates all the libraries into a single Library panel. Click the popup button (located at the top of the Library panel) to select from any available library.

See Also

See "Working with the Library Panel" on page 136 for information on using the single library panel and other options.

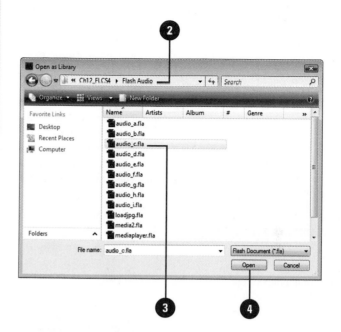

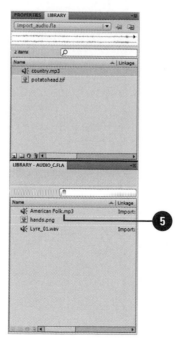

Loading a Sound from a Shared Library

FL 3.4

By default, Flash embeds audio files directly into the published (.swf) file. You have the option of loading audio files from a common Library. This gives you the advantage of using the same sounds in several Flash movies at the same time. For example, you create a Web site using fifteen separate Flash movie files, and each one uses the same background music. Rather than embed the same sound fifteen times, you can simply load the sound, when needed, from a common Library. Shared libraries are simple Flash documents that are set up to share their files between several Flash movies. The process is easy, and the rewards are great, and you don't increase the file size of Flash movies using shared Library elements. Once you've created and defined a Flash document as a shared Library, you can use the items in other Flash movies without increasing the size of the Flash published .swf file.

Create a Shared Audio Library

1. Create a new Flash document.

2. Add the audio files to the document's Library. They do not have to be placed on the Stage.

3. Click the **File** menu, and then click **Save**. Use a distinctive name for the source document.

4. Select an audio file in the Library.

5. Click the **Library Options** button, and then click **Linkage**.

6. Select the **Export For Runtime Sharing** check box.

   ◆ If the check box is not available, clear the **Import for runtime sharing** check box.

7. Enter a distinctive name for the Identifier field or use the default.

8. Enter the name of the published document into the URL field.

9. Click **OK**.

   Repeat steps 4 through 9 until all the audio files are correctly linked.

10. Click the **File** menu, and then click **Publish** to create the Flash .swf file.

11. Close the original source file.

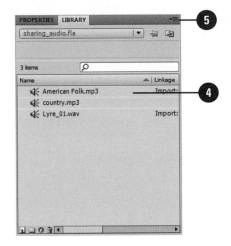

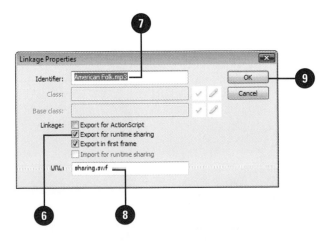

Work with Shared Audio Libraries

1. Click the **File** menu, point to **Import**, and then click **Open External Library**.

2. Select the shared Library, and then click **Open**.

   The items in the external Library will be grayed out, indicated they are sharable items.

3. Drag the audio files from the external Library to the Library of the active document.

4. To display or change link properties for an audio, double-click the audio icon in the Library, click **Advanced** (if necessary), view or change link options, and then click **OK**.

5. When you publish the Flash .swf file, the audio files will be drawn from the common Library, without increasing the size of the Flash movie.

Did You Know?

A Flash Library can be shared with other designers. Since a Library is simply a Flash movie with Library elements, you can create common libraries of often-used elements, and then give them to other designers. When you're working with two or more designers, this is a great way to maintain consistency on a complex project.

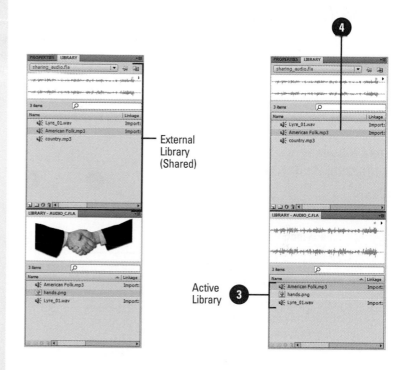

External Library (Shared)

Active Library

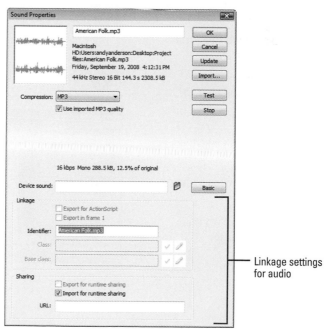

Linkage settings for audio

Using Audio with ActionScript

Sound is a great motivator. For example, a particular piece of music can make you happy, or it can make you sad. In addition, sounds can pull out childhood memories and stir emotions. Sound is a powerful tool, however, different people react differently to sounds, therefore it's important that you think carefully about the sounds you add to your movies. It's equally important to understand how you can control your movies using using ActionScript 3.0 code or ActionScript Behaviors in ActionScript 2.0.

Load a Sound from the Library with ActionScript 3.0

1. Create or open a Flash document (ActionScript 3.0).

2. Click the **Window** menu, click **Library** to open the Library panel, and then select an audio file from the available Library items.

3. Right-click (Win) or Command-click (Mac) the audio sound, and then click **Properties**. Click **Advanced**, if necessary.

4. Enter a distinctive name for the Identifier field or use the default.

5. Select the **Export For ActionScript** check box.

6. Leave the other fields at their default values, and then click **OK**.

7. Click Frame 1 in a layer.

8. Click the **Window** menu, and then click **Actions**.

9. Type the ActionScript code shown in the illustration:

10. Click the **Control** menu, and then click **Test Movie** to test the ActionScript.

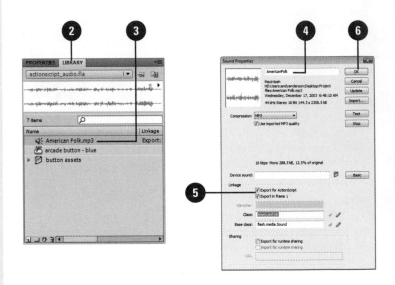

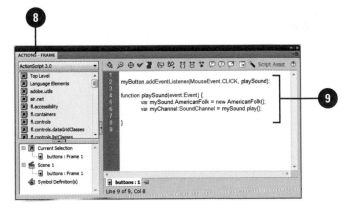

Load a Sound from the Library with an ActionScript Behavior

1. Create or open a Flash document (ActionScript 2.0).

2. Click the **Window** menu, click **Library** to open the Library panel, and then select an audio file from the available Library items.

3. Click the **Library Options** button, and then click **Properties**. Click **Advanced**, if necessary.

4. Select the **Export For ActionScript** check box.

5. Enter a distinctive name for the Identifier field or use the default.

6. Leave the other fields at their default values, and then click **OK**.

7. Click the **Window** menu, and then click **Behaviors** to open the Behaviors panel.

8. Select a button object on the Stage or Timeline keyframe.

9. Click the plus (+) sign, located in the upper-left portion of the Behaviors panel, point to **Sound**, and then click **Load Sound From Library**.

10. Enter the name of the audio file in the Linkage ID field.

11. Enter a unique name in the instance field.

12. Select the **Play This Sound When Loaded** check box.

13. Click **OK**.

14. Select an Event to trigger the sound. If the audio file was added to a Timeline frame, the event field will be disabled.

15. Click the **Control** menu, and then click **Test Movie** to test the ActionScript.

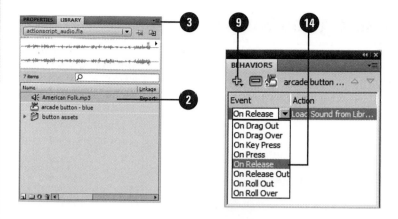

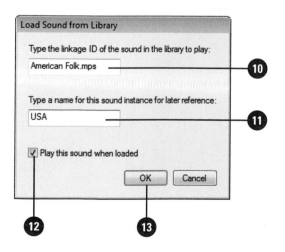

Playing and Stopping Sounds

Whenever you place sounds in a Flash document, it's nice to give your visitors control over the playing and stopping of a specific sound. Giving visitors control over a Flash movie gives them more confidence. Most marketing studies show that if a visitor has more confidence over a Flash document, they'll stay longer. If it's a marketing document, that confidence translates into a greater chance that the visitor will buy what you're selling. If it's a training document, the visitor is more likely to listen to what you're saying, and learn from it. Remember, control leads to confidence, and to better Flash documents.

Play and Stop Sounds

1. Create or open a Flash document (ActionScript 2.0), and then select a sound in the Library.

2. Click the **Library Options** button, and then click **Properties**. Click **Advanced**, if necessary.

3. Select the **Export For ActionScript** check box, and then click **OK**.

4. Select a layer to place the sound.

5. Click the plus (+) sign located in the upper-left portion of the Behaviors panel, point to **Sound**, and then click **Load Sound From Library**.

6. Enter the name of the sound in the Linkage ID field.

7. Give the file a unique instance name.

8. Clear the **Play This Sound When Loaded** check box.

9. Click **OK**.

See Also

See Project 6, "Creating a Context Menu" on page 521 for ActionScript code to play and stop an animation.

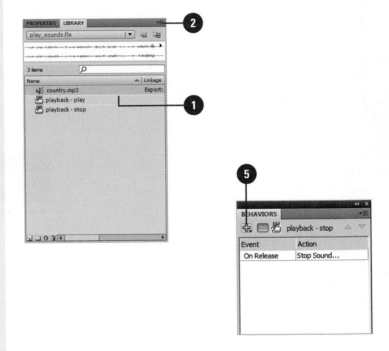

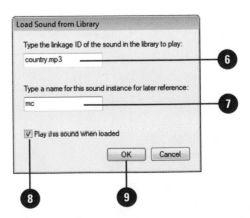

10 Place a Play and Stop button on the Stage.

11 Click the **Play** button.

12 Click the plus (+) sign, located in the upper-left portion of the Behaviors panel, point to **Sound**, and then click **Play Sound**.

13 Enter the name of the sound instance to play.

14 Click **OK**.

15 Select an Event to play the sound.

16 Click the **Stop** button.

17 Click the plus (+) sign, located in the upper-left portion of the Behaviors panel, point to **Sound**, and then click **Stop Sound**.

18 Enter the name of the sound instance to stop.

19 Click **OK**.

20 Select an Event to stop the sound.

21 Click the **Control** menu, and then click **Test Movie** to test the ActionScript.

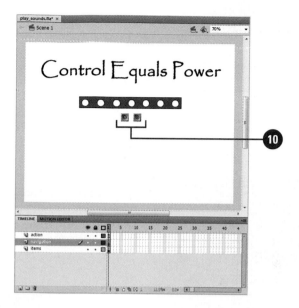

Did You Know?

You can trigger events based on when a sound stops. You can use the onSoundComplete event of the ActionScript Sound object to trigger an event when the sound stops, which can be useful for synchronizing sound to scenes in a presentation, or creating an audio playlist.

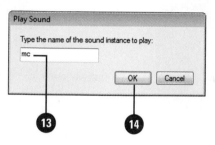

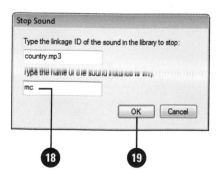

Loading a Streaming MP3 File

FL 4.5

You can load an MP3 music audio file using a built-in Flash behavior. The advantage to this process is that the file is loaded when needed, and it never increases the size of the original Flash movie. Flash performs a calculation on audio files as they are loading. When it has enough of an audio file, it begins playing, while it continues to download the remaining information in the background. For large audio files, this cuts down on long wait times and keeps the visitor from becoming bored. Streaming MP3 files are not part of a pre-existing Flash movie, they're just available from a common location.

Load a Streaming MP3 File with ActionScript 3.0

1. Create or open a Flash document (ActionScript 3.0), and then select a button object on the Stage.

2. Open the **Properties** panel.

3. Enter a distinctive name for the object in the Instance field, such as *myButton*.

4. Click Frame 1 in the actions layer.

5. Click the **Window** menu, and then click **Actions**.

6. Enter the script as shown in the illustration:

7. Click the **Control** menu, and then click **Test Movie** to test the ActionScript.

See Also

See Project 2, "Loading and Formatting Text" on page 511 for ActionScript 3.0 code to load external text.

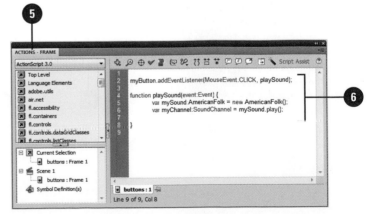

Load a Streaming MP3 File with an ActionScript Behavior

① Create or open a Flash document (ActionScript 2.0), and then select a button object on the Stage or Timeline keyframe.

② Click the plus (+) sign, located in the upper-left portion of the Behaviors panel, point to **Sound**, and then click **Load Streaming MP3 File**.

③ Enter the URL to the source MP3 file.

④ Enter a unique name in the identifier field.

⑤ Click **OK**.

⑥ If you selected a button object, select an Event to trigger the sound.

⑦ Click the **Control** menu, and then click **Test Movie** to test the ActionScript.

Did You Know?

You can stop all sounds using an ActionScript Behavior. Create or open a Flash document (ActionScript 2.0) that contains playing audio files, place a button object on the Stage, and then select it. Click the plus (+) sign in the Behaviors panel, point to Sound, and then click Stop All Sounds. Click OK. Select an Event to stop the sound.

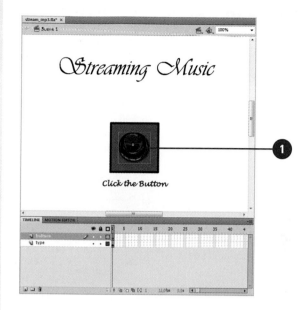

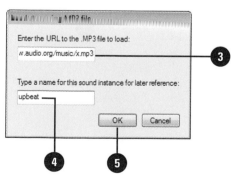

Syncing Sounds to the Timeline

When you sync a sound to the Timeline, you're essentially instructing Flash how to play the sound. Syncing sounds is a fundamental operation because choosing the wrong sync operation can drastically change how the sound plays out during the execution of the Flash movie. Flash gives you the ability to choose a separate sync operation for each individual sound file. When you place the sound on the Timeline, the Properties panel displays the audio properties for the selected sound and lets you define individual properties for every sound in your Flash document. For example, you have a background music sound that's located in several scenes, and you want to make sure it doesn't play on top of itself (Sync: Stop). Or, you have a narration that you want perfectly synced to an animation on the Timeline (Sync: Stream).

Sync Sounds to the Timeline

1. Select the keyframe on the Timeline containing the sound you want to sync.

2. Click the **Window** menu, and then click **Properties** to open the Property Inspector.

3. Click the **Sync** popup, and then select from the following options:

   ◆ **Event.** When you select Event (default) the sound plays when the record head reaches the keyframe containing the sound, and continues to play until the end of the sound. If the record head reaches another keyframe that contains the same sound, it will begin playing on top of the original sound.

   ◆ **Start.** Doesn't allow the sound to play on top of itself.

   ◆ **Stop.** Stops a sound if it is already playing, without affecting any other sounds.

   ◆ **Stream.** The Stream Sync creates sounds synchronized to the Timeline. This is useful for matching sounds to a particular visual event in the movie. If the video can not keep up with the audio, Flash will automatically drop video frames to keep the audio synchronized.

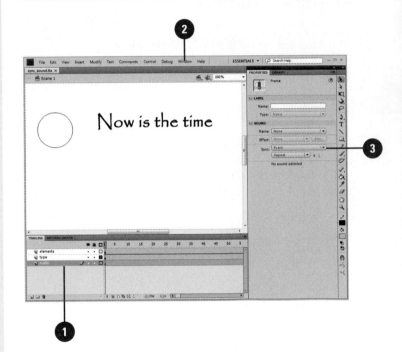

Adding Effects and Looping Sounds

Once a sound is imported into Flash and placed on the Timeline, you can add sound effects and determine the number of loops. When you loop a sound, you're instructing the Flash movie to repeat the sound a given number or times, or to loop the sound forever. Some sounds loop better than others. For example, you create some background music, and you want it to continue to play for as long as the visitor is on that particular page, but you don't want the sound to have a definable beginning or end. In addition to loops, you can also add effects to a sound, including fades in and out, and fade to the left or right channel. The effects applied will only modify the selected audio file. Each copy of an audio file dragged into a Flash movie is controlled independently.

Add Effects and Loop Sounds

1. Select the keyframe on the Timeline containing the sound you want to change.

2. Click the **Window** menu, and then click **Properties** to open the Property Inspector.

3. To add effects to the sound, click the **Effect** popup, and then select an option:

   ◆ **Left Channel/Right Channel.** Plays sound in the left or right channel.

   ◆ **Fade Left To Right/Fade Right To Left.** Changes sounds from one channel to the other.

   ◆ **Fade In.** Increases volume.

   ◆ **Fade Out.** Decreases volume.

   ◆ **Custom.** Creates custom in and out sound points using the Edit Envelope.

4. To loop a sound, click the popup, and then select an option:

   ◆ **Loop.** Click **Loop** to force the sound into an infinite loop.

   ◆ **Repeat.** Click **Repeat**, and then enter the number of times you want the sound to loop (up to 65,535).

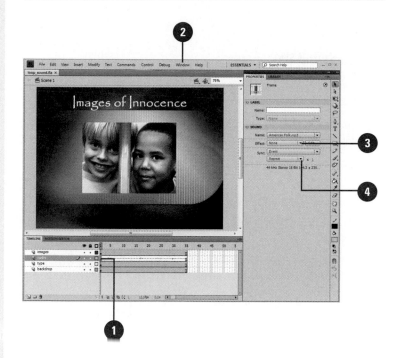

Publishing Documents Containing Audio

Sooner or later, you're going to want to export your Flash movie that contains audio as an SWF file. The process of publishing is relatively painless; however, there are a few considerations as to the compression of the files, which will be important to the size and playability of the Flash movie. Publishing requires knowledge of where the document will be used. For example, if the document is to be streamed over the Internet, and your visitors have relatively low bandwidth, you would want to choose compression settings that would significantly reduce the size of the audio files. It's possible that the Flash document is intended for playing off a CD/DVD; in that case, you could increase the compression settings. When you're designing a Flash document, it's imperative that you understand the end game and design the document toward that goal. Always remember that you can design a Flash document, but it's your visitors that ultimately will see, and use it.

Publish Sound Documents

1. Click the **File** menu, and then click **Publish Settings**.

2. Click the **Formats** tab, and then select the **Flash (.swf)** check box.

3. Click the **Flash** tab.

4. Click the **Set** buttons for Audio Stream or Audio Event.

5. Select other sound options as desired:

   ◆ Select the **Override Sound Settings** check box to override any sound settings applied to the individual sound files within the active Flash document.

   ◆ Select the **Export Device Sounds** check box to export sounds suitable for devices, such as mobile devices, instead of the library sound.

6. Click the **Compression** popup, and then select from the following options:

   ◆ **Disable.** Turns off all sound compression options and instructs Flash not to export sounds.

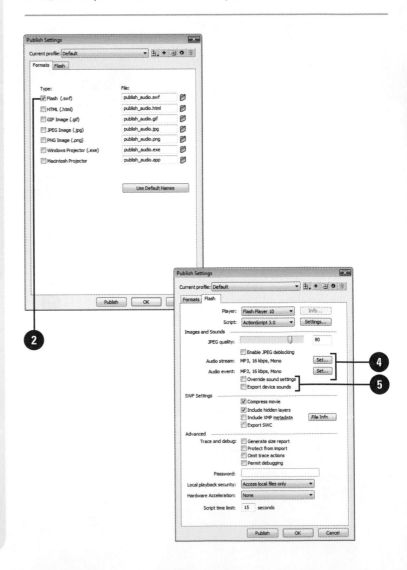

- ◆ **ADPCM.** Performs minor compression to the audio files.

- ◆ **MP3.** Creates audio files, especially music files, with excellent quality in a small file size.

- ◆ **Raw.** Leaves the sounds intact without any compression schemes applied.

- ◆ **Speech.** Creates optimized files for the human voice.

7 Select the **Convert Stereo To Mono** check box for the ADPCM and RAW compression formats.

8 Based on your Compression selections from step 5, select the following options:

- ◆ **Sample Rate.** Available for ADPCM, Raw, and Speech compression. The higher the sample rate the better the quality, but the bigger the file.

- ◆ **ADPCM bits.** Higher bit values translate into better quality audio, but larger file sizes.

- ◆ **Quality.** Available for MP3 compression. The Best option gives the finest quality, but produces a larger file.

- ◆ **Bit Rate.** Available for MP3 compression. The higher the value, the better the quality and the bigger the file.

9 Click **OK**.

10 Select the **Override Sound Settings** check box to take priority over the individual settings applied to the audio files.

11 Select the **Export Device Sounds** check box to export device sounds with the published Flash movie.

12 Click **OK**.

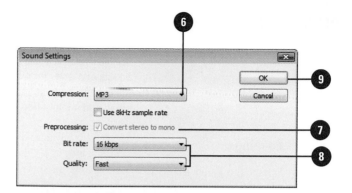

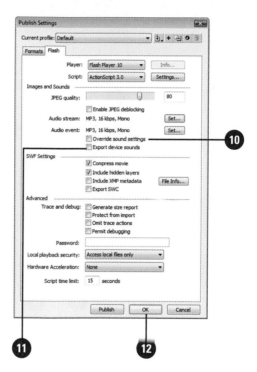

For Your Information

Changing Audio File Quality

You cannot publish a Flash movie with audio files that are better quality than the originals. For example, if the MP3 audio files you're using have a Bit rate of 16kbps, increasing that to 48kbps does not create a better quality audio file. In fact, that's true of most Flash objects, not just audio. To increase the quality of an audio file would require the use of an audio application. You can find sound programs at *www.downloads.com*.

Editing Sounds

Flash is not a major sound editing application. For example, you can't trim or cut audio files, nor can you enhance audio or reduce hum and background noises. Flash expects all that to be done before you import the file. However, you do have some control over when the sound begins and ends (time in, and time out), and you do have control over the volume (fade in and fade out). Making sure that your audio file is clean and smooth flowing will help with the quality of your audio file.

Work with Edit Envelope

1. Select a keyframe on the Timeline that contains an audio file.

2. Click the **Window** menu, and then click **Properties** to open the Property Inspector.

3. Click the **Edit** button.

4. Click the **Effect** popup, and then select a channel, fade, or custom effect.

5. Drag the **Time In** marker to the right to change where the audio file begins.

6. Drag the **Time Out** marker to the left to change where the audio file ends (the Time Out marker appears at the end of the audio file).

7. Click the **Envelope** lines to adjust the volume on the right or left channels.

8. Use the **Zoom** buttons to increase or decrease the size of the audio file in the edit window.

9. Click the **Play** or **Stop** buttons to test the changes to the audio file.

10. Click the **Time Marker** buttons to change the marker code from frames to seconds.

11. Click **OK** to save your changes.

> **IMPORTANT** *Adjusting an audio file using Edit Envelope only impacts the select instance of the audio file. The original audio file (in the Library) is unaffected by these changes.*

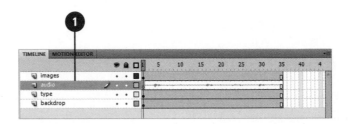

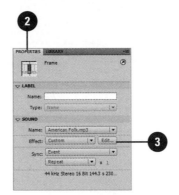

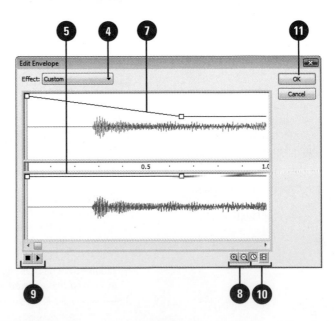

Editing Sounds Using Soundbooth

Adobe Soundbooth is a program that allows you to record and modify sound files. If you have Soundbooth CS4 installed on your computer, you can edit imported sounds in Soundbooth directly from within Flash (**New!**). When you're done editing the sound file in Soundbooth, you can save the file and your changes automatically appear in Flash. If you change the name or format of a sound after editing it, you'll need to re-import the modified file back into Flash. You can edit all different sound file formats in Soundbooth. If you want to non-destructively edit sounds, then use the default sound file format (ASND) in Soundbooth for the best results.

Edit a Sound Using Adobe Soundbooth

1. Click the **Window** menu, and then click **Library** to open the Library panel.

2. Right-click (Win) or Control-click (Mac) the sound file you want to edit, and then click **Edit with Soundbooth**.

   The sound file opens in Adobe Soundbooth.

3. Edit the sound file using Soundbooth tools and commands.

   ◆ Use Help in Soundbooth to edit the sound file the way you want.

4. When you're done, save the sound file in Soundbooth. Click the **File** menu, and then click **Save**.

   ◆ To save the changes in a non-destructive format, save the file using the ASND file format, the default in Soundbooth.

   ◆ If you change the name or format of a sound after editing it, you'll need to re-import the modified file back into Flash.

5. Quit (Mac) or exit (Win) Soundbooth to return to Flash and view the edited version of the sound file in the Library panel.

Working with Video

13

Introduction

The Flash Video Import Wizard lets you import a video clip as a file that is streamed from a Flash server, progressively downloaded from a Web server, embedded (stored in movie) or linked (stored out of movie). It guides you through the steps for the specific deployment method. During the import process, you have the ability to compress the video using user-defined profiles, or preset values, set cue points, and trim excess video. It's important to understand that although Flash can import a video file, it can't make the quality of the video any better than the original. If you receive your video from outside sources, there is little you can do; however, if you're the one shooting the footage, pay close attention to lighting, camera angles, and distractions within the video. The more time and attention you spend taking the video, the better the video will be when imported into Flash. If you do need to tweak a video file, video-editing applications such as Adobe's Premiere (Mac/Win), and Apple's Final Cut Pro (Mac) are excellent choice for the budding movie director.

If you have a video-editing application and Flash, you can create a movie against a blue screen and then mask the area out using alpha channel masks. They do this in the movies all the time. The process involves opening the image within a video-editing application, and creating the transparency using a specific color (referred to as blue or green screening), using luminosity levels, or actually creating a mask in an image-editing application such as, Adobe Photoshop, and then importing the mask. When you open the movie in Flash, any other background you place behind the movie will replace the original green screen.

Using the Video Import Wizard

FL 3.4

Importing video into Flash is not much more difficult than importing a graphic or audio file. The Video Import Wizard is Flash's way of helping you through the process of importing video files into Flash. When you import video, the Wizard lets you import a video clip as a file that is streamed from a Flash server, progressively downloaded from a Web server, embedded (stored in movie) or linked (stored out of the movie). It guides you through the steps for the specific deployment method. During the import process for some methods, you have the ability to compress the video using user-defined encoding profiles, set cue points, and trim excess video. You can choose to accept the Wizard's recommendations or make changes. You can also attach movie play-back controls with different looks, known as **skins**. The Wizard seamlessly uses the Skinning component to attach movie controls.

Use the Video Import Wizard

1. Click the **File** menu, point to **Import**, and then click **Import Video**.

   ◆ For the FLV format, use **Import To Library** since the file is native to Flash and doesn't need to be encoded.

   Flash saves the video in the active document's Library.

2. Select a video file location option:

   ◆ Click the **On Your Computer** option, click **Browse** to manually locate the video file.

   Choose a video method from the following options:

   ◆ Load external video with playback component.

   ◆ Embed FLV in SWF and play in timeline.

   ◆ Import as mobile device video bundled in SWF.

   ◆ Click the **Already deployed to a web server, Flash Video Steaming Service, or Flash Media Server** option, and then enter in the file's URL.

3. Click **Next**.

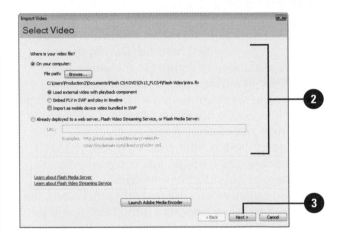

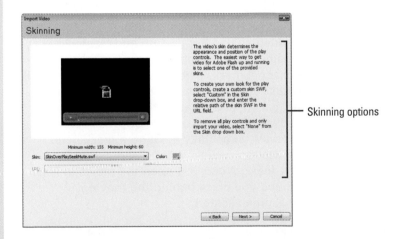

Skinning options

4 Options vary depending on the deployment method; select the ones you want.

◆ **Skinning.** Specify the appearance and position of the play controls.

◆ **Embedding.** Specify a symbol type, and other embedding options.

5 Click **Next**.

6 Click **Finish**.

Flash will automatically create an FLV component, and drop it into the active layer on the Timeline.

7 Click the **Control** menu, and then click **Test Movie** to view the video file as it will appear.

See Also

See "Working with the Video Encoder" on page 342 for information on Flash video encoding settings.

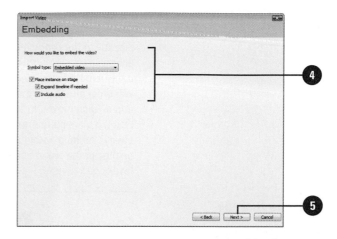

Supported Video Formats

Extension	Description
.avi	Audio Video Interleaved
.dv	Digital video
.flv	Adobe Flash Video
.mpg, .mpeg	Moving Picture Experts Group
.mov	QuickTime (version 7 for Mac and version 6.5 for Win)
.wmv, .asf	Windows Media file (Win only with DirectX 9 or later)

Working with Video on the Timeline

FL 3.4

When you import video into a source document, Flash stores a copy of the video in the active document's Library. Even if you import the video directly to the Stage, Flash will still place a copy in the Library. It's always best to import video files first into the Library; that way you have control of the video and how it's brought onto the Stage. Moving a video file directly to the Stage is the easiest way to incorporate video into a Flash movie. In fact, once the video file has been imported into Flash, it's a simple drag and drop operation. However, video files should always be held within a separate layer. That gives you control over the display of the video and lets you place other Flash elements in other layers.

Move a Video File Directly to the Stage

1. Open a Flash source document (.fla) that contains one or more video files in the Library.

   IMPORTANT *To work directly with video files on the Timeline, you will have to Import them using the Embed video in SWF and play in Timeline (see Using the Video Import Wizard).*

2. Click the **Window** menu, and then click **Library** to open the Library panel.

3. Click the **Insert Layer** button, and then name the new layer video_1.

4. Select the new layer.

5. Drag the video file from the Library onto the Stage.

6. Click **Yes**, if prompted to a dialog box indicating how many frames the video file will occupy on the Stage.

7. Click the **Control** menu, and then click **Test Movie** to view the video file as it will appear.

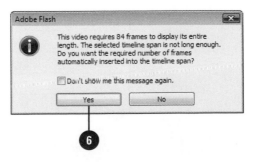

326

Using Movie Clips with Video Files

While placing a video file directly onto the Stage may be an easy way to bring a video file into a Flash movie, the best way to control video is to first place it into a movie clip, and then drag the movie clip onto the Stage. That gives you control of the clip with two Timelines: the Timeline on the Stage, and the Timeline of the movie clip.

Use Movie Clips with Video Files

1. Click the **Window** menu, and then click **Library** to open the Library panel.

2. Click the **Insert** menu, and then click **New Symbol**.

3. Name the new symbol, and then click the **Movie Clip** option.

4. Click **OK**.

5. Drag a video file from the Library into the movie clip Library.

6. Click **Yes** when Flash instructs you as to how many frames the video file will occupy in the movie clip.

7. Return to the current scene by clicking the **Scene** button, located in the upper-left corner of the Flash window.

8. Click the **Insert Layer** button, and name the new layer video 1.

9. Select the new layer.

10. Drag the movie clip from the Library onto the Stage.

    The movie clip occupies a single frame.

11. Click the **Control** menu, and then click **Test Movie** to view the video file as it will appear.

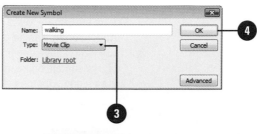

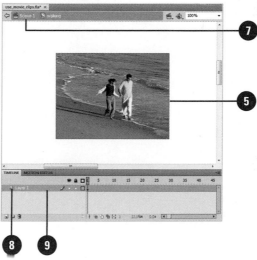

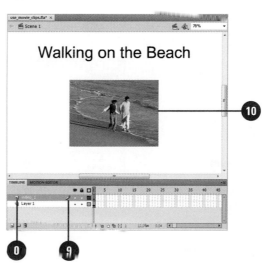

Using Video with ActionScript

Playing a video file inside a Flash movie is one thing, controlling the movie, or better yet, letting your visitors control the movie is something quite different. Control of a movie requires knowledge of Flash's ActionScript language. ActionScript is a control language that instructs Flash what to do, and when to do it. For example, you could create an ActionScript that instructs Flash to play or stop a movie, or you could add buttons to move the video backward or forward, one frame at a time. One way to display video in a Flash Movie is to drag it directly from the Library to the Timeline. Once the video is on the Timeline, ActionScripts can be created to start and stop the video. Since you're using the active document's Timeline to control the video, any other layers containing animation sequences on the Timeline will stop and start along with the video.

Control Video from the Timeline

1. Create or open a Flash document, create a new layer to hold the video file, and then select the layer.

2. Drag the video file from the Library to the Stage.

3. Create a new layer to hold the navigation buttons, and then select the layer.

4. Drag the Play, Stop, and Rewind buttons into the Navigation layer from the Library, and then place them underneath the video.

5. Click the **Window** menu, and then click **Actions** to open the Actions panel.

6. To display scripting language commands for the scripting language you want to use, click the **Language** button, and then select the language you want.

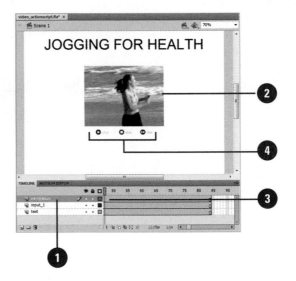

AS 3.0

Did You Know?

You can check the syntax of any script with the click of a button. Click the Check Syntax button, located at the top of the Actions panel, and Flash will check the syntax of the your script.

7 Do either of the following depending the your ActionScript version:

◆ **ActionScript 2.0.** select the Play, Stop, and Rewind buttons individually, and then enter the ActionScript 2.0 script as shown in the illustration.

◆ **ActionScript 3.0.** Click Frame 1 in a layer, and then enter the ActionScript 3.0 script as shown in the illustration.

IMPORTANT *ActionScript is a relatively easy language to learn, but it is also a very unforgiving language. For example, the gotoAndStop script must be written exactly as shown, including the capital "A" and "S". While ActionScripting, remember to keep an eye on syntax.*

8 Click the **Control** menu, and then click **Test Movie** to test the ActionScript.

IMPORTANT *Although working with embedded video is a common practice, large video files can cause audio sync problems when the file is published and played. It's always wise to thoroughly test your published document.*

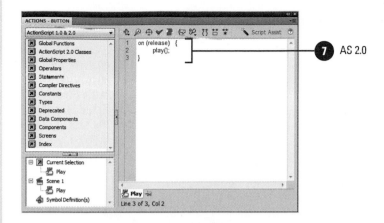

7 AS 2.0

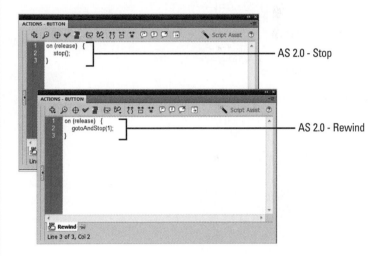

AS 2.0 - Stop

AS 2.0 - Rewind

Did You Know?

Flash contains several sets of pre-designed buttons. Click the Window menu, point to Common Libraries, and then click Buttons. Flash's button Library contains folders with dozens of buttons, including arcade buttons and buttons for controlling a Flash movie.

For Your Information

Referencing Movie Clips in the Timeline

Since movie clips have independent Timelines, referring to them can sometimes be confusing. When you are working on a movie clip in the Timeline for the main Flash document, you refer to it with ActionScript with _root. However, if you are working on a movie clip in another Timeline, you refer to it with _parent. _parent always refers to the Timeline that contains the movie clip.

Controlling Video Through Movie Clips

While it's an easy matter to drag a video file onto the Stage and then use start and stop ActionScripts to control the playing of the video, it's better to create a movie clip, and then load the video file into the clip. It's a bit more work, but the additional rewards are great. For example, you can instruct a movie clip to stop playing without affecting anything else on the Stage. As a matter of fact, you can have as many movie clips on the Stage as you want, and each one can be controlled individually. It's exactly that kind of control that leads to awesome Flash movies. To control a video using a movie clip you will need to have a flash document that contains one or more video files, in the Library.

Control Video Through Movie Clips

1. Create or open a Flash document, click the **Insert** button, and then click **New Symbol**.

2. Name the symbol, and then click the **Movie Clip** option.

3. Click **OK**.

4. Drag a video file from your Library into the movie clip symbol.

5. Click the **Scene** button to return to the Stage of the active scene.

6. Create a new layer to hold the video, and then select the layer.

7. Drag the movie clip to the Stage, and then select the clip.

8. Enter a unique Instance name in the Property Inspector.

   IMPORTANT *The Instance name you enter will be used in the ActionScript to identify the movie clip to the button object "with (instance name)".*

9. Create a new layer to hold the navigation buttons, and then select the layer.

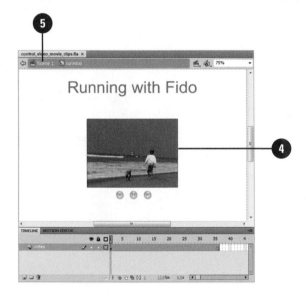

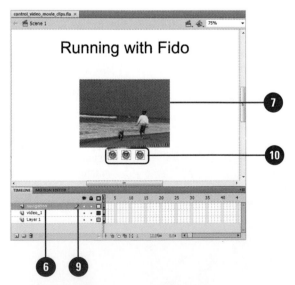

10. Drag Play, Stop, and Rewind buttons into the Navigation layer from the library, and then place them underneath the video.

11. Click the **Window** menu, and then click **Actions**.

12. To display scripting language commands for the scripting language you want to use, click the **Language** button, and then select the language you want.

13. Do either of the following depending the your ActionScript version:

    ◆ **ActionScript 2.0.** select the Play, Stop, and Rewind buttons individually, and then enter the ActionScript 2.0 script as shown in the illustration.

    ◆ **ActionScript 3.0.** Click Frame 1 in a layer, and then enter the ActionScript 3.0 script as shown in the illustration.

    IMPORTANT *ActionScript is a relatively easy language to learn, but it is also a very unforgiving language. For example, the gotoAndStop script must be written exactly as shown, including the capital "A" and "S". While ActionScripting, remember to keep an eye on syntax.*

14. Click the **Control** menu, and then click **Test Movie** to test the ActionScript.

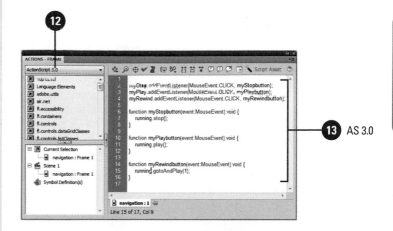

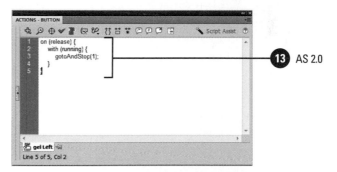

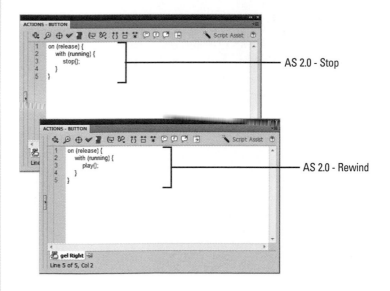

Working with the Flash Player Component

Instead of importing video into Flash, you can also use the FLVPlayback components to dynamically play external FLV files in Flash Player. The FLVPlayback component is the display area (made up of a customizable skin with playback controls) in which you view video. Simply export your movie as an FLV file from Flash or a video editing programs using the FLV Export plug-in, and then use the FLVPlayback component in Flash to play it back. If you want to include closed captioning (W3C standard XML format Timed Text), you can use the FLVPlayback Captioning component

Work with the FLV Playback Component

① Create or open a Flash document.

② Click the **Window** menu, and then click the **Components** and **Component Inspector** to open the panels.

③ Click the **Video** plus sign (**+**) to expand the list.

④ Drag the **FLVPlayback** component onto the Stage, and then select the component.

⑤ In the Component Inspector panel, click the **Parameters** tab.

⑥ Click the **contentPath** (2.0) or **Source** (3.0) value field, and then click the **Magnifying Glass** icon.

⑦ Click the **Browse folder** icon, navigate to and select the FLV video file that you want to use, and then click **Open**.

⑧ Click **OK**.

⑨ Select from the following FLVPlayback parameters:

♦ **align (3.0).** Specify FLV file alignment in the player.

♦ **autoPlay.** Specify True or False to automatically play the FLV file.

♦ **autoRewind (2.0).** Specify True or False to automatically rewind the FLV file upon completion.

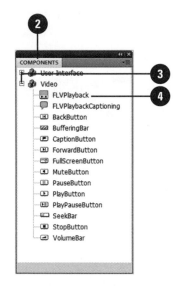

FLVPlayback component

- **autoSize (2.0).** Specify True or False to resize the component at runtime.

- **bufferTime.** Specify the number of seconds to buffer before beginning playback.

- **cuePoints.** Specify a string with the cue points for the video.

- **isLive.** Specify True or False whether the FLV is streaming live.

- **preview (3.0).** Creates a preview for authoring purposes.

- **maintainAspectRatio (2.0)** or **scaleMode (3.0).** Specify True or False to retain the source video aspect ratio.

- **skin.** Select a skin and color for the FLV video player.

- **skinAutoHide.** Specify True or False to automatically hide or show the skin.

- **skinBackground Alpha (3.0).** Specify a background alpha channel for the skin.

- **skinBackgroundColor (3.0).** Specify a background color for the skin.

- **volume.** Specify a volume setting for the video.

10 Click the **Control** menu, and then click **Test Movie** to test the video in the Flash player.

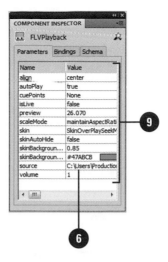

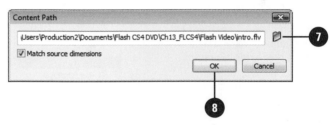

Working with the Media Player for Streaming Video

It seems obvious that you would want to keep Flash movies that contain video relatively small, in order to minimize the download time of the file. However, since Flash uses streaming technology (the file begins playing before it's totally downloaded), it's more important to think about the amount of time before the movie plays. For example, a Flash movie that might take three minutes to download may only take about fifteen seconds before it starts playing. That's what streaming is all about. The Flash Media Player component (ActionScript 2.0) lets you load and control streaming media files in the FLV or MP3 formats into a Flash movie. The media components require Flash Player 6 or later and don't support accessibility.

Work with the Media Playback Component

1. Create or open a Flash document (ActionScript 2.0).

2. Click the **Window** menu, and then click the **Components** and **Component Inspector** to open the panels.

3. Click the **Media** plus sign (+) to expand the list.

4. Drag the **MediaPlayback** component onto the Stage, and then select the component.

Did You Know?

The MediaPlayback component (2.0) is a combination of the MediaDisplay and MediaController components. The combination provides the functionality to stream the video.

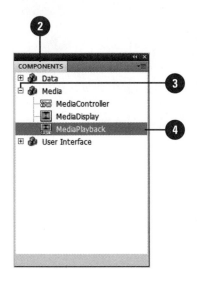

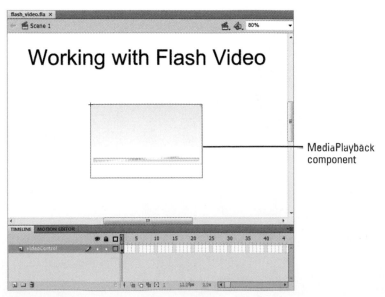

MediaPlayback component

5 In the Component Inspector panel, click the **Parameters** tab.

6 Click the **FLV** option.

7 Enter the URL of the Flash movie file.

8 Select the **Automatically Play** check box to have the video automatically play when loaded.

9 Select the **Use Preferred Media Size** check box to display the video using the original file's width and height.

10 Select the **Respect Aspect Ratio** check box to keep the video's width and height in proportion.

11 Click the **Top**, **Bottom**, **Left**, or **Right** option for the placement of the control panel.

12 Click the **Auto**, **On**, or **Off** option to control when the control panel appears with the video.

13 Click the plus sign (**+**) button to add cue points to the video file, using hours, minutes, seconds, and milliseconds.

14 Click the **Control** menu, and then click **Test Movie** to test the video in the Flash player.

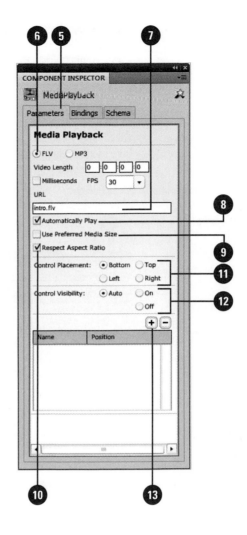

See Also

See "Exporting as a FLV File" on page 346 for information on creating FLV video files.

For Your Information

Streaming Video

Flash gives you three ways to control streaming video files: the Media Player, Media Controller, and Media Display. Each of these components lets you control video (or audio) as a separate file that is loaded into the Flash movie. Flash media components support files in the FLV (video) or MP3 (audio) formats, and since the components must use Adobe Flash Communications Server technology, the Flash files must be saved in the Flash 7 player or later.

Working with the Media Controller Component

The Flash Media Controller component (ActionScript 2.0) lets you control a streaming media file that has been loaded using a Media Display component. The Media Display component gives you an easy way to create a placeholder for a video file, without any play, pause, or rewind buttons. The Media Controller component provides you with standard controls (play, pause, and rewind) for playback of any video on the screen. The Media Controller component is an excellent choice for controlling video and audio files placed on the screen using the Media Display component. The media components require Flash Player 6 or later and don't support accessibility.

Work with the Media Display and Media Controller Components

1. Create or open a Flash document (ActionScript 2.0).

2. Click the **Window** menu, and then click the **Components** and **Component Inspector** to open the panels.

3. Click the **Media** plus sign (+) to expand the list.

4. Drag the **Media Display** component onto the Stage, and then select the component.

5. In the Property Inspector, enter a unique instance name for the Display component.

Did You Know?

You can use the Media components to give you control over precise placement of the controller. Drag the Media Controller on the Stage and place it anywhere you like. The advantage of the Media Controller is that you decide the placement of the controls in relationship to the player. This gives you a distinct design advantage over using the Media Player component.

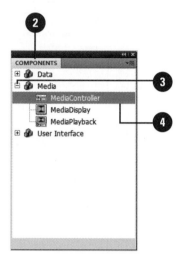

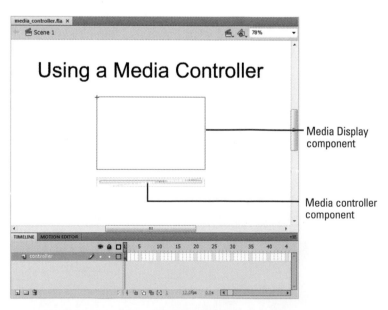

Media Display component

Media controller component

6 In the Component Inspector panel, click the **Parameters** tab.

7 Click the **FLV** option.

8 Enter the URL of the Flash movie file.

9 Clear the **Automatically Play** check box to play the video when loaded.

10 Select the **Use Preferred Media Size** check box to display the video using the original file's width and height.

11 Select the **Respect Aspect Ratio** check box to keep the video's width and height in proportion.

12 Click the plus sign (+) button to add cue points to the video file, using hours, minutes, seconds, and milliseconds.

13 Drag the Media Controller component onto the Stage, and select the component.

14 In the Property Inspector, enter a unique instance name for the Controller component.

15 Click the **Add Behavior** button (+), in the Behaviors panel, point to **Media**, and then click **Associate Display**.

16 Select the instance name given to the Media Display component, and then click **OK**.

This associates the controller with the correct video.

17 Click the **Control** menu, and then click **Test Movie** to test the video in the Flash player.

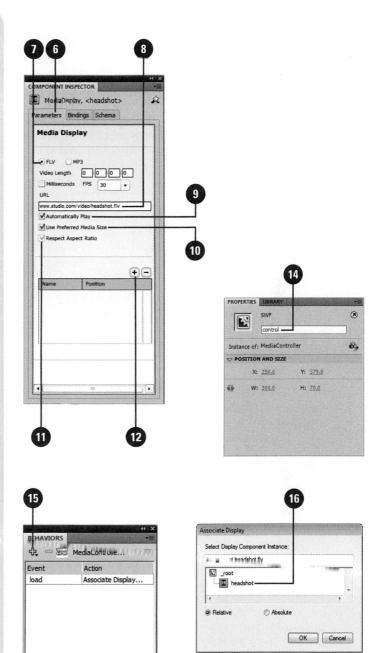

Exporting as a QuickTime Video

Flash makes it easy to export a Flash document to a QuickTime video using the QuickTime Export Settings dialog box. By default, Flash creates a QuickTime video of the complete source document with the same dimensions. However, you can change the export options. In the QuickTime Export Settings dialog box, you can set movie dimensions, ignore stage color, specify when to stop exporting and where to store temporary data, and set advanced QuickTime settings. The advanced QuickTime settings are set for optimal playback. If you have experience using QuickTime, you can set the advanced settings to customize the results you want.

Export Flash as a QuickTime Video

1. Click the **File** menu, point to **Export**, and then click **Export Movie**.

2. Click the **Format** popup (Mac) or **Save As Type** list arrow (Win), and then click **QuickTime**.

3. Type the new file name.

4. Navigate to the drive or folder location where you want to save the document.

5. Click **Save**.

   The QuickTime Export Settings dialog box opens.

6. If available, specify the width and height in pixels you want for the QuickTime video.

   ◆ To maintain the same ratio of width and height, select the **Maintain Aspect Ratio** check box.

7. To create an alpha channel using the Stage color, select the **Ignore Stage Color (Generate Alpha Channel)** check box.

   The alpha channel is encoded as a transparent track, letting you overlay the exported QuickTime movie on top of other content to alter the background color or scene.

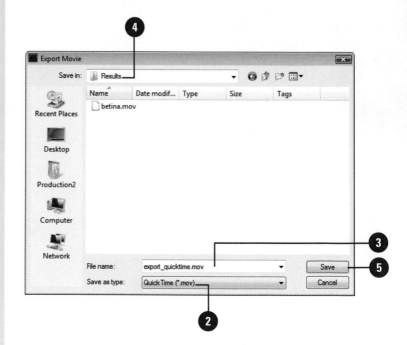

8　Click the **When Last Frame Is Reached** or **After Time Elapsed** option and then specify the time you want in the format (hh:mm:ss.msec), where hh is hours, mm is minutes, ss is seconds, and msec is milliseconds.

9　Click the **In Memory** or **On Disk** option to specify where you want to store temporary data.

10　Click **QuickTime Settings**.

11　Select the **Video** check box, and then click the buttons where you want to make video option changes.

◆ **Settings**. Select video compression type, quality, frame rate, and data rate.

◆ **Filter**. Select a video filter, such as blur, emboss, sharpen, and special effects.

◆ **Size**. Select a standardized size, such as NTSC, PAL, etc.

12　Select the **Sound** check box, and then click the buttons where you want to make audio option changes.

◆ **Settings**. Select sound compression, sample rate, sample bit size, and usage (mono or stereo).

13　To optimize for Internet streaming, select the **Prepare For Internet Streaming** check box, and then select the option you want.

14　Click **OK**.

15　Click **Export**.

16　Upon completion, click **OK**.

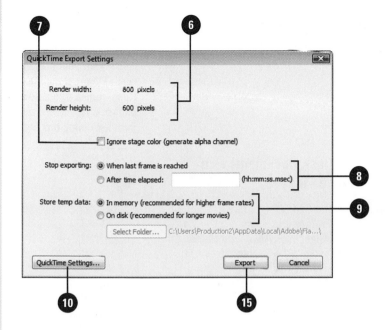

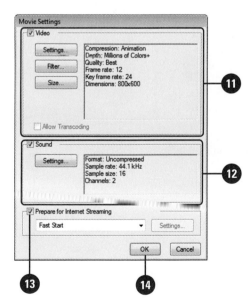

Publishing as a QuickTime Video

If you have QuickTime software developed by Apple Computer installed on your computer, you can publish a Flash document to Flash 5 or earlier as a QuickTime video in the same format you have installed. The Flash document plays in the QuickTime video the same as it does in the Flash Player. If the Flash document also contains a QuickTime video, Flash copies it to its own track in the published QuickTime video file. To publish a QuickTime video, you use the QuickTime tab in the Publish Settings dialog box, where you can set the options you want.

Publish Flash Documents as a QuickTime Video

1. Click the **Edit** (Win) or **Flash** (Mac), click **Preferences**, click **QuickTime**, click **Advanced Media Types**, select the **Enable the use of Flash Tracks** check box, and then click **OK** twice.

2. Click the **File** menu, and then click **Publish Settings**.

3. Click the **Formats** tab.

4. Select the **QuickTime with Flash Track (.mov)** check box.

   ◆ If a warning appears, click **OK**. Click the **Flash** tab, click the **Version** popup, and then select **Flash Player 5**. However, this may change when a newer version of the QuickTime Player is released.

5. Click the **QuickTime** tab.

6. Select the **Match Movie** check box or specify the width and height in pixels you want for the QuickTime video.

7. Click the **Alpha** popup, and then select from the following options:

   ◆ **Auto.** Creates a transparent Flash track when it's on top of any other tracks, or an opaque track when it's at the bottom or the only track.

   ◆ **Alpha-transparent.** Creates a transparent Flash track SWF file and shows any content in tracks behind it.

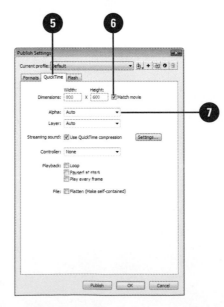

340

- ◆ **Copy.** Creates an opaque Flash track and masks all content in tracks behind it.

7 Click the **Layer** popup, and then select from the following options:

- ◆ **Auto.** Puts the Flash track in front of other tracks when Flash objects are in front of video objects, or behind other tracks when Flash objects are not in front.

- ◆ **Top.** Puts the Flash track on top of all other tracks.

- ◆ **Bottom.** Puts the Flash track at the bottom behind all other tracks.

8 To stream the video/sound, select the **Streaming sound** check box.

9 If you select Streaming sound, click **Settings**, select sound compression, sample rate, sample bit size, and usage (mono or stereo), and then click **OK**.

10 Click the **Controller** popup menu, and then select the type of QuickTime controller you want to use to play the video: **None**, **Standard**, or **QuickTime VR**.

11 Select the playback options you want:

- ◆ **Loop.** Select to repeat the video when it reaches the last frame.

- ◆ **Paused At Start.** Select to pause the video at the start until the user clicks a button.

- ◆ **Play Every Frame.** Select to play every frame, which maintains time and does not play sound.

12 To combine the Flash content and imported video into a single QuickTime video, select **Flatten (Make Self-Contained)** check box.

13 Click **OK**.

Streaming sound settings

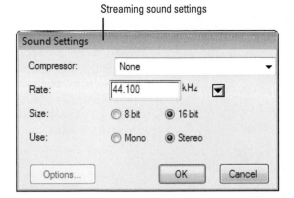

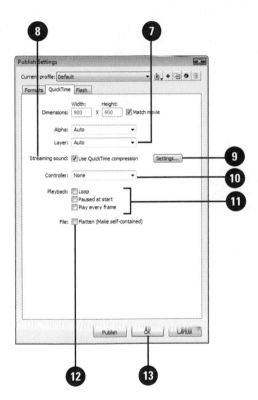

Working with the Video Encoder

To improve workflow for those of us who love to work with video, Adobe Media Encoder CS4 (**New!**) includes a stand-alone video encoder that you can install on a computer dedicated to video encoding. The Adobe Media Encoder CS4 lets you batch process video encoding, allowing you to encode several video clips, using different codecs at the same time. The Adobe Media Encoder CS4 also lets you edit video clips, add cue points (to trigger other actions), and crop (change viewable area of video) and trim (edit beginning and end points) the video.

Work with the Video Encoder

1. Open the Adobe Media Encoder CS4.
   - Use the Start menu (Win) or Applications folder (Mac).
   - If you're importing a video, click **File**, point to **Import**, click **Import Video**, and then click **Launch Adobe Media Encoder**.

2. Click **Add** to add video files to the batch list
   - Click the **File** menu, and then click **Add Adobe Premiere Pro Sequence** or **Add Adobe After Effects Composition** to add these file types.

3. Click **Duplicate** to make a copy of the selected video file, which saves the same video file using different compression settings.

4. Click **Remove** to remove the selected video file from the batch list.

5. Select the video that you want to change settings.

6. Click the **Format** menu, and then select a format with which to encode the video or audio clip.

   The selected format displays a list of available presets designed for the delivery format.

7. Click the **Preset** menu, and then select an encoding preset for your intended application.

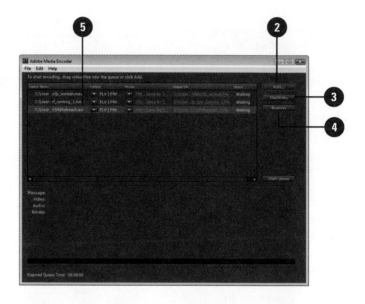

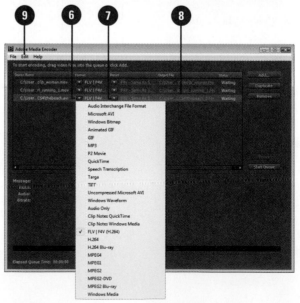

8 Click the **Output** filename, specify a location and file name for the encoded file or use the default filename from the source clip.

9 Click the **Edit** menu, and then click **Export Settings**.

The Export Settings dialog box appears, displaying tabs for Source and Output.

10 Click the **Advanced Mode** button.

This button toggles between Simple Mode and Advanced Mode.

11 Click the **Source** tab.

12 Select the **Export Video** check box, click the **Video** tab, and then specify a frame rate, and other video options.

13 Select the **Export Audio** check box, c lick the **Audio** tab, and then select a kbps data rate, quality setting, and other options.

14 Click the **Crop** button, enter edge values to crop the video, and then drag the in and out point markers below the scrubber bar to set the video trim points.

Click the **Output** tab to preview the cropped image. Use the **Crop Setting** popup to select an option.

15 Use the cursor to move the playback head to the frame location you want to embed, click **Add Cue Point**, and then specify the type of cue point you want.

16 Click **OK**.

17 Click **Start Queue** to begin batch processing all the files in the batch list. Click **Stop Queue** to halt the process.

The status column provides information for each video during the encoding process.

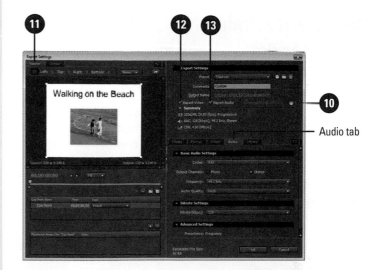

Audio tab

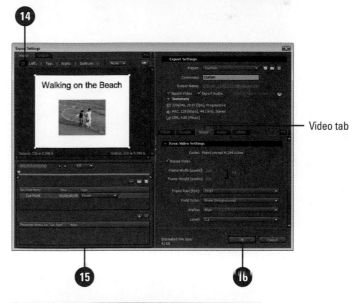

Video tab

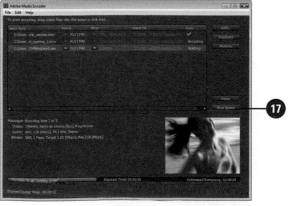

Working with Alpha Channel Masks

One of the cool features in Flash is its ability to work alpha channel masks. Alpha masks are typically created within video-editing applications, such as Apple's Final Cut Pro or Adobe's Premiere. The process involves opening the image within the video-editing application and creating the transparency using a specific color (referred to as blue or green screening), using luminosity levels, or actually creating a mask in an image-editing application such as Adobe Photoshop, and then importing the mask. For example, you could film yourself against a green screen, and then mask those areas out. When you open the movie in Flash, any other background you place behind the movie will replace the original green screen. They do this in the movies all the time.

Work with Alpha Channel Masks

① Open your video-editing application, and create a specific alpha channel mask.

The mask represents the areas of the movie for which you want to maintain transparency.

② Use your video-editing Export command and then select the Flash FLV format.

③ Click **Options** or select options for exporting a Flash FLV file.

◆ If Options is not available, open the Adobe Media Encoder CS4 (from the desktop), add the FLV file to the queue select a FLV preset format, and then open the Export Settings dialog box. Click the **Edit** menu, and then click **Export Settings**.

The Export Settings dialog box appears, displaying tabs for Source and Output.

④ Click the **Advanced Mode** button.

This button toggles between Simple Mode and Advanced Mode.

⑤ Click the **Source** tab.

⑥ Select the **Export Video** check box.

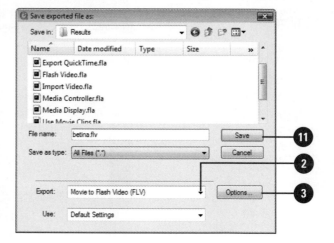

7. Click the **Video** tab.

8. Click the **On2 VP6** option.

9. Select the **Encode Alpha Channel** check box.

10. Click **OK**.

11. Click **Save** to save the file.

12. Open Flash Professional.

13. Click the **File** menu, point to **Import**, and then click **Import Video**.

14. Use the steps outlined in "Using the Video Import Wizard" on page 324.

15. Move to the Timeline and create a new layer directly underneath the video layer, and name it backdrop.

16. Place an image in the backdrop layer.

17. Click the **Control** menu, and then click **Test Movie** to view the video file as it will appear.

When you view the movie, the areas designated as transparent by the alpha channel mask will display the contents of the backdrop layer, directly through the running video.

See Also

See "Using the Video Import Wizard" on page 324 for more information on using the Video wizard.

See "Working with the Video Encoder" on page 342 for information on Flash video encoding settings.

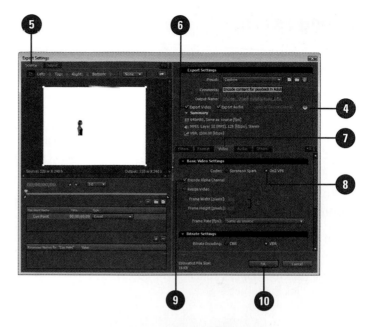

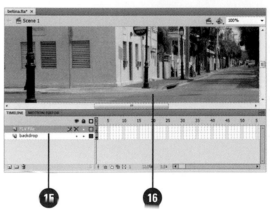

FLV masked movie   Backdrop image

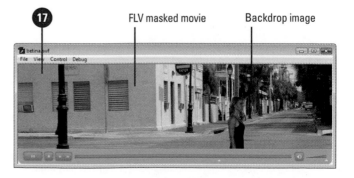

Exporting as a FLV File

The FLV (Flash Video) file format allows you to import or export a static video stream including encoded audio. For example, you could use the FLV format to save video for use with communications applications, such as video conferencing. When an FLV clip is exported with streaming audio, the audio is compressed using the Streaming Audio settings in the Publish Settings dialog box, and the file is compressed. FLV files can be used with Flash's new media components to create streaming video files directly in a Flash movie. In order to use the FLV format, you must first set up the video files for exporting. Any Flash document that contains video clips will work.

Export Video Clips into the FLV File Format

1. Select a video clip in the Library panel.

2. Click the **Libraries Options** button, and then click **Properties**.

3. Click **Export**.

4. Enter a name for the exported file.

5. Select a location where it will be saved.

6. Click **Save**.

7. Click **OK**.

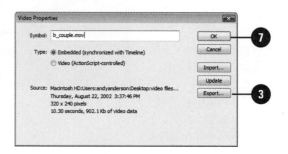

Did You Know?

You can use the Property Inspector to modify a Flash FLV video clip. Drag the FLV video file onto the Stage, select the video clip, and then open the Property Inspector. The Property Inspector lets you give the clip an instance name; change the width, height, and registration point of the clip; and even swap a video clip with another video clip.

Progressive Downloads

When FLV video files are played back, they're handled as a progressive download—Progressive downloads begin playing as soon as a certain percent of the complete file has been transferred. The playback is not as quick as that provided by streaming video, but it's not as slow as complete file download formats such as the MPEG video.

Using Basic ActionScripts

14

Introduction

Flash's programming language is called ActionScript. **ActionScript** lets you create detailed instructions on how the Flash movie will perform. ActionScripts can use an event to trigger the specific action. Say you create a button, and you want the ActionScript to trigger an instruction that will stop the movie, but only when the user clicks the button object. The defined event is the user clicking his mouse, and the action would be to stop playing the movie. ActionScript is not that difficult to learn because it uses logical phrases. For example, the command to stop playing a Timeline is:

```
stop() ;
```

That's pretty simple, but remember that syntax is very important. For example, the ActionScript for moving to a specific frame on the Timeline is:

```
gotoAndPlay(2) ;
```

Notice the capitalization of the letters A and P and how the words are grouped together without any spaces. ActionScript is a relatively easy language to learn, but a very precise language to code, so pay close attention to the syntax.

The good news is that once you master the language and the syntax, the full power of Flash is available to you. You can create ActionScripts that are triggered (the event) by specific data, or information typed in by a visitor. You can even create ActionScripts that are sensitive to variables such as date and time. Flash helps you by giving you functions (English-like script) and as your ActionScript skills grow, you can even create and call your own functions. Each new version of Flash moves the ActionScripting language closer and closer to JavaScript. The power of Flash is fully realized when you write ActionScripts and incorporate them in your Flash documents.

What You'll Do

Use Object-Oriented Programming

View the Actions Panel

Understand Properties and Methods

Work with Objects and Classes

Apply Properties and Methods to an Object

Use Dot Syntax

Apply Dot Syntax to a Movie Clip

Understand Event Handlers

Attach a Mouse Event to a Button

Work with Frame Events

Understand a Clip Event

Attach a Clip Event to a Movie Clip

Understand Data Types

Use Functions

Understand Loops

Work with For Loops

Work with While Loops and Using Loop Exceptions

Use Conditional Statements

Work with ActionScript Behaviors

Using Object-Oriented Programming

 FL 4.2, 4.3

Objects are the key to understanding object-oriented programming. In object-oriented programming (OOP), an object is just as real as an object in this world. For example, your dog, or even your computer are objects that exist in the real world. Real-world objects share two characteristics with objects in the computer world: They have a specific state and behavior. For example, dogs have a state such as their name, color, breed, and if they're hungry. Dog behaviors would be: barking, fetching, and wagging their tails. All objects in the real and computer worlds have a behavior and a state.

Computer objects are modeled after real-world objects in that they also have a specific state and behavior. A **class** is a representation of an object that stores information about its data type, state, and behaviors. A class can include three types of characteristics: properties, methods, and events. A **property** represents different data associated with an object. A **method** is an action that can be performed by an object. An **event** is a system, application, or user action, such as a mouse click, that triggers an action related to an object.

After you create a class, you can also create new classes based on the existing one, known as **subclassing** or extending a class. The subclass inherits all the properties and methods of the parent class, known as the **superclass**. For example, you could create a superclass called Parents, and a subclass called Children. Inheritance allows one class definition (subclass) to include all the functionality of a different class definition (superclass). You can also additional methods and properties to the subclass as well as override

methods inherited from a superclass, which is called **polymorphism**.. Inheritance and subclassing are very useful for large projects where you can share similar functionality and reduce the amount of code.

An object maintains its state using one or more variables. A **variable** is an item of data named by an identifier, and an object performs its behavior with methods. Everything an object understands (its state) and what it can do (its behavior) is expressed by the variables and the methods within that object.

An object that represents a speeding car would have variables that instruct the object as to speed, direction, and color. These variables are known as instance variables because they contain the state for a particular object, and in object-oriented terminology, a particular object is called an **instance**. In addition to its variables, the car would have methods assigned to change speed and turn on the lights. These methods are formally known as instance methods because they inspect or change the state of a particular instance.

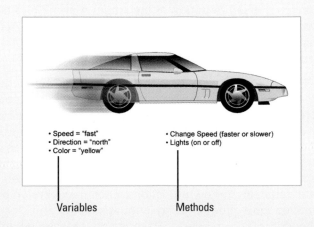

- Speed = "fast"
- Direction = "north"
- Color = "yellow"

- Change Speed (faster or slower)
- Lights (on or off)

Variables   Methods

Viewing the Actions Panel

The Actions panel is gives the Flash designer control of a Flash document by allowing him/her to create and edit actions for an object or frame. To use the Actions panel, select an object on the stage, or select a frame on the Timeline, click the Window menu, and then click Actions. Scripts can be typed directly into the Actions panel using the Script pane, or augmented by using a list of installed Actions in the Toolbox.

- ◆ **Toolbox.** Supplies a list of all installed actions, organized into a folder for either ActionScript 1.0 & 2.0 or ActionScript 3.0

- ◆ **Script pane.** Enter the Actions into the Script pane.

- ◆ **Script Navigator pane.** Gives reference to all the Scripts in the active movie.

- ◆ **Current Script tag.** Indicates which script is being edited.

- ◆ **Pin Script.** Adds a tab for a selected script.

- ◆ **Options menu.** Contains options that control and format the Actions panel.

- ◆ **Add Statement.** Lets you add script elements to the current action.

- ◆ **Find, and Find and Replace.** Searches the active script.

- ◆ **Insert Target Path.** Inserts a specific target clip into the action.

- ◆ **Check Syntax.** Checks the current action for syntax errors.

- ◆ **Auto Format.** Cleans up the script by auto indenting.

- ◆ **Show Code Hint.** Gives you hints to the syntax of the action as you type.

- ◆ **Debug Options.** Add or remove breakpoints into the action to pause on the specified line of code.

- ◆ **Collapse and Expand.** Collapse between braces, collapse selection, or expand all.

- ◆ **Comments.** Apply a block or line comment.

- ◆ **Script Assist for 3.0.** Script assist provides a visual interface for editing scripts that includes syntax completion and parameter descriptions.

- ◆ **Help.** Provides online help.

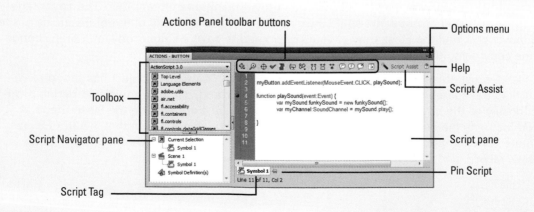

Actions Panel toolbar buttons

Options menu

Help

Script Assist

Toolbox

Script Navigator pane

Script Tag

Script pane

Pin Script

Understanding Properties and Methods

 FL 4.2

Objects in Flash are defined using two primary identifiers: properties and methods. The **properties** of an object define its characteristics. In the real world, a house would be an object, and its properties would be things like its color, style, and number of windows and doors. In Flash, it would be written something like this:

```
house.color = "green";
house.style = "ranch";
house.windows = "12";
house.doors = "2";
```

In this example, the word *house* is a unique instance name for the house object, and the words *color*, *style*, *windows*, and *doors* represent the properties assigned to this instance. Think of an instance as a copy of a Library item. When you create a movie clip, the object is created in Flash's Library. When you return to the Stage, you can then drag the movie clip from the Library to the Stage (technically, you're moving a Library symbol, created using the movie clip behavior). Once the movie clip is moved to the Stage, it is defined as an instance of the original Library item. When you select an instance on the Stage, Flash's Properties panel lets you give it a unique name. In the previous example, "house" is the unique name.

Giving a Library symbol a unique name gives you a lot of control. For example, you could move two instances of the same movie clip onto the Stage, give each of them its own unique name (house1, house2) in the Properties panel, and then define different properties for each one. Something like this:

```
house1.color = "green";      house2.color = "blue";
house1.style = "ranch";      house2.style = "tudor";
house1.windows = "12";       house2.windows = "8";
house1.doors = "2";          house2.doors = "4";
```

As a matter of fact, you could create an entire town using one Library item. The advantage to this approach is enormous. You could create a Flash movie with 100 different instances of the same movie clip, and the Flash movie would only need to save a single copy, and then change that one copy using different properties.

In Flash, most objects have properties. For example, the MovieClip object has property values such as transparency, horizontal and vertical position, and visibility. You might define properties loosely as the physical appearance of a movie clip, as it appears on the Flash Stage. A **method** instructs the object to perform some task. A method is a function that is part of a class definition. For example, if a DVD player is an object, then the methods would be something like: play, record, and stop. Flash methods are written like this:

```
play();
record();
stop();
```

Some methods require parameters within the parenthesis. The following method instructs the play head to move to frame 6 on the Timeline and stop:

    gotoAndStop(6);

Attaching the method to a specific object requires identifying the object in the ActionScript code:

    myDVD.gotoAndStop(6);

ActionScript is a language, and just like learning any foreign language, all the words and syntax might seem strange at first; however, the longer you work with the language, the simpler it becomes.

Introducing ActionScript 3.0

Flash 8 uses ActionScript versions 1.0 and 2.0. In CS3, Flash introduced ActionScript 3.0, a robust programming model familiar to developers with a basic knowledge of object-oriented programming. ActionScript 3.0 allows you to create highly complex applications with large data sets and object-oriented, reusable code bases. ActionScript 3.0 provides a new architecture, core language features, and an improved Flash Player API for better low-level control. Some of the enhancements include more run-time exceptions for common error conditions, added use of run-time type information, improved use of properties and classes with sealed classes, added use of method closures for event handling, added use of industry standard ECMAScript for XML, more support for regular expressions, and added primitive types (int and uint). For specific details about using an ActionScript language, click the Help menu, click Flash Help, and then look in the *Programming ActionScript 2.0 or 3.0* or the *ActionScript 2.0 or 3.0 Language and Components Reference* online chapter.

While ActionScript 3.0 is not required for content that runs in Adobe Flash Player 9 or later, it allows performance improvements that are available only with the ActionScript Virtual Machine (AVM2). ActionScript 3.0 code can execute up to ten times faster than legacy ActionScript code.

Compatibility

The older version of ActionScript Virtual Machine (AVM1) executes ActionScript 1.0 and ActionScript 2.0 code. Flash Player 9 supports AVM1 for backward compatibility with existing and legacy content. Flash Player 7 and 8 only support AVM1 and not AVM2. However, there are a few things you need to know about compatibility. A SWF file cannot combine ActionScript 1.0 or 2.0 with ActionScript 3.0 code, and ActionScript code can load an SWF file with ActionScript 1.0 or 2.0, but it cannot access the file's variables and functions (except you can use the loadMovieNum() command and pass a level parameter). If you have ActionScript 1.0 or 2.0 code and want to use version 3.0 code, you need to migrate all the old code to version 3.0. If you want to use behaviors, you need to use ActionScript 2.0; behaviors are not available for ActionScript 3.0.

Working with Objects and Classes

 FL 4.1, 4.2, 4.3, 4.4

With ActionScript 3.0, you specify a class definition, either document or object level, to work with objects using ActionScript code. To create your own class, you need to follow a certain syntax. First, you enter a package statement to indicate where your class will be found. Then, you enter a class statement to define the name of the class. At this point, you define each property in the class by using variables, and each method by using functions. When you define a class element, such as a property or method, you can also specify an attribute. A private attribute can be called only by code within the class, while a public attribute can be called by any code in the program. After you define a class, you can define a subclass that inherits all the properties and methods of the parent class, or superclass. In the subclass, you can add methods and properties and override others from the superclass, known as polymorphism. If you want to trigger actions based on events, you can use the EventDispatcher class to keep track of event listeners and notify them of events.

Work with Objects and Classes in ActionScript

1. Create or open a Flash document (ActionScript 3.0).

2. Open the Properties panel.

3. Click the Stage.

4. In the Class field, type the name of the ActionScript file to create a document class definition.

   IMPORTANT *Be sure not to include the .as extension.*

5. Open the Library panel.

6. Right-click (Win) or ⌘-click (Mac) the object you want to control in ActionScript, and then click **Properties**.

7. Click **Advanced**, if available. (Button name changes to Basic.)

8. Enter a name for the object.

9. Select the **Export for ActionScript** check box.

   The Class appears with the same name as the object, and the Base class appears with object type.

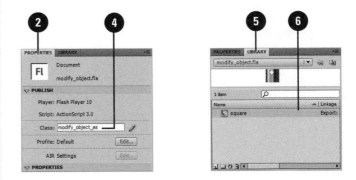

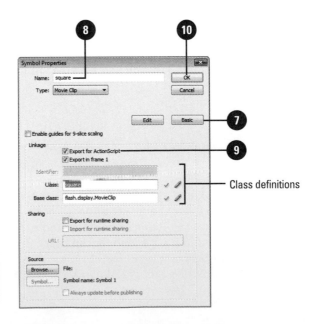

Class definitions

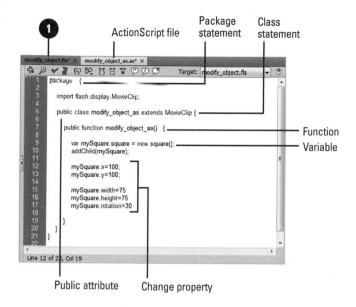

1

ActionScript file

Package statement

Class statement

Function

Variable

Public attribute

Change property

10 Click **OK**.

11 If prompted, click **OK** to define the new class.

12 Click the **File** menu, and then click **Save**.

13 Click the **File** menu, click **New**, and then click the **General** tab.

14 Click **ActionScript File**.

15 Click **OK**.

16 Click the **File** menu, and then click **Save As**.

17 Navigate to the folder with the Flash document, and then name the file (same as the one in Step 4).

18 Click **Save**.

19 In the Actions panel, enter the script as shown in the illustration.

IMPORTANT *ActionScript 3.0 is case-sensitive, so upper- and lower-case make a difference.*

20 Click the **File** menu, click **Save**, and then close the ActionScript file.

21 Click the **Control** menu, and then click **Test Movie**.

Did You Know?

You can define accessor methods. For advanced ActionScripting, you can also define accessors methods, which are a cross between a method and property (defined like a method, yet creates an instance like a property).

Common Syntax in ActionScript 3.0

Command	Description
Dot syntax	Access the properties and methods of an object. myDotEx.method ();
Slash syntax	Not supported in ActionScript 3.0.
Literals	A value that appears directly in your code. "text", true, false, 10
Semicolon (;)	Terminates (ends) a statement. var a:int = 2;
Parentheses	Indicates order of operation, evaluates a series of expressions, or pass parameters.
Comments	Documents code. Single-line comments begin with //, while multi-line comment begin with /* and ends with */.
Keywords	Reserved words you cannot use as identifiers. as, class, const, if, var, true, in
Constants	A fixed value. const MINIMUM:int = 0; ActionScript defines constants with all CAPS with words separated by an underscore. const MOUSE_DOWN:String = "mouseDown";

Applying Properties and Methods to an Object

Once you've gotten the hang of writing ActionScripts, the next step is to apply properties and methods to objects in a Flash document. You can have an object and let your visitor control its color. Changing the color is an example of changing an object's properties. To make an object change color, you will need a Flash document that contains a MovieClip and button symbols. An easy script translation would be: Flash, when my visitor clicks (release) on the button, I want you to assign a new color to an object that I gave a unique instance name (change it), and I'm defining that property as objectColor, and change the color (setRGB) to red (0x990000). When you attach ActionScripts to buttons, you're not limited to just a single use. For example, you could drag three instances of the same button symbol on the Stage and repeat the previous code with one exception: change the SetRGB value of one to (0x990000) for red, another to (0x009900) for green, and the third one to (0x000099) for blue.

Apply Properties and Methods

1. Drag the movie clip onto the Stage.

2. Enter a unique instance name in the Properties panel.

3. Drag the button symbol onto the Stage, and then select the symbol.

4. Click the **Window** menu, and then click **Actions** to open the Actions panel.

Did You Know?

You can now edit ActionScript code using external editor applications. MetaData (Windows), BBEdit (Macintosh), or any editor that saves files using the .as (ActionScript) extension gives you the ability to edit and save ActionScript code. The file can then be opened in Flash (click the File menu, and then click Open) or imported into the Flash Actions panel (click the Actions Options button, and then click Import Script).

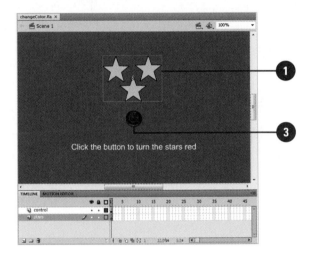

5 Enter the script (ActionScript 2.0) as shown in the illustration.

◆ ActionScript 3.0 example files are available on the Web at *www.perspection.com*.

6 Click the **Control** menu, and then click **Test Movie**.

7 Click the button to change the color of the object to red.

IMPORTANT *Button objects can have triggering events other than a user click. You can create a button instance that uses the rollover event, and have an object change color as the user rolls over the button. Or, you can create an invisible button with a rollover event that triggers a property change when the user rolls over a specific portion of the image.*

See Also

See "Creating Invisible Buttons" on page 153 for information on creating invisible buttons.

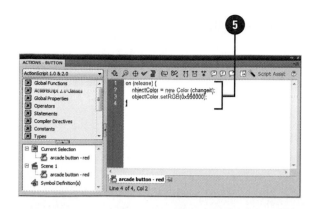

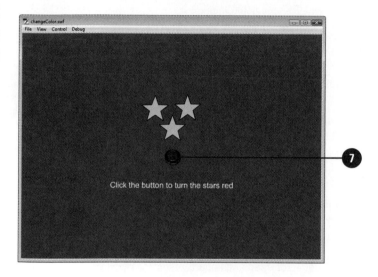

Setting ActionScript Preferences

Since ActionScripting is so important, Flash gives you the ability to control the Actions panel through preferences. ActionScript preferences give you the ability to control the font and size of the text typed into the Actions panel, as well as using syntax coloring to help you visualize the code. You can also set AutoFormat preferences to specify the automatic formatting you want for your ActionScript code.

Set ActionScript Preferences

1 Click the **Flash** (Mac) or **Edit** (Win) menu, and then click **Preferences**.

2 Click the **ActionScript** category,

3 Select from the following options:

◆ **Automatic Indentation.** Instructs Flash to perform syntax indentation.

◆ **Tab Size.** Enter a value for the number of spaces used.

◆ **Code Hints.** Gives you on-screen hints as you type.

◆ **Delay.** Delay before showing a code hint. Drag slider to select a value (0 to 4) in seconds.

◆ **Font.** Select a font and size for the ActionScript text.

◆ **Open/Import and Save/Export.** Select UTF-8 or Default encoding for open and import operations (UTF-8 is best).

◆ **Reload Modified Files.** Click to be prompted when Flash needs to reload a modified file.

◆ **Syntax Coloring.** Choose the syntax-coloring scheme.

◆ **Language.** Click ActionScript 2.0 or ActionScript 3.0 to modify the ActionScript sub-settings.

4 Click the **Auto Format** category.

5 Select the format check boxes you want and view the effect in preview.

6 Click **OK**.

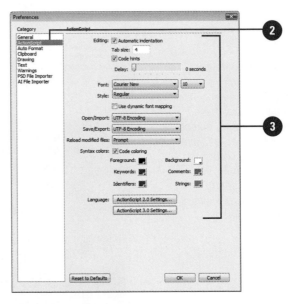

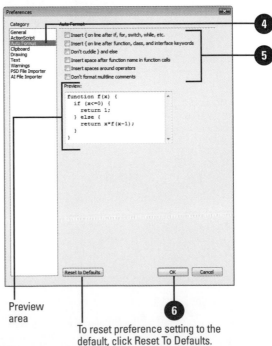

Preview area

To reset preference setting to the default, click Reset To Defaults.

Using Dot Syntax

ActionScript, just like any human language, has rules you should follow. However, in ActionScripts, you have to follow the rules or it won't work. One of the more important rules to follow is the use of dot syntax. The use of dots (.) in a script serves several purposes. First, is to specify the target path to a particular Timeline. For example, **_root.america.kansas.wichita** defines a movie clip on the main (_root) Timeline with the name america, containing a movie clip named kansas, which in turn contains a movie clip named wichita. Dot syntax is used to create a road map for Flash to follow. Dot syntax is a separator between two or more parts of a Flash script.

Another use of dot syntax is to change the properties and methods for a specific object. Since ActionScript, by definition is an object-oriented language, Flash performs its responsibilities by instructing an object to do something (method), or by changing a property. For example, **star._rotation = 90;** instructs Flash to rotate the MovieClip instance named *star*, 90 degrees (property). To instruct the star MovieClip instance to play (method), you would enter the following code: **star.play();**

Movie Clip with Instance Name: *MovieA*

ActionScript 2.0

ActionScript 3.0

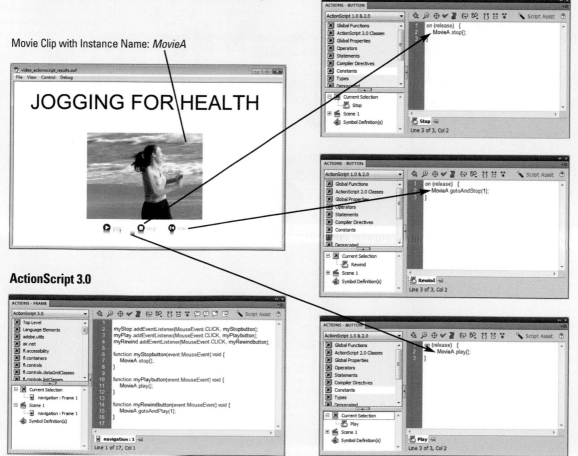

Applying Dot Syntax to a Movie Clip

When you use dot syntax, you gain control over a Flash ActionScript. For example, you have a movie clip of a car, and the wheels of the car are separate movie clips. In other words, you've dragged a movie clip symbol (the wheels), into a movie clip (the car), and you want to use a button to stop and start the wheels movie clip. To do this will require using dot syntax to identify the path to the correct movie clip, and then use the play or stop methods on the wheels.

Use Dot Syntax

1 Open the file *movingCar.fla,* and then open the car movie clip symbol in the Flash Library.

See "*Real World Examples*" on page xviii in the Introduction for information on downloading practice files from the Web.

2 Create a new layer, and then select the new layer.

3 Drag the wheel movie clip symbol into the car movie clip, and then place one copy for the front and one copy for the back wheels.

4 Select and give each of the wheel symbols a unique name in the Properties panel.

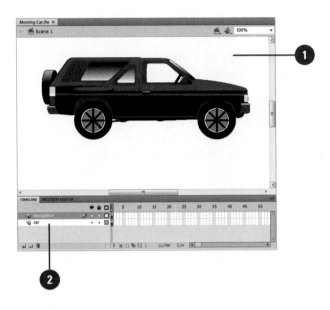

5 Return to the Stage, drag the car movie symbol onto the Stage, and then select the symbol.

6 Give the car movie symbol a unique name in the Properties panel.

7 Drag the Play button symbol onto the Stage, and then select the symbol.

8 Enter the script (ActionScript 2.0) as shown in the illustration.

IMPORTANT *Transportation is the instance name of the car symbol on the Stage, and front wheel and back wheel are the instance names for the wheel movie clips as defined in the Library.*

9 Drag the Stop button symbol onto the Stage, and then select the symbol.

10 Enter the script (ActionScript 2.0) as shown in the illustration.

◆ ActionScript 3.0 example files are available on the Web at *www.perspection.com*.

11 Click the **Control** menu, and then click **Test Movie**.

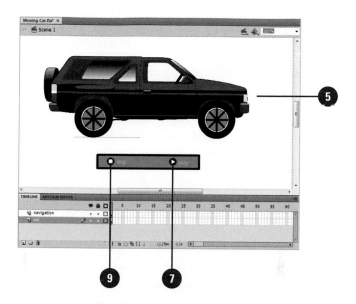

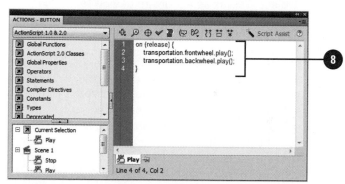

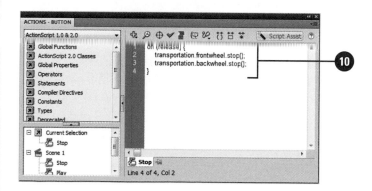

Understanding Data Types

When you use ActionScripts, you have the ability to work with data. Data can be information entered in by a visitor in an input data field, or it can be computer information such as the current position of the mouse, or the date and time. When you work with data, you have 4 possible data types:

- ◆ **String.** Allows for the entering of text values.

- ◆ **Number.** Allows for the entering of numeric values.

- ◆ **Boolean.** A Boolean state has two values; typically true or false.

- ◆ **Object.** Serves as a storage device for any data type, including other objects.

Use Data Types to Control Information

Since data types control the type of information that can be entered into a data field, you can use them to validate the data someone is entering. For example, you want to create a calculator to convert between degrees Fahrenheit and Celsius. To do this, you will need an input field for someone to enter the current temperature in Fahrenheit, a button that would perform the calculation, and then a dynamic text field for the result, and one for an error message.

1. Select the Input Field, and then give it a unique variable name in the Properties panel.

2. Select the Error Dynamic Text Field and give it a unique variable name in the Properties panel.

3. Select the Results Dynamic Text Field, and give it a unique variable name in the Properties panel.

4. Select the button instance, and then enter a script into the Actions panel (see the example file for script details).

When the movie is played, the visitor will enter a value into the data field, and it will be evaluated as to whether it's purely numeric. If it isn't, an error message will display in the dynamic error field. If the field contains numbers, then the calculation will perform the conversion and display the results displayed in the output field.

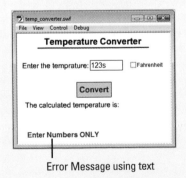

Error Message using text

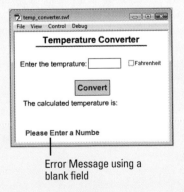

Error Message using a blank field

Correct data...no error message

Using Functions

A **function** is a block of ActionScript code that can be reused anywhere in a SWF file. If you pass values as parameters to a function, the function will operate on those values. A function can also return values. Flash contains built-in functions that let you access certain information and perform certain tasks, such as getting the version number of Flash Player hosting the SWF file (getVersion()). Functions that belong to an object are called methods. Functions that don't belong to an object are called top-level functions and are found in the Functions category of the Actions panel.

Each function has its own characteristics, and some functions require you to pass certain values. If you pass more parameters than the function requires, the extra values are ignored. If you don't pass a required parameter, the empty parameters are assigned the undefined data type, which can cause errors when you export a script. To call a function, it must be in a frame that the playhead has reached.

To call a function, simply use the function name and pass any required parameters. The following code describes a common syntax for creating functions:

```
function firstFunction (x, y, z) {

    // place all actions here;

}
```

Calling a Function

Functions begin with the word function, followed by the name of the function (user-defined). The area enclosed by parenthesis is used for passing parameters to the function actions. If the parameters are left blank, you're essentially creating a generic function that will function the same way every time it's called. If the function contains parameters, it will perform in a unique way each time it's called. When you call a function, you're instructing Flash to execute all of the actions within that function. Therefore, if firstFunction contained 20 actions, all of them would be executed by using a single line of script. To call a function, simply add this line to the action:

```
myFunction ();
```

Passing Parameters to a Function

If the function has been defined to accept parameter information, you can use the following line of script:

```
myFunction (parameter 1, parameter2);
```

Once a Function is defined, it can be called anytime it's needed. Therefore, it's a good practice to define all of your functions in frame 1 of the active Flash document. That way they can be called anytime after that.

Understanding Event Handlers

Event handlers, also known as event listeners, control when events in Flash occur. When you create a script, some event will be invoked to trigger that particular action.

Event Handlers with ActionScript 3.0

For ActionScript 3.0, event handlers are functions (also known as listener functions) that respond to specific events. For example,

function clickHandler(event:MouseEvent):void { }

After you create a listener function, you use the addEventListener() method to register the function with the target event. For example,

addEventListener (MouseEvent.CLICK, clickHandler);

Event Handlers with ActionScript 2.0

For ActionScript 2.0, event handlers come in three different types: mouse events, frame events, and clip events. Mouse events trigger actions when the mouse interacts with a button or movie clip instance. The following events can be associated with mouse events:

- **on (press).** The acton is triggered when the mouse is pressed.

- **on (release).** The action is triggered when the mouse is released.

- **on (releaseOutside).** The action is triggered when the mouse is pressed on a object (button), and then released outside.

- **on (keyPress).** The action is triggered when the visitor presses a key.

- **on (rollOver).** The action is triggered when the visitor rolls over an object.

- **on (rollOut).** The action is triggered when the visitor rolls out of an object.

- **on (dragOver).** The action is triggered when the visitor clicks and then drags into an object.

- **on (dragOut).** The action is triggered when the visitor clicks on an object, and then drags out.

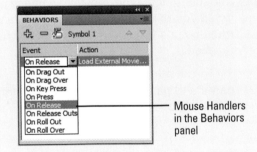

Mouse Handlers in the Behaviors panel

Mouse Handlers in ActionScript 3.0

Mouse Handlers in ActionScript 2.0

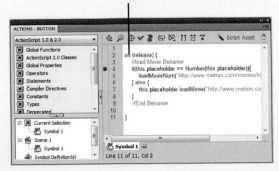

Attaching a Mouse Event to a Button

Attaching a mouse event to a button is probably the easiest of all the event handlers. For example, you have a movie clip of a dog that contains a barking audio file. When the movie clip plays, the dog barks. The trick is to have the dog bark when the visitor rolls their mouse over the dog's face. To do this, you will need to create an invisible button and then attach the mouse event to the invisible button.

Attach an Event to a Button

1. Click the **Insert** menu, and then click **New Symbol**.

2. Select the **Button** type, and then name the symbol.

3. Click **OK**.

4. Create a blank keyframe in the Hit state of the button, and then create a shape.

   Leave the Up, Over, and Down states blank.

5. Exit the Symbol editing mode, and then return to the Stage.

6. Drag a movie clip onto the Stage.

7. Create a new layer, and then name the layer.

8. Drag the invisible button onto the Stage, and then place it over the area of the image you want to use as a button.

9. Enter the script (ActionScript 2.0) as shown in the illustration.

   ◆ ActionScript 3.0 example files are available on the Web at *www.perspection.com*.

   When the visitor rolls into or out of the invisible button, the rollOver or rollOut event handlers will trigger the playing or stopping of the dog movie clip.

10. Click the **Control** menu, and then click **Test Movie**.

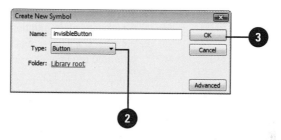

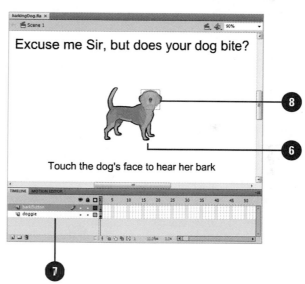

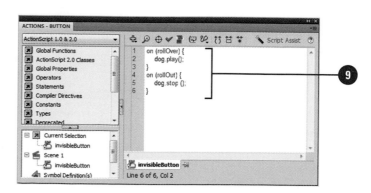

Working with Frame Events

Frame event handlers are easy to understand. When an action is attached to a frame, the action is triggered when the play head hits the frame. For example, you want to create a frame event that swaps images on the Stage, and you want the images to swap every 40 frames. You can attach an ActionScript that swaps the image, and place the action every 40 frames. When the play head hits the frame, the action executes. When you attach an ActionScript to a frame, you'll need a blank keyframe on the Timeline, and it is strongly recommended that you always place ActionScripts in a separate layer from access and control. In addition, if you're planning to swap images in a Flash movie, it's always best to use a blank movie clip (called a placeholder) to hold the images.

Attach an ActionScript to a Frame

1. Drag a blank movie clip onto the Stage, and then select the clip.

2. Give the movie clip a unique instance name in the Properties panel.

3. Create a new layer, and then name the layer.

4. Create blank keyframes at frame numbers 1, 21, 41, and 61.

5. Select a frame, click the **Insert** menu, point to **Timeline**, and then click **Blank Keyframe**.

6. Select frame 1, and then enter the script (ActionScript 2.0) as shown in the illustration.

    ◆ ActionScript 3.0 example files are available on the Web at *www.perspection.com*.

7. Select frames 21, 41, and 61, and then repeat the script, except change the name of the image you want to load (image_b.jpg, image_c.jpg, image_d.jpg).

8. Click the **Control** menu, and then click **Test Movie**.

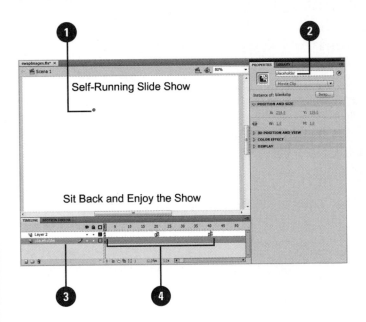

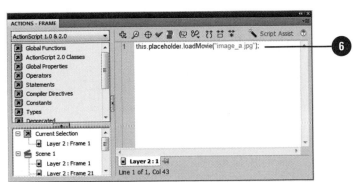

Working with Clip Events

If you're working with ActionScript 2.0 (not supported in ActionScript 3.0), you can attach clip events to movie clips, which triggers an action specified in the onClipEvent handler. You might want a specific movie clip to stop playing when another movie clip loads on the Stage, or when the user clicks or moves their mouse.

The Clip Event is one of a series of event handlers that Flash uses to create actions within a Flash movie. You can attach event handlers directly to a button or movie clip instance by using the onClipEvent() or the on() handlers. The onClipEvent() handles movie clip events, and on() handles button events. To use an on() or onClipEvent() handler, attach it directly to an instance of a button or movie clip on the Stage, and then specify the event you want to handle for that instance. For example, the following on() event handler executes whenever the user clicks the button the handler is attached to.

```
on(press) {
    trace("The button has been pressed.");
}
```

You can specify two or more events for each on() handler, separated by commas. The ActionScript in a handler executes when one of the events specified by the handler occurs. For example, the following on() handler attached to a button will execute whenever the mouse rolls over or out of the button.

```
on(rollOver, rollOut) {
    trace("mouse rolled in or out");
}
```

If you want different scripts to run when different events occur, you have the option to attach more than one handler to an object. You can attach onClipEvent() handlers to the same movie clip instance. The first would execute when the movie clip first loads (or appears on the Stage); the second executes when the movie clip is unloaded from the Stage.

```
onClipEvent(load) {
    trace("loaded");
}
onClipEvent (unload) {
    trace("unloaded");
}
```

Assigning a Clip Event using the Behaviors panel

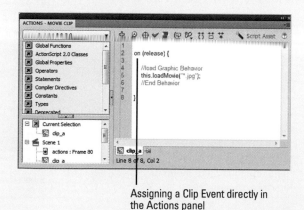

Assigning a Clip Event directly in the Actions panel

Attaching a Clip Event to a Movie Clip

For ActionScript 2.0, you can only attach an onClipEvent() to a movie clip instance that has been placed on the Stage. You can't attach an onClipEvent() to a movie clip instance that is created at runtime; for example, using the attachMovie() method. However, you can still attach multiple event handlers. Using different event handlers within the same Flash document do not conflict with each other. You could have a button with an on(press) handler that tells the .swf file to play, and the same button can have an onPress method, for which you define a function that tells an object on the Stage to rotate. When the button is clicked, the SWF file plays, and the object will rotate. Being able to consolidate different event handlers with a single instance gives you greater control, as well as less Stage clutter.

Attach an onClipEvent to a Movie Clip

1. Create or open a Flash document (ActionScript 2.0), place a movie clip on the Stage, and then select the movie clip.

2. Give the movie clip a unique instance name in the Properties panel.

3. Move down the Timeline and add a keyframe at frame 80.

4. Click the **Insert** menu, point to **Timeline**, and then click **Keyframe**.

5. Add a second movie clip to the Stage, and then select the second movie clip.

6. Enter the script as shown in the illustration.

7. Click the **Control** menu, and then click **Test Movie**.

   When the playhead hits frame 80 it loads the second movie clip. The loading of the movie will trigger the onClipEvent handler, and stop the playing of the movie clip with the unique instance name of movie2.

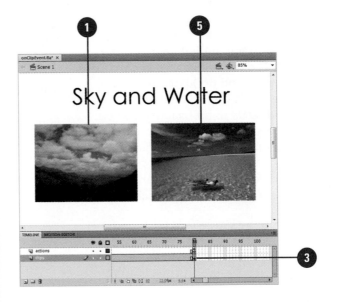

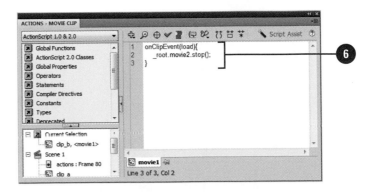

Creating Loops

Loops allow Flash to perform an action repeatedly. You can use a loop to create a dynamic drop-down menu, validate data, search for text, duplicate movie clips, and even detect collisions in games that have projectiles and objects. **Conditional statements** let you execute an action based on a specific condition. You can have a specific action continue to loop until a certain condition is met. For example, continue to search for a specific text string until it is found or the end of the text document is reached. Loops come in two forms—While loops and For loops—it doesn't matter what type of loop is chosen, they will both require a conditional statement to start and stop.

- **While Loops.** While loops continue to execute while a certain condition exists (keep looping or searching) until a specific value is reached.

  ```
  i = 4;
  while (var i > 0) {
      my_mc.duplicateMovieClip("newMC" + i, i );
      i--;
  }
  ```

- **For Loops.** For loops are self-contained counters. For example, loop (repeat the action) ten times and then stop.

  ```
  x = x;
  for (x=0; x<=10, ++x)  {
      myClip.duplicateMovieClip ("myClip" + x, x);
      myClip._rotation =45 + x * 10;
  }
  ```

Working with For Loops

The For loop works with an increasing or decreasing numeric value. For example, you could use a For loop to create several copies of a movie clip on the Stage. Letting the For loop control movie clips to the Stage is far more efficient than having to move them one at a time. In addition, the visitor can control when the items appear on the Stage using a button.

Work with For Loops

1. Drag a movie clip from the Library to the Stage, and then select the movie clip.

2. Enter a unique instance name for the movie clip in the Properties panel.

3. Place a button on the Stage, and then select the button.

4. Enter the script (ActionScript 2.0) as shown in the illustration.

   ◆ ActionScript 3.0 example files are available on the Web at *www.perspection.com*.

When you play the movie, clicking on the button causes the action to loop 10 times. Each time it loops, it duplicates the original movie clip and rotate it by 45 degrees plus the current value of x times 10.

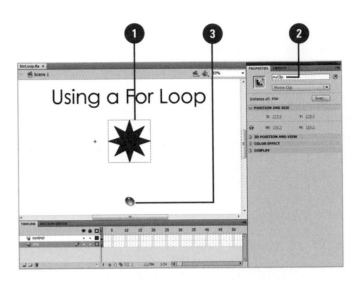

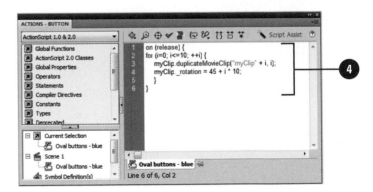

Did You Know?

You can use a For Loop to pause a Flash movie. Select a value, instruct the loop to increment by 1, and then loop until the value is reached. Use a loop timer for such items as a Flash slide show, where you want the slides to display on the stage for a given number of seconds before moving to the next slide.

Working with While Loops and Using Loop Exceptions

While loops wait for a specific condition to start or stop the loop. That may sound similar to the For loop, with one exception: The For Loop is self-contained, and the While loop works with an external condition, or one outside the scope of the loop. For example, to have a While loop perform the same action as the previous For loop, you would use the following script:

```
x = 0;
while (x<10) {
  myClip.duplicateMovieClip ("myClip" + x, x);
  myClip._rotation =45 + x * 10;
  x=x+1;
}
```

When you create a Looping action, you can further control the loop by using the following loop exceptions:

◆ **Continue.** The continue exception lets you stop the current loop from performing its actions and jump directly to the next cycle of the loop.

◆ **Break.** The break exception is used to exit a loop, even if the original condition that is driving the loop is still true.

For example, if you create a While loop using the following script:

```
total = 0;
i = 0:
while (++i <=20) {
  if (i == 10) {
    continue;
  }
  total +=i;
}
```

The results would be a script that executes and adds 1 to total; unless the value of i equaled 10. This would create a sequence of numbers 1 2 3 4 5 6 7 8 9 11 12 13 14 15 16 17 18 19 20. If you had used the break exception in place of continue, the values would read: 1 2 3 4 5 6 7 8 9. Therefore, it loops whether For or While are controlled by internal or external conditions, and using a break or continue exception gives you further control over the loop.

Using Conditional Statements

Conditional statements in ActionScript are a critical part of interactivity. They let you program a script based on any number of conditions. For example, in the morning, you say good day, or good morning to someone you meet. In doing so, you made a conditional choice.

ActionScript does the same thing. You can create an ActionScript that checks the time of day. If it's before noon, Flash responds with a Good Morning message. If it's from noon to 5, Flash says Good Afternoon, or from 5 till midnight, Flash says Good Evening. This type of condition is known as an if/else condition. If this happens, do this... else do that. Since a variable can be almost anything you can measure on a computer, and a conditional statement is made up of two or more variables, ActionScript can be taken to a point where it almost thinks for itself. The previous example could be expressed in flow charting the following way:

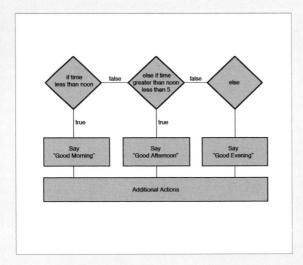

Typically, when you're creating a conditional statement, you're comparing one element against another using operators. The following operators are available to create conditional statements:

◆ == Checks for equality between two values (is time of day equal to 5).

◆ != Checks for inequality between two values.

◆ < Checks for less than (is value A less than value B).

◆ > Checks for greater than (is value A greater than value B).

◆ <= Checks for less than or equal to between two values.

◆ >= Checks for greater than or equal to between two values.

◆ **&&** Checks for a logical AND (if day == "Friday" && time > 5).

◆ || Checks for a logical OR (if day == "Saturday" || day == "Sunday").

Using these operators to check between two or more values, you can create complex ActionScripts that react differently based on the available data. To create a dynamic field that checks the time, and responds with the appropriate answer, you would enter the following code:

```
if (time > "0000 &&  time < 1200) {
    response = "Good Morning";
} else if (time >1200 && time < 1700) {
    response = "Good Afternoon";
}else if (time > 1700 && time < 2400);
    response = "Good Evening"
}
```

Working with ActionScript Behaviors

Behaviors are time-savers because they give you sections of ActionScript 2.0 code (not supported in ActionScript 3.0) for common Flash tasks. Behaviors are a great way to introduce yourself to the wonderful world of ActionScripting without having to write all the code. For example, if you want to add a Play ActionScript to a button, you can do it using the Add button in the Behaviors panel, or you can write out the code on your own; see the example code below. Using Behaviors, as opposed to writing the code by hand, is not better, it's simply faster. The more time you save doing common Action-Scripting tasks using Behaviors, the more time you will have for the creative process.

Using the Behaviors Panel

You use the Behaviors panel to apply the behavior to a triggering object, such as a button. You specify the event that triggers the behavior, such as releasing the mouse. Next select a target object, such as the movie clip instance, and then select settings for behavior parameters, such as a frame number or label, or a relative or absolute path. Flash comes with built-in behaviors, such as Load Graphic, Duplicate Movieclip, and GotoAndPlay At Frame Or Label. To add and configure a

behavior, select a trigger object, and then step through the following general instructions (steps may vary depending on the behavior):

1. Click the **Window** menu, and then click **Behaviors**.

2. Click the **Add (+)** button, and then select a behavior from the menu.

3. If necessary, select settings for the behavior parameters, and then click **OK**.

4. Under Event, click **On Release** (the default event), and then select a mouse event from the menu.

Add button   Click to select a mouse event.

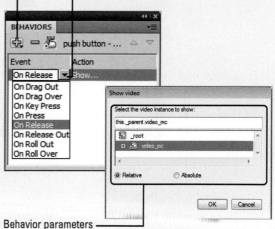

Behavior parameters

Example Play ActionScript code

```
on (release) {
    if(this.video_1._parent._currentframe == this.video_1.parent._totalframes){
        this.video_1parent.gotoAndPlay(1);
    } else {
        this.video_1._parent.play();
    }
}
```

Using an ActionScript Behavior

You can use behaviors (ready-made scripts) to help you get started with ActionScript 2.0 (not supported in ActionScript 3.0). Here's an example. The Start and Stop Dragging Movieclip Behaviors are a novel way to give Flash visitors the chance to interact with your site. The behaviors can be attached to objects on the screen. When the visitor clicks and drags an object, it is dragged along for the ride. For example, you could create a puzzle, and let the visitors assemble the puzzle. To begin the process, you will need an ActionScript 2.0 Flash document that contains one or more movie clips (for dragging).

Use the Start and Stop Dragging Behaviors

1. Create or open a Flash document (ActionScript 2.0), and then select the layer to contain the movie clip or clips.

2. Drag the movie clips from the Library onto the Stage, and then enter a unique instance name for each movie clip.

3. Select a movie clip, click the **Add** (**+**) button in the Behaviors panel, point to **Movieclip**, and then click **Start Dragging Movieclip**.

4. Select the unique instance name for the movie clip.

5. Click **OK**.

6. Click the **Event** list arrow, and then change the event that triggers the behavior to On Press.

7. With a selected movie clip, click the **Add** (**+**) button in the Behaviors panel, point to **Movieclip**, and then click **Stop Dragging Movieclip**.

8. Click **OK**.

9. Click the **Event** list arrow, and then change the event that triggers the behavior to On Release.

   Repeat steps 3 through 9 for all of the movie clips.

10. Click the **Control** menu, and then click **Test Movie**.

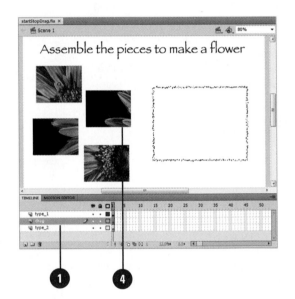

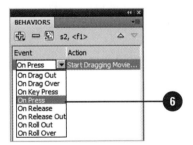

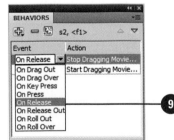

Debugging a Movie

15

Introduction

Flash provides several enhancements that make it easier for you to debug scripts using the ActionScript language. The features include new language elements, improved editing and debugging tools, and the introduction of a more object-oriented programming language; however, not all debugging problems reside in an ActionScript. Debugging a Flash movie is similar to a mechanic attempting to fix the engine on a car. He can hear a knocking or pinging sound, but he's not sure what's causing it, so he brings out his debugging tools to help locate the problem.

A Flash movie is not a car, however, there are similarities. If the movie is not doing what you want: Maybe it's running too slow, or your movie crashes after playing a specific scene; you can bring out Flash's debugging tools to help locate (and fix) the problem. When you design a Flash movie, the fonts, colors, video and audio (if any), along with the overall construction of the movie are very right-brain techniques (your creative side at work). When you debug a Flash movie, you're using a very logical approach to the problem. Like the car mechanic, you're listening for that annoying pinging sound. Flash will not only help you locate the problem, its array of debugging tools will help you fix it and get you back speeding down the electronic highway.

Flash's debugging tools include the Debug workspace (ActionScript 3.0) or Actions panel (ActionScript 2.0) and the Movie Explorer, where you can set breakpoints, view variables, and see how they react during the play of the movie. Flash uses a different debugger for ActionScript 3.0 files than it does for ActionScript 2.0 files. The debugger functionality is similar, but the look and feel is different. The debugger for ActionScript 3.0 uses the Debug workspace while ActionScript 2.0 uses traditional the Actions panel.

What You'll Do

Debug Concepts

Debug with the ActionScript Editor

Use the Movie Explorer

Debug for ActionScript 3.0

Debug for ActionScript 2.0

View Variables

Add Variables to the Watch List

View Properties

Set Breakpoints

Step Through Code

Debug Manually

Debugging Concepts

When you debug a movie, you're not just looking for the obvious problems; you're attempting to see if you can find anything that might happen. Depending on the complexity of the movie, hidden problems can be difficult to find. For example, if you're calling video files into a Flash movie, are all your paths to the files correct? It may function fine when you're testing on your computer, but will it still work when you move it to a CD or Web server? Test it and find out. Here are a few things to consider when going into the debug phase of a Flash Movie:

◆ **Paths to file.** If you're importing external .swf files, image files, video, or audio files into a Flash movie, the best approach is to create a folder to hold the entire Flash project, and then create sub-folders within that folder to hold the movie assets. When you move the Flash project, move the entire folder. That way,

all the path names stay correct, and you always know where everything is, at all times.

◆ **Short, descriptive file names.** Computers allow for file names of unlimited length; however, that does not mean that you need to use large file names. Large file names are harder for you to type in, and there is a greater chance that you will mistype the name. Use short, descriptive names.

◆ **Use smart naming conventions.** Since file names display alphabetically, it's not a bad idea to come up with similar names for similar file types. For example, car_1.jpg, car_2.jpg, car_3.jpg. The name and extension describe (in general terms) the content of the file and file type and will display one after the other. Smart naming conventions won't make your Flash project any

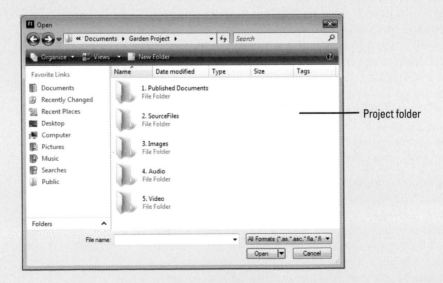

Project folder

better, but they will help to organize some of the confusion that comes with a complicated Flash project.

- **Test and test often.** Debugging does not start at the end of a project, it begins as soon as you click the File menu, and then click New. Flash lets you test a movie whenever you choose. Just click the Control menu and then click Test Movie (to test the entire Flash movie), or click Test Scene (to test just the active scene).When you test a scene or movie, Flash creates a temporary .swf file and then runs the movie in a version of the Flash plug-in. Flash publishes the test movie using the settings in the Publishing dialog box.

- **Bandwidth.** If a project is going out to the Internet, make sure that the size of the finished movie isn't so large that your visitors have to wait a long time for it to download. It's possible you might want to include a pre-loader to entertain the audience while they're waiting.

- **Planning is the key.** If you want your Flash movie to look good, work without error, and be completed in the least amount of time, then plan, plan, and then plan some more. Use the carpenter's adage: Measure Twice... Cut Once. University studies show that planning a project, before you start, cuts the project completion time by 20 percent. Planning involves thinking about what you want to accomplish (what's the message), research and gather all the files and things you'll need to complete the project, and think about where the project will be used (Internet, CD). In addition, a well-planned project will cut down your debugging time by over half.

Smart file naming conventions

Debugging with the ActionScript Editor

FL 5.1, 5.2

The ActionScript editor allows you to edit and debug scripts. When you're debugging a Flash movie, the traditional wisdom is to try to push it until it breaks, and then figure out why it broke. However, once you find out what's broken, it's very possible that you're going to have to work on the ActionScript's that drive the movie. That's where the Actions panel comes into play. The designers of Flash included editing and debugging features to make debugging easier. You can quickly set and remove breakpoints using the Debug Options button to check different parts of your code to determine if it's working correctly. You can also work in the Actions panel in **Script Assist** mode—supported by ActionScript 2.0 and ActionScript 3.0—in which you filled in options and parameters to create code. It is a great way for novice ActionScript coders to learn programming. To make working with code easier, you can use collapse and expand buttons to show and hide sections of code. In addition, you can use buttons to quickly add comments to a line of code or a block of code to document your work.

Use the ActionScript Editor

1. Click the **Window** menu, and then click **Actions** to open the ActionScript Editor.

2. **Script Assist**. You can view, write, and edit scripts using a visual interface that includes automatic syntax completion and parameter descriptions.

3. **Word wrapping**. Click the Options pop-up menu in the Script pane to enable or disable word wrapping.

4. **Viewing context-sensitive Help**. When your pointer is positioned over an ActionScript element in the Actions toolbox or in the Script pane, you can click the Reference button in the context menu to display an element help page.

5. **Importing scripts**. When you select Import Script from the pop-up menu in the Actions panel, the imported script is copied into the script at the insertion point.

6. **Single-click breakpoints**. To add a debugging breakpoint before a line of code in the Debugger panel or the Script pane of the Actions panel, click in the left margin.

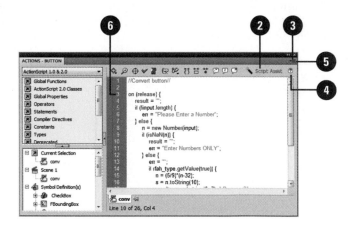

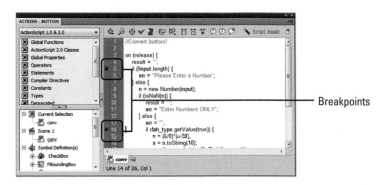

Breakpoints

7 **Pinning multiple scripts**. You can pin multiple scripts within a FLA file along the bottom of the Script pane in the Actions panel.

8 **Script navigator.** The Script navigator is a visual representation of the structure of your Flash (.fla) file; you can navigate through the file to locate the ActionScript code.

9 **Integrated Script window for editing external files**. You can use the ActionScript editor in a Script window (separate from the Actions panel) to write and edit external script files.

10 **Syntax coloring**. Syntax coloring utilizes a user-defined set of colors to display the code entered into the Script pane. Click the Flash menu, and then click Preferences (Mac), or click the Edit menu, and then click Preferences. Click the ActionScript Preferences tab to modify the syntax coloring, font and size, or the scripting text.

11 **Instant Syntax Checking**. Click the Check Syntax button to get an instant evaluation of the current script.

12 **Code Hint**. Click the Show Code Hint button, and then Flash will give you a hint of what to do next.

13 **Debug Options**. Click the Debug Options button to set and remove breakpoints.

14 **Collapse and Expand**. Click the Collapse Between Braces, Collapse Selection, or Expand All buttons.

15 **Comments**. Click the Apply Block Comment, Apply Line Comment, and Remove Comment buttons.

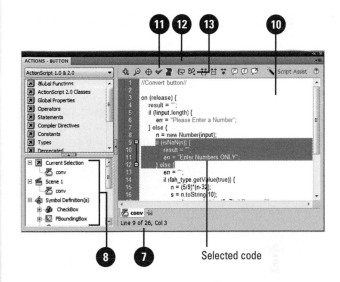

Selected code

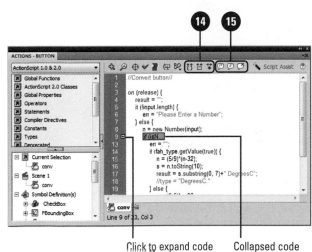

Click to expand code   Collapsed code

Using the Movie Explorer

Flash's Movie Explorer gives you an easy way to view and organize the contents of an .fla document, and even select elements for modification. It contains a display list of currently used elements, arranged in a tree hierarchical structure. The Movie Explorer gives you the ability to filter which categories of items in the document are displayed: text, graphics, buttons, movie clips, actions, and imported files. You can even display selected categories as individual scenes, concise symbol definitions, or both. When you select an item in the Movie Explorer panel, the item will be selected in the Flash document. If you double-click on an ActionScript, Flash opens the script in the Actions panel. If you double-click on a Library item, Flash opens the item in the Library.

Use the Movie Explorer

1. Click the **Window** menu, and then click **Movie Explorer** to open the panel.

2. Click the Movie Explorer **Options** menu, and then select from the following options:

   - **Go To Location.** Takes you to the selected layer, scene, or frame in the active document.

   - **Go To Symbol Definition.** Takes you to the symbol definition for a symbol that is selected in the Elements area.

   - **Select Symbol Instances.** Takes you to the scene containing instances of a symbol that is selected in the Definitions area.

   - **Find In Library.** Select to highlight the selected symbol in the document's Library.

   - **Rename.** Select to enter a new name for a selected element.

   - **Edit In Place.** Select to edit a selected symbol on the Stage.

   - **Edit In New Window.** Select to edit a selected symbol in a new window.

   - **Show Movie Elements.** Displays document elements organized into scenes.

- ◆ **Show Symbol Definitions.** Select to display all the elements associated with a symbol.

- ◆ **Copy All Text To Clipboard.** Select to copy selected text to the Clipboard.

- ◆ **Cut, Copy, Paste, And Clear.** Select to perform these functions on a selected element.

- ◆ **Expand Branch.** Select to expand the navigation tree at the selected element.

- ◆ **Collapse Branch.** Select to collapse the navigation tree at the selected element.

- ◆ **Collapse Others.** Select to collapse the branches in the navigation tree not containing the selected element.

- ◆ **Print.** Select to print the hierarchical display list currently displayed in the Movie Explorer.

③ The Show buttons give you the option to show or hide different elements of the movie. These options will only impact the Movie Explorer, not the Flash Stage.

- ◆ **Show Text**

- ◆ **Show Buttons, Movie Clips, and Graphics**

- ◆ **Show ActionScripts**

- ◆ **Show Video, Sounds, and Bitmaps**

- ◆ **Show Frames and Layers**

④ Click the **Customize Which Items To Show** button to customize what items display in the Movie Explorer window.

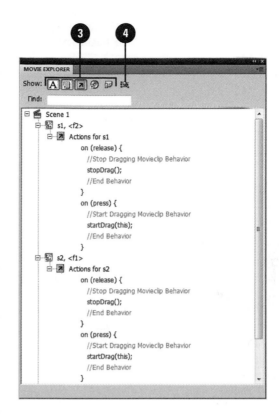

Debugging for ActionScript 3.0

FL 5.2

The designers of Flash included editing and debugging features to make debugging easier. You can quickly set and remove breakpoints to check different parts of your code to determine if it's working correctly. Flash uses a different debugger for ActionScript 3.0 files (FLA or AS) than it does for ActionScript 2.0 files. The functionality is similar, but the look and feel is different. The debugger for ActionScript 3.0 uses the Debug workspace that displays the Debug Console, Variables, and Output panels along with the Actions panel or Script window. The Debug Console displays the call stack, scripts containing the functions in the call stack, and contains buttons to step through the code. The call stack shows the current list of nested function calls ready for execution. The Variables panel displays variables and their current values. When a problem is encountered, Flash displays the line of code in the Compiler Errors panel. Double-click the error to view it in the code.

Use the Debugger for ActionScript 3.0

1. Create or open a Flash document (ActionScript 3.0).

   ◆ To debug an ActionScript 3.0 file (AS), open the file in the Script window, select the associated Flash file from the Target menu.

2. Click the **Debug** menu, and then click **Debug Movie**.

   ◆ You can access many debugging commands on the Debug menu.

3. Add or remove breakpoints to interrupt the execution of the scripting code.

   ◆ **Add.** Click in the left margin next to the line of code.

   ◆ **Remove.** Click the breakpoint in the left margin.

4. To step through the code line by line or step in and out of functions, use any of the following:

   ◆ Step into code line by line. Click the **Step In** button in the Debug Console panel.

   ◆ Step over a function call. Click the **Step Over** button in the

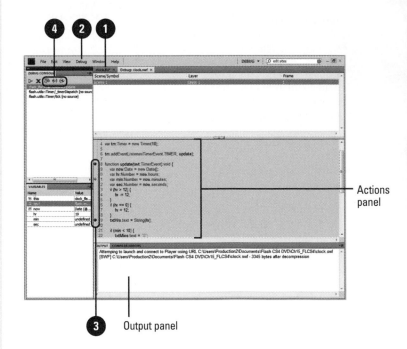

Actions panel

Output panel

◆ **Step out of a function call.** Click the **Stop Out** button in the Debug Console panel.

◆ **Resume normal code execution.** Click the **Continue** button in the Debug Console panel.

⑤ To view the individual scripts that contain each function, double-click the script name in the call stack in the Debug Console panel.

⑥ To view variable values, click the **Options** button on the Variables panel, and then click one of the following:

◆ **Show Constants.** Displays the values constants.

◆ **Show Statics.** Displays variables for the class instead of instances of the class.

◆ **Show Inaccessible Member Variables.** Displays variables that are inaccessible to other classes or namespaces.

◆ **Show Additional Hexadecimal Display.** Displays hexadecimal values instead of decimal values.

◆ **Show Qualified Names.** Displays variable types with both the package name and the class name.

⑦ To edit the values of variables in the Variables panel, double-click the value, enter a new value, and then press Enter (Win) or Return (Mac).

⑧ If an error occurs, double-click it in the Compiler Errors panel.

⑨ To exit debugging mode, click the **End Debug Session** button in the Debug Console panel. To change workspaces, click the Workspace menu, and then select one.

Continue

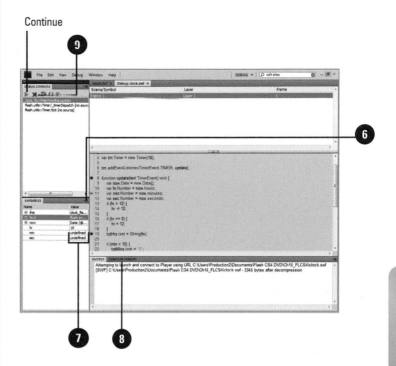

Debugging for ActionScript 2.0

FL 5.2

Flash provides several tools for testing Flash files (ActionScript 2.0). The Debugger panel lets you find and locate errors hidden in an .swf file, while it's running in the Flash Player. You must view your SWF file in a special version of Flash Player called the Flash Debug Player (installed automatically when you install the Flash application). The Debugger panel shows a hierarchical display list of movie clips currently loaded in the Flash Player. You can then use the Debugger to display and modify variables and property values as the .swf file plays. You can insert breakpoints to stop the .swf file and step through the ActionScript code line-by-line. You can even use the Debugger panel to test files on a Web server in a remote location. The Debugger lets you set breakpoints in your ActionScript that stop the Flash Player, and then lets you step through the code as it runs. You can then go back to your scripts and edit them so that they produce the correct results. The Debugger will show you where the problems are, but it doesn't fix them.

Use the Debugger for ActionScript 2.0

1. Create or open a Flash document (ActionScript 2.0).

2. Click the **Debug** menu, and then click **Debug Movie**.

3. The Code View panel displays a message indicating the movie is paused.

4. Click the **Continue** button to start the movie.

5. Click the **Stop Debugging** button to turn off the Debugger panel.

6. Click inside the code, and then click the **Toggle Breakpoint** button to add or remove a breakpoint at the insertion point of the cursor.

   Breakpoints stop the movie from playing and allow you to step through the code line-by-line.

7. Click the **Remove All Breakpoints** button to remove all the breakpoints from the code.

8. Click the **Step Over**, **Step In**, and **Step Out** buttons to step through each line of an ActionScript.

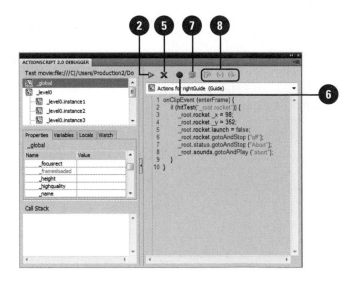

For Your Information

Testing Your Movie

When you use the Test Movie command to test movies that implement keyboard shortcuts, click the Control menu, and then click Disable Keyboard Shortcuts. This prevents Flash from interpreting keystrokes, and lets them pass through to the player. For example, you can have a Flash document that uses Ctrl+U to display a file or video. However, Flash uses Ctrl+U to display the Preferences panel. If you don't Disable Keyboard Shortcuts, pressing Ctrl+U in the Flash player will actually open Flash Preferences.

Viewing Variables

When you work in the debugger, you have the option of viewing any variables used in the Flash movie. The Variables tab (ActionScript 2.0) or Variables panel (ActionScript 3.0) displays the names and values of any global and variables in the .swf file. If you change the value of a variable, you can see the change reflected in the .swf file while it runs. This gives you the ability to test new data variables and their impact on the Flash player document.

View Variables

1. Click the **Debug** menu, and then click **Debug Movie**.

2. Select the movie clip containing the variable from the display list.

3. Select an item in the display frame to view the variables' names and values.

4. Click the **Continue** button to observe the variables as the Flash movie runs.

5. Click the **Variables** tab (ActionScript 2.0) or open the Variables panel (ActionScript 3.0).

   IMPORTANT *The display list updates automatically as the .swf file plays. When a movie clip is removed from the .swf file at a specific frame, the movie clip, variable and variable name are removed from the display list in the Debugger panel. This lets you focus on the current variables. When you're viewing a complex Flash movie that contains a lot of variables, only having to view the current variables cuts down on the visual clutter and helps you to focus on the immediate problem.*

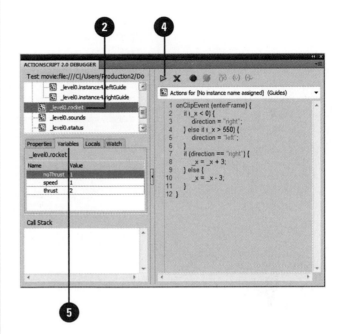

Variables panel
(ActionScript 3.0)

Adding Variables to the Watch List

In any complex Flash movie, there will probably be a set of critical variables that you want to keep an eye on. You can monitor critical variables in a controllable way by marking them to appear in the Debugger panel Watch list (ActionScript 2.0). The Watch list displays the absolute path to the variable and its current value, and just like the Variables tab, you can enter a new variable value at any time during the debugging process. If you add a local variable to the Watch list, its value appears only when Flash Player is stopped at a line of ActionScript where that variable is in scope. All other variables appear while the .swf file is playing. If the Debugger can't find the value of the variable, it will list the value as undefined.

Add Variables

1. In a Flash document (ActionScript 2.0), click the **Debug** menu, and then click **Debug Movie**.

2. Click the **Variables** or **Locals** tab, and then select a variable.

3. Click the **Debugger Options** button, and then click **Watch**.

4. Click the **Watch** tab.

5. Click the **Debugger Options** button, and then click **Add Watch**.

6. Enter the target path to the variable name and the value in the fields.

    IMPORTANT *To remove variables from the Watch list, select a variable on the Watch tab, click the Debugger Options button, and then click Remove Watch.*

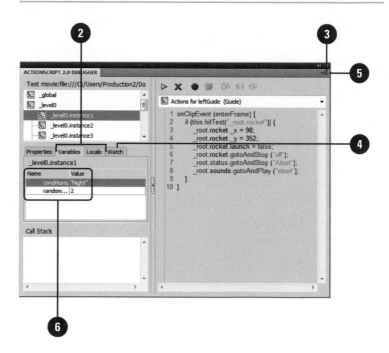

Viewing Properties

The Properties tab in the Debugger panel displays all property values of any movie clip on the Stage. Properties are modifiable script elements such as _alpha (controls transparency) or _rotation (controls the rotation of an object). The Properties tab lists all the properties including their current values. You can then view and adjust the values as the Flash movie is running to judge their impact. This gives you a tremendous amount of control over the debugging process.

View Properties

1. In a Flash document (ActionScript 2.0), click the **Debug** menu, and then click **Debug Movie**.

2. Select an available movie clip from the Display list.

3. Click the **Properties** tab to view all the properties, and their associated values.

4. Double-click on a value, and then enter a new value in any available property.

5. Click the **Continue** button to view how the Properties change as the Flash movie executes.

   IMPORTANT *The Property value is picky about what you enter. For example, you can enter a value of 100 or text within quotes such as: "newvalue", but you cannot enter expressions such as: y + 10, or on array of values such as: 1, 2, 3.*

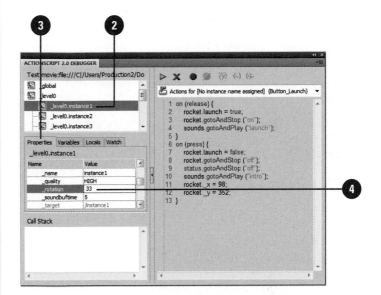

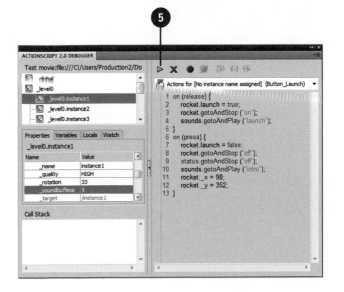

Setting Breakpoints

 FL 5.3

Breakpoints are instructions to the Debugger to halt the running of a Flash movie. For example, you're watching how the .swf file plays using the debugger, however, it's moving so fast it's difficult to watch everything. By inserting a breakpoint, you instruct the Debugger to halt the movie, and any variables and properties will display the values associated with that point in time. You can then change the values, and instruct the Debugger to continue playing the movie, using the modified values.

Set Breakpoints

1. Click the **Debug** menu, and then click **Debug Movie**.

2. Click in the left margin next to the line of code where you want the breakpoint (red dot) to appears.

   ◆ You can also click the **Toggle Breakpoint** button (ActionScript 2.0) to add/remove a breakpoint.

3. To remove a breakpoint, click the existing breakpoint (red dot) in the left margin.

4. Click the **Continue** button to begin playing the Flash .swf file.

   The Debugger will stop the movie at each breakpoint.

Did You Know?

You can set or remove breakpoints in the Actions panel. In the Actions panel (ActionScript 2.0), click in the line you want, click the Debug Option button, and then select a command to set or remove breakpoints.

You cannot set a breakpoint on a comment line. If you set a breakpoint in a comment (or empty line) in the Actions panel, the breakpoint will be ignored by the Debugger.

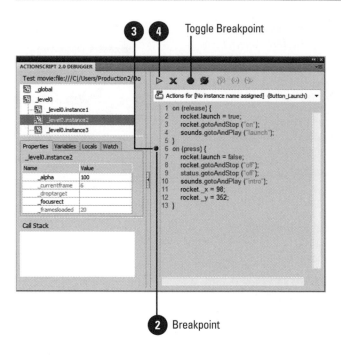

Toggle Breakpoint

Breakpoint

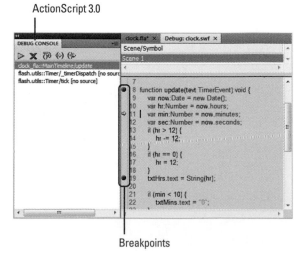

ActionScript 3.0

Breakpoints

Stepping Through Code

 FL 5.3

Step Through Code

① Click the **Debug** menu, and then click **Debug Movie**.

② Add breakpoints by clicking in the left margin next to the line of code where you want the breakpoint. To remove a breakpoint, click it.

③ Click the **Continue** button.

   Flash will stop at the first breakpoint.

④ Select from the step options:

   ◆ **Continue**. Click to leave the line at which the player is stopped and continue playing.

   ◆ **Stop Debugging**. Click to deactivate the Debugger, but continue to play the SWF file.

   ◆ **Step In**. Click to step into and execute a function (works only for user-defined functions).

   ◆ **Step Out**. Click to move out of a function (works only if you are currently stopped in a user-defined function).

   ◆ **Step Over**. Click to skip over a line of code.

   IMPORTANT *If you want to know where the Debugger stopped, keep an eye on the yellow arrow. A yellow arrow along the left side of the Debugger's code view indicates the line at which the Debugger stopped.*

When you open the Debugger, the Flash Player is automatically paused. This gives you the opportunity to set breakpoints in the script (see previous lesson: Setting Breakpoints). Once the breakpoints are set, you can click the Continue or Play button, and the Debugger will play the .swf file until it encounters a breakpoint. When a breakpoint is reached, the Debugger again pauses the movie. You now have the option to step in, out, or through the breakpoint script.

Current breakpoints

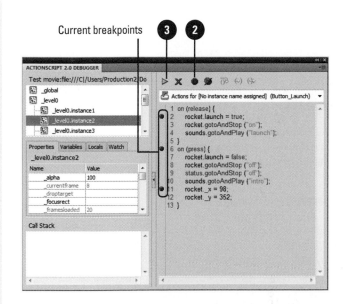

Continue   Stop Debugging

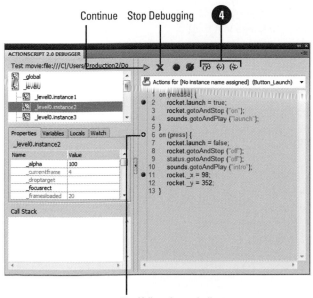

The Yellow Arrow indicates where the Debugger stopped.

Debugging Manually

Debugging a Flash movie manually means exactly what it implies. You can open the movie and take it for a test drive. Debugging a movie manually gives you a chance to be the visitor, and experience your movie exactly as they would. When you manually test a Flash movie, you want to experience the wait time for downloading, you want to forget that you created this masterpiece, and you want to come at it just as if you were a first-time viewer. A Flash movie is composed of text, video, audio, images, animation, and ActionScript. Your visitors will never see the ActionScript code, and most do not care how it was written; but they will care if it doesn't work properly. For example, your visitor clicks a button to load a video file, and the video never loads, or it takes so long to load that they get bored and leave. Problems like these are what manual debugging can solve.

Debug Manually

1 Click the **Control** menu, and then click **Test Movie** to test the entire Flash movie, or click **Test Scene** to test the active scene.

> **IMPORTANT** *Flash uses the settings described in the Publish Settings dialog box to test the movie. Use different settings such as Flash plug-in, to test the movie against earlier versions of the Flash plug-in.*

2 Test the movie for any structural failures. Click all the buttons, and then do all the things you think a visitor would do.

3 Note any problems on paper (remember this is manual) in a list, called a debug, or edit list. The list can then be used to edit the document, using Flash's standard editing tools.

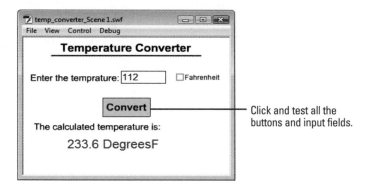

Click and test all the buttons and input fields.

See Also

See Chapter 20, "Publishing a Movie" on page 465 for information on modifying publishing settings.

For Your Information

Debugging Flash Player

When Adobe Flash is installed, the debug version of the Adobe Flash Player is installed for the application as well as any browser specified. While this debug version of the player can be very useful when authoring, there may be situations where the standard player is desired. If you would like to uninstall the debug player, point your browser to: *http://www.adobe.com/support/flash/ts/documents/remove_player.htm*, and then follow the on-screen instructions. You can then point your browser to: *http://www.adobe.com/shockwave/download/download.cgi?P1_Prod_Version=ShockwaveFlash*, and download the current version of the player.

Adding Display Components

16

Introduction

Components are building blocks that you can use to create interactive, dynamic Flash documents. Think of a component as a movie clip with modifiable parameters, which are set during the design of a Flash document, and ActionScript APIs (APIs allow you to customize the component at runtime). Since components are reusable, they give developers the ability to share code between projects. Since components are rooted in ActionScript code, Flash comes with a set of components for ActionScript 2.0 and another one for ActionScript 3.0, and you cannot mix components in the same Flash document.

You can use components created by Adobe, download components created by other developers or, with a bit of practice create your own components. Flash comes packaged with many components, some of them new, such as: the FLVPlayback, and customized User Interface skins, as discussed in Chapter 13, "Working with Video." Other Flash components provide the ability to add check boxes, radio buttons, and even create sophisticated menus and labels with a minimum of scripting experience.

Suppose you want to create a list of options from which a visitor would be able to click and choose. You can open the Actions panel, and then create the list by typing in about forty or more lines of script, or you can use Flash's built-in component to create the list. The difference is not in the quality of the list, but the amount of time it took to create it. Spending less time on creating dynamic, interactive Flash elements gives you more time to concentrate on design features. To a Flash visitor, it's not about the code or how long it took you to create it, it's about the design, and it will always be about the design.

Understanding Basic Components

 FL 2.8, 2.9

If you're the type of Flash designer who wants to create Rich Internet Applications, while writing as little ActionScript as possible, then Flash components are just what you've been looking for all these years. You can drag components into a document, set a few parameters in the Property or Component Inspector panel, attach an on() handler directly to a component in the Actions panel to handle component events, and you're finished. If you think components sound too good to be true, then think again. Components are not just a way to get out of coding, they're an excellent way to create consistency in your design; and since components are based on pre-tested code, they will work the same way every time.

When you work with Flash components, you can create Flash content that is accessible to users with disabilities using Flash accessibly features. As you design accessible Flash applications, consider how your users will interact with the content. Visually impaired users might rely on additional technology, such as screen readers, while hearing-impaired users might read text and captions in the document. To make a Flash Component accessible, click the Window menu, point to Other Panels, and then click Accessibility to open the Accessibility panel. For more information on creating accessible compliant documents, open your browser and visit *www.w3.org/WAI/*, or for information on Flash, open your browser and visit *www.adobe.com/*, go to the Flash Exchange, and then type the word "accessibility" in the keyword field.

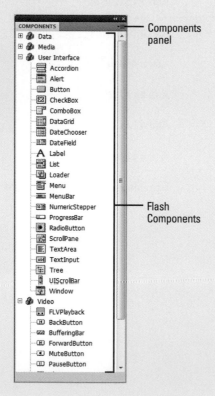

Components panel

Flash Components

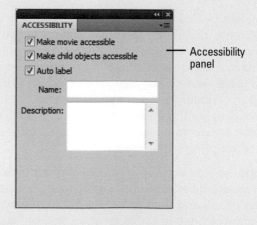

Accessibility panel

Components are added to the Stage using the Components panel. To add an Alert component to the Stage, you would open the Components panel, expand the UI Components list, and then drag the Alert icon onto the Stage. Since components are based on ActionScript code, Flash comes with a set of components for ActionScript 2.0 and another one for ActionScript 3.0, and you cannot mix components in a Flash document. You specify the components type by selecting an ActionScript version in the Publishing Settings dialog box.

There are four categories of components for ActionScript 2.0—user interface, data, media, and video—and two categories of components for ActionScript 3.0—user interface and video. ActionScript 3.0 provides similar components as ActionScript 2.0. However, the parameters associated with a component may vary. User interface components allow you to interact with an application (RadioButton, Checkbox, and TextInput). Data components (ActionScript 2.0) allow you to load and manipulate information from data sources (WebServiceConnector and XMLConnector). Media components (ActionScript 2.0) allow you to play back and control streaming media (MediaController, MediaPlayback, and MediaDisplay). Video components allow you to add video playback controls, such as FLVPlayback, Back, Forward, Mute, Pause, Play, Play/Pause, Seek Bar, Stop, and Volume Bar.

Customizing a Component

Some of the components, such as Scroll bars, include a skin, or look and feel, which you can customize to suit your own artistic nature. See Project 1, "Creating and Customizing Scrollable Text," on page 509 for a step by step example.

Using the Component Inspector

Once the component is on the Stage, it is controlled through the Component Inspector panel. The Component Inspector panel has three tabs: Parameters, Bindings, and Schema. Each tab gives you modifiable elements to help control the look and functionality of the component. The Parameters tab lists the most commonly used properties and methods; others parameters can be added using the ActionScript panel. The Bindings tab gives you a way to bind, or link two or more components together. For example, you can bind an external database to a display component for on-screen viewing of the data. The Schema tab contains a list of a component's bindable properties, data types, internal structure, and other special attributes.

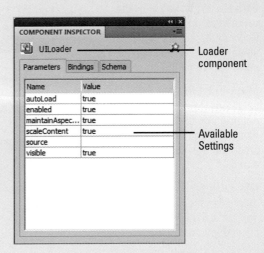

Loader component

Available Settings

Adding a Text Input

The TextInput component works with the ActionScript TextField object. Once a TextInput component is added to the Stage, you can use styles to customize the font, size, and color. A TextInput component can be formatted using HTML, or even as a password field that disguises the text. When a TextInput field has focus, visitors can use the arrow keys to move through information in the field, and they can use the tab key to move the focus to the next object, or Shift+Tab to move to the previous object. TextInput fields can be used to hold information. For example, you could use a group of TextInput components as the basis for creating an interactive form for fields such as: name, address, city, state, and zip code.

Add a TextInput Component

1. Open the **Components** panel.

2. Click the **User Interface** plus (+) sign to expand the list.

3. Drag the **TextInput** component onto the Stage, and then select the component.

4. Open the **Component Inspector** panel, and then click the **Parameters** tab.

5. Select from the following Text Input parameters:

   ◆ **editable.** When you click the value field, and select true, the field can be edited. If you select false, the field can be selected but not edited.

   ◆ **password.** When you click the value field, and select true, text entered into the field appears as dots. If you select false, text typed into the field appears as typed.

   ◆ **text.** Click the value field, and then enter the text that will appear in the field when the Flash document opens.

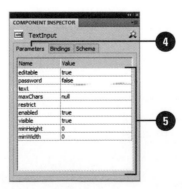

◆ **maxChars.** Click the value field, and then enter a numerical value indicating the max characters allowed in the TextInput field.

◆ **restrict.** Click the value field, and then enter any characters that cannot be entered into the TextInput field.

◆ **enabled.** When you select true, the field can be edited. If you select false, the field appears grayed out and is not selectable or editable.

◆ **visible.** When you click the value field, and select true, the field can be viewed. If you select false, the field is invisible.

◆ **minHeight (2.0).** Click the value field, and then enter a minimum height for the TextInput box.

◆ **minWidth (2.0).** Click the value field, and then enter a minimum width for the TextInput box.

6 Click the **Control** menu, and then click **Test Movie**.

IMPORTANT *Although you can change the size of any component using the Free Transform tool, since the TextInput component is a single-line component, changing its height does not impact how many lines of text you can type.*

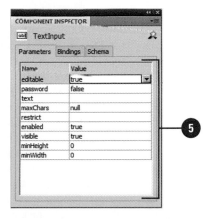

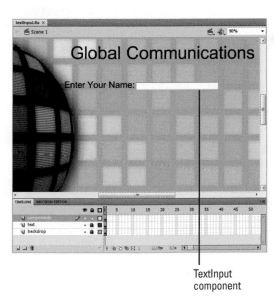

TextInput
component

Adding a Combo Text Box

The ComboBox component creates a drop-down list of selectable options. They can be either static or editable. The static ComboBox component allows a user to make a single selection from a drop-down list. An editable ComboBox component lets users enter text into a text field located at the top of the list, as well as selecting an item from a drop-down list. A ComboBox component is composed of three subcomponents: Button, TextInput, and List components. When a visitor selects an item, the label of the selection is automatically copied to the text field at the top of the combo box. The ComboBox component is an excellent way to offer several choices to a user, without the necessity of them having to type in a response. For example, a ComboBox could be used to list all of the states in the union in a drop-down box, giving the user the chance to select his home state. When the ComboBox displays in a Flash document, it appears as a single line; clicking the triangle to the right of the line expands the box and displays all the available options.

Add a ComboBox Component

1. Open the **Components** panel.

2. Click the **User Interface** plus (+) sign to expand the list.

3. Drag the **ComboBox** component onto the Stage, and then select the component.

4. Open the **Component Inspector** panel, and then click the **Parameters** tab.

5. Select from the following ComboBox parameters:

   ◆ **data.** Click the value field, and then enter an array in the Values dialog box. Click the plus (+) sign to add values and the minus sign (-) to remove a value. Data values are used to populate the drop-down list.

   ◆ **editable.** When you click the value field, and select true, the field can be edited. If you select false, the field can be selected but not edited.

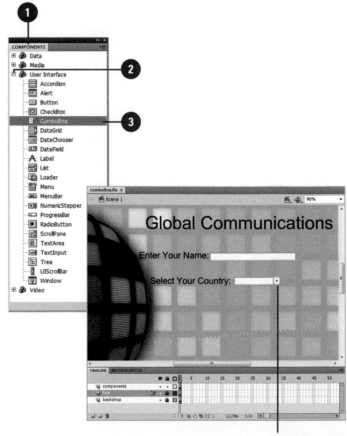

ComboBox component

◆ **labels (2.0).** Click the value field, and then enter an array in the Values dialog box. Click the plus (+) sign to add values, and the minus sign (-) to remove a value. Data values are used as the selectable items in the list.

◆ **rowCount.** Click the value field, and then enter a number to determine the maximum height of the drop-down list.

◆ **enabled.** When you click the value field, and select true, the items in the list can be selected. If you select false, the field appears grayed out and is not selectable.

◆ **visible.** When you click the value field, and select true, the field can be viewed. If you select false, the field is invisible.

◆ **minHeight (2.0).** Click the value field, and then enter a minimum height for the ComboBox box.

◆ **minWidth (2.0).** Click the value field, and then enter a minimum width for the ComboBox box.

IMPORTANT *If there is not enough room for the ComboBox to open without hitting the bottom of the document, it will open up instead of down.*

6 Click the **Control** menu, and then click **Test Movie**.

When you click the Select Your Country list arrow, the list will open, and a selection can be made by clicking on one of the available options.

Click to add values

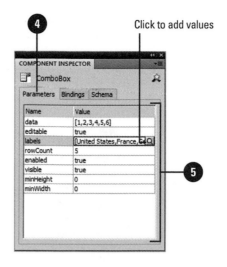

Use to add, remove and order values

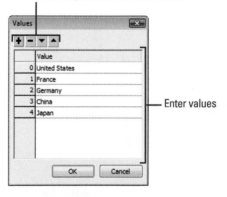

Enter values

Adding a Check Box

A check box is simply a square box that the user can select or deselect. When it is selected, a check mark appears in the box. When a selected check box is clicked, the check mark is removed. The state of a CheckBox component does not change until the mouse is released over the component.

Add a CheckBox Component

1. Open the **Components** panel.

2. Click the **User Interface** plus (+) sign to expand the list.

3. Drag the **CheckBox** component onto the Stage, and then select the component.

Did You Know?

You can control the state of a CheckBox component without the mouse. If the CheckBox component has focus (selected), pressing the Spacebar selects or deselects the check mark.

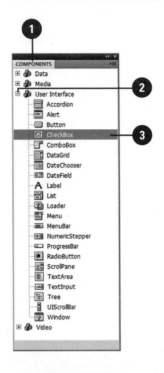

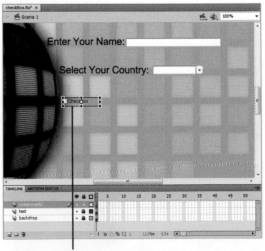

CheckBox component

4) Open the **Component Inspector** panel, and then click the **Parameters** tab.

5) Select from the following CheckBox parameters:

  ◆ **enabled (3.0).** When you click the value field, and select true, the items in the list can be selected. If you select false, the field appears grayed out and is not selectable.

  ◆ **label.** Click the value field, and then enter a label for the check box.

  ◆ **labelPlacement.** Click the value field, and then select between right, left, top, or bottom for the placement of the label text.

  ◆ **selected.** Click the value field and select between true (field appears with a checkmark), or false (field appears without a check mark).

  ◆ **visible (3.0).** When you click the value field, and select true, the field can be viewed. If you select false, the field is invisible.

6) To change the width and height of the check box component, select the component, and then drag a resize handle to change the width and height.

7) Click the **Control** menu, and then click **Test Movie**.

  Click in the CheckBox component to add a check mark, and then click a second time to remove the check mark.

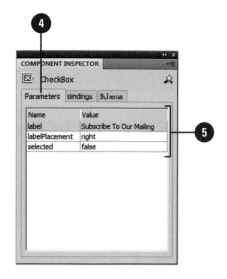

Adding a Radio Button

The RadioButton component lets you do something that the CheckBox component cannot do: force a user to make a single choice within a set of choices. The RadioButton component must be used in a group of at least two RadioButton instances, and only one member of the group can be selected at any given time. Selecting one radio button in a group will deselect the currently selected radio button in the group. For example, a radio button options for Gender can be Male, Female. There can be only one answer to that question, so you would group the two items using RadioButton components.

Add a RadioButton Component

1. Open the **Components** panel.

2. Click the **User Interface** plus (+) sign to expand the list.

3. Drag one or more **RadioButton** components onto the Stage, and then select one at time.

4. Open the **Component Inspector** panel, and then click the **Parameters** tab.

Did You Know?

A visitor can control a radio button selection with the keyboard. Click the Tab key until one of the buttons within the group receives focus (is selected), and then use the left and right arrow keys to change the selection within the group. Having the ability to use the keyboard makes Flash components compliant with the current rules on accessibility as set by the U.S. Congress.

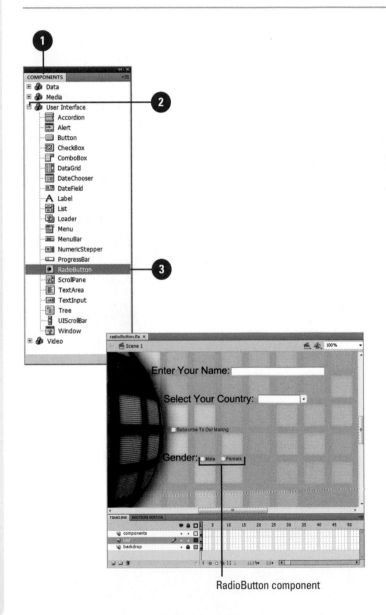

RadioButton component

5 Select from the following RadioButton parameters:

- **data (2.0)** or **value (3.0)**. Click the value field, and then enter a value that will be used to populate the RadioButton.

- **groupName.** Click in the value field, and then enter a group name for the button. When you associate a group name to several RadioButton components, the visitor will only be able to select one button in the group.

- **label.** Click the value field, and then enter a label for the RadioButton.

- **labelPlacement.** Click the value field, and then select between right, left, top, or bottom for the placement of the label text.

- **selected.** Click the value field, and then select between true (field appears selected), or false (field appears unselected).

- **enabled (3.0).** When you click the value field, and select true, the items in the list can be selected. If you select false, the field appears grayed out and is not selectable.

- **visible (3.0).** When you click the value field, and select true, the field can be viewed. If you select false, the field is invisible.

6 Click the **Control** menu, and then click **Test Movie**.

Since the RadioButton components both use the same Group name, you can only select one button.

Adding a Text Area

The TextArea component works with the ActionScript TextField object. Once a TextArea component is added to the Stage, you can use styles to customize font, size, and color. In addition, a TextArea component can be formatted using HTML. If this sounds similar to the TextInput component, you're right. In fact, the major difference between a TextInput and a Text Area field is the ability of the TextArea field to generate multiple lines. TextArea fields can be used to hold information. For example, you can use a TextArea component to create a comment or a suggestion field on an interactive form.

Add a TextArea Component

1. Open the **Components** panel.

2. Click the **User Interface** plus (+) sign to expand the list.

3. Drag the **TextArea** component onto the Stage, and then select the component.

4. Open the **Component Inspector**, and then click the **Parameters** tab.

5. Select from the following TextArea parameters:

   ◆ **condenseWhite (3.0).** When you click the value field, select true to remove extra white space (spaces, line breaks) in a text field. If you select false, the white space remains.

   ◆ **editable.** When you click the value field and select true, the field can be edited. If you select false, the field can be selected but not edited.

   ◆ **html.** When you click the value field, select true to allow HTML to control the formatting of the data. If you select false, the field cannot be modified using HTML.

   ◆ **text.** Click the value field, and then enter the initial text that will appear in the TextArea component.

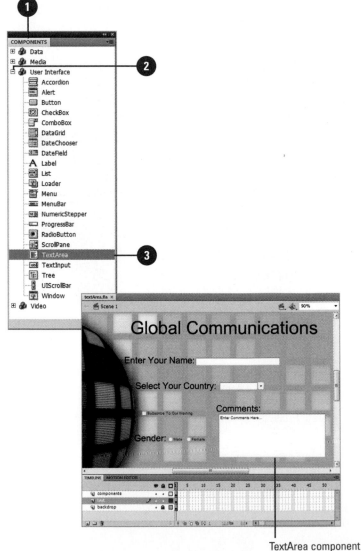

TextArea component

- **wordWrap.** When you click the value field and select true, the text typed by the visitor wraps in the TextArea box. If you select false, the text will not wrap.

- **maxChars.** Click the value field, and then enter the maximum number of characters that can be typed into the TextArea component.

- **restrict.** Click the value field, and then enter any characters that cannot be entered into the TextArea field.

- **enabled.** When you click the value field and select true, the field can be edited. If you select false, the field appears grayed out and is not selectable, or editable.

- **visible.** When you click the value field and select true, the field can be viewed. If you select false, the field is invisible.

- **minHeight (2.0).** Click the value field, and then enter a minimum height for the TextArea.

- **minWidth (2.0).** Click the value field, and then enter a minimum width for the TextArea.

- **horizontal or vertical ScrollPolicy (3.0).** Click the value field, and then select auto, on, or off to show or hide scroll bars.

6 Click the **Control** menu, and then click **Test Movie**.

In the example, visitors can type as much information as needed, and when the box fills up, scroll bars appear to the right of the box; allowing them to maneuver up and down through the document.

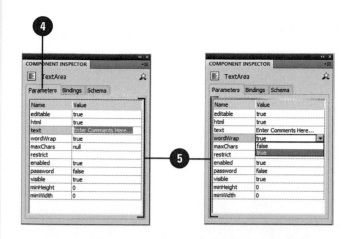

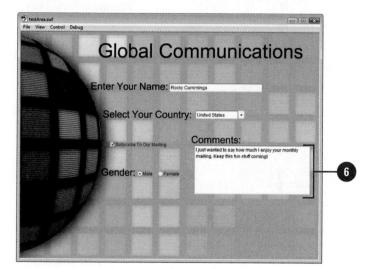

Adding a Button

The Button component is a clickable rectangular button, which can be resized. If you desire, you can add a custom icon to the Button component. In addition, you can change the behavior of a Button component from push to **toggle**. A toggle button stays pressed when clicked and returns to its up state when clicked again. All of these options are accomplished through the Component Inspector panel.

Add a Button Component

1. Open the **Components** panel.

2. Click the **User Interface** plus (+) sign to expand the list.

3. Drag the **Button** component onto the Stage, and then select the component.

4. Open the **Component Inspector** panel, and then click the **Parameters** tab.

5. Select from the following Button parameters:

   ◆ **icon (2.0).** Click the value field, and then enter the full path name to an icon file.

   ◆ **emphasized (3.0).** Click the value field and then select true to add a border around the button. If you select false, the button is normal.

   ◆ **label.** Click the value field, and then enter a label for the Button component.

   ◆ **labelPlacement.** Click the value field, and then select between right, left, top, or bottom for the placement of the Button component text.

   ◆ **selected.** When you click the value field and select true, the button appears selected. If you select false, the button is normal or deselected.

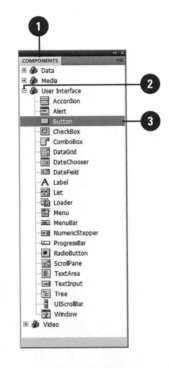

Button component

- ◆ **toggle.** When you click the value field, and select true, the button, when selected, returns a true value. If you select false, the button returns false when selected.

- ◆ **enabled.** When you click the value field and select true, the button can be clicked. If you select false, the button is grayed out and cannot be clicked.

- ◆ **visible.** When you click the value field and select true, the Button can be viewed. If you select false, the Button is invisible.

- ◆ **minHeight (2.0).** Click the value field, and then enter a minimum height for the Button.

- ◆ **minWidth (2.0).** Click the value field, and then enter a minimum width for the Button.

6 Click the **Control** menu, and then click **Test Movie**.

In the example, when you click the button, it changes color, just like a typical rollover button. You could now attach an ActionScript to the button to load another scene or movie.

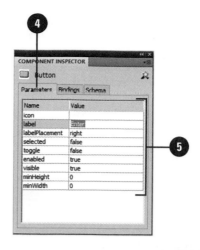

Adding a Menu Bar

The Menu component (ActionScript 2.0) lets a visitor select items from a menu. The Menu component opens in an application when a user rolls over or clicks a button-like menu activator. Flash conserves valuable space by creating Menu components dynamically at runtime. Menu components have an obvious advantage over static menus: They only display information when requested, and they give a sense of order to a site that requires the visitor to select from many choices.

Add a MenuBar Component

1. Open the **Components** panel.

2. Click the **User Interface** plus (+) sign to expand the list.

3. Drag the **MenuBar** component (2.0) onto the Stage, and then select the component.

4. Open the **Component Inspector** panel, and then click the **Parameters** tab.

> **IMPORTANT** *Menus represent the navigation, or steering wheel, of your Flash document. Visitors require a powerful, yet easy-to-understand way to navigate. Not only should your menus be easy, they should be designed to allow visitors to get to any page, scene or document within three clicks. It's called the three-click rule (of course), and it keeps visitors from getting frustrated trying to navigate through your site. Remember, build it, and they will come... make it easy to navigate, and they will stay.*

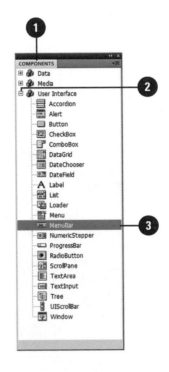

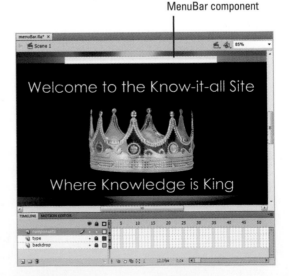

MenuBar component

5 Select from the following MenuBar parameters:

- **labels.** Click the Zoom button to the right of the value field, and then enter the labels used in the Menu Bar. Click the plus (+) sign to add a label, and the minus sign (-) to remove a label. Click the up and down arrow keys to reorder the values.

- **enabled.** When you click the value field and select true, the menu can be used. If you select false, the menu is grayed out and cannot be used.

- **visible.** When you click the value field and select true, the menu can be viewed. If you select false the menu is invisible.

- **minHeight.** Click the value field, and then enter a minimum height for the menu.

- **minWidth.** Click the value field, and then enter a minimum width for the menu.

6 Click the **Control** menu, and then click **Test Movie**.

In the example, when you roll over the menu, the buttons change color. You can now attach ActionScripts to the buttons to load other scenes or movies.

Click to add labels

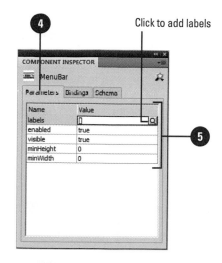

Use buttons to add, remove, and order labels

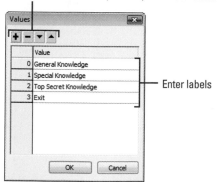

Enter labels

Adding an Alert

The Alert component (ActionScript 2.0) lets you create a popup window that presents the user with a message and response buttons. An Alert window can have any combination of Yes, No, OK, and Cancel buttons. Alert components are used when it's important to get a piece of information to the user. For example, a data validation routine indicates that the user is not entering in their zip code; you can create an Alert component that informs them of their error, and makes them go back and type in their zip code.

Add an Alert Component

1. Open the **Components** panel.

2. Click the **User Interface** plus (+) sign to expand the list.

3. Drag the **Alert** component (2.0) onto the Stage, and then select the component.

4. Press the Backspace key to delete the Alert window from the Stage. This removes the Alert component from the Stage, but keeps the component as a complied clip in the Library.

5. Select the first keyframe in the Flash document.

See Also

See Chapter 14, "Using Basic ActionScripts" on page 347 for more information on writing ActionScripts.

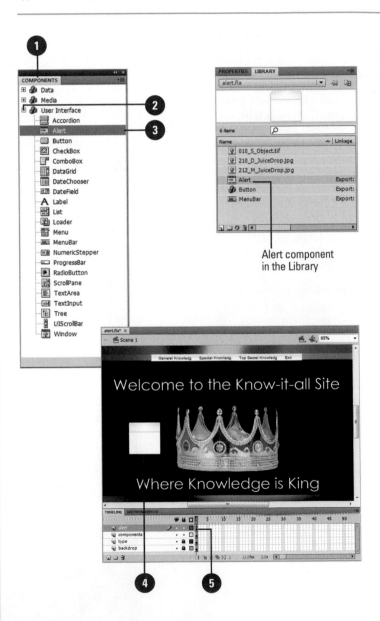

Alert component in the Library

6 Open the **Actions** panel, and then enter the script as shown in the illustration.

This code creates an Alert window with OK and Cancel buttons. When either button is pressed, the myClickHandler function is called. But when the OK button is pressed, the startKnowledgeApplication() method is called. In this test, a trace box opens and displays the message "Launch Knowledge Application."

7 Click the **Control** menu, and then click **Test Movie**.

IMPORTANT *Since Alert components are only visible when called, it is standard procedure to first drag the Alert component to the Stage and then delete it. It is the Alert component in the Library that is called, not the one on the Stage.*

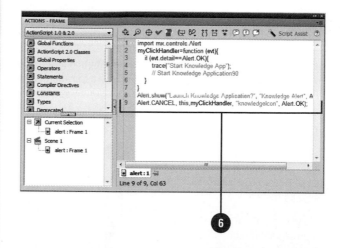

Adding a List

The List component is a scrollable box that lets users select one or more items in the list. Lists are similar to the ComboBox component, except List components can be formatted to display all of the available items at once, where as the ComboBox component uses a drop-down (or up) feature to display the items only when requested (clicking the triangle button to the right of the list).

Add a List Component

1. Open the **Components** panel.

2. Click the **User Interface** plus (+) sign to expand the list.

3. Drag the **List** component onto the Stage, and then select the component.

4. Open the **Component Inspector** panel, and then click the **Parameters** tab.

   IMPORTANT *The List component reduces the clutter of a typical data screen by allowing you to control the height of a data box. For example, if you wanted a visitor to select their home State from a list, you wouldn't want all 50 States permanently displayed on the screen. You would create a more manageable box size, and make the visitor scroll up or down to select the correct State.*

5. Select from the following List parameters:

   ◆ **data.** Click the value field, and then enter an array in the Values dialog box. Click the plus (+) sign to add a value, and the minus sign (-) to remove a value. Data values are used to populate the list labels.

   ◆ **enabled (3.0).** When you click the value field and select true, the field can be clicked. If you select false, the field is grayed out and cannot be clicked.

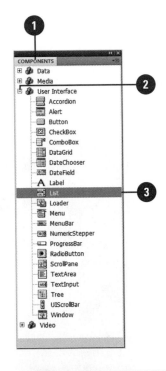

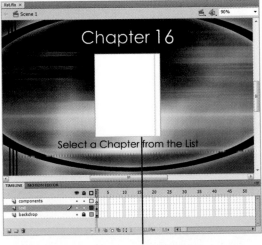

List component

- ◆ **labels (2.0).** Click the value field, and then enter an array in the Values dialog box. Click the plus (+) sign to add a value, and the minus sign (-) to remove a value. Data values are used as the selectable items in the list.

- ◆ **multipleSelection.** When you click the value field, and select true, the visitor can select more than one item in the list. If you select false, the visitor can only select a single item.

- ◆ **rowHeight (2.0).** Click the value field, and then enter a number to determine the spacing between items in the list. The higher the value, the more space between items.

- ◆ **horizontal or vertical ScrollPolicy (3.0).** Click the value field, and then select auto, on, or off to show or hide scroll bars.

- ◆ **horizontal or vertical Line or Page ScrollSize (3.0).** Click the value field, and then enter a number for the scroll size.

- ◆ **visible (3.0).** When you click the value field, and select true, the list can be viewed. If you select false the list is invisible.

6️⃣ Click the **Control** menu, and then click **Test Movie**.

In the example, click on a Chapter, and then select that chapter. You can now attach an ActionScript to the list to load the correct chapter.

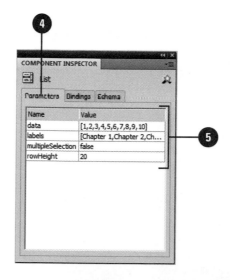

Adding a Label

A Label component consists of a single line of text. You can specify that a label be formatted with HTML. You can also control alignment and sizing of a label. Label components do not have borders, nor do they contain input that can be changed by the user. They are simply text information. Labels can be used to identify data input fields, or they can contain visitor information important to the understanding of a form. Labels can change what they display, as the Flash movie plays.

Add a Label Component

1. Open the **Components** panel.

2. Click the **User Interface** plus (+) sign to expand the list.

3. Drag one or more **Label** components onto the Stage, and then select the component, one at a time.

4. Open the **Component Inspector** panel, and then click the **Parameters** tab.

5. Select from the following Label parameters:

   ◆ **autoSize.** Click the value field, and then select between left, center, right, or none. The autoSize parameter uses this information when automatically resizing the text.

   ◆ **condenseWhite (3.0).** When you click the value field, select true, to remove extra white space (spaces, line breaks) in a text field. If you select false, the white space remains.

   ◆ **enabled (3.0).** When you select true, the field can be edited. If you select false, the field appears grayed out and is not selectable, or editable.

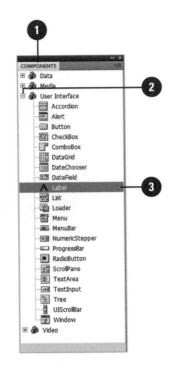

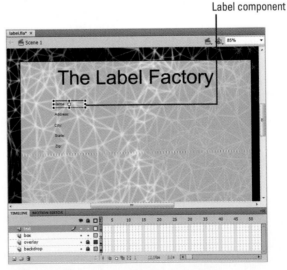

Label component

- **html.** When you click the value field, select true to allow HTML to control the formatting of the text. If you select false, the field cannot be modified using HTML.

- **text.** Click the value field, and then enter the text that will appear in the field when the Flash document opens.

- **selectable (3.0).** When you click the value field and select true, the field text is selectable. If you select false, the field text is not selectable.

- **visible.** When you click the value field and select true, the field can be viewed. If you select false, the field is invisible.

- **minHeight (2.0).** Click the value field, and then enter a minimum height for the Label.

- **minWidth (2.0).** Click the value field, and then enter a minimum width for the Label.

- **wordWrap (3.0).** When you click the value field and select true, the text typed by the visitor wraps in the TextArea box. If you select false, the text will not wrap

6) Click the **Control** menu, and then click **Test Movie**.

In the example, the Label components represent visitor information in which the labeling fields require visitor input.

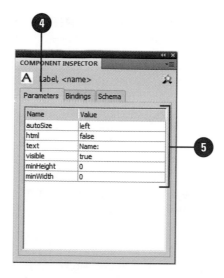

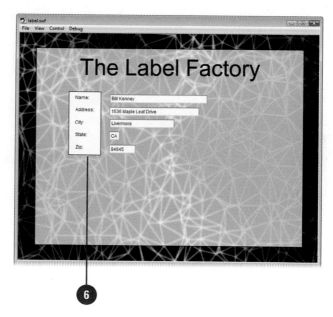

Using Components to Build a Form

When you create a form, you're incorporating all the various Flash components onto the Stage. Flash components make creating a form easy; however, there are still design considerations to be made. For example, what information do you need to extract from your visitors, and how will you receive it? Does your audience primarily speak and read English, or do you need to make the form multi-lingual (that's possible by creating label components that display text in a language selected by the visitor). And what about handicap and accessibility standards, how do you handle them? Yes, Flash does make the creation of a form easy, but you are still responsible for the overall design, and that includes images, backgrounds, colors, fonts and sizes, readability, and accessibility. The following Flash document is an example of incorporating multiple components to create an interactive form.

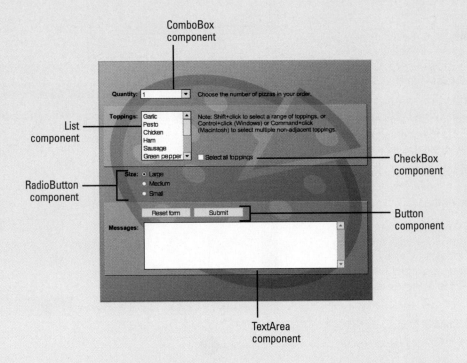

When you create a form, it is a good programming practice to isolate components onto separate layers. That way, they're easier to locate and edit, and you can always lock the component's layer to prevent accidental tampering.

Adding Advanced Display Components

17

Introduction

Components are composed of two elements: a movie clip and parameters, allowing you to modify the components' appearance and behavior. Components run the gamut from a radio button to a scroll pane. Components equalize the designer's playing field, enabling anyone to build complex applications, even if they do not have a complete understanding of the ActionScript language. As easy as it is to simply drag the component you need from the Components panel onto the Stage, it is just as easy to customize the look and feel of components to suit your design needs. Since components are rooted in ActionScript code, Flash comes with a set of components for ActionScript 2.0 and another one for ActionScript 3.0, and you cannot mix components in the same Flash document.

Components let you easily and quickly build strong applications with a consistent appearance and behavior. Each component comes with predefined parameters, located in the Component Inspector panel, which let you control how the object looks and operates. Each component also includes a set of API (application programming interface) methods and properties that allows you to set parameters and additional options at runtime. This is typically accomplished by adding the scripts to Frame 1 in the Flash Timeline. It is said that Flash components finally allow for the separation of coding and design.

Components allow ActionScript writers to create functionality that designers can use in applications, and designers with little programming skill can incorporate Rich Media Content to their Flash documents with a minimum of coding experience. If the components that ship with Flash are not enough, you can always download additional components built by members of the Flash community by pointing your browser to: *http://www.adobe.com/cfusion/exchange/ index.cfm* at the Adobe Exchange.

What You'll Do

Add a Data Grid

Use a Local Data Provider

Add a Loader

Add a Numeric Stepper

Add a Progress Bar

Add a Scroll Pane

Add a Tree

Add a Window

Modify DataGrid Options

Adding a Data Grid

The DataGrid component allows you to create strong data-enabled displays and applications. You can use the DataGrid component to create a recordset (retrieved from a database query in ColdFusion, Java, or .Net) using Adobe Flash Remoting and display it in columns. You can also use data from a data set or from an array to fill a DataGrid component. The DataGrid component includes horizontal scrolling, event support (including event support for editable cells), sorting capabilities, and performance optimizations. The data for a grid can come from a recordset that is fed from a database query in Adobe ColdFusion, Java, or .Net using Flash Remoting, a data set or an array. To pull the information into a DataGrid, you set the DataGrid.dataProvider property to the recordset, data set, or array.

Add a DataGrid Component

1 Open the **Components** panel.

2 Click the **User Interface** plus (+) sign to expand the list.

3 Drag the **DataGrid** component onto the Stage, and then select the component.

Did You Know?

You can create shapes directly on the Stage in Drawing mode. If you plan to design your interface using Flash's drawing tools, you can now create shapes directly on the Stage that will not interfere with other shapes on the same Stage by using Drawing mode.

You can use Script Assist mode to help you write a script. If you're having problems writing your own ActionScripts, simply click the Script Assist button (located in the upper-right corner of the Action panel, and let Flash give you a hand.

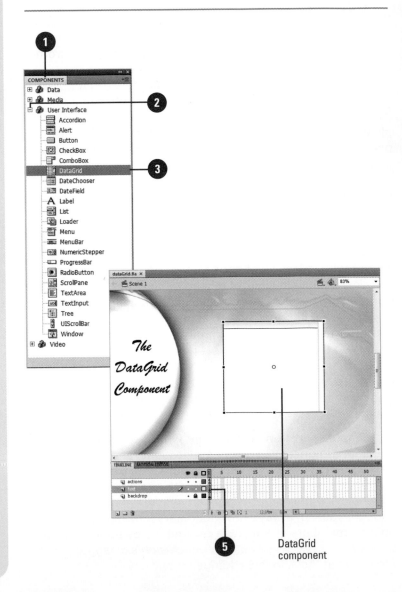

DataGrid
component

④ Enter a unique instance name for the DataGrid component in the Property Inspector.

⑤ Select Frame 1 in the actions layer in the Timeline.

⑥ Open the **Actions** panel, and then enter the script as shown in the illustration.

The Flash Remoting recordset recordSetInstance is assigned to the dataProvider property of myDataGrid.

See Also

See "Modifying DataGrid Options" on page 430 for more information on changing DataGrid parameters.

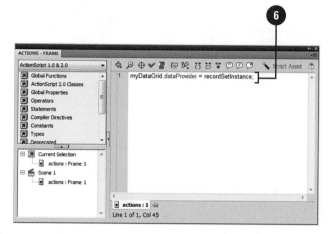

For Your Information

Dragging a DataGrid

When you drag a DataGrid onto the Stage, the component displays at a pre-defined width and height. If you want to resize the instance, just select the Transform tool from the toolbox, and then use the resize nodes to change the width and height. If you drag another DataGrid component onto the Stage, it will display using the default width and height. If you want an exact copy of the one you first placed on the stage, select the Selection tool, hold down the Alt key (Win), Option key (Mac), and then drag the component. Flash will create an exact copy of the modified component.

Using a Local Data Provider

The DataGrid component lets you provide data using a local (embedded in the document) data provider. The data is read into the grid from a pre-written ActionScript, and since Flash components are on the Stage, the ActionScript would typically be entered into the first frame of the Flash Timeline.

Use a Local Data Provider

1. Open the **Components** panel.

2. Click the **User Interface** plus (+) sign to expand the list.

3. Drag the **DataGrid** component onto the Stage, and then select the component.

4. Enter a unique instance name for the DataGrid component in the Property Inspector.

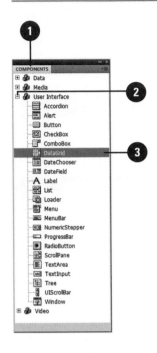

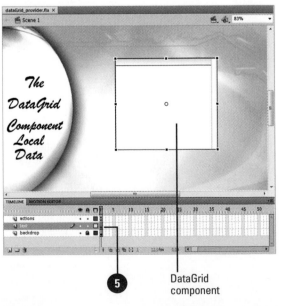

DataGrid component

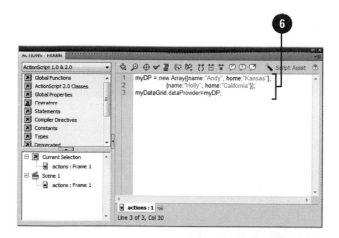

5 Select Frame 1 in the actions layer in the Timeline.

6 Open the **Actions** panel, and then enter the script as shown in the illustration.

7 Click the **Control** menu, and then click **Test Movie**.

The name and home fields are the column headings for the DataGrid component, and the values fill the cells in each row.

IMPORTANT *It's smart programming to create a separate layer to hold the ActionScript for the DataGrid. That way you have much easier access to the script.*

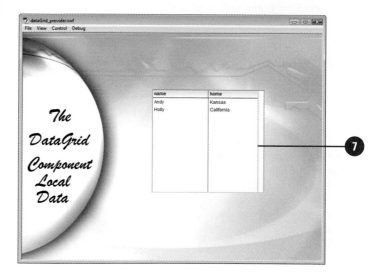

For Your Information

Data Provider

Data Provider, such as adding data within an ActionScript, makes the Flash document display the same data every time the Flash document is displayed. You can always modify the data as the movie plays, by adding additional ActionScript instructions on the Timeline, and therefore, create a more dynamic Data Provider.

Adding a Loader

The Loader component is a container that can display a .swf or a .jpg. You use the Loader component when you want to pull in external content into a Flash movie. For example, you can bring in a product introduction (.swf) or a company logo (.jpg) at the beginning of a movie. In addition, you can scale the contents of the loader, or resize the loader itself, to accommodate the size of the contents. By default, the contents are scaled to fit.

Add a Loader Component

1. Open the **Components** panel.

2. Click the **User Interface** plus (+) sign to expand the list.

3. Drag the **Loader** (2.0) or **UILoader** (3.0) component onto the Stage, and then select the component.

4. Select the **Free Transform** tool to size the Loader to the dimensions of the image file.

Did You Know?

You can use a preloader with components. Components are set to load before the first frame of a Flash movie. You can create a custom preloader by setting an export frame option to the frame containing your components. To change the export frame option, click the File menu, click Publish Settings, set ActionScript version to ActionScript 2.0, click Settings next to it, and then change the Export Frame For Classes value to the frame number where your components first appear.

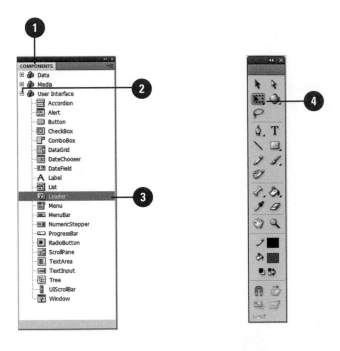

Loader component

5 Open the **Component Inspector** panel, and then click the **Parameters** tab.

6 Enter the path to the .jpg or .swf file in the contentPath value (2.0) or source (3.0) field.

7 Click the **Control** menu, and then click **Test Movie**.

Flash displays the selected image in the Loader component.

Did You Know?

You can use ActionScript to load external SWF and image files. To load an SWF or image file into a movie, use the loadMovie() or loadMovieNum() global function, the loadMovie() method of the MovieClip class. For example, loadMovie("intro.swf", video_mc) loads the movie named *intro* into the movie clip instance named *video_mc*. For another example, loadMovie("http://www.company.com /images/logo.jpg", image_mc) loads an image named *logo* into the movie clip instance named *image_mc*.

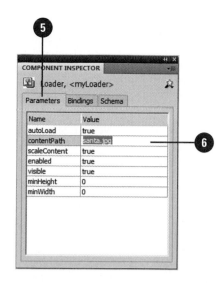

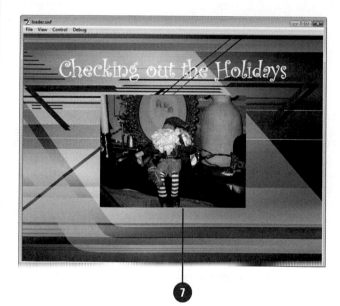

Adding a Numeric Stepper

The NumericStepper component allows a user to step through an ordered set of numbers. The component consists of a number displayed beside small up and down arrow buttons. You can decide the maximum and minimum values along with the step value. When the visitor clicks the up or down buttons, the value changes until the maximum or minimums are reached. As its name implies, the numeric stepper component only handles numbers, text or special characters are not allowed. The NumericStepper component has many uses; for example, a site that books rooms for a major hotel chain would use a stepper for letting the visitor indicate how many people are staying, or an airline for how many people are flying.

Add a NumericStepper Component

1. Open the **Components** panel.

2. Click the **User Interface** plus (+) sign to expand the list.

3. Drag the **NumericStepper** component onto the Stage, and then select the component.

4. Open the **Component Inspector** panel, and then click the **Parameters** tab.

   IMPORTANT *The NumericStepper component can be used to change the properties of items on the stage. You could link a NumericStepper instance to the property value of a dynamic text box, and then use the stepper to change the size of the text. This can be useful for people who require larger, readable text.*

NumericStepper component

420

5 Select from the following NumericStepper parameters:

◆ **maximum.** Click the value field, and then enter the maximum value associated with the NumericStepper.

◆ **minimum.** Click the value field, and then enter the minimum value associated with the NumericStepper.

◆ **stepSize.** Click the value field, and then enter a numerical value for stepping between numbers. For example, a stepSize value of 2, would cause the values to step by 2 (2, 4, 6, 8).

◆ **value.** Click the value field, and then enter the first number value that appears in the NumericStepper.

◆ **enabled.** When you click the value field and select true, the field can be selected. If you select false, the field appears grayed out and is not selectable.

◆ **visible.** When you click the value field and select true, the field can be viewed. If you select false, the field is invisible.

◆ **minHeight (2.0).** Click the value field, and then enter a minimum height for the NumericStepper.

◆ **minWidth (2.0).** Click the value field, and then enter a minimum width for the NumericStepper.

6 Click the **Control** menu, and then click **Test Movie**.

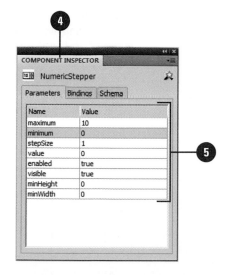

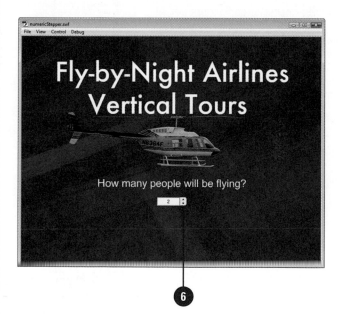

Adding a Progress Bar

The ProgressBar component is a necessity for Flash documents that require a long time to download, because they display the loading progress while a user waits. Web designers live under what is called the "ten-second rule." What that implies is that visitors to your Web site have very little patience, and they want to see things happening. When you add a ProgressBar component, the visitor sees a moving representation (a bar), letting them know the information is being downloaded.

Add a ProgressBar Component

1. Open the **Components** panel.

2. Click the **User Interface** plus (+) sign to expand the list.

3. Drag the **ProgressBar** component onto the Stage, and then select the bar.

4. Give the ProgressBar component a unique instance name in the Property Inspector.

5. Open the **Component Inspector** panel, and then click the **Parameters** tab.

6. Click the **Mode** list arrow, and then click **Event**.

Did You Know?

The ProgressBar component doesn't make a good preloader. A preloader is a custom progress bar that shows the loading status of an entire movie, and is usually smaller in file size than the ProgressBar component.

The loading process can be determinate or indeterminate. A determinate progress bar is linear, tracking progress over time. Use this when the amount of content is known. Indeterminate progress bar is used when the amount of content is unknown.

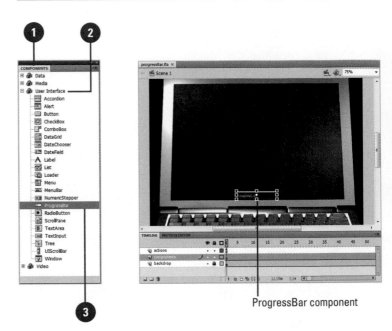

ProgressBar component

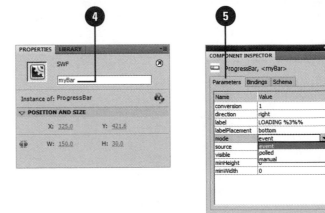

7 Drag a Loader component from the Components panel onto the Stage.

8 Give the Loader component a unique instance name in the Property Inspector.

9 Select the ProgressBar component.

10 Click the **Parameters** tab in the Component Inspector panel, and then enter the instance name of the Loader into the Source value field.

11 Select Frame 1 in the actions layer in the Timeline.

12 Open the **Actions** panel, and then enter the script as shown in the illustration that will load a .jpg, or .swf file into the Loader component.

When executed, the ProgressBar component will display a horizontal bar, and the percentage of the file that's loaded.

13 Click the **Control** menu, and then click **Test Movie**.

When executed, the ProgressBar component will display a moving horizontal bar, and a percentage which displays how much of the file has loaded.

IMPORTANT *Notice that you're not adding scripts to the components on the Stage. The key is that these components are activated by scripts in Frame 1 on the Timeline, and are identified by using unique instance names for each component.*

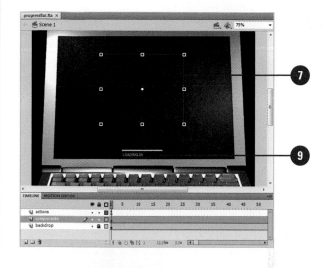

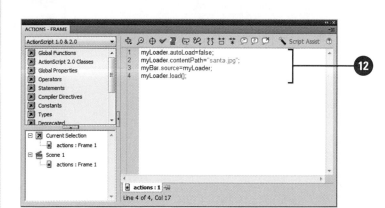

Adding a Scroll Pane

The ScrollPane component can be used for displaying large movie clips, .jpg files, and .swf files that need a scrollable area to display, or that you want to confine to a specific area on the Flash Stage. You have the ability to display images in a limited area, using scroll bars, and the content loaded into the ScrollPane can be from a local location, or over the Internet.

Add a ScrollPane Component

1. Open the **Components** panel.

2. Click the **User Interface** plus (+) sign to expand the list.

3. Drag the **ScrollPane** component onto the Stage, and then select the pane.

4. Open the **Component Inspector** panel, and then click the **Parameters** tab.

5. Select from the following ScrollPane parameters:

   ◆ **contentPath (2.0)** or **source (3.0).** Click the value field, and then enter the full path name to the movie clip, .jpg, or .swf file.

   ◆ **hLineScrollSize.** Click the value field, and then enter the number of pixels to move the content when the left or right arrow in the horizontal scroll bar is pressed.

   ◆ **hPageScrollSize.** Click the value field, and then enter the number of pixels to move the content when the track in the horizontal scroll bar is pressed.

   ◆ **hScrollPolicy.** Click the value field, and then select whether the horizontal scroll bar is always present (on), never present (off), or appears automatically according to the size of the image (auto).

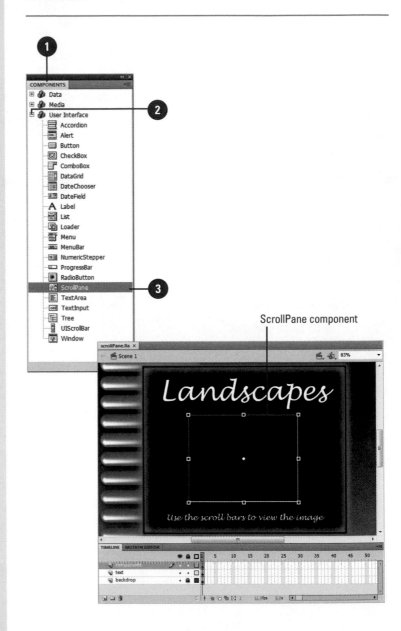

ScrollPane component

- ◆ **scrollDrag.** Click the value field, and then select whether there is scrolling when a user presses and drags within the ScrollPane (true), or no scrolling (false).

- ◆ **vLineScrollSize.** Click the value field, and then enter the number of pixels to move the content when the up or down arrow in the vertical scroll bar is pressed.

- ◆ **vPageScrollSize.** Click the value field, and then enter the number of pixels to move the content when the track in the vertical scroll bar is pressed.

- ◆ **vScrollPolicy.** Click the value field, and then select whether the vertical scroll bar is always present (on), never present (off), or appears automatically according to the size of the image (auto).

- ◆ **enabled.** When you click the value field and select true, the field can be selected. If you select false, the field appears grayed out and is not selectable.

- ◆ **visible.** When you click the value field and select true, the field can be viewed. If you select false, the field is invisible.

- ◆ **minHeight (2.0).** Click the value field, and then enter a minimum height for the ScrollPane.

- ◆ **minWidth (2.0).** Click the value field, and then enter a minimum width for the ScrollPane.

6 Click the **Control** menu, and then click **Test Movie**.

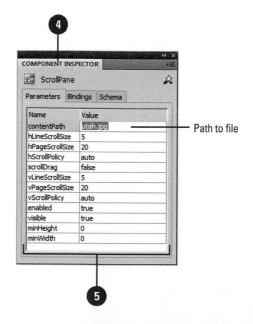

Path to file

Adding a Tree

The Tree component (ActionScript 2.0) allows a user to view hierarchical data. The tree appears within a box like the List component, but each item in a tree is called a node and can be either a leaf or a branch. By default, a leaf is represented by a text label beside a file icon and a branch is represented by a text label beside a folder icon with a disclosure triangle that a user can open to expose children. The children of a branch can either be leaves or branches themselves.

Add a Tree Component

1. Open the **Components** panel.

2. Click the **User Interface** plus (+) sign to expand the list.

3. Drag the **Tree** component (2.0) onto the Stage, and then select the tree.

4. Open the **Component Inspector** panel, and then click the **Parameters** tab.

5. Select from the following Tree parameters:

   ◆ **multipleSelection.** Click the value field, and then select whether the visitor can select multiple items (true), or single items (false).

   ◆ **rowHeight.** Click the value field, and then enter a numerical value for the height of each row in pixels.

6. Create a unique instance name for the Tree component in the Property Inspector.

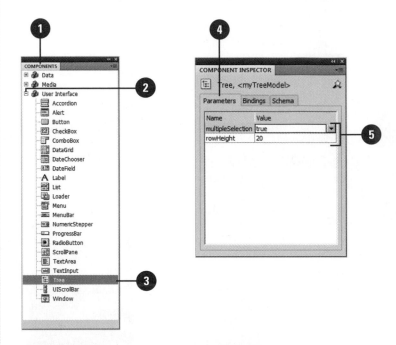

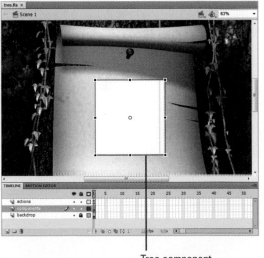

Tree component

7 Open the **Actions** panel, and then enter the script (ActionScript 2.0) as shown in the illustration into Frame 1 on the Timeline.

This Script creates a trace action inside the handler and sends a message to the Output panel every time an item in the tree is selected.

8 Add the remaining script to Frame 1 in the Timeline to complete the Tree component structure.

The previous code creates an XML object called myTreeDP. Any XML object on the same frame as a Tree component automatically receives all the properties and methods of the TreeDataProvider API. The second line of code creates a single root node called Local Folders.

9 Click the **Control** menu, and then click **Test Movie**.

In the .swf file, you can see the XML structure displayed in the Tree. Click the triangle next to Local Folders to expand the list. Each time you click on an item in the list, the trace action in the change event handler sends the data "was selected" to the Output panel.

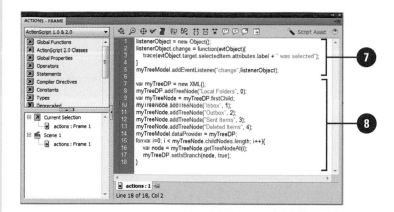

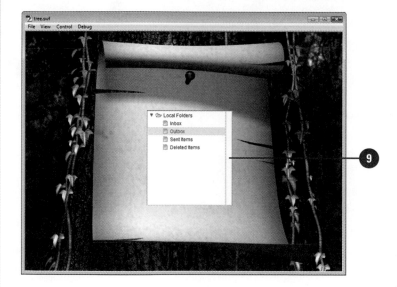

See Also

See Chapter 18, "Adding and Modifying Data Components" on page 431 for information on working with data components.

Adding a Window

The Window component (ActionScript 2.0) lets you display the contents of a movie clip inside a window using a title bar, a border, and a Close button (optional). The Window component lets you create complex Flash documents with one or more windows controlling the viewing of multiple movie clips. Since a movie clip can contain anything from a static image to video, the Window component gives you the creative freedom to choose what design elements best suit your Flash document, and then incorporate them on the Stage. Since movie clips can contain their own play, stop, and rewind buttons, you can use the Window component to load the movie clip, and then use the clip's internal controls to play the movie. Finally, use the Close button on the Window component to unload the clip when finished.

Add a Window Component

1. Open the **Components** panel.

2. Click the **User Interface** plus (+) sign to expand the list.

3. Drag the **Window** component (2.0) onto the Stage, and then select the window.

4. Open the **Component Inspector** panel, and then click the **Parameters** tab.

5. Select from the following Window parameters:

   ◆ **closeButton.** Click the value field, and then select whether the Close button is available (true) or disabled (false).

   ◆ **contentPath.** Click the value field, and then enter the full path name to the movie clip you want to display.

   ◆ **title.** Click the value field, and then enter the name that will appear in the title bar.

   ◆ **enabled.** When you click the value field and select true, the Window can be accessed. If you select false, the Window appears grayed out and is not usable.

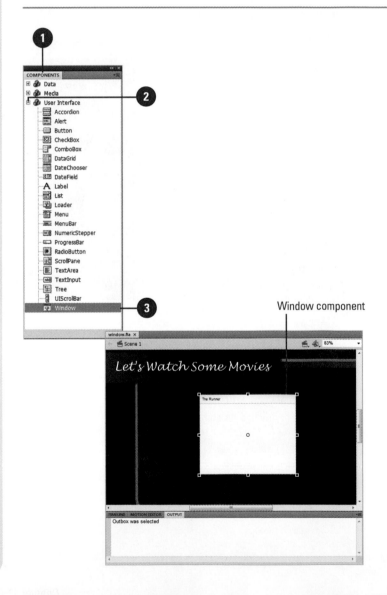

Window component

- ◆ **visible.** When you click the value field and select true, the Window can be viewed. If you select false, the Window is invisible.

- ◆ **minHeight.** Click the value field, and then enter a minimum height for the Window.

- ◆ **minWidth.** Click the value field, and then enter a minimum width for the Window.

- ◆ **skinCloseDisable.** The value field represents the name of the formatting .fla document used for the Close button, when disabled.

- ◆ **skinCloseDown.** The value field represents the name of the formatting .fla document used for the Close button, when down.

- ◆ **skinCloseOver.** The value field represents the name of the formatting .fla document used for the Close button, when the mouse is over.

- ◆ **skinCloseUp.** The value field represents the name of the formatting .fla document used for the Close button, when Up.

- ◆ **skinTitleBackground.** The value field represents the name of the formatting .fla document used for the title background.

- ◆ **TitleStyleDeclaration.** Click the value field, and then enter the path to a style declaration that formats the title bar of a window (CSS).

6 Click the **Control** menu, and then click **Test Movie**.

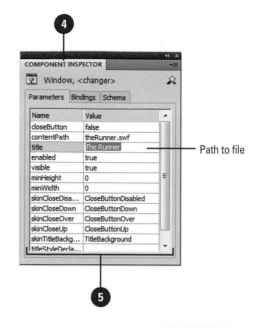

Path to file

Modifying DataGrid Options

Just like any other Flash component, the DataGrid has parameters that can be modified. However, as the previous example illustrates, using the Actions panel and entering scripts can give you further control over the modification of a Flash component. The Parameters available from the Component Inspector panel give you a start at how you can modify a component.

Modify DataGrid Options

1. Select the DataGrid component, and then open the **Component Inspector** panel.

2. Click the **Parameters** tab.

3. Select from the following DataGrid parameters:

   ◆ **editable.** When you click the value field and select true, the field can be edited. If you select false, the field can be selected but not edited.

   ◆ **mutipleSelection.** When you click the value field and select true, the visitor can select more than one item in the list. If you select false, the visitor can only select a single item.

   ◆ **rowHeight.** Click the value field, and then enter a number to determine the spacing between items in the list. The higher the value, the more space between items.

See Also

See "Adding a DataGrid" on page 414 for more information on using DataGrid components.

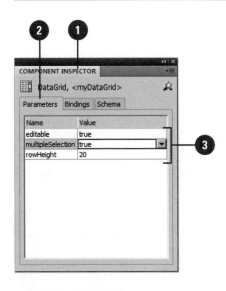

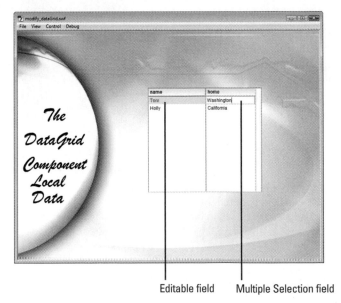

Editable field   Multiple Selection field

Adding and Modifying Data Components

18

Introduction

Flash comes with various components. To provide Rich Internet Applications to developers, Adobe provided developers with greatly advanced tools for video and advanced data components. The Data Connection Kit contains three components—Connector, Dataset, and Resolver. The Connector component is used to connect to and retrieve data from a remote data source, the Dataset component is used to manage the data in Flash, and the Resolver sends the updated data back to the original data source, all with a minimum of programming skills on the part of the designer.

In addition, there is included support for XML and Web Services (WSDL). In fact, any visual component in Flash can be bound to data. **Data Binding** is a concept where the property of one component can be bound to the property of another component: if the property of the one component changes, so will the property of the other component or components. Flash comes with several Data components such as the DataHolder, the WebServicesConnector, and the XMLConnector. In fact, you can point your browser to www.adobe.com, and then go to the Flash Exchange to download even more components.

The power of a component is its ability to change. Components can be modified directly in the Component Inspector panel, or they can be modified dynamically, as the Flash movie runs. The Component Inspector panel has three areas to modify a component—Parameters, Bindings, and Schema. These three tabs allow you to attach components to data files, change or modify the text on a button, or create drop-down menus and lists. Since components are rooted in ActionScript code, Flash comes with a set of components for ActionScript 2.0 and another one for ActionScript 3.0, and you cannot mix components in the same Flash document.

What You'll Do

Use the Data Holder

Understand Web Services

Use XML in Flash

Use the Web Service Connector

Use the XML Connector

Use the Component Inspector

Work with Parameters

Modify Parameters

Create Bindings

Modify Bindings

Understand Schema

Modify Schema

Modify a Component's Attributes

Using the Data Holder

The DataHolder component (ActionScript 2.0) holds various types of data and lets you generate events based on how the data changes. The main function of the DataHolder component is to hold data and act as a conduit between other components utilizing data binding. You can assign any type of data to a DataHolder property, either by creating a binding between the data and another property, or by using your own ActionScript code. Whenever the value of that data changes, the DataHolder component generates an event with a name equal to the property name. Any bindings associated with that property are executed. You could have a DataHolder that keeps the current system time and has several display fields bound to that information. One of the fields is simply a display of the time in hours, minutes, and seconds, and another field might be a calculated field that displays good morning, afternoon, or evening, depending on the data sent from the DataHolder field. When you create a DataHolder, it comes with one bindable property named data; you can add more properties to create a group of data information fields, which can transmit their data to other components.

Use the DataHolder Component

1. Open the **Components** panel.

2. Click the **Data** (2.0) plus (+) sign to expand the list.

3. Drag the **DataHolder** component onto the Stage, and then select the component.

4. Give the DataHolder component a unique name in the Property Inspector.

5. Click the **User Interface** plus (+) sign to expand the list.

6. Drag a **DataGrid** component onto the Stage, and then select the component.

7. Give the DataGrid component a unique name in the Property Inspector.

8. Select the DataHolder component.

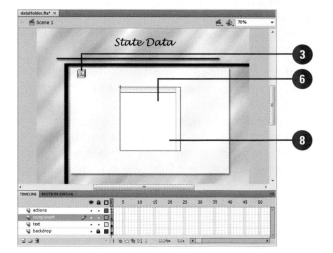

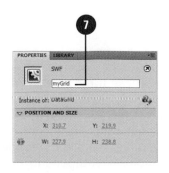

9. Open the **Component Inspector** panel, and then click the **Schema** tab.

10. Click the **Add Component Property** (+) button located at the top of the Schema tab.

11. Enter a unique name in the Field Name field.

12. Select **Array** from the Data Type popup menu.

13. Click the **Bindings** tab in the Component Inspector panel, and then add a binding between the property of the DataHolder component and the data provider property of the DataGrid component.

14. Click **OK**.

15. Select Frame 1 on the Timeline, and then enter the script as shown in the illustration.

16. Click the **Control** menu, and then click **Test Movie**.

See Also

See Chapter 18, "Adding and Modifying Data Components" on page 431 for more information on using Schema and Binding options.

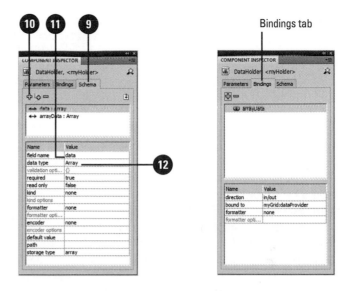

Bindings tab

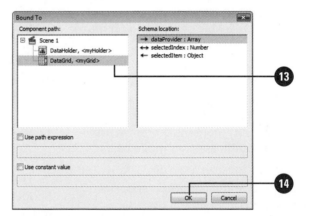

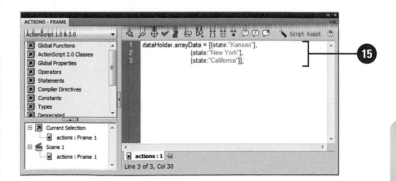

Understanding Web Services

Communication is an important part of our daily life. Think of a society where everyone spoke a different language. While most people that live in a country have a single language to communicate with, the Internet is still struggling with standardizing many of its communication features. However, as communication protocols and message formats become more and more consistent, it is becoming possible to describe the exchanges between two or more computer systems in a structured way. WSDL (Web Services Descriptive Language) addresses this need by defining an underlying XML grammar (a standard communication system) for describing network services as collections of communication standards capable of exchanging messages.

A Flash WSDL compliant document defines Web services to be a collection of network endpoints. This translates into a better system of transferring data between two endpoints, or ports; components therefore are more reliably bound, and can move easier between systems.

The protocol and data format specifications for a particular endpoint become a reusable binding. An endpoint, or port is defined by associating a network address with a reusable binding, and collections of ports define a Web service. Think of the endpoints as the connection between two computers: Two computers connected together by a communications cable. When one computer speaks to the other, Web Services ensures that they are speaking the same language.

Flash WSDL compliant documents use the following elements to define a Web service:

◆ **Types.** A container for data type definitions using some type system (such as XSD).

◆ **Message.** An abstract, typed definition of the data being communicated.

◆ **Operation.** An abstract description of an action supported by the service.

◆ **Port Type.** An abstract set of operations supported by one or more endpoints.

◆ **Binding.** A concrete protocol and data format specification for a particular port type.

◆ **Port.** A single endpoint defined as a combination of a binding and a network address.

◆ **Service.** A collection of related endpoints.

While all of this may seem a bit overwhelming, it translates into an easier way to move data between two points. Eventually, transferring information on the Internet will be as easy as talking over the fence to your next-door neighbor. For more information on Web Services, point your browser to *http://www.w3c.org*, and type in "*Web Services*" into the search field.

The good news about Web Services is that Adobe Flash takes care of all the hard stuff with the WebServicesConnector component which is detailed in the next section: Using the WebServiceConnector Component.

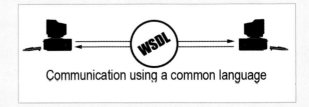
Communication using a common language

Using XML in Flash

Extensible Markup Language (XML) is a simple, but very flexible, text information system. Originally designed to meet the challenges of large-scale electronic publishing, XML also plays an important role in the exchange of a wide variety of data on the Web and elsewhere; including Flash documents.

The main difference between XML and HTML is that XML was designed to carry data. XML is not a replacement for HTML. XML and HTML were designed with different goals: XML was designed to describe data and to focus on what data is, and HTML was designed to display data and to focus on how data looks. In other words, HTML is about displaying information, while XML is about describing information. It was created to structure, store and to send information.

The following is an example of XML:

```
<memo>
<to>Holly</to>
<from>Andy</from>
</description>Reminder</description>
<body>Keep up the great work!</body>
</memo>
```

The note has a header and a message body. It also contains a sender and receiver. Understand that the XML document doesn't do anything. It's simply information wrapped in programmer-defined XML tags. To make all this work, someone must write a piece of software to send, receive or display the information, and that's where Flash's XMLConnector component comes into play. XML is simply a cross-platform, software and hardware independent tool for transmitting information.

XML is a tool for transmitting information in a way that all systems can understand. Again, it's all about communication. When computers were born (followed closely by the birth of the Internet), everyone spoke a different language, and the moving of information was a difficult venture. With the inception of XML and WSDL, all of those communication problems are quickly becoming a thing of the past, and Flash is at the forefront of implementing these new technologies.

Using the Web Service Connector

The WebServiceConnector component enables you to access remote methods offered by a server using the industry-standard SOAP (Simple Object Access Protocol) protocol. This gives a Web service the ability to accept parameters and return a result back to the generating script. By using the Flash Professional authoring tool and the WebService-Connector component, you can access and bind data between a remote Web service and your Flash application. To save programming time, a single instance of WebServiceConnector component can be used to make multiple calls to the same operation. All you would have to do is to use a different instance of the WebServiceConnector for each different operation you wanted to call. You can use the WebServiceConnector to connect to a Web service, and make the properties of the Web service available for binding to properties of Flash UI components within your application. Think of a Web Service as a database of information, which can be downloaded—using the WebServiceConnector—and then displayed inside a Flash movie. For example, the Virginia Department of Parks and Recreation has a Web service (large database) that contains information in the WSDL format that you can download and display within a Flash document. Since the connection to the service is live, every time the Park Service changes information such as the opening and closing times for the park, the Web Service would send that information to your Flash document (called listening) and automatically update the page.

Use the WebServiceConnector Component

1. Click the **Window** menu, point to **Other Panels**, and then click **Web Services**.

2. Click the **Define Web Services** button.

3. Click the **Add (+)** button to add the path for a Web service WSDL file.

4. Add a call to a method of the Web service by selecting the method, Control-clicking (Mac) or right-clicking (Win), and then selecting Add Method Call from the context menu.

5. Click **OK**.

   This will create a WebService-Connector component instance in your application.

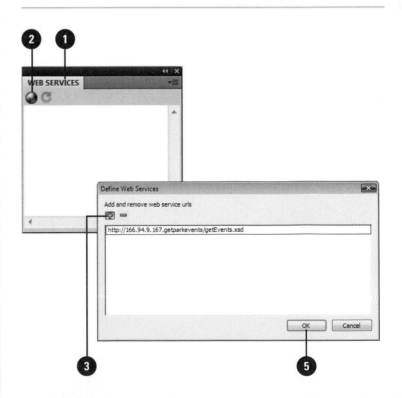

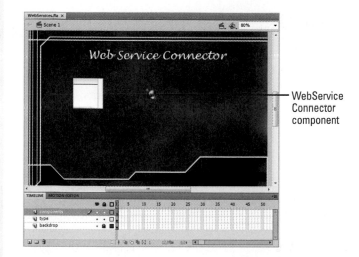

WebService Connector component

6. Click the **Parameters** tab in the Component Inspector panel to edit these properties as needed. For example, you can provide additional formatting or validation settings.

7. Use the **Bindings** tab in the Component Inspector panel to bind the Web service parameters and the results that are now defined in your schema to UI Components within your application, such as a DataGrid.

8. Click **OK**.

9. Add a trigger to initiate the data binding operation by attaching the trigger to a button.

You can add an ActionScript on the WebServiceConnector component or create a binding between a Web service parameter and a UI control. Set its Kind property to AutoTrigger.

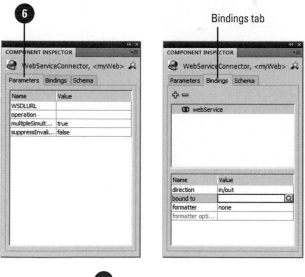

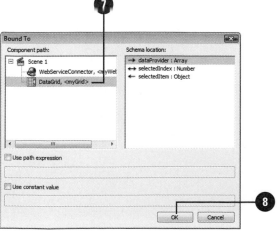

Using the XML Connector

The XMLConnector component (ActionScript 2.0) is designed to read or write XML documents using standard HTTP protocol, get operations or post operations. It acts as the connector between other Flash components and external XML data sources. For example, you could use a DataGrid component to format and display information received from a remote site containing an XML document. Since XML (Extensible Markup Language) is a hardware independent language, it's easy to work with, and it can be modified to fit a specific purpose. The XMLConnector communicates with components in a Flash application using data binding features, or ActionScript code. It has properties, methods, and events but no runtime visual appearance. In fact, all of Flash's connector components have no visual presence; they are simply the gateway for passing information from one source to another. The XMLConnector component implements a set of methods, properties, and events that define a simple way to send parameters to, and receive results from an external data source.

Use the XMLConnector Component

1. Open the **Components** panel.

2. Click the **Data** (2.0) plus (+) sign to expand the list.

3. Drag the **XMLConnector** component onto the Stage, and then select the component.

4. Give the XMLConnector component a unique name in the Property Inspector.

5. Open the **Component Inspector** panel, and then click the **Parameters** tab.

6. Enter the full path name to the external XML file.

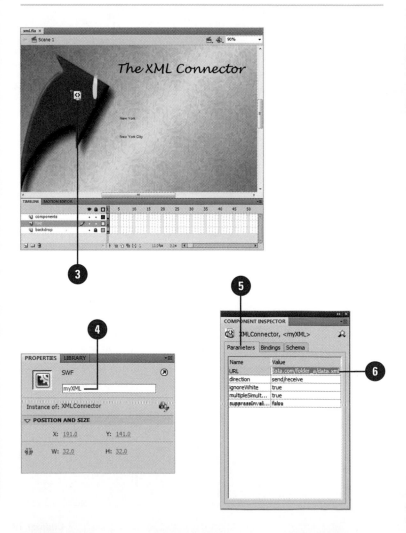

7 Click the **Schema** tab, and then specify a schema for the XML document.

The schema tab lets you create fields to format the XML data.

8 Use the **Bindings** tab to bind the data elements from the XML document to properties of the visual components in your application.

For example, you can connect to an XML document that provides weather data, and bind the Location and Temperature data elements to Label components in your application, so that the name and temperature of a specified city appears in the application at runtime.

9 Click **OK**.

10 Add a trigger to initiate the data binding operation by attaching the trigger behavior to a button, and then add your own ActionScript.

You can also create a binding between an XML parameter and setting a UI component's Kind property to AutoTrigger.

11 Click the **Control** menu, and then click **Test Movie**.

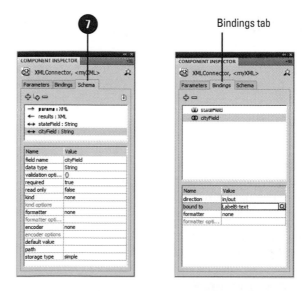

Bindings tab

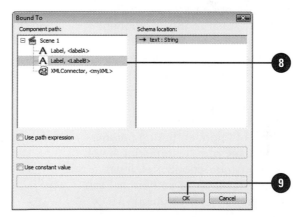

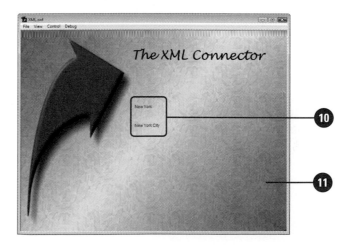

Using the Component Inspector

The Component Inspector panel represents the focus of control for most of Flash's components. After you add an instance of a component to a Flash document, you can use the Component Inspector panel to set and view information for the instance. You can drag a component from the Components panel to the Stage, and then give the component a unique instance name, using the Property Inspector.

Once a component and instance name are established, you can use the Component Inspector panel to set and modify parameters for that particular instance. Parameters represent the instance's appearance and behavior. Parameters that appear in the Component Inspector panel are known as authoring parameters. **Authoring parameters** represent common things such as the label attached to a Button component, or items displayed when using the MenuBar component. There are other parameters that can be set using ActionScript. In addition, authoring parameters can also be set with ActionScript. If you set a parameter using ActionScript, it will override any value set while authoring. Each Flash component has its own unique set of parameters.

The Component Inspector panel has two additional tabs: Bindings and Schema. The Bindings tab defines a link between two endpoints, a source (external data file, movie clip, graphic) and a destination component (DataGrid, Loader, Label). It listens for changes to the source endpoint and copies the changed data to the destination endpoint each time the source changes. The Schema tab lets you view the schema for the selected component. **Schema** is basically a list of the component's binding properties, their data types, their internal structure, and other special attributes, depending on the selected component. This is the information that the Bindings tab needs in order to handle your data correctly. You can drag the DataGrid component onto the Stage, and then use the XMLConnector to pull in data from an external Web site. You can click the Schema tab, define the binding component (DataGrid), and then use the Bindings tab to link the DataGrid component to the external XML file.

Once connected, the XMLConnector would listen for changes to the external XML file, and then pass that information on to the DataGrid component. Since the DataGrid displays visible information in a Flash document, the result would be information that performs live updates to the Flash screen.

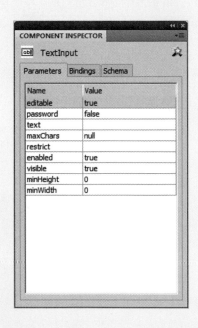

Working with Parameters

After adding an instance of a component to a Flash document, you can name the instance in the Property Inspector, and then specify the parameters for the instance using the fields on the Parameters tab in the Component Inspector panel.

Each component has parameters that you can set to change its appearance and behavior. A **parameter** is a property or method that appears in the Property Inspector and Component Inspector panel. The most commonly used properties and methods appear

as authoring parameters; others can be set using ActionScript. Think of authoring parameters as the most common parameters.

Additions parameters include the ability to change an instance's font, color, and size. Additional parameters are added by selecting the instance on the Stage and typing the script into the Actions panel. Adding parameters directly to the component instance will only impact the selected instance. If you add the script to Frame 1 in the Timeline, you can create global changes to instance parameters.

Components panel

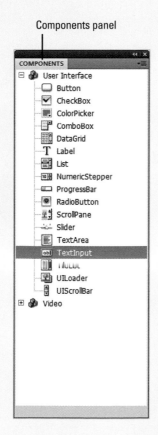

Component Inspector panel

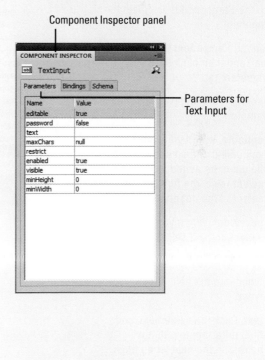

Parameters for Text Input

Modifying Parameters

To modify the parameters of a component, you must first create an instance of the component. For example, if you want to modify a TextInput field, you would first open the Components panel, and then drag a TextInput component onto the Stage. Next, you would give the component a unique instance name by selecting the component and then entering the name in the Property Inspector. Finally, you would open the Component Inspector panel, click the Parameters tab, and then make the changes. Understand that each component will have its own unique parameters, and changing parameters in the Component Inspector panel only changes the selected instance.

Modify Parameters

① Open the **Components** panel.

② Click the **User Interface** plus (+) sign to expand the list.

③ Drag the **TextInput** component onto the Stage, and then select the component.

④ Open the **Component Inspector** panel, and then click the **Parameters** tab.

⑤ Select from the following TextInput parameters:

◆ **editable.** When you click the value field and select true, the field can be edited. If you select false, the field can be selected but not edited.

◆ **password.** When you click the value field and select true, text entered into the field appears as dots. If you select false, text typed into the field appears as typed.

◆ **text.** Click the value field, and then enter the text that will appear in the field when the Flash document opens.

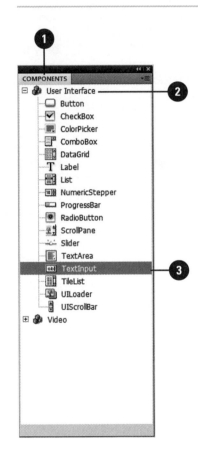

- **maxChars.** Click the value field, and then enter a numerical value indicating the max characters allowed in the TextInput field.

- **restrict.** Click the value field, and then enter any characters that cannot be entered into the TextInput field.

- **enabled.** When you click the value field and select true, the field can be edited. If you select false, the field appears grayed out, and is not selectable or editable.

- **visible.** When you click the value field and then select true, the field can be viewed. If you select false, the field is invisible.

- **minHeight (2.0).** Click the value field, and then enter a minimum height for the TextInput box.

- **minWidth (2.0).** Click the value field, and then enter a minimum width for the TextInput box.

6 Click the **Control** Menu, and then click **Test Movie**.

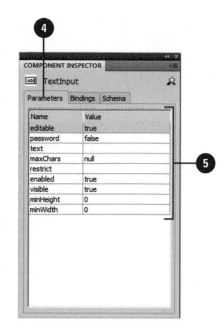

Did You Know?

You can change the properties of an instance from the Properties panel.
Select an instance of a component on the Stage, and then open the Property Inspector. Click the Window menu, and then click Properties.

Creating Bindings

Data binding is a simple way of connecting Flash components to each other. Components can be viewed as containers that transfer information (images, text, numbers, video, graphics) from one to the other. In the Component Inspector panel, the Bindings tab controls the two containers, so that when property X of component A changes, it will copy the new value to property Y of component B. You can do data binding within the Component Inspector panel using the Bindings tab. The Bindings tab lets you add, view, and remove bindings for the selected component. Although data binding works with any component, its main purpose is to connect Component panel UI components to external data sources such as Web Services and XML documents. These external data sources are available as components with properties, which you can bind to other component properties. The Component Inspector panel is the main tool that is used within Flash for data binding. It contains a Schema tab for defining the schema for a component and a Bindings tab for creating bindings between component properties. The following example demonstrates how to create basic data binding by connecting one UI component to another.

Create Bindings

1. Open the **Components** panel.

2. Click the **User Interface** plus (+) sign to expand the list.

3. Drag the **NumericStepper** component onto the Stage, and then select the component.

4. Give the NumericStepper a unique instance name in the Property Inspector.

5. Drag a second NumericStepper onto the Stage, and then give it a unique instance name.

6. Select the first NumericStepper component.

See Also

See Chapter 18 on "Adding and Modifying Data Components" on page 431 for more information on XML and Web Services.

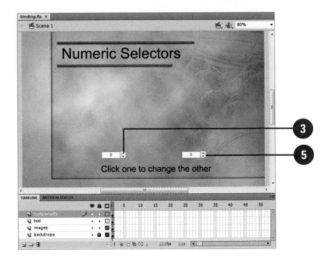

7. Open the **Component Inspector** panel, and then click the **Bindings** tab.

8. Click the **Add Binding (+)** button to add a binding.

9. In the Add Binding dialog box, select **Value**.

10. Click **OK**.

11. Move to the Name/Value section, located at the bottom of the Bindings tab.

12. Click the **Bound To** item under Name, and then click the **Magnifying Glass** icon.

13. In the Bound To dialog box, select the **NumbericStepper** component B.

14. Click **OK**.

15. Click the **Control** menu, and then click **Test Movie**.

When you click the up and down buttons on the first NumericStepper, the value changes automatically in the second NumericStepper.

IMPORTANT *You can use the Bindings tab to link two or more components together. If you want to add another component, just click the Add Binding (+) button to bind a second, or third component. There is no limit to the number of components that can be bound together.*

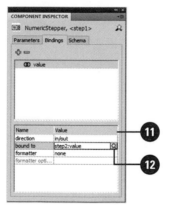

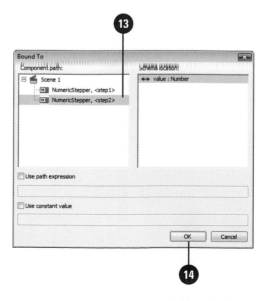

Modifying Bindings

Once you create a binding between two components or between a component, such as a DataGrid, and an external file, you can control the binding through the binding options. For example, you may not want the exchange of data either way, or you may wish to control what type of data is entered or received. The Binding options, located on the Bindings tab, give you several author-controllable options.

Modify Bindings

1. Open the **Components** panel.

2. Click the **User Interface** plus (+) sign to expand the list.

3. Drag the **NumericStepper** component onto the Stage, and then select the component.

4. Give the NumericStepper a unique instance name in the Property Inspector.

5. Drag a **TextInput** component onto the Stage, and then give it a unique instance name.

6. Select the NumericStepper component.

7. Open the **Component Inspector** panel, and then click the **Bindings** tab.

8. Click the **Add Binding** (+) button to add a binding.

9. In the Add Binding dialog box, select **Value**.

10. Click **OK**.

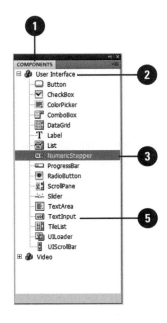

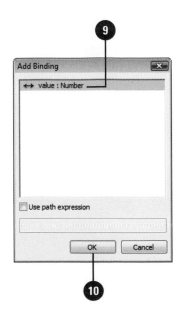

11 Move to the Name/Value section, located at the bottom of the Bindings tab.

12 Click the **Bound To** item under Name, and then click the **Magnifying Glass** icon.

13 In the Bound To dialog box, select the **TextInput** component.

14 Click **OK**.

15 Click the **Control** menu, and then click **Test Movie**.

If you click the up and down arrows on the NumericStepper, the value in the TextInput field changes. If you enter a value into the TextInput field and press Return or Tab, the value in the NumericStepper changes.

16 Close the Flash movie, and then select the NumericStepper.

17 Select **Value** at the top of the Component Inspector panel, click the **Direction** option, and then change the value from in/out to out.

18 Click the **Control** menu, and then click **Test Movie**.

If you click the up and down arrows on the NumericStepper, the value in the TextInput field changes. If you enter a value into the TextInput field and press Return or Tab, the value in the NumericStepper no longer changes.

IMPORTANT *Data binding is supported only between components that exist in Frame 1 of the main Timeline, Frame 1 of a movie clip, or Frame 1 of a screen.*

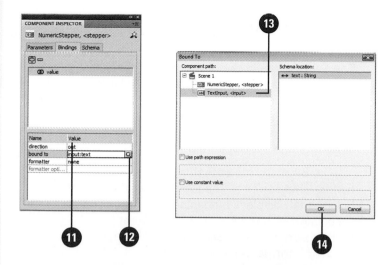

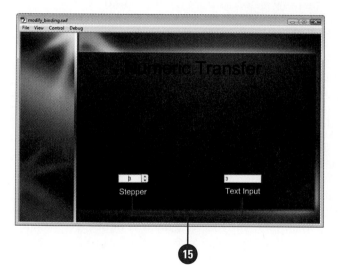

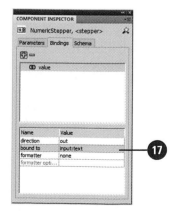

Understanding Schema

The Schema tab in the Component Inspector panel lets you view the schema for a selected component. The schema tab contains a list of what are known as a component's bindable properties, along with data types, internal structure, and special attributes.

The Bindings tab uses this information to handle data correctly. The top portion of the Schema tab displays bindable properties associated with the selected component. The bottom portion of the Schema tab, displays detailed information about the selected schema item (selected from the top portion of the Schema tab).

A component's schema describes the structure and type of data, independent of exactly how the data is stored. For example, the Schema tab identifies data, but not if the data is stored using XML objects, or possibly ActionScript code.

Schemas are important because they help create a communication link between other components, using the Bindings tab. For example, you can use the XMLConnector and DataGrid components to pull data from an XML document, and then display that information on the Stage. The XMLConnector provides the communication link to the external data file, and the DataGrid provides you with an easy way to organize and display the information, but not until you define the data using the Schema tab, and then bind the XMLConnector to the DataGrid using the Bindings tab.

A component's schema simply represents the properties and fields that are available for data binding. Each property or field contains settings that control validation, formatting, type conversion, and other features that affect how data binding and the data management components handle the data of a field. The bottom pane of the Schema tab presents these settings, and gives you the ability to view or edit them.

Schema tab

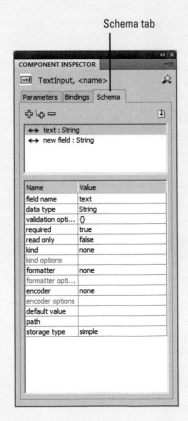

Modifying Schema

To modify the schema of a component, you must first select an instance of the component. For example, if you want to modify the schema of a DataGrid component panel, you first select the component, open the Component Inspector panel, click the Schema tab, and then make the changes. Each component has its own unique schema, and changing parameters in the Component Inspector panel only changes the selected instance.

Modify Schema

1. Select a unique instance of a component on the Stage.

2. Open the **Component Inspector** panel.

3. Click the **Schema** tab.

4. Click the **Add A Component Property** (+) button to add additional fields to the schema list.

5. Click the **Add A Field Under The Selected Field** (+) button to add an additional field that's nested within the selected field.

6. Click the **Delete The Selected Field Or Property** (-) button to remove the selected field or property from the schema.

7. Select an item in the upper portion of the Schema tab, and then modify its options in the lower portion of the Schema tab.

Did You Know?

The Schema tab displays data based on the selected component. Although all components have properties, by default, the Schema tab only displays properties that contain dynamic data. Dynamic data properties are called bindable properties. Flash lets you bind to any property by adding it to the schema panel yourself (using the Add Field (+) button), or using ActionScript code.

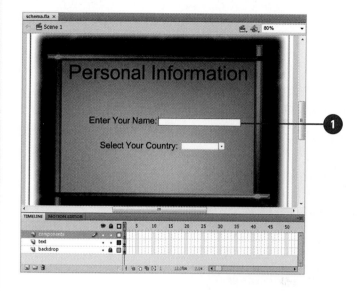

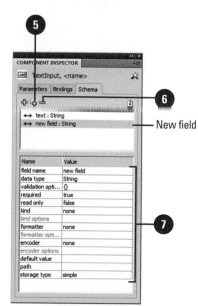

New field

Modifying a Component's Attributes

You can write ActionScript code to change the properties for any Flash component instance. For example, you can change the color of text of a label instance named myLabel using the following code:

myLabel.setStyle("color", "0x990000")

The preceding code would instruct Flash to change the color of the text used in the Label component instance named *myLabel* to red. Changes to the properties of a component can be attached to the instance on the Stage (influences only the one instance), or they can be used to globally change all instances, by placing the script in Frame 1 on the Timeline.

Modify Attributes

① Open the **Actions** panel.

② Select an instance or Frame 1 on the Timeline.

③ Enter the script as shown in the illustration.

④ Click the **Control** menu, and then click **Test Movie**.

The following table is a list of the available ActionScript options for changing the attributes of a component instance.

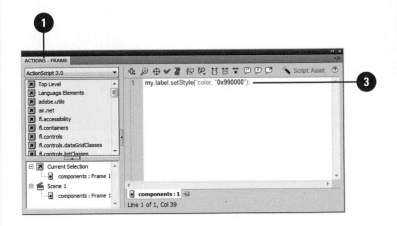

Available Flash Attributes

backgroundColor	marginLeft
borderColor	marginRight
borderStyle	scrollTrackColor
buttonColor	shadowColor
color	symbolBackgroundColor
disabledColor	symbolBackgroundDisabledColor
fontFamily	symbolBackgroundPressedColor
fontSize	symbolColor
fontStyle	symbolDisabledColor
fontWeight	textDecoration
highlightColor	textIndent

Automating Your Work

19

Introduction

The History panel helps you work more efficiently in Flash. As you work, the History panel tracks all the steps you take in Flash. With the History panel, you can undo or redo steps to correct mistakes, replay selected steps for new tasks to streamline repetitive work, and record steps for replay from the Commands menu to automate your work. In addition, Flash allows you to use Object-level undo modes. Which means you can undo steps to a specific object without having to undo the changes made to other main objects on the Stage.

You can open the History panel from the Other Panels submenu on the Window menu. Each step you take in the active document during a work session appears on a separate line in the History panel. You can undo or redo a single step or series of steps quickly with the Undo/Redo slider, which you can drag up to undo a series of steps or drag down to redo a series of steps. You can also select a series of steps in the History panel and replay them to the same object or to a different object in the document.

Do you often repeat the same series of steps? Rather than repeat the same actions, you can work faster by saving the entire series of steps as a command on the Commands menu, which you can reuse again and again. Flash stores the commands you save for future use. After you save steps as a command, you can select the command name on the Commands menu to run it, or use the Manage Saved Command dialog box to rename or delete commands.

Due to the complex nature of some steps, such as adding a gradient to a shape or modifying document size, Flash cannot replay or save (as a command) all steps in the History panel. For these steps, a red X appears in the icon for a step in the History panel. Even though Flash cannot replay or save all steps, it can undo and redo all steps.

What You'll Do

Examine the History Panel

Use the History Panel

Undo and Redo Steps

Replay Steps

Save Steps and Use Commands

Copy Steps Between Documents

Work with Object-Level Undo Mode

Examining the History Panel

The History panel helps you automate and streamline the way you work in Flash. As you work in Flash, the History panel is tracking all your steps for the entire document or only on individual or all objects behind the scenes. With the History panel, you can do any of the following:

◆ Undo or redo steps to correct mistakes.

◆ Replay selected steps for new tasks to streamline repetitive work.

◆ Record steps for replay from the Commands menu to automate your work.

The History panel doesn't replace the Undo, Redo, and Repeat commands on the Edit menu, it simply tracks every step you perform in Flash. When you undo or redo one or more commands, the History panel displays the results; the Undo/Redo slider moves

according to the commands you select.

You can open the History panel using the Window menu like any of the other panels in Flash. Each step you take in the active document during a work session (since you created or opened the document) appears on a separate line in the History panel. The first step you perform in a work session appears at the top of the list and the last step appears at the bottom. If a red X appears in the icon for a step, it indicates Flash cannot save or replay the step. Unlike other panels in Flash, the History panel includes a slider on the left side that you can use to undo/redo steps; the Undo/Redo slider initially points to the last step you performed. The bottom of the History panel includes buttons to replay selected steps, copy selected steps to the Clipboard, and create a command from selected steps. The Options menu displays commands, such as Clear History, specific to the History panel.

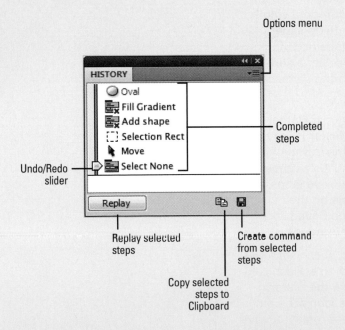

Options menu

Undo/Redo slider

Completed steps

Replay selected steps

Copy selected steps to Clipboard

Create command from selected steps

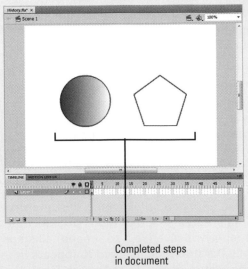

Completed steps in document

Using the History Panel

You can use the Window menu to open the History panel like any of the other panels in Flash; the History panel appears on the Other Panels submenu. Each step you take in the active document during a work session appears on a separate line in the History panel. Steps you take in other Flash documents don't appear in other History panel lists. If you no longer need the steps in the History panel, you can erase the entire list. When you close a document, Flash clears the History panel.

Open and Close the History Panel

- To open the History panel, click the **Window** menu, point to **Other Panels**, and then click **History**.

  TIMESAVER *Press* ⌘+F10 *(Mac) or Ctrl+F10 (Win) to open the History panel.*

- To close the panel, click the **Close** button, or click the **Options** menu, and then click **Close Panel**.

Close button

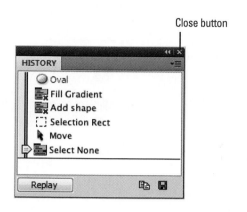

Clear the History Panel

1. Open or expand the **History** panel.

2. Click the **Options** menu, and then click **Clear History**.

3. Click **Yes** to confirm the operation.

4. When you're done, click the **Close** button on the History panel.

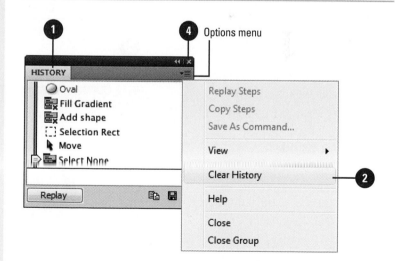

Undoing and Redoing Steps

You can undo or redo a single step or a series of steps quickly with the History panel. The History panel contains the Undo/Redo slider which you can drag up to undo (restore previous steps) a series of steps, or drag down to redo (restore steps you've undone) a series of steps. You can also undo and redo previous steps one at a time using the Undo and Redo commands on the Edit menu. When you use these commands, the steps in the History panel change based on the command results. The History panel and the Undo command can undo steps up to a maximum number (from 2 to 9999) set in the General tab of the Preferences dialog box.

Undo Steps with the History Panel

1. Open or expand the **History** panel.

2. Drag the **Undo/Redo** slider up until the slider points to the last step you want to keep.

   TIMESAVER *Position the pointer in the gray area to the left of a step, and then click the gray area to make the slider point to the step.*

   Flash undoes and grays out each selected step, starting from the bottom.

3. When you're done, click the **Close** button on the History panel.

Did You Know?

You can undo steps using the Undo command. Click the Edit menu, and then click Undo, or press ⌘+Z (Mac) or Ctrl+Z (Win).

See Also

See "Examining the History Panel" on page 452 for information on different elements in the History panel.

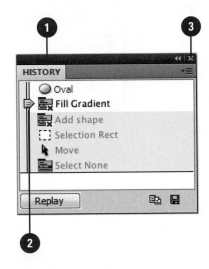

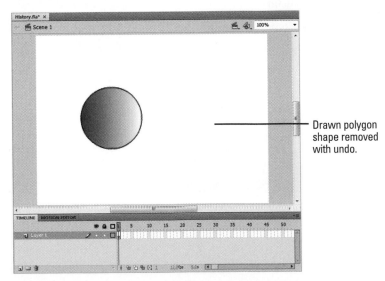

Drawn polygon shape removed with undo.

Redo Steps with the History Panel

1. Open or expand the **History** panel.

2. Drag the **Undo/Redo** slider down until the slider points to the last step you want to redo.

   Flash redoes and removes the gray highlighting for each selected step.

3. When you're done, click the **Close** button on the History panel.

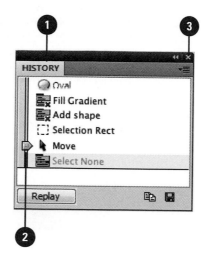

Did You Know?

You can redo steps using the Redo command. Click the Edit menu, and then click Redo, or press ⌘+Y (Mac) or Ctrl+Y (Win).

You can change the number of undo levels for the Undo command. Click the Flash (Mac) or Edit (Win) menu, click Preferences, click the General tab, enter a number (from 2 to 9999) in the Undo Level box, and then click OK.

For Your Information

Saving Documents After Using Undo

When you delete an object in a document, the file size of the document doesn't change. The document still includes the size of the object you just deleted to preserve the possibility you might want to undo the step and restore the deleted item. If you know that you don't want the steps in the History panel, you can use the Save And Compact command on the File menu to clear the History panel, reduce the file size, and save the document. If you want to save the document and keep the steps in the History panel for the current session, use the Save command on the File menu.

Replaying Steps

You can replay steps from the History panel to the same object or to a different object in the document. You can replay steps only in the order in which you performed them; you can't rearrange the order of the steps in the History panel. If a red X appears in the icon for a step, it indicates Flash cannot save or replay the step. The Repeat command on the Edit menu allows you to apply your previous step to another object. For example, if you fill a shape with a color or pattern, you can fill another shape with the same color or pattern by selecting the other shape and using the Repeat command.

Replay Steps to the Same Object or Another Object

1. Open or expand the **History** panel.

2. Select the steps you want:

   ◆ **One step.** Click a step.

   ◆ **Adjacent steps.** Drag from one step to another or click the first step, hold down the Shift key, and then click the last step.

   ◆ **Nonadjacent steps.** Hold down the ⌘ (Mac) or Ctrl (Win) key, and then click steps.

3. Select the same object used in the History steps or another object.

4. Click **Replay** in the History panel.

   The steps are replayed in order, and a new step called Replay Steps appears in the History panel.

5. When you're done, click the **Close** button on the History panel.

See Also

See "Copying Steps Between Documents" on page 460 for information on replaying steps in a different document.

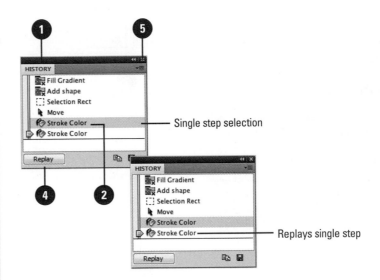

Single step selection

Replays single step

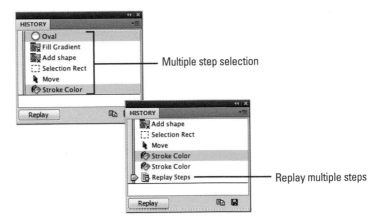

Multiple step selection

Replay multiple steps

Repeat the Previous Step on Another Object

1. Select an object, and then perform a command.

2. Select another object to which you want to perform the same previous command.

3. Click the **Edit** menu, and then click **Repeat**.

   The command is performed on the selected object.

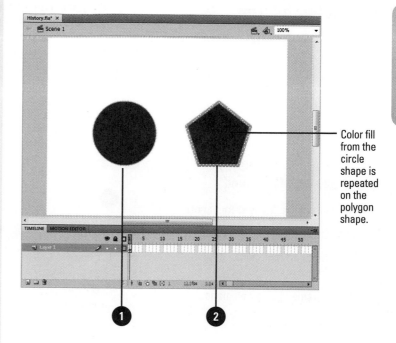

Color fill from the circle shape is repeated on the polygon shape.

Saving Steps and Using Commands

The History panel records the steps you take in the order in which you performed them in Flash. If you perform the same set of steps several times while you work on a document, you can save the steps in the History panel as a command on the Commands menu, which you can reuse again and again. Flash stores the commands you save for future use (even if you close the document). Some steps, including selecting a frame or modifying a document size, can't be saved as commands, but they can be undone and redone. If a red X appears in the icon for a step, it indicates Flash cannot save or replay the step. After you save steps as a command, you can run, rename, or delete commands.

Save Steps as a Command

1. Open or expand the **History** panel.

2. Select the steps you want to save.

3. Click the **Save As Command** button in the History panel.

4. Enter a name for the command.

5. Click **OK**.

   The command is available on the Commands menu and saved as a JavaScript file with the extension .jsfl in the Commands folder, which is located in Adobe\Flash CS4\First Run\.

6. When you're done, click the **Close** button on the History panel.

Did You Know?

You can delete a name from the Command menu. Click the Commands menu, click Manage Saved Commands, select the command you want to remove, click Delete, click Yes, and then click OK.

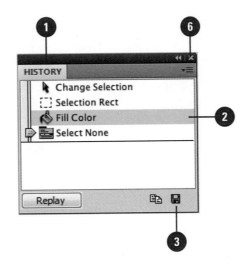

Run a Command

① Click the **Commands** menu.

② Click a command name from the list.

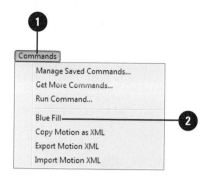

Did You Know?

You can run JavaScript or Flash JavaScript commands. Click the Commands menu, click Run Command, navigate to the script file, and then click Open.

Edit the Names of Commands

① Click the **Commands** menu, and then click **Manage Saved Commands**.

② Select a command to rename.

③ Click **Rename**.

④ Enter a new name for the command.

⑤ Click **OK**.

⑥ Click **OK**.

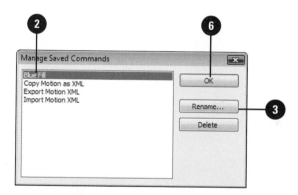

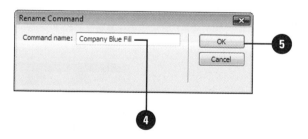

Did You Know?

You can download commands from the Web. The Flash Exchange Web site contains commands developed by other users you can download (some for a fee) and use in your documents. Click the Commands menu, and then click Get More Commands to quickly access the Adobe Web site.

Copying Steps Between Documents

Each document only tracks its own set of steps in the History panel. When you close a document, Flash clears the History panel. If you want to use a set of steps in another document, you need to copy them from one History panel and paste them to another document. You can use the Copy Steps button on the History panel or the same command on the Options menu to complete the task. When you paste steps into another document, Flash replays the steps and the History panel shows the steps as only one step called Paste Steps (Mac) or Paste (Win).

Copy Steps Between Documents

1 Open a document containing the steps you want to copy.

2 Open or expand the **History** panel.

3 Select the steps in the History panel you want to copy.

4 Click the **Copy Steps** button in the History panel.

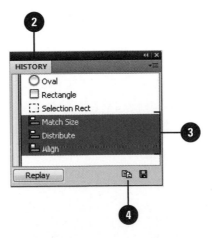

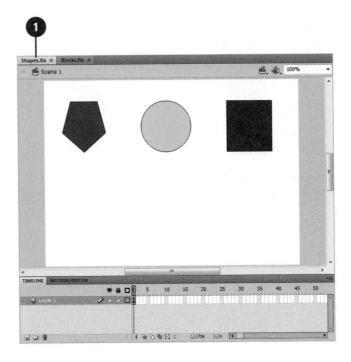

5. Open the document into which you want to paste the steps.

6. Select the objects to which you want to apply the steps.

7. Click the **Edit** menu, and then click **Paste In Center**.

   The steps play in the document as Flash pastes the steps into the History panel of the document. The steps appear in the History panel as a single step called Paste Steps (Mac) or Paste (Win).

8. When you're done, click the **Close** button on the History panel.

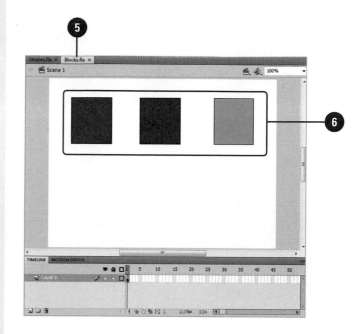

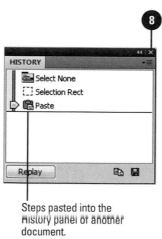

Steps pasted into the History panel of another document.

Working with Object-Level Undo Mode

The Flash History panel now allows you to keep track of the changes made in Flash on a per-object basis. When this mode is activated in the General Preferences dialog box, each object on the Stage and even objects in the Library panel have their own undo list. Think about just what this means. You can now undo the changes you make to an object without having to undo changes to any other object.

Set Object-Level Undo

1. Click the **Flash** (Mac) or **Edit** (Win) menu, and then click **Preferences**.

2. Click the **General** category.

3. Click the **Undo** popup, and then click **Object-Level Undo**.

4. Click **OK** to confirm changing from Document to Object level undo will delete your current undo history.

5. Click **OK** to set object level undo or click **Cancel** to keep document level undo.

   As you work, Flash keeps a per-object record of the history of each main Flash object.

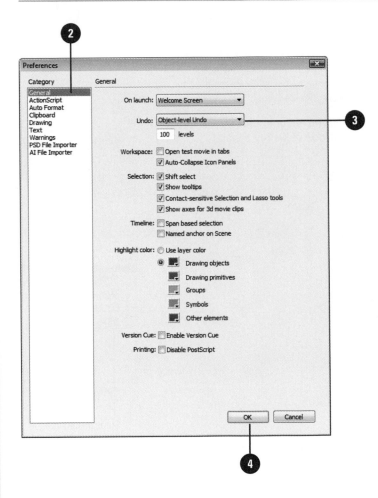

Work with Object Level Undo

1. Set object level undo in General preferences, and then open a new or existing Flash document.

2. Begin working with an object.

   As you work, Flash keeps a per-object record of the history of each main Flash object.

3. Open the **History** panel.

4. Use the Undo, Redo, or Repeat commands on the Edit menu.

   TROUBLE? *You cannot undo some object-level actions, such as working in a library or a scene. Check Flash Help for specifics.*

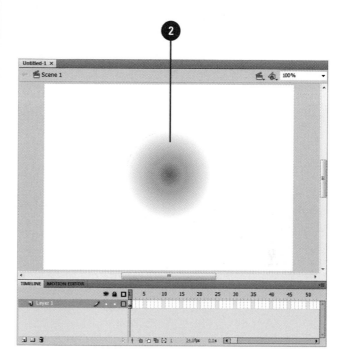

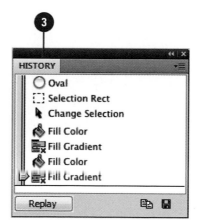

Publishing a Movie

20

Introduction

When you design a Flash movie, you're actually working with two documents: a source document (.fla), and a publish document (.swf). The source document is the working document that the Flash application uses to edit the movie data. The published document is the compressed player document that, once created, can be inserted into an HTML document, burned onto a CD, DVD, or DVS, or played directly from your hard drive.

You can publish a Flash document in one step, by clicking the File menu, and then clicking Publish. However, before publishing, it's a good idea to first check the publish settings by clicking the File menu, and then clicking Publish Settings. Using the Publish Settings dialog box, you can easily change the way your file is published. For example, the default settings for publishing a Flash document are to publish using the latest Flash plug-in, and to create an HTML container document to hold and play the published movie. Additional options include the ability to generate a JPEG, GIF, or PNG image of a selected frame in the Flash source document. You can even create a self-running player document for Macintosh or Windows. Publishing is not only necessary to create a Flash movie; it can be used to test the movie using different settings.

Once the correct publish settings are found, you can export the settings into a separate file, and then use them on new Flash documents. This not only makes the publishing process fast, it gives you consistency between documents.

What You'll Do

Publish Considerations

Modify Publish Settings

Specify Flash Options

Specify Adobe AIR Options

Insert File Information

Specify HTML Options

Specify GIF Options

Specify PNG Options

Specify JPEG Options

Create a Projector

Create a Publishing Profile

Edit Profile Properties

Export and Import a Profile

Duplicate a Profile

Test a Movie

Use the Bandwidth Profiler

Print from the Flash Player

Export a Movie to Different Formats

Publishing Considerations

 FL 1.2, 5.4

Publishing a Flash movie is the last step in a long journey from inception to the final product. Along the publishing road, you'll encounter detours, and stoplights and even get lost once in awhile. However, if you've had the foresight to plan your project, then the journey becomes one more of pleasure than pain.

Planning a project requires knowledge of where the final published document is headed. You might be designing a Flash movie, where the intended audience is the Web, or it could be a project where the final destination is a CD or DVD. It could be an interactive form, or an animated cartoon. It's even possible that your goals for this project involve more than one destination.

Called Multi-purposing, Flash will help you design a project version that is small enough to run efficiently, as well as a higher-quality version, intended to run directly off the hard drive. It really doesn't matter where the project is headed, because Flash's advanced publishing options will effortlessly guide you through the process.

Before you ever open Flash, create your first graphic, or write your first piece of text, always remember to plan the project. In other words, begin the project with the end in mind. That's not new, but it bears remembering. If you plan for the end of a project, you will create a road map that will accurately guide you to your final destination.

When you are ready to publish a Flash movie, you can use Flash publishing settings and tools in this chapter to make the job easier. You can also use the Adobe Flash deployment kit to post Flash Player (.swf) files to your Web site and control the experience of visitors who do not have the Flash Player installed in their browser. Flash standardizes the method used for detection of the plug-in on the client-side, reducing the amount of code that must be written to implement the detection option. If you're interested in working with the Flash Development Kit, simply point your browser to *http://www.adobe.com/devnet/devices/development_kits.html*. Since Flash is always creating new ways for us to design great Flash documents, this site is constantly changing to reflect the latest technologies.

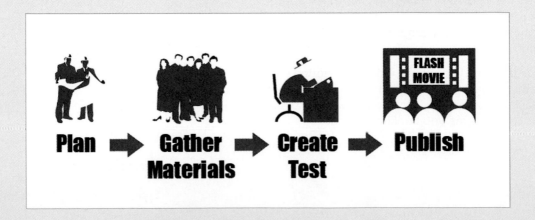

Modifying Publish Settings

FL 1.2, 5.4

Once you've determined how your project will be published, it's time to let Flash assist you with all the details of getting your project from conception to an output file suited to your needs. Flash's publishing settings go far beyond converting a Flash source file (.fla) into a published movie (.swf); they give you the ability to adjust the output to a specific version of the Flash player, incorporate specific Flash compression features, and even save screen shots of the source file's frames in several different formats. And, if a Flash movie is not what you're after, you can even save a Flash source file as a QuickTime movie (.mov). To utilize this feature, you may need to download the latest version of the QuickTime player; point your browser to *www.quicktime.com*. It's free and works equally well within the Windows or the Macintosh environments.

Modify Publish Settings

1. Open a Flash source document.

   Generic publish settings are initially linked to a specific Flash file.

2. Click the **File** menu, and then click **Publish Settings**.

3. Select or clear the option check boxes to enable or disable the Publish Settings.

4. Enter a name for the individual options in the File name input box.

5. To revert the names to default, click the **Use Default Names** button.

   The default name refers to the name of the source document.

6. Click **OK** to save the changes.

   IMPORTANT *When you publish a Flash movie, the changes only affect the published .swf document, never the .fla source document. If you delete or misplace the .fla source document, you will never be able to re-edit, or republish the movie.*

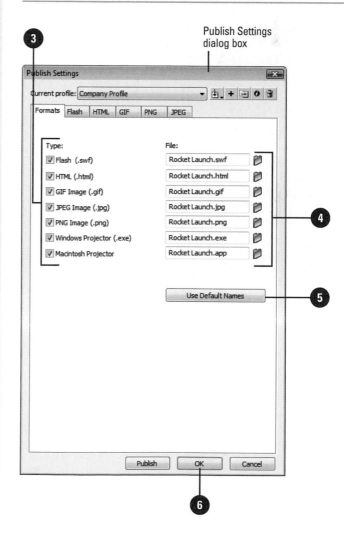

Publish Settings dialog box

Specifying Flash Options

Specify Flash Options

1. Click the **File** menu, and then click **Publish Settings**.

2. Select the **Flash** check box, and then click the **Flash** tab.

3. Click the **Player** popup, and then select the version of the player to publish the Flash document.

4. Click the **Script** popup, and then select the version to publish the Flash document.

5. Drag the **JPEG Quality** slider to increase or decrease the amount of compression applied to the image.

   The lower the value, the more information is removed from the image.

6. Select the **Enable JPEG deblocking** check box to reduce the appearance of common artifacts found in highly compressed JPEG files (**New!**).

7. Select from the following options:

   ◆ Click **Set** to modify the Audio Stream settings for the active Flash document.

   ◆ Click **Set** to modify the Audio Event settings for the active Flash document.

   ◆ Select the **Override Sound Settings** check box to override any sound settings applied to the individual sound files within the active Flash document.

A Flash document is like a fingerprint: no two Flash movies are the same. So it stands to reason that different Flash documents would require different publish settings. Flash gives you the ability to conform a Flash document using specific output settings. Everything from the version of the Flash player plug-in and ActionScript to the movie compression and quality of embedded JPEG images are available options in the Publish Setting dialog box.

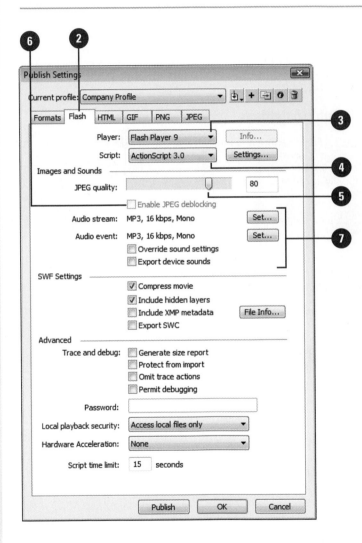

8. Select from the following options:

- **Compress Movie.** Compresses the movie (only for movies played with Flash 7 player).

- **Include Hidden Layers.** Includes hidden layers in the Flash document.

- **Include XMP metadata.** Includes XMP data (**New!**). Click File Info to view the data.

- **Export SWC.** Exports a .swc file, which is used for distributing components made up of ActionScript code.

- **Generate Size Report.** Creates a frame-by-frame size report for the active document.

- **Protect From Import.** Prevents the published Flash document from being reopened in the Flash application.

- **Omit Trace Actions.** Prevents trace actions from being carried over to the published document.

- **Permit Debugging.** Permits debugging of the Flash movie.

9. Enter a password for the Flash document (2.0).

This option is available if Protect From Import or Permit Debugging are selected in step 10.

10. Click the **Local Playback Security** popup, and then select the local only or network only option.

11. Click the **Hardware Acceleration** popup, and then select an option to take advantage of available hardware for better playback performance (**New!**).

12. Click **OK** to save the settings.

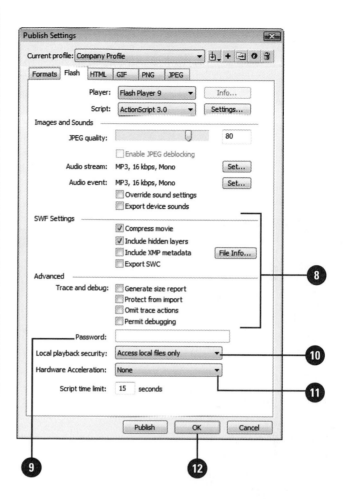

For Your Information

Security Options

The Flash Player 8 and later incorporates a security option that allows you to determine the local and network playback security for published SWF files. SWF files have read access to local files and networks by default, but they cannot communicate with the network. In the Flash tab on the Publish Settings dialog box, you can select a Local Playback Security option to access network resources, which allows the SWF file to send and receive information. If you select the option to access network resources, local access is disabled for security reasons. Flash also provides buffer overrun protection, which prevents misuse of external files, such as a virus. The player also provides stricter security; SWF files with nonsecure protocols (HTTP) cannot access content loaded using secure protocols (HTTPS).

Specifying Adobe AIR Options

Adobe AIR is a cross-operating system runtime that allows you to leverage your existing web development skills in Flash to build and deliver Rich Internet Applications (RIAs) to more devices, including the web, mobile, and desktop. You can create a new Flash file for AIR (**New!**) from the Welcome page or the New dialog box by clicking Flash File (Adobe AIR), or use an existing Flash file (ActionScript 3.0), and then convert it to an Adobe AIR file through the Publish Settings dialog box. Before you can publish a file to Adobe AIR, you need to have a digital certificate that represents the application publisher's identify. Flash CS4 only supports and publishes to AIR 1.1, while Flash CS3 only supports and publishes to AIR 1.0.

Create a New Adobe AIR Document

1. Click the **File** menu, and then click **New**.

    TIMESAVER *Click Flash File (Adobe AIR) on the Welcome screen to create a new blank document.*

2. Click the **General** tab.

3. Click **Flash File (Adobe AIR)**.

    IMPORTANT *The Adobe AIR is a Flash file ActionScript 3.0 by default. You can convert an ActionScript 2.0 file, but it will not be able to use AIR specific APIs.*

4. Click **OK**.

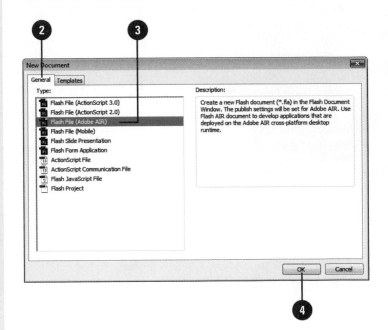

Did You Know?

You can preview an Adobe AIR file. Set the Player setting in the Publish Settings dialog box to Adobe Air, click Settings, specify the options you want, click OK, and then click OK. Click the Control menu, and then click Test Movie or press Control+Enter.

Publish to Adobe AIR

1. Click the **File** menu, and then click **Publish Settings**.

2. Select the **Flash** check box, and then click the **Flash** tab.

3. Click the **Player** popup, and then click **Adobe AIR 1.1**.

4. Click **Settings**.

   ◆ If you have an application descriptor file (an XML file), select the **Use custom application descriptor file** check box, and then skip to Step 8.

5. Enter the following file information: File name, Name, Version, ID (a unique identifier, no spaces or special characters), Description, Copyright, and Window style.

6. Click **Select Icon Images**, select an application icon, and then click **OK**.

7. Click **Settings**, specify any associated file types, initial window settings, install and program menu folders, and then click **OK**.

8. Select from the following Installer settings:

   ◆ **Digital signature**. All Adobe Air applications must be signed to be installed on another system. Click **Set**, and then specify a digital certificate or use AIR Intermediate for temporary use.

   ◆ **Destination**. Specifies where to save the AIR file.

   ◆ **Included files**. Specifies which additional files and folders to include in the AIR file.

9. Click **Publish AIR File** to publish it, or click **OK**, and then click **OK** to save settings.

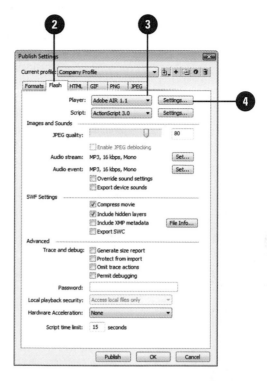

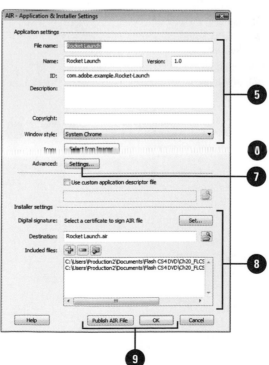

Inserting File Information

When you save a document, you have the ability to save more than just Flash information. You can save copyright, camera, and even image category information. This data is saved with the file as metadata in the XMP format (Extensible Metadata Platform) in SWF files, and can be recognized and accessed by any application, such as Adobe Bridge, that reads XMP metadata (**New!**). In addition, if an image is a photograph, you can save data specifying the type of image, where it was shot, or the camera used. You can even get information on shutter speed and f-stop. You can do the same with video and audio data too. That information will not only protect your intellectual property, but will supply you with vital statistics on exactly how you created that one-of-a-kind image.

Insert File Information into a Flash Document

1. Open a document.

2. Click the **File** menu, and then click **File Info**.

3. Click the **Description** tab, and then enter information concerning the author and any copyright information.

4. Click the **IPTC** tab to enter information concerning the image's creator, description and keywords, location where photograph was taken, date created, copyright, and usage terms.

5. Click the **Camera Data** tab, which reveals information about the camera that took the image.

6. Click the **Video Data** tab or **Audio Data** tab to reveal information about video and audio data, and then enter your video and audio data.

7. Click the **Mobile SWF** tab or **Audio Data** tab, and then enter file information for a mobile SWF.

8. Click the **Categories** tab, and then enter category keywords for search purposes.

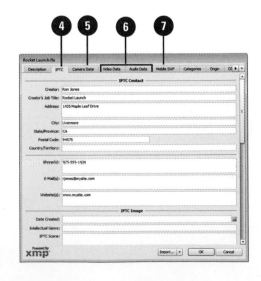

9 Click the **Origin** tab, and then enter data pertaining to the origin of the image.

10 Click the **DICOM** tab, and then enter data pertaining to the Digital Imaging and Communications in Medicine.

11 Click the **History** tab to view historical information about the active document, such as dates last opened and saved, and a list of image adjustments.

12 Click the **Illustrator** tab, and then select an Illustrator profile.

13 Click the **Advanced** tab to view additional information on the active document, such as EXIF, and PDF document properties.

14 Click the **Raw Data** tab to view raw RDF/XML information.

15 Click **OK**.

Did You Know?

You can add metadata to files saved in the PSD, PDF, EPS, PNG, GIF, JPEG, and TIFF formats. The information is embedded in the file using XMP (eXtensible Metadata Platform). This allows metadata to be exchanged between Adobe applications and across operating systems.

You can use the XMP Software Development Kit to customize the creation, processing, and interchange of metadata. You can also use the XMP kit to add fields to the File Info dialog box. For information on XMP and the XMP SDK, check the Adobe Solutions Network.

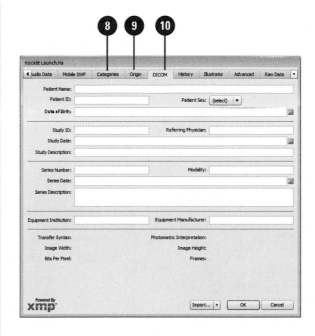

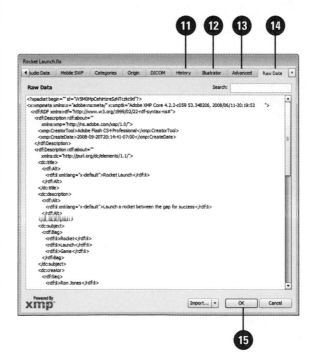

Specifying HTML Options

The most common way to display a Flash movie is on the Internet, using an HTML document as the movie container. HTML creates tags that embed the Flash movie in an HTML document for viewing on the Web. Flash publish settings give you the ability to create an HTML document specifically tailored to the active Flash document; including options to use an HTML template, and control the playback and quality of the final published document. You can also set options to specify the scale and alignment of the movie as well as the way it opens.

Specify HTML Options

1. Click the **File** menu, and then click **Publish Settings**.

2. Select the **HTML** check box, and then click the **HTML** tab.

3. Click the **Template** popup, and then select a Flash container template (including templates for PocketPC devices).

4. Click the **Dimensions** popup, and then click **Match Movie**, **Pixels**, or **Percent**. If Pixels or Percent, enter width and height.

    The Match Movie option matches the size of the Flash movie. The Pixels option sets the exact size. The Percent option allows for scaling within a browser.

5. Select from the following Playback options:

    ◆ **Paused At Start.** Select this option to pause the Flash movie, when loaded.

    ◆ **Loop.** Select this option to cause the Flash movie to loop, when loaded.

    ◆ **Display Menu.** Select this option to have the HTML document display a control menu for the Flash document.

    ◆ **Device Font.** Select this option to use device fonts in the Flash document.

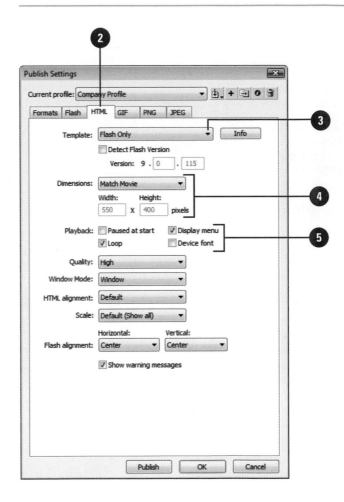

6 Click the **Quality** popup to select a quality level for the document.

- ◆ **Low** No anti-alias.
- ◆ **Auto Low.** Starts with no anti-alias, but changes as needed.
- ◆ **High.** Allows anti-alias.
- ◆ **Auto High.** Starts with anti-alias, but changes down as needed.
- ◆ **Medium.** Anti-aliases most items, but does not smooth bitmaps.
- ◆ **Best.** Anti-aliases everything.

7 Click the **Window Mode** popup to select a mode (Window, Opaque Windowless, or Transparent Windowless) for opening the Flash document.

8 Click the **HTML Alignment** popup to select the alignment of the HTML page.

9 Click the **Scale** popup to select how to scale the Flash document, when loaded into the HTML page.

- ◆ **Default.** Shows entire document; keeps proportions.
- ◆ **No Border.** Fills area to the border; keeps proportions.
- ◆ **Exact Fit.** Fills entire SWF movie; doesn't keep proportions.
- ◆ **No Scale.** SWF remains the same size if Player window is resized.

10 Click the **Horizontal** and **Vertical** popups to select how the Flash document is aligned with in the HTML page.

11 Click **OK** to save HTML settings.

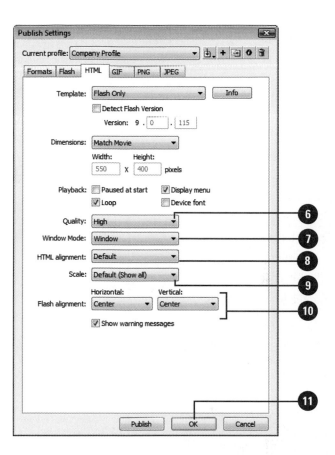

Specifying GIF Options

When you publish a Flash document, you're not limited to just the creation of the Flash movie, you can instruct Flash to create a GIF image of the Flash movie, based on the currently selected frame. The GIF file format (Graphics Interchange Format) is used primarily for clipart, text, and line art, or for images that contain areas of solid color. Once the image is created, you can open and use it in any application that supports the GIF file format.

Specify GIF Options

1. Select a specific frame on the Timeline.

2. Click the **File** menu, and then click **Publish Settings**.

3. Select the **GIF** check box, and then click the **GIF** tab.

4. Enter a **Width** and **Height** (in pixels) for the JPEG image, or select the **Match Movie** check box to create a JPEG image that matches the size of the Flash movie.

5. Select from the following Playback options:

   ◆ **Static.** Prevents the GIF animation from playing.

   ◆ **Animated.** Animates the GIF document.

   ◆ **Loop Continuously.** Forces the animation into a continuous loop.

   ◆ **Repeat.** Enter a value representing the number of times the file loops.

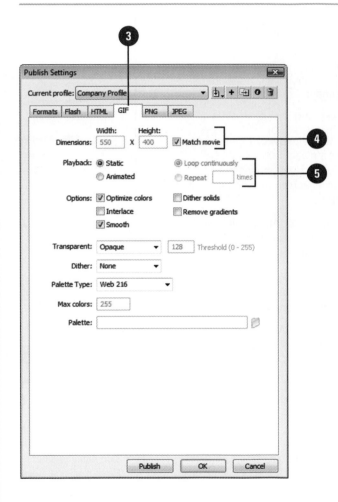

6. Select from the following Options:

- ◆ **Optimize Colors.** Creates an optimized (smaller) set of colors for the active document.

- ◆ **Interlace.** Creates an interlaced image where the file, when displayed on a Web page, loads in three passes.

- ◆ **Smooth.** Uses a color dithering scheme to create visually smoother color transitions.

- ◆ **Dither Solids.** Dithers (mixes) solid colors if they fall outside of the viewable color gamut.

- ◆ **Remove Gradients.** Removes gradients from the active image.

7. Click the **Transparent** popup, and then click **Opaque**, **Transparent**, or **Alpha**.

   The Alpha transparency mask generates transparent areas within the GIF image.

8. Click the **Dither** popup, and then click **None**, **Ordered**, or **Diffusion**.

9. Click the **Palette Type** popup, and then click **Web 216**, **Adaptive**, **Web Snap Adaptive**, or **Custom**.

10. Enter a number for the Maximum Colors.

    This is available for Adaptive and Web Snap Adaptive. Flash lets you select how many colors are available for the image's color table.

11. Click to select a color table file for the Custom Palette Type.

12. Click **OK** to save the GIF settings.

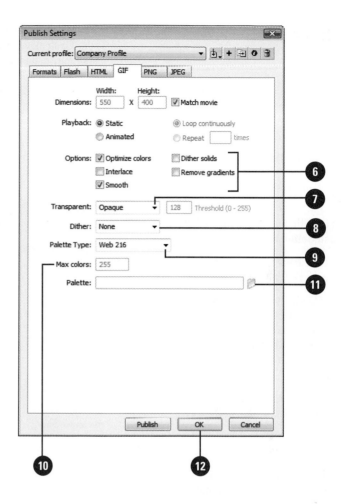

Palette Type Options

Option	Use
Web 216	Creates an image with only Web Safe colors.
Adaptive	Creates an image where the color table (CLUT) adapts to the image colors.
Web Snap Adaptive	Creates a color table that adheres closely to the Web Safe Color palette.
Custom	Creates a customized color palette.

Specifying PNG Options

When you publish a Flash document, you're not limited to just the creation of the Flash movie. You can instruct Flash to create a PNG image of the Flash movie, based on the currently selected frame. The PNG file format (Portable Network Graphic) is a hybrid format designed to save clip art, photographic images, text, and line art. Once the image is created, you can open and use it in any application that supports the PNG file format.

Specify PNG Options

1. Select a specific Frame on the Timeline.

2. Click the **File** menu, and then click **Publish Settings**.

3. Select the **PNG** check box, and then click the **PNG** tab.

4. Enter a **Width** and **Height** (in pixels) for the PNG image, or select the **Match Movie** check box to create a PNG image that matches the size of the Flash movie.

5. Click the **Bit Depth** popup, and then select **8-bit**, **24-bit**, or **24-bit With Alpha**.

6. Select from the following Options:

   ◆ **Optimize Colors.** Creates an optimized (smaller) set of colors for the active document.

   ◆ **Interlace.** Creates an interlaced image where the file, when displayed on a Web page, loads in three passes.

   ◆ **Smooth.** Uses a color dithering scheme to create visually smoother color transitions.

   ◆ **Dither Solids.** Dithers (mixes) solid colors, if the colors fall outside of the viewable color gamut.

   ◆ **Remove Gradients.** Remove any gradients from the active image.

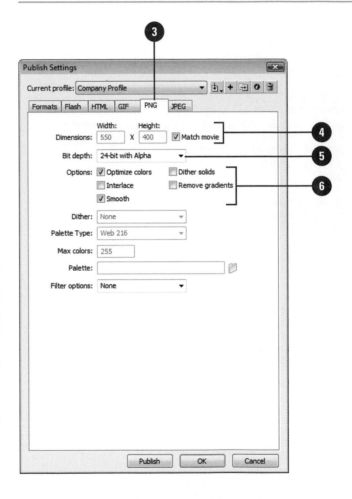

Bit Depth Choices	
Option	**Selection**
8-bit	Maximum of 256 colors
24-bit	Maximum of 16.7 million colors
24-bit with Alpha	Maximum of 16.7 colors and supports the alpha transparency

7 Click the **Dither** popup, and then click **None**, **Ordered**, or **Diffusion** to dither (mix) colors that fall outside the viewable color gamut.

8 Click the **Palette Type** popup, and then click **Web 216**, **Adaptive**, **Web Snap Adaptive**, or **Custom** to select a specific palette type.

9 Enter a number for the Maximum Colors.

This is available for Adaptive and Web Snap Adaptive. Flash lets you select how many colors are available for the image's color table.

10 Click to select a color table file for the Custom Palette Type.

11 Click the **Filter Options** popup, and then select from the available filter options to control the filtering of the colors in the active image.

12 Click **OK** to save the PNG settings.

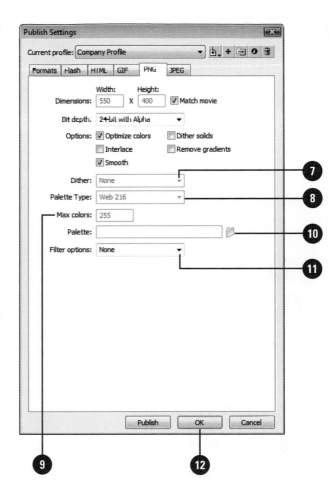

Specifying JPEG Options

When you publish a Flash document, you're not limited to just the creation of the Flash movie, you can instruct Flash to create a JPEG image of the Flash movie, based on the currently selected frame. The JPEG file format (Joint Photographic Experts Group), is used primarily to reduce the size of photographic images. Once the image is created, you can open and use it in any application that supports the JPEG file format. You can select a quality option to compress the file size, which reduces download time over the Internet. You can specify a quality value between 1 and 100. A higher value preserves image quality, but retains a higher file size.

Specify JPEG Options

1. Select a specific frame on the Timeline.

2. Click the **File** menu, and then click **Publish Settings**.

3. Select the **JPEG** check box, and then click the **JPEG** tab.

4. Enter a **Width** and **Height** (in pixels) for the JPEG image, or select the **Match Movie** check box to create a JPEG image that matches the size of the Flash movie.

5. Drag the **Quality** slider to increase or decrease the amount of compression applied to the image.

   The lower the value, the more information (quality) is removed from the image.

6. Select the **Progressive** check box to create a progressive JPEG image. The file, when displayed on a Web page, loads in three passes.

7. Click **OK** to save the JPEG settings.

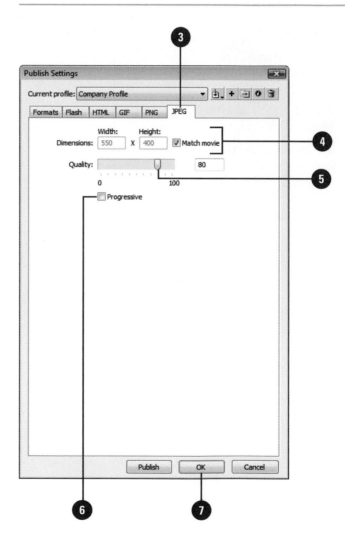

Creating a Windows or Macintosh Projector

The Flash publish settings gives you the ability to create a self-contained player document for the Macintosh or Windows operating system. When you publish a document using the projector options, Flash creates a Flash movie according to your setting, and embeds the player application into the file. Creating a projector document increases the size of the final document by almost 1MB, so this option would not be used to create Internet documents, but for movies destined for playing on a hard drive, or burned onto a CD. When you publish using the Projector options, there are no additional options.

Create a Windows or Macintosh Projector

1. Click the **File** menu, and then click **Publish Settings**.

2. Select the **Windows Projector (.exe)**, and/or **Macintosh Projector** check boxes.

3. Click **Publish**.

   Flash generates the Macintosh or Windows Projectors documents, and saves them in the same location as the original source document.

Did You Know?

You can play Flash SWF files different ways. Besides playing SWF files in a stand-alone projector, you can also play Flash content in an Internet browser, such as Internet Explorer or Firefox; in Director, Microsoft Office and other ActiveX applications with the Flash ActiveX; and as part of a QuickTime video.

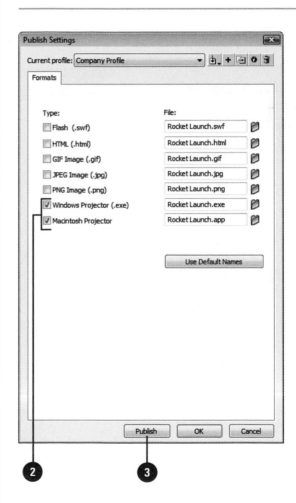

Creating a Publishing Profile

Flash lets you generate profiles for often-used publish settings within a Flash source file. For example, you're creating a multi-purpose Flash document and you need specific settings to create a fast-loading Internet version, as well as a version designed to run on a CD. You could create a publishing profile to fit both needs, and save them with the source document. The benefits of this are obvious: Not only can you quickly publish a Flash document using different profiles; you're assured the settings will be accurate every time. Fast and accurate are two words which describe Flash publishing.

Create a Publishing Profile

1. Click the **File** menu, and then click **Publish Settings**.

2. Click the **Current Profile** popup to select the profile.

3. Make the necessary changes in the Publish Settings dialog box.

4. Click **OK**.

5. Click the **Create New Profile** button.

6. Enter a unique name in the Profile Name box.

7. Click **OK**.

   IMPORTANT *When you save a Flash profile, it's only available to that specific document.*

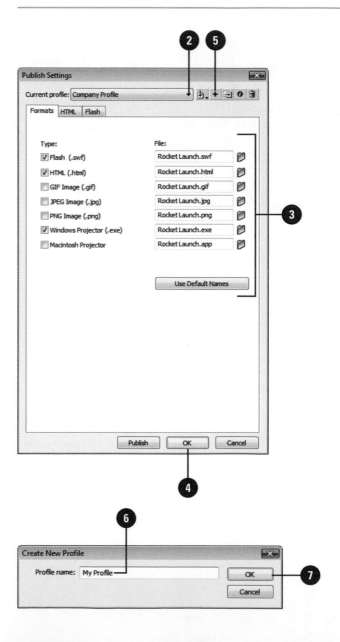

Editing Profile Properties

Once you create a unique profile settings file, it's available for use with the click of the Current Profile popup in the Publish Settings dialog box. Unfortunately, not everything is perfect the first time you do it, and it's possible that after you create a profile, you discover a mistake in the settings. The good news is that you don't have to begin again. All you have to do is edit the profile.

Edit Profile Properties

1. Click the **File** menu, and then click **Publish Settings**.

2. Click the **Current Profile** popup, and then select the profile you want to change.

3. Make the necessary changes in the Publish Settings dialog box.

4. Click **OK**.

5. Select the **File** menu, and then click **Save**.

    Flash profiles are saved when you save the Flash source document.

    IMPORTANT *Profile properties are recorded as you change them, and then saved when you save the file. If you change your mind after modifying the profile, your choices include manually changing the profile back to its original settings, or closing the file without saving. However, if you've also made changes to the Flash document, closing without saving will also cause you to lose those changes.*

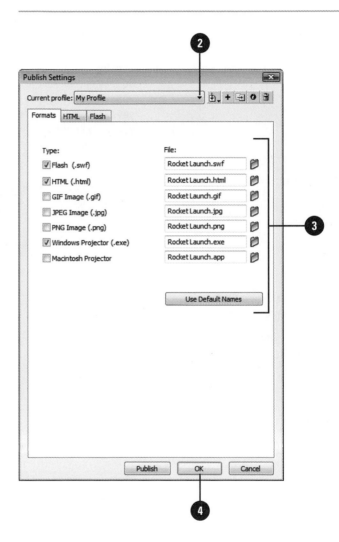

Exporting and Importing a Profile

Saving Flash profiles is a great way to cut down on repetitive publish settings. However, the disadvantage is the user-defined settings only relate to the original source document. If you open a new file, you're starting from scratch. It would be great to be able to create a series of setting files, and then use them over and over again on new Flash document. Flash understood this need and gave Flash users the ability to create settings files, and then export them as a separate file. Then, if you need to use the settings in a new Flash document, all you have to do is import the settings file. Exporting Dreamweaver profiles gives you the ability to import and use the profile on multiple Flash projects. In addition, you can send copies of exported profiles to other Flash users, so they can benefit from your efforts. When you export a Flash profile, you have the ability to reuse it, via the Import option. It's a good idea to save (export) all of your profiles into a single location. That way, when you go to import a specific profile, you will know exactly where to point your finder.

Export a Profile

1. Click the **File** menu, and then click **Publish Settings**.

2. Click the **Current Profile** popup, and then select the profile you want to export.

3. Click the **Import/Export Profile** button, and then click **Export**.

4. Navigate to the drive or folder location where you want to save the exported profile.

5. Click **Save**.

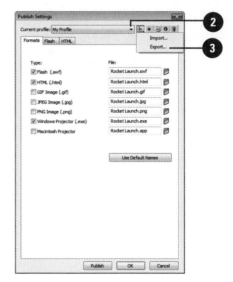

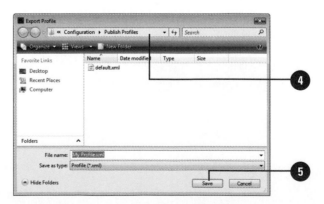

Import a Profile

1. Click the **File** menu, and then click **Publish Settings**.

2. Click the **Current Profile** popup, and then select the profile you want to import.

3. Click the **Import/Export Profile** button, and then click **Import**.

4. Navigate to the drive or folder where the profile is located.

5. Select the file name of the exported profile.

6. Click **Open**.

   IMPORTANT *Once a profile is imported into a Flash document, it becomes a copy of the original item. You can use it in the active document, or make some minor adjustments, and export it out as a new profile.*

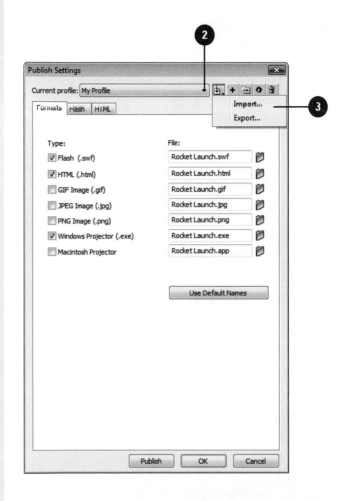

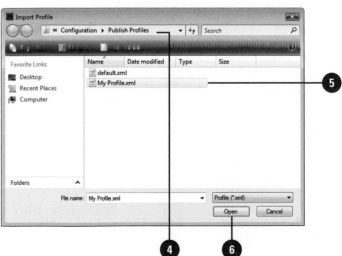

Duplicating a Profile

When you work with a profile, you're creating a time-saving file that lets you use the same settings over and over again. Not only does Flash make the creation of a profile easy; it will let you create a duplicate of the file. In truth, a duplicate file would not serve much of a purpose: Why would you want an exact copy of something that already exists? Actually, creating a duplicate can be a very smart thing to do. For example, say you create a profile for a specific job that involved several changes to the default settings, and you name it: Output_A. Then, two weeks later you need another profile that's almost exactly the same as Output_A, with one or two minor changes. Rather than start from scratch, you create a duplicate of Output_A, make the minor changes, and Export it using the name: Output_B. It's fast and easy, it and means you're working smart.

Duplicate a Profile

1. Click the **File** menu, and then click **Publish Settings**.

2. Click the **Current Profile** popup, and then select the profile you want to duplicate.

3. Click the **Duplicate Profile** button.

4. Give the duplicate a new name.

5. Click **OK**.

See Also

See "Exporting and Importing a Profile" on page 484 for more information on how to export a Flash publishing profile.

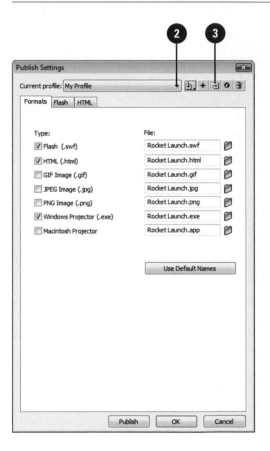

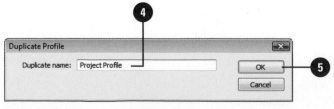

Testing a Movie

Testing a Flash movie is an important part of the design process. As you work, you should periodically stop and test the movie. It's also a good idea to periodically save your document. In fact, you should always save the Flash document before testing. That way, if there happen to be any problems, it's an easy matter of restoring the file from the last-saved version. To preview your Flash SWF file with the publishing format and settings you've selected, you can use the Publish Preview command. This command exports the file and opens the preview within the default browser.

Test a Movie

1. Click the **File** menu, point to **Publish Preview**, and then select from the following options:

- **Default (HTML)**. Select this option to display the Flash document within an HTML document.

- **Flash**. Select this option to create and play a Flash .swf file.

- **HTML**. Same as Default (HTML).

- **GIF**. Select this option to create a GIF version of the currently selected frame in the Timeline.

- **JPEG**. Select this option to create a JPEG version of the currently selected frame in the Timeline.

- **PNG**. Select this option to create a PNG version of the currently selected frame in the Timeline.

- **Projector**. Select this option to display the Flash document in a self-contained projector file.

- **QuickTime**. Select this option to open QuickTime, and play the Flash movie as a QuickTime file.

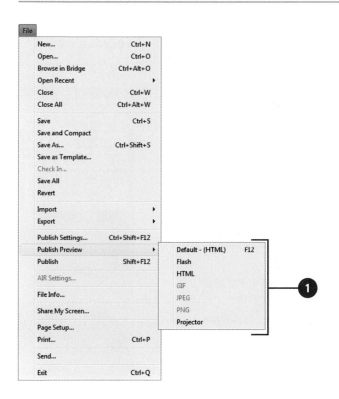

Using the Bandwidth Profiler

To view the performance of a Flash document using a graph, use the Bandwidth Profiler. The Bandwidth Profiler displays how much data is sent for each frame in the active Flash document, according to the modem speed you specify. The Bandwidth Profiler has two windows. The left window shows information about the active document and the current download settings, and the right window displays information about each frame in the document. In addition, the Bandwidth Profiler lets you view how the page loads, based on a specific bandwidth. For example, you could specify to load the Flash document using a modem speed of 28.8Kbps. To maintain an accurate download test, the Bandwidth Profiler compensates for added compression support applied to .swf files, which reduces the file size and improves streaming performance.

Use the Bandwidth Profiler

1. Click the **Control** menu, and then click **Test Movie**.

2. Click the **View** menu, and then click **Bandwidth Profiler**.

3. Click the **View** menu, point to **Download Settings**, and then select from the available bandwidth options, or click **Customize**, and then create a user-defined setting.

4. Click the **View** menu, and then click **Simulate Download**.

   This tests the load of the Flash movie against the current settings.

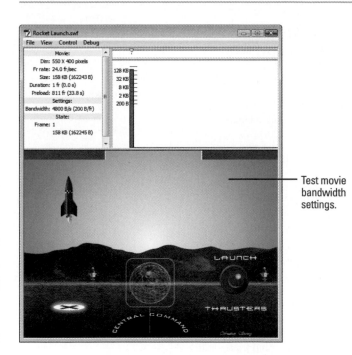

Test movie bandwidth settings.

Printing from the Flash Player

In your browser, you can press Control+click (Mac) or right-click (Win) a Flash movie in a Flash Player to display a contextual, or shortcut, menu. The menu contains Flash Player related commands, such as Print. You can give viewers the option to print some, or all of your movie. By default, the Print command prints every frame in the movie unless you restrict printing to specific frames by labeling them as printable in the Flash document before you publish it. You label frames as printable by typing #p in the Frame box of the Property Inspector. By default, the movie's Stage size determines the print area.

Label Frames as Printable and Print from the Flash Player

1. Open a document.

2. Select the frames or keyframes in the Timeline you want to label as printable.

3. Type **#p** in the Frame box in the Property Inspector.

4. Repeat steps 2 and 3 for each keyframe you want to label as printable.

5. Publish your movie using the Publish command on the File menu, and then view it in your browser using the Flash Player.

6. Press Control+click (Mac) or right-click (Win) anywhere in the movie window, and then click **Print**.

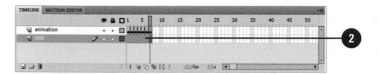

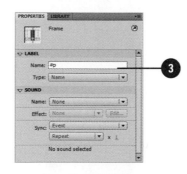

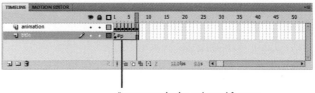

#p appears in the selected frames.

Did You Know?

You can disable printing from the Flash Player. Open the Flash document, select a frame in the Timeline, open the Frame Property Inspector, and then type **!#p** in the Label box.

You can disable the contextual menu in the Flash Player. Click the File menu, click Publish Setting, click the HTML tab, clear the Display Menu check box, and then click OK.

For Your Information

Printing with ActionScript

You can also print with ActionScript using the following commands: print (target, bounding box), printasBitmap (target, bounding box), or Printjob class. The target is the Movie Clip Timeline (or specific frames) and bounding box is bmovie (frame with a #b used as print area), bframe (each frame used as print area), or bmax (one big print area).

Exporting a Movie to Different Formats

Flash can export an entire movie or frame to several different formats that are not included in the Publish Settings dialog box. These formats include Adobe Illustrator, EPS, DXF, PICT, Quick Time (MOV), Enhanced Metafile (EMF), Windows Metafile (WMF), Windows AVI, and WAV (for Windows only). When you export a movie or image (frame), some file formats require you to select additional format specific options, such as resolution (dots per inch) and number of colors or color bit depth, to complete the operation. To set the resolution to match your monitor, select Match Screen.

Export a Movie Frame to Different Formats

1. Open a document.

2. Select a frame you want to export in the Timeline.

3. Click the **File** menu, point to **Export**, and then click **Export Image**.

4. Navigate to the location where you want to save the file.

5. Enter a name in the Save As (Mac) or File Name (Win) box.

6. Click the **Format** popup (Mac) or the **Save As Type** list arrow (Win), and then select a file format.

7. Click **Save**.

    Some file formats require you to select additional format specific options to complete the operation.

8. If a dialog box appears, select the options you want, and then click **OK**.

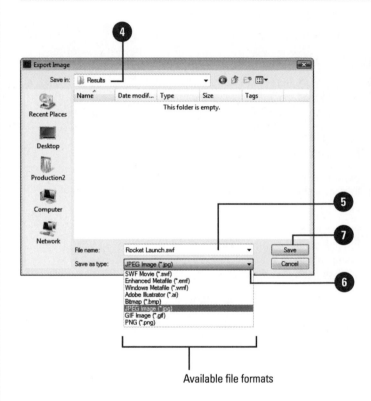

Available file formats

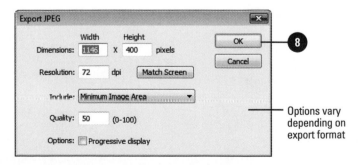

Options vary depending on export format

Export a Movie to Different Formats

① Open a document.

② Click the **File** menu, point to **Export**, and then click **Export Movie**.

TIMESAVER *Press Option+ Shift+⌘+S (Mac) or Ctrl+Alt+ Shift+S (Win) to export a movie.*

③ Navigate to the location where you want to save the file.

④ Enter a name in the Save As (Mac) or File Name (Win) box.

⑤ Click the **Format** popup (Mac) or the **Save As Type** list arrow (Win), and then select a file format.

⑥ Click **Save**.

Some file formats require you to select additional format specific options to complete the operation.

⑦ If a dialog box appears, select the options you want.

⑧ Click **OK** or **Export**.

When you export a movie, Flash creates a separate file for each frame of the movie and numbers them in sequential order.

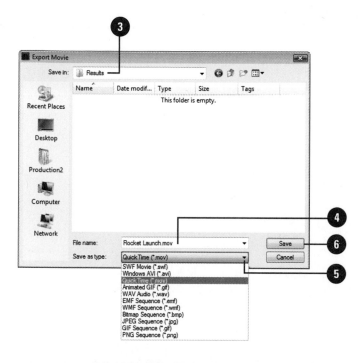

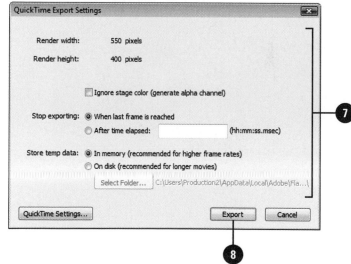

Using Advanced Flash Features

21

Introduction

Flash was created with the advanced Web designer in mind. It provides project management tools that allow for the optimization of the workflow between the members of a Web team. In addition, a Screen-based visual development environment makes designing Flash applications simpler. Add to that the ability to export Flash movies directly into the FLV (Flash Video File) format, advanced video features, application binding components, and sound management, and you have a program suited for the most demanding of Flash designers.

Flash lets you create two different types of screens within the active document: slide screens and form screens. A slide presentation uses the slide screen, and a Flash form application uses the form screen as the default screen type. If you're creating a Flash document with a combination of slides and forms, you have the ability to mix both screen types within a single Flash document. When you work with screens, you're creating complex applications without the use of multiple frames and layers on the main Timeline. As a matter of fact, screen applications can be created without ever viewing the main Timeline. When you create a slide or form screen document, Flash opens the document with the main Timeline collapsed, and the addition of slides or form components is accomplished using a control dialog box, located to the left of the document window.

If you want to develop content for mobile devices, you can use Flash templates to help you create the document and Adobe Device Central CS4 to test it. Adobe Device Central allows you to test your content on a variety of mobile devices. Flash uses the right settings from Device Central to create the content you want.

Creating a Slide Presentation

The Slide Screen feature allows you to create a Flash document using sequential content like a slide show. The default behavior of a screen lets the visitor navigate between screens using the arrow keys. This is accomplished by automatically attaching a key object to the visitor's keyboard. To increase functionality, sequential screens can actually overlay each another so that the previous screen remains visible when the next slide is viewed.

Create a Slide Presentation

1. Click the **File** menu, and then click **New**.

2. Click the **General** tab.

3. Click **Flash Slide Presentation**.

4. Click **OK**.

5. Create, or select a backdrop for the slide show, and then place it on the presentation main page (optional).

6. Select Slide 1.

7. Drag an image from the Library onto the Slide 1 Stage, or click the File menu, and then click Import to select an image from an external source.

Did You Know?

Graphics aren't the only items that can be placed on a slide. You can display video clips, Flash movie clips, even audio on a slide. It's totally up to you. The animation, video, or audio files will begin to play when the visitor clicks to access the slide.

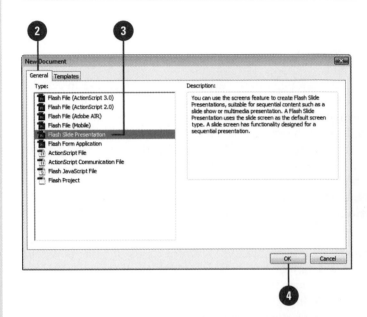

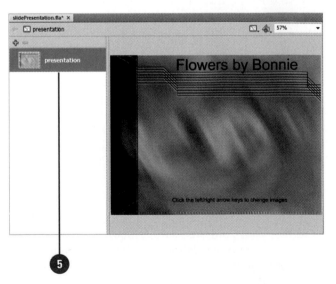

8 Click the **Insert Screen (+)** button.

9 Select Slide 2, and then add another image.

10 Click the **Insert Screen (+)** button, and then repeat steps 5 through 7 to add as many slides as required.

11 Select a slide, and then click the **Delete Screen (-)** button to remove the slide from the set.

12 Click and drag a slide up or down to reorder the slide within the stack.

13 Click the **Control** menu, and then click **Test Movie**.

14 Use the left and right arrow keys to maneuver between slides.

IMPORTANT *If you right-click on a slide, you can choose to insert a nested screen. Nested screens are always visible, but appeared grayed out when viewed.*

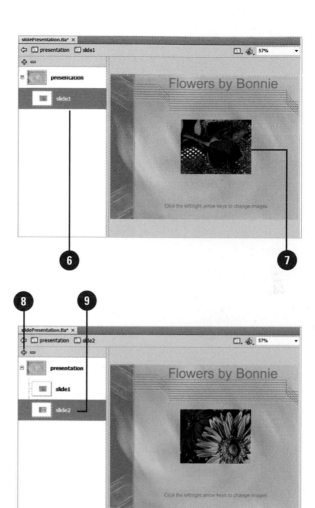

Creating a Form Screen

Flash Professional lets you create form screens for documents, such as online registration forms or e-commerce forms. Form screens are containers that add structure and organization to a form-based application. A form screen has functionality designed for a nonlinear, form-based application, with multiple options available in one visual space. Use form screens when you want to manage the visibility of individual screens yourself. For example, you could use forms to create an interactive search engine, or an interactive data collection form.

Create a Form Screen

1. Click the **File** menu, and then click **New**.

2. Click the **General** tab.

3. Click **Flash Form Application**.

4. Click **OK**.

   This creates a default application with two nested form screens.

5. Add a backdrop to the application form by creating it directly in Flash, or by using a graphic image (optional).

6. Select form1.

7. Add the required User Interface components to form1.

   IMPORTANT *The application form is the parent of the other forms within the application. Anything you put on that form will also appear on any of its child forms.*

See Also

See Chapter 16 , "Adding Display Components" on page 389 for more information on adding interactive components to a Flash document.

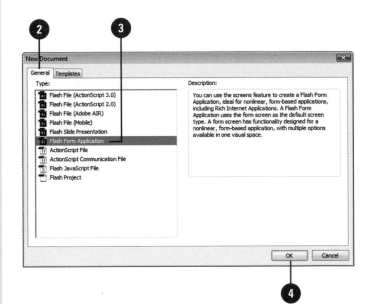

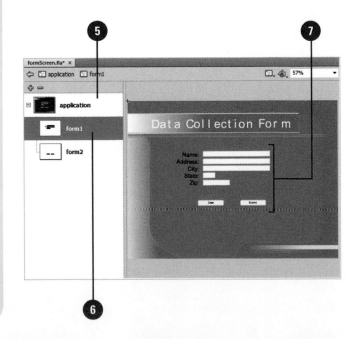

496

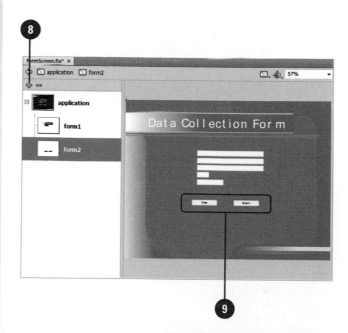

8 Click the **Insert Screen (+)** button.

9 Add component buttons to the second screen, and then use the Component Inspector panel to link the buttons to the form.

10 Click the **Control** menu, and then click **Test Movie**.

See Also

See Chapter 18, "Adding and Modifying Data Components" on page 431 for more information on binding components.

Creating Content for a Mobile Device

Flash content deployment is expanding from the Web to other mediums, such as cell phones, PDAs, and other mobile devices. In conjunction with Adobe Device Central CS4, Flash allows you to create and test content for mobile devices. You use the New Document dialog box to create a blank Flash document for mobile devices or one of the available templates. Flash comes equipped with a template library of cell phone and PDA interfaces in the following categories: BREW Handsets, Consumer Devices, and Global Handsets. Each template provides a brief description of device support and screen resolution. Flash uses the right settings from Device Central to create the content you want. To display content on mobile devices, Flash uses Flash Lite, a specialized player for mobile devices. After you create your mobile content, you can test it using Adobe Device Central and Flash Lite.

Create a Document for a Mobile Device

1. Click the **File** menu, and then click **New**.

2. Follow the instructions for the type of Flash mobile file you want:

   ◆ **Blank.** Click the **General** tab, and then click **Flash File (Mobile)**.

   ◆ **Template.** Click the **Templates** tab, select a mobile templates category, and then select a template.

3. Click **OK**.

   If you selected a blank Flash File (Mobile), Adobe Device Central CS4 opens, where you can select the device and any options you want.

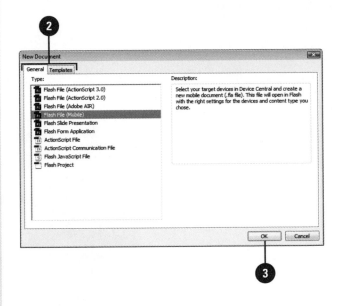

Mobile templates

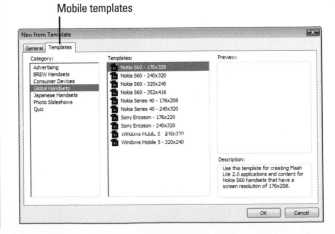

4 Select the device you want and check the device profile for support and compatibility issues.

5 Click **Create**.

The new document appears in Flash, where you can develop your content.

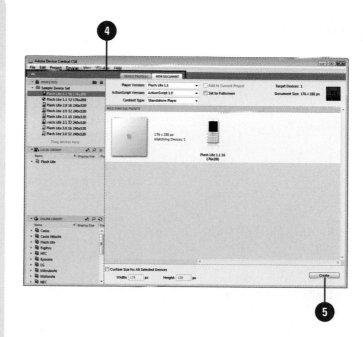

Device Profiles tab

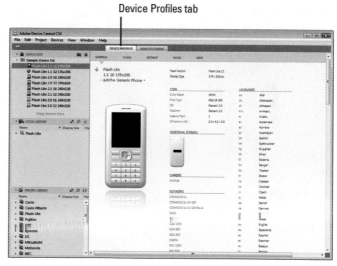

Mapping MIDI Device Sounds

Every day the world is getting smaller, and mobile devices are getting smaller, and smarter. Using Flash, you can include event sounds when creating documents for playback on mobile devices. Flash does not support sound file formats used for mobile devices (such as MIDI and others); when authoring for mobile devices, you must temporarily place a proxy sound in a supported format such as .mp3, .wav, or .aif in the Flash document. The proxy sound in the document is then mapped to an external mobile device sound, such as a MIDI file. During the document publishing process, the proxy sound is replaced with the linked external sound. The .swf file generated contains the external sound and uses it for playback with Flash Lite on a mobile device. Flash Lite is the Flash Player for mobile devices.

Map MIDI Sounds on a Mobile Device

1. Click the **File** menu, point to **Import**, click **Import to Library**, and then import one or more sounds into the Flash Library.

2. Press Control+click (Mac) or right-click (Win) the sound you want to work with, and then click **Properties**.

3. Enter a path to the location where the mobile device sound is located.

4. Click **OK**.

5. Add a button instance to the Stage.

   IMPORTANT *You can use a pre-made Flash button. Click the Window menu, point to Common Libraries, and then click Buttons.*

6. Open the button in the Library, and then add the linked sound to the Hit frame of the button.

7. Click the **File** menu, and then click **Publish Settings**.

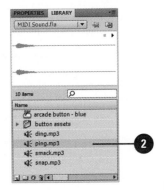

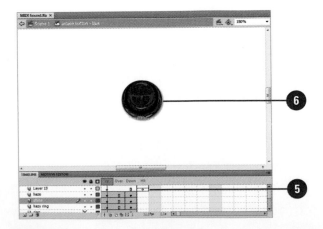

8 Click the **Flash** tab.

9 Click the **Player** popup, click **Flash Lite 1.x** or **Flash Lite 2.x**, and then select the ActionScript version you want, if necessary.

The Export device sounds option is automatically selected.

Flash Lite is a player for mobile devices.

10 Click **OK**.

The .swf file now contains the linked mobile device sound.

11 Click the **Control** menu, and then click **Test Movie**.

When you execute a Flash document using Flash Lite, Flash opens Adobe Device Central CS4 to emulate the display with the currently selected mobile device.

When Adobe Device Central CS4 opens, its displays an emulator of the currently selected mobile device, or asks you to select one.

12 If necessary, select the device you want and check the device profile for support and compatibility issues.

13 Use the Device Central controls to test out your Flash document on the mobile device.

The mobile device sound has been modified to emulate the Flash .swf file sound.

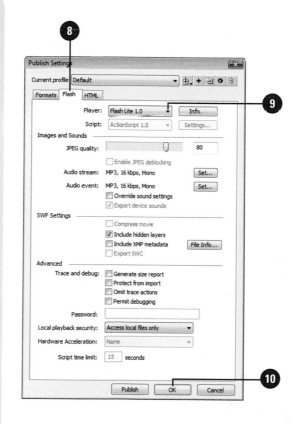

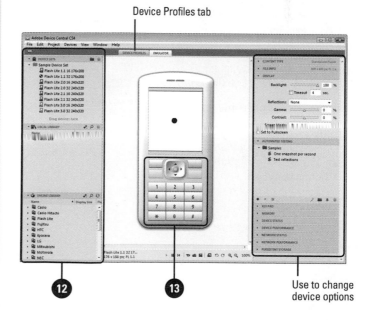

Device Profiles tab

Use to change device options

Creating and Managing a Project

In Flash, you can manage multiple document files within a Flash Project. A Flash Projects lets you group multiple, and related files together to help you keep track of complex applications (**New!**). Flash lets you apply version-control to ensure that the correct file versions are used during editing and to prevent accidental overwriting. A Flash Project is essentially a collection of any Flash or other file types, including Flash SWF and FLA files and even other Flash projects. When you open an existing project, the Project panel gives you instant access to all the various parts of the project. The Flash Project panel is used to create and manage projects. The Project panel displays the contents of a Flash Project using a collapsible tree structure. Flash limits you to opening or creating one project at a time. Any changes made to the project are automatically saved to the project file, so it's not necessary to perform a Save operation.

Create and Manage a Project

1. Click the **Window** menu, point to **Other Panels**, and then click **Project** to open the Project panel.

   ◆ **Quick Project.** You can create a quick project. A quick project is based on the currently open FLA file. Click the **Projects** popup in the Project panel, and then click **Quick Project**.

2. Click the **Projects** popup, and then click **New Project**.

3. Name the new project, locate and select a root folder location for the project file, and then click **OK**.

   Any folders in the selected root folder appear in the Project panel.

4. Click the **ActionScript version** popup, and then click **ActionScript 3.0** or **ActionScript 2.0**.

5. Click **Create Project**.

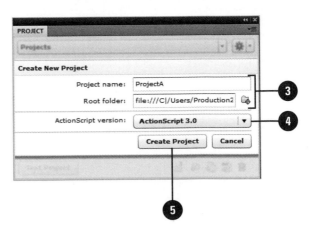

Did You Know?

You can open a project. Click the Projects popup in the Project panel, and then click Open Project, browse to the project folder, and then click OK.

6 Manage a project using any of the following options:

- ◆ **Add Folder.** Click the **New Folder** button, type the folder name, and then click **Create Folder**.

- ◆ **Delete Folder.** Select the folder, click the **Delete** button to delete a selected project asset.

- ◆ **Close Project.** Click the **Options** menu, and then click **Close Project**.

- ◆ **Delete Project.** Open the project, click the **Options** menu, and then click **Delete Project**. Select a delete content option, and then click **Yes**.

- ◆ **Rename Project.** Click the **Options** menu, and then click **Rename Project**, type a name, and then click **OK**.

- ◆ **Switch Open Projects.** Click the **Project** popup, and then click the open project name.

- ◆ **Project Properties.** Click the **Options** menu, click **Project Properties**, specify options on the different tabs (Classes, Locations, and Paths), and then click **OK**.

7 Click the **Close** button on the Project panel.

Did You Know?

You can convert previous projects to the new project format. In previous versions of Flash, projects used an XML file with a .FLP extension. To convert it, simply open it in Flash CS4. Open the Project panel, click the Project popup, click Open Project, navigate to the folder with the project, and then click OK.

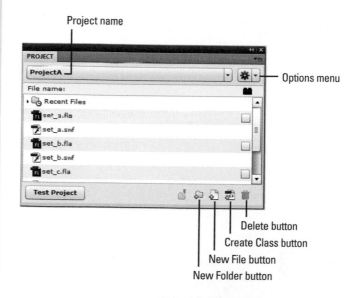

Project name

Options menu

Delete button

Create Class button

New File button

New Folder button

Create a new folder

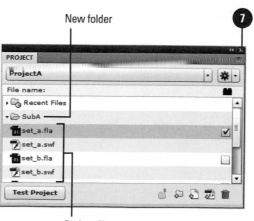

New folder

Project files

Managing Project Files

A project is a collection of files that you can manage directly from Flash (**New!**). The Project panel displays files by filename extension. By default, the Project panel only shows Flash documents type (FLA, SWF, SWC, AS, JSFL, ASC, MXML). If you want to display other types, you can change settings in Panel Preferences. You can also hide files or folder by preceding the file or folder name with a special character, such as an underscore, and enabling the option in Panel Preferences. When you work with the same project, the Project Panel shows all recently opened files in the Recent Files folder for easy access. You can create files, including Flash and ActionScript, from the Project panel.

Manage Project Files

1 Click the **Window** menu, point to **Other Panels**, and then click **Project** to open the Project panel.

2 Manage files using any of the following options:

- ◆ **Create File.** Select the folder where you want the file (no selection is the root), click the **New File** button, enter a name, select a file type, and then click **Create File**.

- ◆ **Open File.** Double-click the file in the Project panel.

- ◆ **Delete File.** Select the file, click the **Delete** button, and then click **Yes** to delete a selected project asset.

- ◆ **Publish.** Select or clear the file check box on the right to add or remove the file to/from the publishing list.

- ◆ **Pin a Directory.** Select a folder, and then click the **Pin Directory** button; click again to unpin.

3 Click the **Close** button on the Project panel.

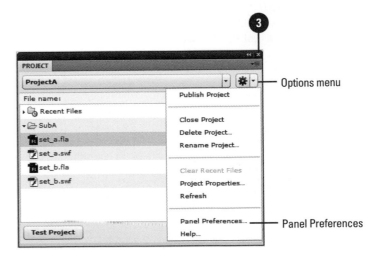

Options menu

Delete button

New File button

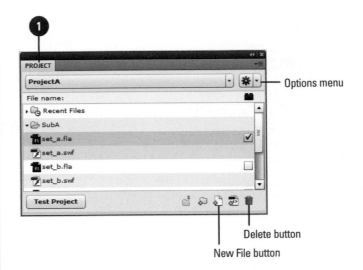

Options menu

Panel Preferences

Did You Know?

You can clear the Recent Files list. In the Project panel, click the Options menu, and then click Clear Recent Files.

Change Project Properties

1. In the Project panel, click the **Options** menu, click **Project Properties**.

2. Click any of the following tabs:

   - **Classes.** Specify the ActionScript version, and class file folder locations.

   - **Locations.** Specify additional source folder locations.

   - **Paths.** Specify the location Flex SDK files for use in Flash to create skins and other visual elements in Flex.

3. Click **OK**.

Change Panel Preferences

1. In the Project panel, click the **Options** menu, and then click **Panel Preferences**.

2. Click any of the following tabs:

   - **Classes.** Specify the ActionScript version, and class file folder locations.

   - **Settings.** Change defaults filters, hide files or folders based on the name, and show or hide classes folder, hidden files, or recent files.

   - **Locations.** Specify additional source folder locations.

3. Click **OK**.

Testing a Project

A project is a collection of files that constitute a complex project. For example, you can create a Flash project that contains 5 Flash documents, with interactive buttons on the pages to call the other pages. If all of the FLA files are located within the same project, it's an easy matter to test the entire project. You must first select one of the files as the main file, and then simply click the Test Project button. Flash will automatically publish all of the Flash documents in the project, display the main file, and then allow you to test its operation. It's that simple.

Test a Project

1. Click the **Window** menu, point to **Other Panels**, and then click **Project** to open the Project panel.

2. If the project you want to test is not open, click the **Project** popup and click **Open Project** in the Project panel, and then select the appropriate file.

3. Click **Open**.

   IMPORTANT *Since testing a project involves moving among different Flash movies, your published documents will have to have interactive buttons linked to all the other pages within the project, or the test will not work.*

4. Right-click (Win) or Control-click (Mac) one of the FLA or HTML files in the project.

5. Click **Make Default Document** from the available options.

6. Click **Test Project**.

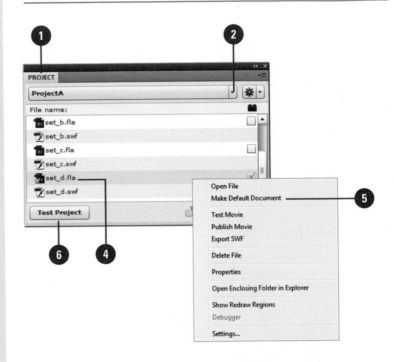

See Also

See Chapter 15, "Debugging a Movie" on page 373 for more information on how to perform debugging operations on a running Flash movie.

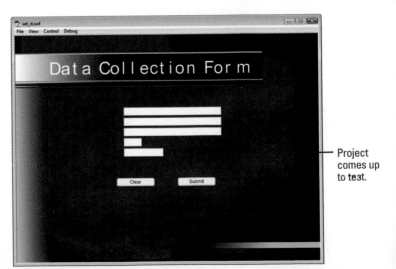

Project comes up to test.

Sending a Document Using E-Mail

After you finish making changes to a document, you can quickly send it to another person for review using e-mail. Flash allows you to send documents out for review as an attachment using e-mail from within the program so that you do not have to open your e-mail program. An e-mail program needs to be installed on your computer before you begin. When you send your document out for review, reviewers can add comments and then send it back to you.

Send an Office Document Using E-Mail

1 Click the **File** menu, and then click **Send**.

- ◆ If prompted, click **Yes** to save your Flash document.

IMPORTANT *To complete the following steps, you need to have an e-mail program installed on your computer and an e-mail account set-up.*

Your default e-mail program opens with your document attached.

2 Enter your recipients and subject (appears with document name by default).

3 Enter a message for your reviewer with instructions.

4 Click the **Send** button.

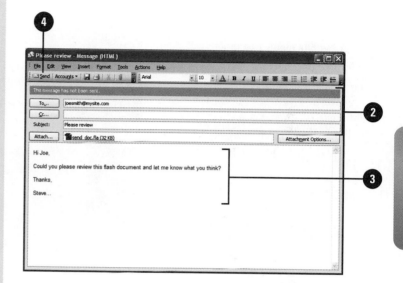

Sharing My Screen

The Share My Screen command (**New!**) on the File menu allows you to connect to Adobe ConnectNow, which is a secure Web site where you can start an online meeting and collaborate on any design project across platforms and programs. You can share and annotate your computer screen or take control of an attendee's computer. During the meeting, you can communicate by sending chat messages, using live audio, or broadcasting live video. In addition, you can take meeting notes, and share files.

Share My Screen

1. Click the **File** menu, and then click **Share My Screen**.

2. Enter your Adobe ID and password.

   ◆ If you don't have an Adobe ID and password, click the Create a Free Adobe ID link, and then follow the online instructions.

3. Click **Sign In**.

   ◆ If prompted, sign in to ConnectNow.

4. To share your computer screen, click the **Share My Computer Screen** button.

5. Use the ConnectNow toolbar to do any of the following:

   ◆ **Meeting.** Use to invite participants, share my computer screen, upload a file, share my webcam, set preferences, and end a meeting, and exit Adobe ConnectNow.

   ◆ **PODS.** Use to show and hide pod panels.

   ◆ **Help.** Use to get help, troubleshoot problems, and set account and Flash Player settings.

6. Click the participant buttons at the bottom to specify roles, remove a user, or request control of a user's computer.

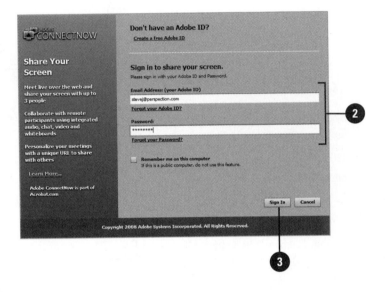

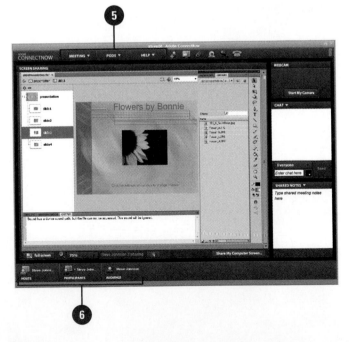

Workshops

Introduction

The Workshop is all about being creative and thinking outside of the box. These workshops will help your right-brain soar, while making your left-brain happy; by explaining why things work the way they do. Exploring Flash's possibilities is great fun; however, always stay grounded with knowledge of how things work. Knowledge is power.

Getting and Using the Project Files

Each project in the Workshop includes a start file to help you get started with the project, and a final file to provide you with the results of the project so you can see how well you accomplished the task.

Before you can use the project files, you need to download them from the Web. You can access the files at *www.perspection.com* in the software downloads area. After you download the files from the Web, uncompress the files into a folder on your hard drive to which you have easy access from Flash.

Project 1: Creating and Customizing Scrollable Text

Skills and Tools: Flash component and ActionScripting

Flash comes with a set of built-in components—Button, CheckBox, Label, RadioButton, and UIScrollBar—that make it easy to add elements and controls to a Flash document. The components are available in the Components panel. There is a set of components for use with Flash documents (ActionScript 2.0) and another one for use with Flash documents (ActionScript 3.0). However, each set contains many of the same components. Some of the components include a skin, or look and feel, which you can customize to suit your own artistic nature.

The Project

In this project, you'll learn how to create scrollable text using the UIScrollBar component, and then customize the component.

The Process

1. Open Flash CS4, create a new document (3.0), and then save it as **scroll_text_component.fla**.

2 Select the **Text** tool on the Tools panel.

3 Draw a text box on the Stage, and then select the text box.

4 Open the Properties panel.

5 Enter *scrollableText* in the instance box.

6 Click the **Text type** popup, and then click **Dynamic Text**.

7 Select the **Selection** tool on the Tools panel.

8 Right-click (Win) or Control-click (Mac) the text box, and then click **Scrollable**.

9 Click the **Window** menu, and then click **Components**.

10 Click the **User Interface** plus sign (+), and then click **UIScrollBar**.

11 Drag the **UIScrollBar** component onto the text box named *scrollableText*.

12 Click the **Close** button on the Components panel.

13 Drag the UIScrollBar component object to the right side of the text box.

14 Resize the text to line up with the length of the UIScrollBar component object.

15 Select the **Text** tool on the Tools panel.

16 Type text in the text box until the number of lines goes beyond the height of the text box.

17 Click the **File** menu, and then click **Save**.

18 Click the **Control** menu, and then click **Test Movie**, or press Ctrl+Enter (Win) or ⌘+Return (Mac).

19 Use the scroll bar in the Flash movie to display all the text.

20 Click the **Close** button in the test movie window.

21 Double-click the UIScrollBar component object.

The component symbol opens.

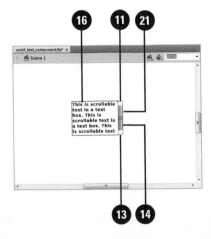

W

22 Double-click one of the scroll arrows, and then double-click the same scroll arrow again.

23 Select the **Zoom** tool on the Tools panel, and then click to zoom in on the scroll arrow that you selected.

24 Double-click the arrow again until the graphic object appears.

25 Click the **Fill Color** button on the Tools panel, and then select a color (red).

26 Select the **Paint Bucket** tool on the Tools panel, and then click in the arrow to change the color from black to red.

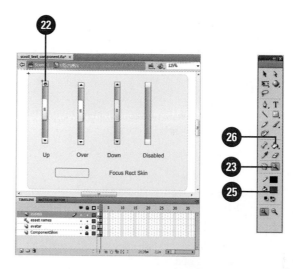

27 Select the **Zoom** tool on the Tools panel, and then Alt-click (Win) or Option-click (Mac) to zoom in on the scroll arrow that you selected.

All the arrows in the different scroll bar states appear in red. You can modify other parts of the scroll from here too.

28 Click the **Scene 1** button on the Edit bar.

29 Click the **File** menu, and then click **Save**.

30 Click the **Control** menu, and then click **Test Movie**.

The arrows on the scroll bar appear in red.

31 Click the **Close** button in the test movie window.

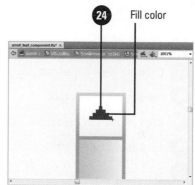

Fill color

The Results

Finish: Compare your completed project file with the movie in **scroll_text_component_fnl.swa**. ☞

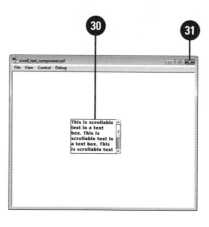

Project 2: Loading and Formatting Text

Skills and Tools: ActionScripting

You can create a scrollable text box and then manually enter the text that you want to display, or you can use ActionScripting to load the text for you. If you have text that frequently changes, you can store the text into an external text file, which is easy to open and change, and dynamically load the text into your Flash document. After you load the text from the document, you can use Action-

Scripting to format the text the way you want it to appear on the screen. To load a text file, you need to store the text file in the same folder as the Flash document, or you need to know the path location to the text file.

The Project

In this project, you'll use ActionScripting to load text from an external file into a scrollable text box, and then format the text.

The Process

1. Open the file **load_text_start.fla** in Flash CS4, and then save it as **load_text.fla** in the same Project folder.

   The Flash document opens with a scrollable text box. The scrollable text box uses the UIScrollBar component and named scrollableText. See project "Creating and Customizing Scrollable Text" for details on how to create one.

2. Select the text layer in the Timeline.

3. Click the **New Layer** button.

4. Name the layer *actions*.

5. Click Frame 1 in the actions layer.

6. Click the **Window** menu, and then click **Actions**.

7. Type the following ActionScript code exactly as shown:

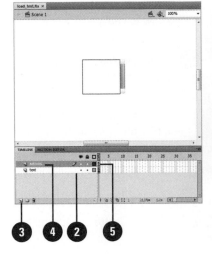

   ```
   var loader:URLLoader = new URLLoader();

   loader.load(new URLRequest("externalText.txt");

   loader.addEventListener(Event.COMPLETE, onGetText);

   function onGetText(event:Event):void {

       scrollableText.text =
   event.target.data;

   }
   ```

   The text file *externalText.txt* is located in the same folder as Flash document, so no path is necessary. The scrollable text box is named *scrollableText*.

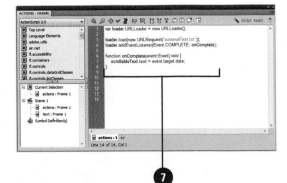

W

8 Click the **File** menu, and then click **Save**.

9 Click the **Control** menu, and then click **Test Movie**, or press Ctrl+Enter (Win) or ⌘+Return (Mac).

The text from the document appears in the scrollable text box.

10 Use the scroll bar in the Flash movie to display all the text.

11 Click the **Close** button in the test movie window.

12 In the Actions panel, type the following ActionScript code exactly as shown:

```
var format:TextFormat = new
TextFormat();

format.font = "Arial";

format.size = 18;

scrollableText.defaultTextFormat =
format;
```

13 Click the **File** menu, and then click **Save**.

14 Click the **Control** menu, and then click **Test Movie**, or press Ctrl+Enter (Win) or ⌘+Return (Mac).

The text from the document appears in the scrollable text box with the Arial font at the 18 point size.

15 Use the scroll bar in the Flash movie to display all the text.

16 Click the **Close** button in the test movie window.

The Results

Finish: Compare your completed project file with the movie in **load_text_fnl.swa.** 👉

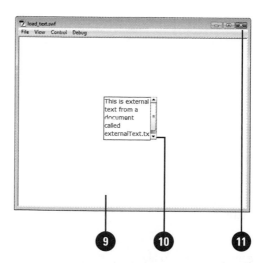

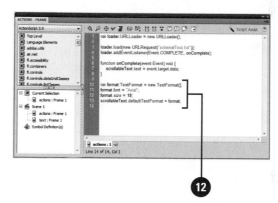

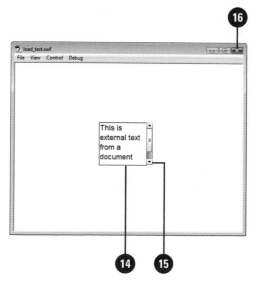

Project 3: Playing Internal and External Sounds

Skills and Tools: ActionScripting

You can use ActionScript to play a sound from the Library or an external location. When a sound is small and doesn't affect the size of the Flash document, the best way to go is to import the sound into the Flash document and then play it. If the sound is large, you might want to play the sound from an external folder location. If the external sound file remains in the same location, this is the best way to go, otherwise I would import it into the Flash document. Either way, you can use Action-Script to play it.

The Project

In this project, you'll use ActionScript to play a sound from the Library, and then play a sound from an external audio file.

The Process

1. Open the file **play_sound_start.fla** in Flash CS4, and then save it as **play_sound.fla** in the same Project folder.

2. Select the Play Sound button on the Stage.

3. Open the **Properties** panel.

4. Name the object *myButton*.

5. Click the **File** menu, point to **Import**, and then click **Import to Library**.

6. Navigate to the Project folder where the sound is located.

7. Select the file **funky.mp3**.

8. Click **Open**.

9. Open the **Library** panel.

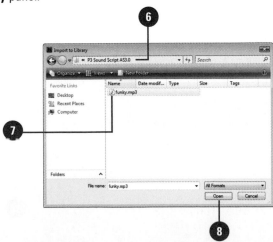

10 Right-click (Win) or Command-click (Mac) the sound named **funky.mp3**, and then click **Properties**.

11 Click **Advanced**, if available. The button toggles to Basic (as shown in the illustration).

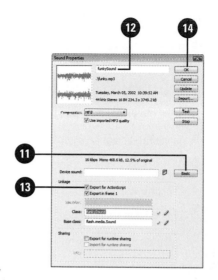

12 Name the sound *funkySound*.

13 Select the **Export for ActionScript** check box.

The Export in frame 1 check box is enabled and selected. The Class appears with the same name as the sound element *funkySound*, and the Base class appears as *flash.media.sound* indicating type information.

14 Click **OK**.

15 If an ActionScript Class Warning dialog box appears, click **OK** to define the new class.

16 Click Frame 1 in the actions layer.

17 Click the **Window** menu, and then click **Actions**.

18 Type the following ActionScript code exactly as shown:

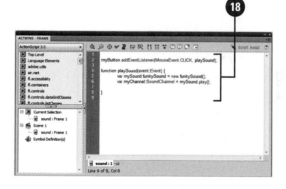

```
myButton.addEventListener
(MouseEvent.CLICK, playSound);

function playSound(event:Event) {

    var mySound:funkySound = new
funkySound();

    var myChannel:SoundChannel =
mySound.play();

}
```

19 Click the **File** menu, and then click **Save**.

20 Click the **Control** menu, and then click **Test Movie**, or press Ctrl+Enter (Win) or ⌘+Return (Mac).

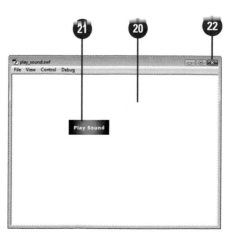

21 Click the Play Sound button in the movie.

22 Click the **Close** button in the test movie window.

The Results

Finish: Compare your completed project file with the movie in **play_sound_fnl.swf**. 👉

Playing External Sound

1. Open the file **external_sound_start.fla** in Flash CS4, and then save it as **external_sound.fla** in the same Project folder.

2. Select the Play External Sound button on the Stage.

3. Open the **Properties** panel.

4. Name the object *myButton*.

5. Click Frame 1 in the actions layer.

6. Click the **Window** menu, and then click **Actions**.

7. Type the following ActionScript code exactly as shown:

```
myButton.addEventListener(MouseEvent.CLICK, playSound);

var myExternalSound:Sound = new Sound();

var req:URLRequest = new URLRequest("funky.mp3");

myExternalSound.load(req);

function playSound(event:Event) {

    myExternalSound.play();

}
```

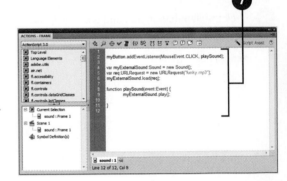

8. Click the **File** menu, and then click **Save**.

9. Click the **Control** menu, and then click **Test Movie**, or press Ctrl+Enter (Win) or ⌘+Return (Mac).

10. Click the Play External Sound button in the movie.

11. Click the **Close** button in the test movie window.

The Results

Finish: Compare your completed project file with the movie in **external_sound_fnl.swf**. ☞

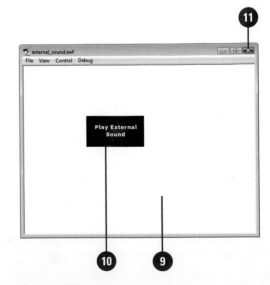

516

Project 4: Modifying an Object with ActionScript

Skills and Tools: ActionScripting

With ActionScript 3.0, you specify a class definition, either document or object level, to work with objects using ActionScript code. A class is a representation of an object that stores information about its data type, state, and behaviors. A class can include three types of characteristics: properties, methods, and events. A property represents different data associated with an object. A method is an action that can be performed by an object. An event is a system, application, or user action, such as a mouse click, that triggers an action related to an object. You can store ActionScript code in the Flash document or in a separate ActionScript file (.as).

The Project

In this project, you'll create an ActionScript file, enter a script, and then use it in a Flash document to control an object.

The Process

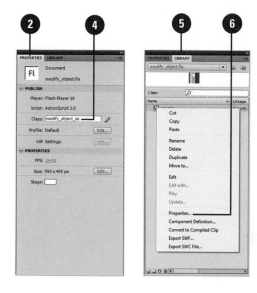

1. Open the file **modify_object_start.fla** in Flash CS4, and then save it as **modify_object.fla** in the same Project folder.

2. Open the Properties panel.

3. Click the Stage.

4. In the Class field, type *modify_object_as*.

   This indicates the name of the ActionScript file with the scripting code.

5. Open the **Library** panel.

6. Right-click (Win) or Command-click (Mac) the sound named **square**, and then click **Properties**.

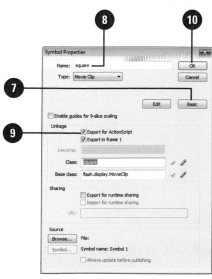

7. Click **Advanced**, if available. The button toggles to Basic (as shown in the illustration).

8. Name the sound *square*.

9. Select the **Export for ActionScript** check box.

   The Export in frame 1 check box is enabled and selected. The Class appears with the same name as the object *square*, and the Base class appears as *flash.media.MovieClip* indicating type information.

10. Click **OK**.

11 If an ActionScript Class Warning dialog box appears, click **OK** to define the new class.

12 Click the **File** menu, and then click **Save**.

This saves the Flash document. Now, lets create an ActionScript file to store the ActionScript code.

13 Click the **File** menu, and then click **New**.

14 Click the **General** tab.

15 Click **ActionScript File**.

16 Click **OK**.

17 Click the **File** menu, and then click **Save As**.

18 Navigate to the Project folder, and then name the file *modify_object_as*.

19 Click **Save**.

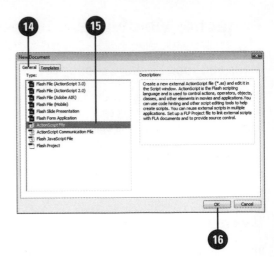

20 In the Actions panel, type the following ActionScript code exactly as shown:

```
package      {

    import flash.display.MovieClip;

    public class modify_object_as extends MovieClip        {

    public function modify_object_as()     {

            var mySquare:square = new square();

            addChild(mySquare);

            mySquare.x=100;

            mySquare.y=100;

            mySquare.width=75;

            mySquare.height=75;

            mySquare.rotation=30;

        }

    }

    }
```

ActionScript file

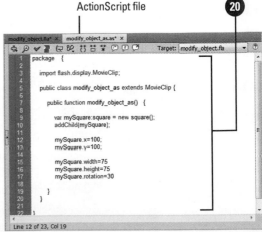

21 Click the **File** menu, and then click **Save**.

22 Click the **File** menu, and then click **Close** to close the ActionScript file.

W

23 In the Flash document, click the **Control** menu, and then click **Test Movie**, or press Ctrl+Enter (Win) or ⌘+Return (Mac).

24 Click the **Close** button in the test movie window.

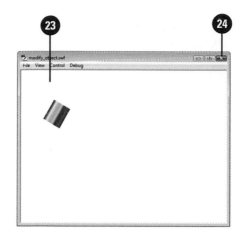

The Results

Finish: Compare your completed project file with the movie in **modify_object_fnl.swa**. 👉

Project 5: Moving a Button with ActionScript

Skills and Tools: ActionScripting and Button Component

Flash comes with a set of built-in components—Button, CheckBox, Label, RadioButton, and UIScrollBar—that make it easy to add elements and controls to a Flash document. The components are available in the Components panel. After you insert a component into a Flash document, you can use ActionScript to move and modify it. The component is automatically set up for use with ActionScript. All you need to do is give it an instance name and write the script.

The Project

In this project, you'll place a button component on the Stage and then use ActionScript to move the button when you click it.

The Process

1 Open Flash CS4, create a new document (3.0), and then save it as **move_button.fla**.

2 Click the **Window** menu, and then click **Components**.

3 Click the **User Interface** plus sign (+), and then click **Button**.

4 Drag the **Button** component onto the Stage.

5 Click the **Close** button on the Components panel.

6 Select the **Selection** tool on the Tools panel.

7 Select the button components object.

8 Open the Properties panel.

9 Enter *myButton* in the instance box.

10 Name the layer *button*.

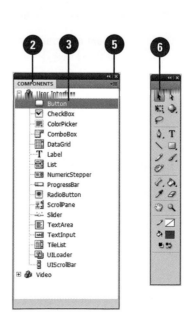

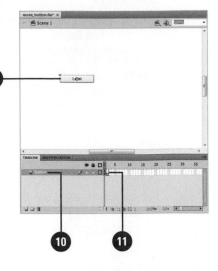

11 Click Frame 1 in the actions layer.

12 Click the **Window** menu, and then click **Actions**.

13 Type the following ActionScript code exactly as shown:

import flash.events.MouseEvent;

myButton.addEventListener(MouseEvent.CLICK, moveButton);

function moveButton(event:MouseEvent):void {

    myButton.x=myButton.x+50;

    myButton.y=myButton.y+50;

}

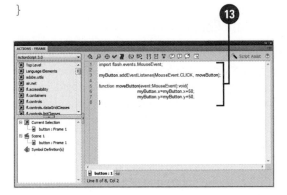

14 Click the **File** menu, and then click **Save**.

15 Click the **Control** menu, and then click **Test Movie**, or press Ctrl+Enter (Win) or ⌘+Return (Mac).

16 Click the button to watch it move by 50 pixels to the right and down.

17 Click the **Close** button in the test movie window.

The Results

Finish: Compare your completed project file with the movie in **move_button_fnl.swa**. 👉

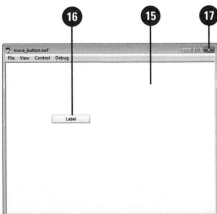

Project 6: Creating a Context Menu

Skills and Tools: ActionScripting

In addition of executing commands using buttons and other components, you can also execute commands using a context menu, which is also known as a shortcut menu. A context menu appears when you right-click (Win) or Control-click (Mac) an item on the screen. With ActionScript, you can create a custom context menu, and execute the commands using functions.

The Project

In this project, you'll create a context menu using ActionScript to execute a command in a Flash movie.

The Process

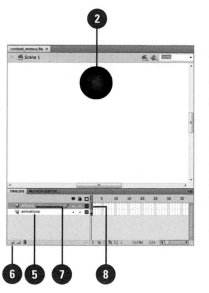

1. Open the file **context_menus_start.fla** in Flash CS4, and then save it as **context_menus.fla** in the same Project folder.

2. Select ball object on the Stage.

3. Open the Properties panel.

4. Enter *myAnimation* in the instance box.

5. Select the animations layer in the Timeline.

6. Click the **New Layer** button.

7. Name the layer *actions*.

8. Click Frame 1 in the actions layer.

9. Click the **Window** menu, and then click **Actions**.

10. Type the following ActionScript code exactly as shown:

    ```
    var menuItem1:ContextMenuItem = new ContextMenuItem("Stop");

    var menuItem2:ContextMenuItem = new ContextMenuItem("Play Again");

    menuItem1.addEventListener(ContextMenuEvent.MENU_ITEM_SELECT, stopCommand);

    menuItem2.addEventListener(ContextMenuEvent.MENU_ITEM_SELECT, playCommand);

    var myContextMenu:ContextMenu = new ContextMenu();
    ```

```
myContextMenu.hideBuiltInItems();

myContextMenu.customItems.push(menuItem1);

myContextMenu.customItems.push(menuItem2);

this.contextMenu = myContextMenu;

function stopCommand(event:ContextMenuEvent):void {

    myAnimation.stop();

}

function playCommand(event:ContextMenuEvent):void {

    myAnimation.gotoAndPlay(1);

}
```

⑪ Click the **File** menu, and then click **Save**.

⑫ Click the **Control** menu, and then click **Test Movie**, or press Ctrl+Enter (Win) or ⌘+Return (Mac).

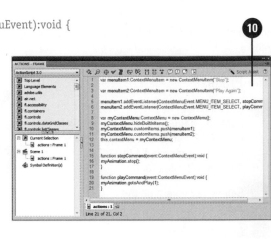

⑬ Right-click (Win) or Control-click (Mac) the animation, and then click **Stop**.

⑭ Right-click (Win) or Control-click (Mac) the animation, and then click **Play Again**.

⑮ Click the **Close** button in the test movie window.

The Results

Finish: Compare your completed project file with the movie in **context_menus_fnl.swf**. 👉

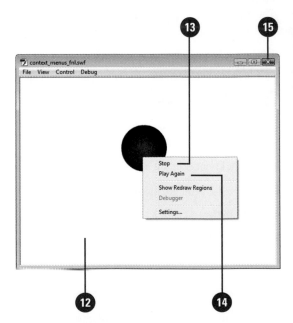

Want More Projects

You can access and download more workshop projects and related files at *www.perspection.com* in the software downloads area. After you download the files from the Web, uncompress the files into a folder on your hard drive to which you have easy access from Flash.

Get Everything on DVD

Instead of downloading everything from the Web, which can take a while depending on your Internet connection speed, you can get all the files used in this book and much more on a Flash CS4 On Demand DVD. The DVD contains task and workshop files, tips and tricks, keyboard shortcuts, and other goodies from the author.

To get the Flash CS4 On Demand DVD, go to *www.perspection.com*.

New! Features

Adobe Flash CS4 Professional

Adobe Flash CS4 Professional means superior results faster, with new features and enhancements that help you create and manage your images more easily and efficiently. The indispensable new and improved features help graphic web designers, photographers, and video professionals create the highest quality images, with the control, flexibility, and capabilities that you expect from the professional standards in desktop digital imaging.

Each new release of Flash brings with it new features, improvements, and added sophistication. This edition is aimed at the Web designer, interactive media professional, or subject matter expert developing multimedia content, and the application developer.

Only New Features

If you're already familiar with Flash CS3, you can access and download all the tasks in this book with Adobe Flash CS4 New Features to help make your transition to the new version simple and smooth. The Flash CS4 New Features as well as other Flash CS3 to Flash CS4 transition helpers are available on the Web at *www.perspection.com*.

What's New

If you're searching for what's new in Flash CS4, just look for the icon. New!. The new icon appears in the table of contents and throughout this book, so you can quickly and easily identify a new or improved feature in Flash CS4. The following is a brief description of each new feature and its location in this book.

Flash CS4 Professional

- **Multi-language installer (p. 3)** The installer includes a new language option which allows for the installation of different resource sets for international languages.

- **Flash Configuration Folders (p. 3)** When you install Flash CS4, two configuration folders are created. One folder is for language configuration content and the other is for common configuration content. The common configuration folder is located at ...\Adobe\Adobe Flash CS4\Configuration, and the language specific configuration folder is located at ...\Adobe\Adobe Flash CS4\en\Configuration. Where en is the language code, in this case English.

◆ **Flash Player 10 (p. 3)** In addition to playing movies with the Flash Player 10 on any computer, you can also preview movies in the Flash authoring tool by using the Test Movie command.

◆ **Open dialog box (p. 14)** The Flash Open dialog box can open XFL and XML files.

◆ **XFL support (p. 14)** You can create a Flash file by importing a XML file. The XML file is a packaged XML representation of a FLA file along with the assets for that file. An XFL file is essentially a ZIP package containing the XML and the assets for a FLA file. To view the actual XML and assets of the FLA file, change the .XFL file extension to .ZIP and unzip the folder.

◆ **Property Inspector (p. 16, 30-31, 54)** You can display the Property Inspector, also known as the Properties panel, horizontally (like previous versions of Flash) or vertically. In the Property Inspector, you can also apply filters, such as gradient controls, to text, buttons, and movie clips.

◆ **User Interface improvements (p. 18, 28, 33, 53, 56)** The Close button for a document appears on the document tab. You can close a panel by using the Close Panel or Close Group commands on the Options menu. You can automatically collapse an expanded panel to icons by using the Auto-Collapse Icon Panels or Auto-Show Hidden Panels commands. You can access workspaces from the Workspace menu on the menu bar.

◆ **Community Help (p. 24-25)** Flash Help uses a Community Help site on the web at *adobe.com* (which is updated regularly) to help you find the information you need. When you start Flash Help, your browser opens, displaying a web site with Flash help categories and topics. Along with help text, some help topics include links to text and video tutorials. In addition, comments and ratings from users are available to help guide you to an answer.

◆ **Adobe Product Improvement Program (p. 25)** This is an opt-in program that allows you to test Adobe products and make suggestions for future products. This program enables Adobe to collect product usage data from customers while maintaining their privacy.

◆ **Tools Panel (p. 50)** The Tools panel is horizontally and vertically resizeable. You can dock it as a single height row above documents.

◆ **3D support (p. 61, 122-123, 124, 125)** With Flash Player 10, you can create 3D animation of 2D surfaces. There are two tools in the Tools panel: the 3D Translation tool and the 3D Rotation tool. Vanishing Point gives you the ability to move 3D movie clips and still maintain the same visual perspective of the original. With these tools, you can change the Perspective Angle, which affects the size and view of 3D movie clips on the Stage.

◆ **Font Mapping (p. 62)** Set options in Text Preferences to specify the font style, and whether to display a dialog box.

- **Font menu (p. 62, 166-167)** You can select font families and font styles from separate menus in the Property Inspector. The font menu displays font names and previews of each font and style to make it easier to select the fonts you want.

- **Warning dialog boxes (p. 64-65)** Set options in Warning Preferences to specify whether to display a warning dialog box. The new options includes: Warn On Converting Multiple Selection To Symbol For Tween, Warn On Replacing Current Tween Target, Warn On Motion Frame Contains ActionScript, Warn On Motion Target Object Contains ActionScript, and Warn On IK Bones Not Showing.

- **Smooth and Straighten dialogs (p. 76-77)** The Smooth dialog gives the flexibility of maximum and minimum angle to smooth and smoothing strength. The Straighten dialog gives the control of the straighten rate. In addition, both dialogs provide live preview.

- **Kuler (p. 100-101)** Kuler is an extension that provides access to the Kuler online community. The Kuler application is added as a SWF panel in Flash. You can add the Kuler color theme to the Swatches panel.

- **Spray Brush tool (p. 108)** The Spray Brush tool allows you to spray particles onto the Stage using the current fill color. If you want to create a more complex pattern, you can also use a movie clip or graphic symbol from the library as a particle.

- **Deco tool (p. 109)** The Deco tool allows you to apply a kaleidoscopic drawing effect to the Stage or a selected object on the Stage. You can apply several effects: Vine, Grid, or Symmetry.

- **Inverse Kinematic animation: Bone tool and Bind tool (p. 130, 283-288)** Inverse kinematics is the process of animating an articulated structure by calculating the changes needed to achieve its end state. All you need to do is specify the start and end positions to create an animation. Flash uses two tools: the Bone tool and the Bind tool. You can use these tools on either symbol instances or shapes to create an animation.

- **Library panel (p. 136-137)** The improved Library panel allows you to search for and sort Library items, and set properties on multiple Library items at once.

- **Motion tweens (p. 232-233, 236)** Tween paths can be edited directly on the Stage, tweens cannot be broken, tween properties are keyframed independently, and properties are auto keyframed. With the 3D Translation and 3D Rotation tools, you can also apply motion tween to 3D objects. You can control the positions and rotation angles of 3D objects in the tween layer.

- **Motion Presets panel (p. 234-235)** The Motion Presets panel allows you to create, apply, and manage custom tween presets. You can also import and export presets (.XML), so you can exchange them with others. Adobe provides a built-in set of presets to help you animate objects and learn how to use the presets.

- **Motion Editor (p. 238-243)** A new panel provides a place to create and work with motions tweens. In the Motion Editor panel, you have independent control over keyframe options, including rotation, size, scale, position, color effects, filters, and easing in and out.

- ◆ **Sounds library (p. 304-306)**   The Sounds library provides easy access to sample sound effects that you can use in Flash movies.

- ◆ **Edit in Soundbooth (p. 304, 321)**   If you have Soundbooth CS4 installed on your computer, you can edit imported sounds in Soundbooth directly from within Flash. In addition, you can use the Adobe ASND sound file format to non-destructively edit sounds.

- ◆ **Adobe Media Encoder with H.264 support (p. 342)**   Adobe Media Encoder uses tools and advanced controls found in other Adobe video products, such as Premiere Pro and After Effects, to deliver high quality video in Flash.

- ◆ **JPEG deblocking (p. 468)**   This publishing option allows you to reduce the appearance of common artifacts found in highly compressed JPEG files.

- ◆ **Hardware Acceleration (p. 469)**   This publishing option allows you to take advantage of available hardware for better playback performance.

- ◆ **Metadata support (p. 469, 472-473)**   The XMP panel allows you to assign metadata tags to content in a SWF file. The XMP metadata can be recognized by Adobe Bridge and other applications.

- ◆ **AIR publishing (p. 470-471)**   Adobe AIR is a cross-operating system runtime that allows you to leverage your existing web development skills in Flash to build and deliver Rich Internet Applications (RIAs) to the web, mobile, and desktop. You can publish Flash files to Adobe AIR from the Publish Settings dialog box. You can also create a Flash file for AIR from the Welcome page by clicking Flash File (Adobe AIR).

- ◆ **Project Panel (p. 502-506)**   The Project panel allows you to manage and publish files and folders on your file system without leaving Flash. It simplifies creation of ActionScript classes by automatically filling in necessary keywords and compiler directives, and associating those classes with Library symbols as needed. You can access the Project Panel from the Windows and Other Panels menus.

- ◆ **Adobe ConnectNow (p. 508)**   The Share My Screen command on the File menu allows you to connect to Adobe ConnectNow, which is a secure Web site where you can start an online meeting and collaborate on any design project across platforms and programs.

- ◆ **Adobe Drive**   Adobe Drive is an AIR program that allows you to connect to hosted services, such as Version Cue CS4 servers.

- ◆ **Support for Adobe Pixel Bender**   Adobe Pixel Bender is a program that creates unique filters, blends, and fills, which you can incorporate into Flash using ActionScript 3.0.

- ◆ **Collaborate with Flex developers**   You can import code-only ActionScript 3.0 SWC components developed in Flex Builder.

Adobe Certified Expert

About the Adobe Certified Expert (ACE) Program

The Adobe Certified Expert (ACE) program is for graphic designers, Web designers, systems integrators, value-added resellers, developers, and business professionals seeking official recognition of their expertise on Adobe products.

What Is an ACE?

An Adobe Certified Expert is an individual who has passed an Adobe Product Proficiency Exam for a specific Adobe software product. Adobe Certified Experts are eligible to promote themselves to clients or employers as highly skilled, expert-level users of Adobe software. ACE certification is a recognized worldwide standard for excellence in Adobe software knowledge. There are three levels of ACE certification: Single product certification, Specialist certification, and Master certification. To become an ACE, you must pass one or more product-specific proficiency exams and sign the ACE program agreement. When you become an ACE, you enjoy these special benefits:

- ◆ Professional recognition
- ◆ An ACE program certificate
- ◆ Use of the Adobe Certified Expert program logo

What Does This Logo Mean?

It means this book will prepare you fully for the Adobe Certified Expert exam for Adobe Flash CS4 Professional. The certification exam has a set of objectives, which are organized into broader skill sets. The Adobe Certified Expert objectives and the specific pages throughout this book that cover the objectives are available on the Web at *www.perspection.com*.

 FLCS4-3.1

Flash CS4 ACE Exam Objectives

Objective	Skill	Page
1.0	**Planning and designing Flash applications**	
1.1	Given a scenario, choose the appropriate type of image asset and explain when and why you would use that asset type. (Image asset types include: vector, bitmap, SVG)	188-189, 194-199
1.2	Given a requirement based on your audience, determine the appropriate Flash features and options used to meet the needs of your audience. (Audience requirements include: publishing to AIR, accessibility, player version)	8-11, 466-471
2.0	**Creating and managing assets**	
2.1	Given an option in the Library panel, explain the purpose of and how to use that option.	136-137
2.2	Given a tool, create a shape by using that tool. (Tools include: Deco, Spray Brush, Rectangle Primitive)	76-80, 108-109
2.3	Given a tool, work with an existing asset by using that tool. (Tools include: Transform, 3D Rotation, Bone)	118-125, 283-288
2.4	Given an asset, modify individual properties to achieve specific design requirements. (Design requirements include: advanced text controls including anti-aliasing, stroke control and styling)	166-179
2.5	Import external assets into Flash. (External assets include: XFL from InDesign or After Effects, Photoshop files, Illustrator files, and images)	14-15, 188-189 194-199
2.6	Create and manage text fields by using the Text tool.	164-165, 180-182
2.7	Given an asset, convert that asset to a symbol.	138-139
2.8	Given a component, explain the purpose of or how to use that component.	390-391
2.9	Edit the skin of a component.	390-391
3.0	**Creating Flash movies**	
3.1	Create animations by using the Timeline.	236-237, 248-249, 270-271
3.2	Edit animations by using the Motion Editor.	238-243
3.3	Reuse animations by using Motion Presets.	234-235
3.4	Incorporate and manage audio and video in your movie.	304-309, 324-326
3.5	Apply filters and effects to Movie Clips and text.	240-241
3.6	Manage performance by utilizing bitmap techniques.	196-197
3.7	Apply inverse kinematics to objectives by using the Bone tool.	283-288
4.0	**Programming with ActionScript 3.0**	
4.1	Given an ActionScript class, create an instance from and work with the properties of that class.	352-353

Flash CS4 ACE Exam Objectives (continued)

Objective	Skill	Page
4.2	Given an object-oriented concept, explain the definition of or purpose associated with that concept. (Object-oriented concepts include: Classes, Interfaces, Inheritance, Polymorphism, and Packages)	348, 350-353
4.3	Create custom classes. (Options include: Extending, Subclassing)	348, 352-353
4.4	Explain how to use the Document class.	352-353
4.5	Load content and data from external sources. (Sources include: XML, SWF, and remote objects)	314
5.0	**Testing, publishing, and deploying Flash movies**	
5.1	Recognize effective optimization considerations when testing and debugging Flash applications.	374-377
5.2	Test an application by using the Debugger.	376-377, 380-382
5.3	Given a code snippet, find the error in that code snippet.	386-387
5.4	Given a scenario, select the appropriate Publish settings to deploy a Flash movie. (Scenarios include: Web delivery and AIR)	466-471

Choosing a Certification Level

There are three levels of certification to become an Adobe Certified Expert.

◆ **Single product certification.** Recognizes your proficiency in a single Adobe product. To qualify as an ACE, you must pass one product-specific exam.

◆ **Specialist certification.** Recognizes your proficiency in multiple Adobe products with a specific medium: print, Web, or video. To become certified as a Specialist, you must pass the exams on the required products. To review the requirements, go online to *http://www.adobe.com/support/certification/ace_certify.html*.

◆ **Master certification.** Recognizes your skills in terms of how they align with the Adobe product suites. To become certified as a Master, you must pass the exam for each of the products in the suite.

Preparing for an Adobe Certified Expert Exam

Every Adobe Certified Expert Exam is developed from a list of objectives, which are based on studies of how an Adobe program is actually used in the workplace. The list of objectives determine the scope of each exam, so they provide you with the information you need to prepare for ACE certification. Follow these steps to complete the ACE Exam requirement:

1 Review and perform each task identified with a Adobe Certified Expert objective to confirm that you can meet the requirements for the exam.

2 Identify the topic areas and objectives you need to study, and then prepare for the exam.

3 Review the Adobe Certified Expert Program Agreement. To review it, go online to *http://www.adobe.com/support/certification/ace_certify.html*.

You will be required to accept the ACE agreement when you take the Adobe Certified Exam at an authorized testing center.

4 Register for the Adobe Certified Expert Exam.

ACE testing is offered at more than a thousand authorized Pearson VUE and Thomson Prometric testing centers in many countries. To find the testing center nearest you, go online to *www.pearsonvue.com/adobe* (for Pearson VUE) or *www.2test.com* (for Prometric). The ACE exam fee is US$150 worldwide. When contacting an authorized training center, provide them with the Adobe Product Proficiency exam name and number you want to take, which is available online in the Exam Bulletin at *http://www.adobe.com/support/certification/ace_certify.html*.

5 Take the ACE exam.

Getting Recertified

For those with an ACE certification for a specific Adobe product, recertification is required of each ACE within 90 days of a designated ACE Exam release date. There are no restrictions on the number of times you may take the exam within a given period.

To get recertified, call Pearson VUE or Thomson Prometric. You will need to verify your previous certification for that product. If you are getting recertified, check with the authorized testing center for discounts.

Taking an Adobe Certified Expert Exam

The Adobe Certified Expert exams are computer-delivered, closed-book tests consisting of 60 to 90 multiple-choice questions. Each exam is approximately one to two hours long. A 15-minute tutorial will precede the test to familiarize you with the function of the Windows-based driver. The exams are currently available worldwide in English only. They are administered by Pearson VUE and Thomson Prometric, independent third-party testing companies.

Exam Results

At the end of the exam, a score report appears indicating whether you passed or failed the exam. Diagnostic information is included in your exam report. When you pass the exam, your score is electronically reported to Adobe. You will then be sent an ACE Welcome Kit and access to the ACE program logo in four to six weeks. You are also placed on the Adobe certification mailing list to receive special Adobe announcements and information about promotions and events that take place throughout the year.

When you pass the exam, you can get program information, check and update your profile, or download ACE program logos for your promotional materials online at:

http://www.adobe.com/support/certification/community.html

Getting More Information

To learn more about the Adobe Certified Expert program, read a list of frequently asked questions, and locate the nearest testing center, go online to:

http://www.adobe.com/support/certification/ace.html

To learn more about other Adobe certification programs, go online to:

http://www.adobe.com/support/certification

Index